SOUTH CAROLINA
GOES TO WAR
1860–1865

SOUTHERN CLASSICS SERIES
John G. Sproat and Mark M. Smith, Series Editors

SOUTH CAROLINA GOES TO WAR 1860–1865

CHARLES EDWARD CAUTHEN

New Introduction by J. Tracy Power

University of South Carolina Press

Published in cooperation with the Institute for
Southern Studies of the University of South Carolina

Original text © 1950 University of North Carolina Press
New Introduction © 2005 University of South Carolina

Published in Columbia, South Carolina,
by the University of South Carolina Press

Manufactured in the United States of America

17 16 15 14 13 12 11 10 09 08   10 9 8 7 6 5 4 3 2

Library of Congress Cataloging-in-Publication Data

Cauthen, Charles Edward.
    South Carolina goes to war, 1860–1865 / Charles Edward Cauthen ;
new introduction by J. Tracy Power.
        p. cm. — (Southern classics series)
    Originally published: Chapel Hill : University of North Carolina Press, 1950, in
series: The James Sprunt studies in history and political science ; v. 32.
    "Published in cooperation with the Institute for Southern Studies of the University
of South Carolina."
    Includes bibliographical references and index.
    ISBN 1-57003-560-1 (pbk : alk. paper)
    1. South Carolina—History—Civil War, 1861–1865. I. University of South
Carolina. Institute for Southern Studies. II. Title. III. Series.
    E577.C397 2005
    973.7'09757—dc22

                                                                    2005016160

Publication of the Southern Classics series is made possible in part by the generous
support of the Watson-Brown Foundation.

ISBN-13: 978-1-57003-560-9 (pbk)

CONTENTS

SERIES EDITORS' PREFACE   vii

NEW INTRODUCTION   ix

PREFACE TO THE FIRST EDITION   xxiii

CHAPTER

    I. THE SECESSION MOVEMENT BEFORE 1860   1

    II. THE PRESIDENTIAL ELECTION OF 1860   14

    III. PROPAGANDA ON THE EVE OF SECESSION   31

    IV. SOUTH CAROLINA'S DECISION TO LEAD   49

    V. INDEPENDENCE DECLARED   63

    VI. THE REPUBLIC OF SOUTH CAROLINA   79

    VII. FORTS DIPLOMACY   92

    VIII. PREPARATIONS FOR WAR   110

    IX. THE WAR BEGINS   119

    X. THE EXECUTIVE COUNCIL   139

    XI. ABOLITION OF THE COUNCIL   152

    XII. CONSCRIPTION   164

    XIII. IMPRESSMENT OF NEGROES AND SUPPLIES   178

    XIV. STATE FINANCE IN WAR TIME   188

    XV. SOUTH CAROLINA AND THE DAVIS GOVERNMENT   201

    XVI. DESPAIR AND DEFEAT   217

BIBLIOGRAPHY   231

INDEX   247

SERIES EDITORS' PREFACE

Published originally in 1950, Charles E. Cauthen's *South Carolina Goes to War, 1860–1865* explained why the Palmetto State seceded, explored the political dynamics of the secession crisis, and examined little-known aspects of the state's Confederate experience. Evenhanded, considered, and detailed, *South Carolina Goes to War* has stood the test of time. As J. Tracy Power makes clear in his thoughtful introduction, Cauthen's classic work remains essential reading for anyone interested in a reliable understanding of South Carolina's role in the coming of the Civil War.

Southern Classics returns to general circulation books of importance dealing with the history and culture of the American South. Sponsored by the Institute for Southern Studies and the South Caroliniana Society of the University of South Carolina, the series is advised by a board of distinguished scholars who suggest titles and editors of individual volumes to the series editors and help establish priorities in publication.

Chronological age alone does not determine a title's designation as a Southern Classic. The criteria also include significance in contributing to a broad understanding of the region, timeliness in relation to events and moments of peculiar interest to the American South, usefulness in the classroom, and suitability for inclusion in personal and institutional collections on the region.

MARK M. SMITH
JOHN G. SPROAT
Series Editors

NEW INTRODUCTION

Robert Penn Warren has called the Civil War "the single greatest event of our history." He claimed that "with the War the old America, with all its defects and virtues, was dead. With the War the new America, with its promise of realizing the vision inherited from the old America, was born."[1] Many observers before and since Warren have persuasively argued that the war is indeed the central event of American history, that from the beginning a bitter conflict over slavery, the tension between state rights and federal authority, and the very nature of the Union itself was inevitable, and that nothing short of secession and civil war could ever have resolved such issues. If this viewpoint is correct, then understanding South Carolina's role in both disunion and war is vital to understanding how it all unfolded and what it all means. Once the Palmetto State seceded and once state after state followed it out of the Union, one side "would make war rather than let the nation survive, and the other would accept war rather than let it perish," as Abraham Lincoln later said so memorably, adding, "and the war came."[2]

South Carolina had long been a catalyst for, and a symbol of, Southern dreams of a bold new future and an independent new confederacy as well as Northern nightmares of the American experiment gone awry. Most white South Carolinians believed that their economic prosperity, political interests, and social stability were inextricably tied to state rights, the institution of slavery, and the plantation system as it had evolved since the colonial era. For more than thirty years the fire-eaters among them—convinced that Yankee abolitionists wanted to take away their slaves, their self-respect, their freedom, and their liberty—had defended their society against enemies both real and imagined and sought to persuade their fellow Carolinians that a separate Southern nation was their only hope. In 1860, with the election of a "Black Republican" president, the radicals finally found the justification they had sought for so many years and convinced moderates, cooperationists, and even Unionists to join them. It might have taken generations to set things in motion, but once the wheel began turning in earnest it could not be slowed, much less stopped.

This story, or its outline, is at least familiar to those with more than a passing interest in American history, much less Southern or Civil War or South Carolina history. Many people have seen the 1860 broadside printed by the *Charleston Mercury* and reproduced in textbooks and general histories of the Civil War. I first saw it at the age of six in Bruce Catton's *American Heritage Pictorial History of the Civil War* (1960), its caption commenting that the *Mercury* "trumpeted the dire news in what was surely the largest type available"—the one that leaps off the page with the bold words "THE UNION IS DISSOLVED!"[3] Some readers may also recall the claim of Senator James Chesnut that disunion would not necessarily mean war, that "the man most averse to blood might safely drink every drop shed" after secession, or the acerbic, and perhaps apocryphal, comment by staunch Unionist James Louis Petigru, appalled by the cheering crowds celebrating in the streets of Charleston once the Palmetto State had actually seceded, that "South Carolina is too small to be a Republic, and too large to be an insane asylum."[4]

And yet . . . nothing that followed the cataclysmic moment when South Carolina seceded from the Union, not even the bombardment and surrender of Fort Sumter, was quite so significant. That moment was captured forever by the Ordinance of Secession—that engrossed and signed piece of linen with 170 signatures, the one document above all others that visitors to the South Carolina Department of Archives and History want to see and sometimes buy facsimile copies of. Secession seems, almost one hundred and fifty years later, to have been more an end than a beginning, or perhaps simply the beginning of the end. For years many white South Carolinians, and many other white Southerners too, had essentially defined themselves, whether consciously or not, in terms of a society in which some people owned not only the labor of others but owned the others themselves. Fears over whether that society would continue to prosper, or even survive, brought South Carolina and the rest of the South to this moment. The foundation of that society crumbled under the strain of war, and its end was drawn out over four years of disappointment, finally falling apart in defeat, destruction, and despair.

South Carolina had prepared for this moment for so long, almost on its own, that it was as if the last grand gesture was to fire shot and shell at Major Robert Anderson's garrison, now representing a foreign nation, sitting in that fort out in Charleston Harbor. Though its citizens made many military and civilian contributions and personal sacrifices on behalf of the Confederacy over the next four years—and though they displayed a passionate devotion to the Lost Cause from 1865 for the next hundred years and in many ways even into the twenty-first century—South Carolina's time had come and gone.

Almost no one could have dared believe this fact in the exhilarating spring of 1861, when thousands of South Carolinians left their books, their plows, their desks, and various other pursuits to enlist in military units already formed or being raised in every hamlet, town, and city. As soon as Fort Sumter surrendered, a pair of brothers at Wofford College, only days away from their graduation in the class of 1861, left Spartanburg bound for Charleston. Dick and Tally Simpson were among the Wofford students who had organized a volunteer company intending to offer their services to their native state. Reverend Albert M. Shipp, the college president, reluctantly told the Simpsons and their classmates that since they were so close to taking their final examinations and graduating and so determined to leave school, he had no choice but to give them their diplomas and let them go. "There has been so much excitement, I have hardly found time to write," Dick confessed to his mother; then he reassured her, "If the fight ends shortly or if there is a cessation of any length, we have promised Dr. Shipp to return to college."⁵ Two months later, the brothers arrived in Virginia, where it was widely assumed the war would end with one grand battle. Tally proudly wrote his sister about the enthusiasm displayed for their regiment and its home state on its way to Richmond:

South Carolina is a noble state. Her praise is on the lips of all. She always has had a great reputation, but since her secession from the Federal Union—and her attack upon Fort Sumter—her fame has been wafted upon the wings of the wind. . . . Little boys, girls and all follow the men, begging them for palmetto leaves, buttons, and any thing that will remind them of that noble little state.⁶

The Simpson brothers were typical of the South Carolinians and other Americans, South and North, who left their homes that spring wearing bright new uniforms, marching under gaudy silk banners to the sound of drums and horns, with exhortations of bravery ringing in their ears and dreams of martial glory swirling in their heads. What they got instead was nothing as simple and swift or as grand and gallant.

The war lasted for four agonizing years and wrecked an entire generation of South Carolinians. Almost no household went untouched by lives lost by disease or in battle or ruined by disabling wounds or imprisonment. There were about sixty thousand men of military age in South Carolina in 1860, and the state accounted for about that many enlistments before the end of the war. A third of them—between nineteen thousand and twenty-two thousand—died of disease, were killed in battle, or died of their wounds. Many more were wounded, often permanently disabled, or were captured and sent to Northern prisons. Even those who survived the war intact were never the same.

Whether in new volunteer companies organized amid great excitement or in established militia companies, some of them with lineages dating back to the Revolution, many South Carolinians went to Charleston and remained there or in the lowcountry for most of the war. Many more, however, went to Virginia once that state became the major battleground in the East; still others went to Tennessee when that state became the major battleground in the West. In retrospect South Carolina's reputation as a Confederate state owes more to Palmetto State units and generals serving elsewhere—such as the larger-than-life Wade Hampton, longtime second-in-command of J. E. B. Stuart's cavalry in the Army of Northern Virginia, or the too-perfectly-named States

Rights Gist, killed at Franklin while serving in the Army of Tennessee —than it does to Carolinians defending their native soil.

Events in South Carolina and elsewhere helped determine whether the Palmetto State's devotion to a Southern confederacy in the abstract, one envisioned and planned by so many for so long, could transfer itself to and help to sustain a would-be nation fighting to survive. Most white South Carolinians gave their fair share, or more, to the Confederacy. They not only sent their fathers, husbands, sons, and brothers off to war, but also donated food and clothing to soldiers in the field and to their families at home. They furnished gunpowder and lead to the state and Confederate governments; accepted, if sometimes reluctantly, the impressment of their corn, wheat, flour, meal, salt, cows, pigs, chickens, milk, eggs, and butter; and paid taxes levied for the relief of soldiers' families. In return, most of them asked only that the state and Confederate authorities protect them, their homes, and their property.

Nothing demonstrates this feeling quite as well as the way they reacted to the early—and significant—presence of the enemy on and near their coast. Most of them had expected, after the boasts made between Lincoln's election and the surrender of Fort Sumter, that every precious inch of soil up and down the Carolina seaboard would be defended to the last ditch from any vandal invaders. In November 1861, after little more than token resistance, a combined Federal naval and land force captured Port Royal, Beaufort, and the South Carolina sea islands, giving the U.S. Navy a deep-water port on the Atlantic and the U.S. Army a firm foothold on Palmetto soil between Savannah and Charleston, which they kept for the rest of the war.

This catastrophe forced most white residents in the vicinity to leave their homes and most of their property behind—including, of course, their slaves, whose status shifted to being neither truly slave nor truly free but something in between. Union occupation disrupted agricultural production in the region, severed the delicate mutual dependency of master and slave, and sowed the seeds of widespread doubt that military and civil authorities, whether state or Confederate, could adequately protect citizens' property or even their lives. The shock and anger felt by most white South Carolinians, especially those forced to flee from their homes to Columbia, Greenville, or other points in the interior, were profound. The idea that any part of the state could be so vulnerable was almost beyond belief, so much so that many never accepted, much less truly comprehended, what had happened. Within a few months the U.S. Treasury and Northern missionaries were cooperating in an ambitious project, best known as "the Port Royal experiment," intended to train and educate the slaves on the sea islands in order to help them adjust to freedom and become productive members of their communities once the war was over.

Governor Francis W. Pickens was widely criticized by legislators, civilians, and newspaper editors for the Port Royal disaster, which led to a significant yet surprisingly little-known episode in South Carolina Confederate history, during which an executive council—rather than the governor and the General Assembly—essentially governed the state. This council, authorized by an emergency session of the Secession Convention, was the second such body of its type.

Its predecessor had also been authorized by the Secession Convention. The first council was created in early 1861 to assist Pickens in handling the diplomatic and military affairs of South Carolina as long as it was an independent republic, then to cooperate with efforts to establish a central Confederate government. Within a few months, once Confederate military and civilian authorities began assuming responsibilities, the council had outlived its usefulness and was abolished.

The second Executive Council of South Carolina was created in early 1862 amid widespread claims that the Federal capture of Port Royal should have been better contested, if not prevented, and frequent charges that Pickens and his administration were guilty of mismanagement by their incompetence, even timidity. This council assumed much more power than the first, declaring martial law in the lowcountry, establishing quotas for the enlistment of troops, requiring slave owners to loan their slaves out for the war effort, and confiscating food and other supplies as necessary to supply units in need. Under almost constant criticism and controversy from almost all quarters, whether from those who objected to it on constitutional grounds or those who opposed specific actions and policies, the council was abolished by the General Assembly after operating for a little less than a year. For the most part the council did what it was intended to do, which was to coordinate the war effort between the citizens and the state government and between the state and Confederate governments.

Though true governmental power in South Carolina resided in the legislature and not in the governor, the state's three war governors —Pickens until December 1862, Milledge L. Bonham until December 1864, and Andrew G. Magrath in the last few months—were not mere figureheads, not even Pickens in the period when he wrangled with the second council. They were, in most instances, more cooperative and less contentious than Joseph E. Brown and Zebulon B. Vance, their counterparts in Georgia and North Carolina, who were well known for their vocal, though never actually disloyal, opposition to so many Confederate policies and strategies.

There were, of course, legitimate reasons for discontent as the war dragged on, most of them not unique to South Carolina but typical of every Confederate state. The first draft in American history, in which men between ages eighteen and thirty-five (later seventeen and fifty) were liable for military service, was the most unpopular measure of the entire war. The practice of allowing substitutes and many exemptions, some of them questionable, made conscription doubly controversial. Other complaints included rampant speculation and inflation, absenteeism and outright desertion from the army, and the rise of lawlessness and bushwhacking in isolated areas. The *Charleston Mercury* reflected its editors' unwavering, vitriolic, even personal opposition to President Jefferson Davis and his policies, adding their editorials' influence to a climate in which battlefield defeats elsewhere helped magnify pessimism across the state. In most respects, however, South Carolina's record of cooperation with the Confederate establishment stands in contrast to the provincialism, obstructionism, and carping so prominent in wartime Georgia and North Carolina.

Even during the war, South Carolina was more a symbol than a strategic prize or the scene of significant action. The most notable occurrence in the state between the firing on Fort Sumter and the burning of Columbia was the siege of Charleston, which lasted—albeit with interruptions, so that it did not quite measure up to the textbook definition of a siege—from April 1863 to February 1865. The campaign fired the imagination of Northern newspaper editorialists and civilians, who saw Charleston as "that viper's nest and breeding place of rebellion," in many ways second only to Richmond.[7] The uncertainty of life under that sort of pressure often overwhelmed Charlestonians, lowcountry residents, and others who found themselves alternating between hope and despair from one day to the next as Union ships seemed to shell the city with impunity. The most memorable action of the siege was the failed Federal assault on Battery Wagner, an earthwork on the northern tip of Morris Island, in July 1863—remembered primarily as one of the first battles in which black Union soldiers, such as the Fifty-fourth Massachusetts Volunteer Infantry (Colored), commanded by Colonel Robert Gould Shaw, played a prominent role.

The disbelief that followed the occupation of Port Royal, Beaufort, and the sea islands was intensified tenfold, even in the face of ample evidence that defeat was imminent, once William T. Sherman's combined Federal forces crossed the Savannah River into the state in early 1865. Most South Carolinians, from the civil authorities to the military establishment and from newspaper editors to the least-informed civilians, were convinced that the enemy would be hopelessly mired down in the swamps and thickets of the lowcountry and that the March to the Sea from Atlanta to Savannah could never be duplicated from Savannah to Columbia.

They could not have been more wrong. Many Federal enlisted men, and some officers as well, proved themselves eager to take out four years of frustration on South Carolina, believing it responsible for breaking up the Union and starting the war. When Yankees in blue insulted and taunted civilians, ransacked public and private buildings, and stole livestock, household goods, furniture, clothing, books, papers, jewelry, gold, and silver, their behavior confirmed, even exceeded, most white South Carolinians' worst fears of humiliation and subjugation. When Union troops set fire to individual buildings, whole blocks, or large sections of Columbia and other towns, they left ruin and rage smoldering behind them. Incidents such as these were so unthinkable that most white South Carolinians who witnessed them came to cherish the privilege of remembering everything that happened, passing down vivid memories, bits of conversations, embroidered stories, and mementos to generation after generation after generation.

Because South Carolina embraced and identified with the Confederacy from its optimistic beginning to its crushing end, the myths and realities of the Civil War experience still have a remarkable hold on the state and its people almost 150 years later. Charles Edward Cauthen's assessment of the Palmetto State is simple but persuasive:

Through it all South Carolina on the whole stood loyally and courageously for the Confederate cause. . . . The masses of the people remained firm and determined long after the hope of ultimate victory seemed slim indeed.

Probably no state officially coöperated more fully with the Confederate government. Passionately devoted to state rights principles there was nevertheless a disposition, until the very last months of the war, . . . to sacrifice these opinions in the interest of harmony and victory. . . .

To the end South Carolina maintained a sincere confidence in the justice of her cause.[8]

As a portrait of South Carolina politics and government during the secession crisis and the war years, Charles Edward Cauthen's *South Carolina Goes to War, 1860–1865* is a study quite unlike any other published before or since. Published in 1950 by the University of North Carolina Press as a volume in the James Sprunt Series in History and Political Science, Cauthen's book was a revision of "Secession and Civil War in South Carolina: Part I, Political," his 1937 doctoral dissertation at the University of North Carolina. A newspaper article that appeared just before the publication date quoted its author's self-effacing characterization of *South Carolina Goes to War:* "it is not a book with popular appeal . . . but neither is it a text book."[9]

The title, suggested—as Cauthen noted in his preface—by his long-time Wofford colleague Lewis P. Jones, could not be more appropriate —or more accurate. Eight and a half of the book's sixteen chapters and more than half its pages focus on South Carolina's path toward secession, the secession crisis, and the months leading up to the firing on Fort Sumter. As Cauthen pointed out in his preface and as every contemporary reviewer of *South Carolina Goes to War* observed, it is no exaggeration to say that for most of 1860 and the first four months of 1861 South Carolina history is synonymous with American history.

Even so, this book is often more wide ranging, both in its research and its analysis, than the more specialized studies that came before it or after it, many of them focusing on the significant and dramatic events so often associated with the Palmetto State: the Secession Convention, Fort Sumter and the debate over responsibility for "the first shot," the Port Royal experiment, the siege of Charleston, or the burning of Columbia.[10] Perhaps its most valuable chapters are those covering aspects often neglected by those writing about South Carolina's Confederate experience, such as the two executive councils and the impact of the state and Confederate governments on the home front and on the state's contribution to the war effort. Cauthen hoped that this book—his first—would synthesize "information heretofore unavailable in one place but also [make] some contribution to a better understanding of the political history of the state."[11]

That modest assessment is typical of Cauthen's style throughout *South Carolina Goes to War.* Based on years of indefatigable research and mature reflection, the book also benefits from its author's determination to keep a proper distance from his subject. Cauthen's prose is always understated, even when his analysis might justify, and his narrative might sustain, a more forceful approach. He strives to maintain a balance between the opposing views of those prominent in the events he describes and evaluates, and at the same time he tries to maintain a balance between the school of thought that sees South Carolina's central role in the secession crisis and the Civil War as something bold, noble, and ultimately tragic and the school of thought that sees it as reckless, selfish, and ultimately destructive.

Charles Edward Cauthen, whose students often affectionately called him "Doctor Charlie," taught history and political science at Wofford College in Spartanburg from 1943 until shortly before his death in 1964 at the age of sixty-six. Cauthen, whose grandfather and father—the Reverends Andrew Jackson Cauthen Sr. and Jr.—boasted almost eighty-five years of combined service as Methodist ministers in South Carolina, was a 1917 graduate of Wofford. While there he was an excellent student, lettered in both football and baseball, and was described by his classmates as "a specimen of which both class and school are proud . . . an all-round man, always busy."[12]

After serving in the U.S. Navy as a pilot during World War I, Cauthen taught history at Lynchburg High School in Lee County, serving briefly as school principal. He moved to Columbia to become an instructor of history, and later professor of history and department chairman, at Columbia College, where he taught from 1922 to 1943. During his stay at Columbia College, Cauthen received his M.A. from

Columbia University in New York City in 1925, writing his thesis on South Carolina's ratification of the Constitution, and his Ph.D. from the University of North Carolina in 1937, studying under the direction of prominent Southern historian Fletcher M. Green. Cauthen served on the executive committee of the South Carolina Historical Association for several years in the 1930s and 1940s and was president of the association in 1940.

Cauthen returned to his alma mater as professor of history and political science in 1943, becoming only the second professor of history at Wofford and joining David Duncan Wallace, the dean of South Carolina historians, who had taught there since 1899. When Wallace retired in 1947, Cauthen succeeded him as chairman of the department and was named John M. Reeves Professor of History in 1954. Cauthen also served for many years as faculty adviser to the Kappa Alpha Order, and he was chairman of the college centennial committee in 1954.

Cauthen was a member of the South Carolina Archives and History Commission from 1955 to 1962, serving a term as commission chairman. Though *South Carolina Goes to War* is his best known and most often cited work, Cauthen also edited *Family Letters of the Three Wade Hamptons, 1782–1901,* published by the University of South Carolina Press in 1953, and *The Journals of the South Carolina Executive Councils of 1861 and 1862,* a documentary edition published by the South Carolina Department of Archives and History in 1956.[13]

The opening chapters of *South Carolina Goes to War* are an insightful introduction to the period from 1820 to 1860, years in which South Carolina gained its reputation for bold, even reckless, rhetoric defending state rights, the plantation economy, the institution of slavery, and an agrarian society while attacking federal authority, manufacturing and banking, abolitionism, and urbanization. Many South Carolinians began to consider themselves Southern nationalists willing to take great risks to remain true to their own farsighted vision—or version—of the Constitution by upholding the primacy of state rights. Others believed these South Carolinians to be shortsighted radicals willing to risk destroying the Union itself in order to protect their own selfish interests. Cauthen commented that by late 1860, with Lincoln's election all but certain, South Carolinians displayed a remarkable degree of "unity and enthusiasm" for secession but cautioned his readers—and other historians as well—that "it is not easy to explain fully why South Carolina was so much more united in secession than were other Southern states."[14] A desire to defend slavery, both in the real world and the abstract, is part of the answer, but not all. Secession was, in the end, a political answer to a political question, a solution that finally struck a chord with the people, who were ready for it in 1860 but had been unwilling to risk something so drastic in 1828, 1832, 1850, or 1852. As Cauthen explained:

Secession came to South Carolina on the crest of a great wave of popular enthusiasm which all but drowned the voices of the few who urged caution. It did not come at the dictation of a handful of leaders.

That secession in South Carolina was essentially an act of the people can hardly be doubted.[15]

Chapter 4, "South Carolina's Decision to Lead," is the most significant of the five chapters devoted to the coming of the Civil War and the secession crisis. Based in large part on a paper Cauthen delivered at the 1940 meeting of the Southern Historical Association, held in Charleston, and the resulting article published in the *North Carolina Historical Review* the next year under the title "South Carolina's Decision to Lead the Secession Movement," this chapter demonstrates its author's painstaking research, careful arguments, and cogent conclusions about precisely how secessionists and cooperationists were able to work together to take control of the situation in the state, leaving Unionists and undecided moderates stunned at the speed with which events tumbled down on one another once Lincoln was elected president.[16]

Fire-eaters such as Robert Barnwell Rhett, who had once seemed to be the logical political successor to John C. Calhoun, had long been sensitive to charges—not entirely unfounded, to be sure—that they were reckless and headstrong and that time after time they had spoken too loudly, announced their views too openly, and left South Carolina in an isolated, even untenable position somewhere between the Union and the other Southern states. Many who never doubted that secession was desirable, or possible, still questioned whether South Carolina should commit itself to sole action without pledges of support from other states.

Even the state's two influential U.S. senators, James Henry Hammond and James Chesnut, refused to go on record in the months immediately before the election of 1860 as being in favor of immediate and separate action by the Palmetto State. It was not until the week after the election, when South Carolina finally received assurances from Georgia and other states that they would secede once South Carolina led the way, that the legislature voted to call a secession convention before the end of the year.

Chapters 10 and 11, "The Executive Council" and "Abolition of the Council," are still the best analysis of this little known episode in wartime South Carolina, one later ably supplemented by Cauthen's 1956 documentary edition of the 1861 and 1862 executive council journals. With the creation of the 1862 council, the responsibility and authority for the day-to-day operations of the state government was vested in a five-man council made up of the governor, lieutenant governor, and three at-large members appointed by the Secession Convention. It was no accident that the three appointees could always overrule the governor and lieutenant governor on any matter before the council.

Cauthen pointed out that, when the council was formed, its three at-large members—former U.S. senator James Chesnut, former governor William H. Gist, and state attorney general Isaac W. Hayne—were widely respected as men of experience and influence. As Cauthen also made clear, the council soon became controversial—more for the measures it proposed than for any other reason, though there were also objections to it on strictly constitutional grounds. Cauthen observed, "On the whole, it would seem that the council exercised its power with not only considerable energy and wisdom but with restraint as well."[17]

Every contemporary review of *South Carolina Goes to War* commented that Cauthen's research in manuscript and other archival sources was impressive and that his citations of those sources, and published sources as well, supported his conclusions. Reviewers differed slightly, however, on Cauthen's contribution to Civil War and Southern history, over and above his contribution to South Carolina history.

One of the first reviews, published in the *Charleston News and Courier* under the title "Sound Conclusions," observed that *South Carolina Goes to War* "may well tend to give some congenital and inveterate Confederates a severe heart attack"—a comment that the University of North Carolina Press quoted in a letter announcing the book's publication. The reviewer continued, "The thoroughness of Mr. Cauthen's research in the causes of the War Between the States one cannot dispute. His conclusions from his endeavors the reviewer is forced to admit are pretty sound though perhaps somewhat distasteful."[18]

A few reviewers in scholarly journals, who complained that the title was misleading, either misread—or did not agree with—Cauthen's methodology, organization, and overall conception, making such comments as, "Its title notwithstanding, the work emphasizes political rather than military events"; "The title does not cover the contents fully. . . . It is a comprehensive account of South Carolinians neither at the front nor behind the lines," and "less than 100 of his 230 pages of narrative are devoted to the period after 1861."[19] All these reviewers considered the book a contribution to the literature, but they believed it modest rather than comprehensive and analytical—assessments that in some respects say more about the expectations of the historians making them than about the book they were reviewing.

Not a history of South Carolinians in the war or of the war in South Carolina—and never intended to be either—*South Carolina Goes to War* is a thorough examination of the state's political leadership during the years and months leading up to secession and during four years of war and of the state government during that period as well. The book is precisely what Cauthen, whose dual interest in history and political science was central to his scholarship and his teaching, intended it to be: political history, not military history, social history, or any other kind of history that happened to be in vogue among professors and graduate students in 1950. To call *South Carolina Goes to War* "old-fashioned" is a compliment, not a criticism.

Cauthen's students paid tribute to him after his death—and still respect him—for his scholarship, but their memories of him always emphasize his love of teaching and his generosity toward his students more than they do his books. In 1964 A. V. Huff Jr. wrote in a special section of the *Old Gold and Black,* the Wofford newspaper: "Charles Edward Cauthen, the historian, will stand through his scholarship in the annals of South Carolina's historiography. It is 'Doctor Charlie' Cauthen, the teacher and the man, whom his students remember."[20] Forty years later, Huff—a distinguished South Carolina and Southern historian and professor emeritus at Furman University—recalls, "His standards were high, but he was a deeply caring person. He was the perfect embodiment of a teacher and scholar."[21]

In a letter to the members of the South Carolina Historical Association announcing the publication of Cauthen's book, George F. Scheer of the University of North Carolina Press called it an "honest, forthright appraisal of the past," something that would have pleased its author, who could have been described in just those terms himself: honest and forthright, as a scholar, teacher, mentor, and man.[22] *South Carolina Goes to War* is indeed an honest and forthright appraisal of South Carolina's crucial role in secession and Civil War, a book well worth the attention of anyone with an interest in South Carolina, Southern, or American history during the middle period, and one well deserving its place on any bookshelf of Southern classics.

J. TRACY POWER

Notes

1. Robert Penn Warren, *The Legacy of the Civil War* (New York: Random House, 1961; reprinted, Lincoln: University of Nebraska Press, 1998), 3, 47.

2. Abraham Lincoln, Second Inaugural Address, March 4, 1865; quoted in *Encyclopedia of the American Civil War: A Political, Social, and Military History,* ed. David S. Heidler and Jeanne T. Heidler (Santa Barbara, Calif.: ABC-Clio, 2000), 5:2376.

3. Bruce Catton, *The American Heritage Picture History of the Civil War* (New York: American Heritage Publishing Company, 1960), 1:50 (caption), 1:51 (image).

4. James Chesnut, quoted in Cauthen, *South Carolina Goes to War, 1860–1865,* 53–54; James Louis Petigru, quoted in Lacy K. Ford, "James Louis Petigru: The Last South Carolina Federalist," in *Intellectual Life in Antebellum Charleston,* ed. Michael O'Brien and David Moltke-Hansen (Knoxville: University of Tennessee Press, 1986), 281. Ford observed in an endnote (p. 415), "This famous statement was printed, in slightly different forms, in newspapers throughout South Carolina after the Civil War and has become part of the state's oral historical tradition."

5. Richard W. Simpson to Mary Margaret Taliaferro Simpson, April 14, 1861, in *Far, Far from Home: The Wartime Letters of Dick and Tally Simpson, 3rd South Carolina Volunteers*, ed. Guy R. Everson and Edward H. Simpson Jr. (New York & Oxford: Oxford University Press, 1994), 4.

6. Taliaferro N. Simpson to Anna Tallulah Simpson, June 20, 1861, in *Far, Far from Home*, 16.

7. *New York Tribune*, June 9, 1862; quoted in E. Milby Burton, *The Siege of Charleston 1861–1865* (Columbia: University of South Carolina Press, 1970), 99.

8. Cauthen, *South Carolina Goes to War*, 229–30.

9. Betty Tribble, "Dr. Cauthen of Wofford Author of War History," *Spartanburg Herald*, August 28, 1950.

10. See two significant studies that preceded Cauthen's book: Chauncey Samuel Boucher, *South Carolina and the South on the Eve of Secession, 1852 to 1860*, Washington University Studies, Humanistic Series 6, no. 2 (St. Louis: Washington University, 1919), and Dwight L. Dumond, *The Secession Movement* (New York: Macmillan, 1931). See also these relevant studies on different aspects of South Carolina's experience in secession and the Civil War that followed Cauthen's book (arranged in rough chronological order of their subjects): Harold Schultz, *Nationalism and Sectionalism in South Carolina, 1852–1860: A Study of the Movement for Southern Independence* (Durham: Duke University Press, 1950); Steven Channing, *Crisis of Fear: Secession in South Carolina* (New York: Simon & Schuster, 1970); Lacy K. Ford, *Origins of Southern Radicalism: The South Carolina Upcountry, 1800–1860* (Oxford and New York: Oxford University Press, 1988); Eric H. Walther, *The Fire-Eaters* (Baton Rouge: Louisiana State University Press, 1992); David S. Heidler, *Pulling the Temple Down: The Fire-Eaters and the Destruction of the Union* (Harrisburg, Pa.: Stackpole Books, 1994); Charles H. Lesser, *Relic of the Lost Cause: The Story of South Carolina's Ordinance of Secession* (Columbia: South Carolina Department of Archives and History, 1996); Charles B. Dew, *Apostles of Disunion: Southern Secession Commissioners and the Causes of the Civil War* (Charlottesville: University Press of Virginia, 2001); Richard N. Current, *Lincoln and the First Shot*, Critical Periods of History (Philadelphia & New York: Lippincott, 1963); W. A. Swanberg, *First Blood: The Story of Fort Sumter* (New York: Scribners, 1957); Maury Klein, *Days of Defiance: Sumter, Secession, and the Coming of the Civil War* (New York: Knopf, 1997); David Detzer, *Allegiance: Fort Sumter, Charleston, and the Beginning of the Civil War* (New York: Harcourt, 1991); John Hammond Moore, *Southern Homefront, 1861–1865* (Columbia, S.C.: Summerhouse Press, 1988); Willie Lee Rose, *Rehearsal for Reconstruction: The Port Royal Experiment* (Indianapolis: Bobbs-Merrill, 1964); E. Milby Burton, *The Siege of Charleston, 1861–1865* (Columbia: University of South Carolina Press, 1970); Stephen R. Wise, *Gate of Hell: Campaign for Charleston Harbor, 1863* (Columbia: University of South Carolina Press, 1994); John G. Barrett, *Sherman's March through the Carolinas* (Chapel Hill: University of North Carolina Press, 1956); Joseph T. Glatthaar, *The March to the Sea and Beyond: Sherman's Troops in the Savannah and Carolinas Campaigns*, American Social Experience Series (New York: New York University Press, 1985); and Marion Brunson Lucas, *Sherman and the Burning of Columbia*, Texas A&M University Military History Series 10 (College Station & London: Texas A&M University Press, 1976).

11. Cauthen, *South Carolina Goes to War*, xxiii.

12. 1917 *Bohemian;* quoted in L.P.J., Class of 1938 [Lewis P. Jones, Professor of History, Wofford College], Guest Editorial, "Intaminatis . . . ," *Old Gold and Black* (Wofford College, Spartanburg, S.C.), December 18, 1964, 2.

13. Charles E. Cauthen, ed., *Family Letters of the Three Wade Hamptons, 1782–1902* (Columbia: University of South Carolina Press, 1953); *The Journals of the South Carolina Executive Councils of 1861 and 1862* (Columbia: South Carolina Department of Archives and History, 1956). This biographical sketch of Cauthen is compiled from several sources: "Cauthen Edits Letters of Hamptons," *Spartanburg Herald,* November 22, 1953, D-7; "Dr. Cauthen Edits New Volume on S.C. History," *Spartanburg Herald,* July 22, 1956, A-6; Lane Causey, "Dr. Charles Cauthen Has Retired," *Old Gold and Black,* December 11, 1964, 2; "Dr. Charles Cauthen, S.C. History Expert, Dies Here," *Spartanburg Herald Journal,* December 13, 1964, B-1; "Historian Cauthen Dies in Spartanburg," *Columbia State* and *Columbia Record,* December 13, 1964, 15-C; "A Tribute to Dr. Charlie Cauthen," and L.P.J., Guest Editorial, "Intaminatis . . . ," *Old Gold and Black,* December 18, 1964, 2; and "Charles Edward Cauthen, 1897–1964," *Proceedings of the South Carolina Historical Association, 1965* (Columbia: South Carolina Historical Association, 1965), iii.

14. Cauthen, *South Carolina Goes to War,* 31.

15. Ibid., 32.

16. Charles E. Cauthen, "South Carolina's Decision to Lead the Secession Movement," *North Carolina Historical Review* 18 (October 1941): 360–72.

17. Cauthen, *South Carolina Goes to War,* 151.

18. H.E.L., "Sound Conclusions," in "Books in Review," *Charleston News and Courier,* October 29, 1950, 4-F. See also George F. Scheer, University of North Carolina Press, to the members of the South Carolina Historical Association, January 10, 1951, Papers of the University of North Carolina Press, Southern Historical Collection, University of North Carolina, Chapel Hill, N.C.

19. Anonymous, review of *South Carolina Goes to War, 1860–1865,* in *United States Quarterly Book Review* 6 (December 1950): 444; Edward Younger, review of *South Carolina Goes to War, 1860–1865,* in *Journal of Southern History* 17 (February 1951): 94; Francis Butler Simkins, review of *South Carolina Goes to War, 1860–1865,* in *North Carolina Historical Review* 28 (July 1951): 379. See also Rembert W. Patrick, review of *South Carolina Goes to War, 1860–1865,* in *Mississippi Valley Historical Review* [later *Journal of American History*] 38 (June 1951): 127–28.

20. A. V. Huff Jr., Class of 1959, in "A Tribute to Dr. Charlie Cauthen," *Old Gold and Black,* December 18, 1964, 2.

21. Huff, e-mail to the author, October 5, 2004. Thanks also to Allen H. Stokes Jr., Class of 1964, longtime director of the South Caroliniana Library, University of South Carolina, and Marion Chandler, Class of 1966, longtime historian and archivist at the South Carolina Department of Archives and History, for sharing their reminiscences of Cauthen as a scholar and teacher.

22. Scheer to the members of the South Carolina Historical Association, January 10, 1951.

PREFACE TO THE FIRST EDITION

Although the political history of South Carolina from 1860 to 1865 has not heretofore been the subject of a published volume, the field is not an entirely unexplored one. South Carolina history in the period of secession and war is so vitally related to our national history that even the general American historian has necessarily given considerable attention to it. Every study of the secession movement as a whole has required an examination of the South Carolina scene and an appraisal of forces operating within and across the borders of the state. Indeed the success of the larger secession movement was conditioned in no small degree upon developments in South Carolina during the whole generation before 1860 and especially during the last critical weeks of state conventions and secession ordinances. Likewise South Carolina attitudes and policies were perhaps no less important in setting the stage for the Fort Sumter episode than were the decisions made in Washington and Montgomery. And from Fort Sumter to Appomattox the state's history is interwoven with that of the whole country.

The author is indebted not only to those who have written the general history of the United States but also to numerous others who have worked in the more particular field of South Carolina history. David Duncan Wallace, Alexander S. Salley, David E. Houston, Chauncey S. Boucher, Phillip M. Hamer, William A. Schaper, John G. Van Deusen, Laura A. White (to mention only a few), and biographers too numerous to mention have either furnished background or broken the trail for the present writer. But while trying to take full advantage of earlier scholarship in the field, the author has depended primarily on the almost inexhaustible supply of source material pertaining to South Carolina Confederate history. He hopes that the resulting narrative has not only served the purpose of bringing together information heretofore unavailable in one place but also has made some contribution to a better understanding of the political history of the state.

To many friends thanks are due for encouragement and assistance. Special interest in the subject was first aroused by Professor J. G. de Roulhac Hamilton of the University of North Carolina, an inspiring teacher. Of the same faculty Professor Fletcher M. Green was an indispensable counselor in the preparation of a doctoral thesis and has most generously read and constructively criticized the revised study. Several members of the Wofford College faculty have also read part or all of the manuscript. Professor D. D. Wallace was very helpful at a number of points. Professor Lewis P. Jones suggested the title and was also of great assistance in literary revision, as was Registrar S. Frank Logan. The courteous assistance of librarians, especially at the University of North Carolina, Duke University, University of South Carolina, Charleston Library Society, South Carolina Historical Society, and the Library of Congress is also gratefully acknowledged. To *The James Sprunt Studies in History and Political Science* thanks are expressed for aid in publication.

C.E.C.

SOUTH CAROLINA
GOES TO WAR
1860–1865

CHAPTER I

THE SECESSION MOVEMENT BEFORE 1860

It is a commonplace of American history that South Carolina leaders did not always, in the first decades of the Union, defend the extreme state rights doctrines which John C. Calhoun so ably expounded later in the antebellum period. In the convention of 1787 South Carolina delegates played an important part in framing the Constitution. The strong nationalistic spirit which they displayed there was again evidenced in the state convention which ratified the document. And for about three decades thereafter, especially in the years immediately following the War of 1812, there is little evidence of those extreme state sovereignty principles and sectional attitudes which led to nullification in 1832 and eventually to disunion in 1860.

In the period following 1820, however, there was a rising tide of opposition to various powers and policies of the general government, and a strong tendency for the South as a whole and South Carolina especially to seek a defense for threatened economic interests in a narrow interpretation of congressional powers and a corresponding exaltation of the rights of the state. Thus South Carolina, consistently opposing protective tariffs from the first as inequitable[1] and blaming the tariff for the economic decline which soil erosion and destructive competition of the Southwest had more largely caused, came in the middle eighteen twenties to attack protection on constitutional grounds. In 1832 the Calhoun theory of state "interposition" was adopted in an attempt to prevent the operation of a tariff which by that time had come to be very generally regarded in South Carolina as unconstitutional. In the same period the state voiced sharp protests against the construction of roads, canals, and other internal improvements at national expense on the ground that Congress did not possess the taxing power for such purposes.[2]

More important than the tariff in nourishing sectionalism, state rights, and disunion was the necessity of defending a labor system which under the rise of cotton culture came to be regarded as essential to the economic well-being of the state. From the time of the debate over slavery in the Louisiana purchase and the compromise of 1820, and especially after the rise of militant abolitionism in the 1830's, South Carolina was quick to resent anything which even remotely threatened to endanger slavery and therefore her own safety. A philosophical defense of slavery was developed under which the institution was held to

---

[1] John G. Van Deusen, *Economic Bases of Disunion in South Carolina* (New York, 1928), pp. 17 *et seq.*

[2] *Ibid.*, pp. 39-40, 116 *et seq.*

2

be a divinely established system economically beneficial to master, non-slaveholder, and slave. To it was ascribed a wholesome social and political organization which would not otherwise exist. Moreover, emancipation meant Africanization and ruin to Southern civilization in general.[3] State sovereignty principles were seized upon as an obvious defense against interference from outside. As Francis W. Pickens expressed it, "the law of State sovereignty is with us the law of State existence." This, as Professor Wallace suggests, would no doubt have been changed to "the law of national sovereignty is the law of existence" if the slaveowner had been threatened with local opposition against which only the national government could protect him.[4] But once state rights doctrines became firmly established, they were generally accepted and cherished without a consciousness of their economic foundation.

Disunion itself was early suggested by the more radical as a remedy for South Carolina's grievances. Amidst the anti-tariff excitement of 1827, Dr. Thomas Cooper startled the state by his famous declaration that it was "time to calculate the value of the Union." But the idea soon found many supporters. It was inherent in the "Crisis" articles of Robert J. Turnbull (1827), and in the whole nullification movement which looked to secession should nullification be resisted. That the leaders of nullification would be willing and able to carry the threat of secession into effect should the United States resort to force was believed by Joel R. Poinsett, the leader of the unionist party. And many of the unionists while denying the legality of nullification conceded at least the revolutionary right of secession.[5] The whole episode undoubtedly tended to weaken unionism in South Carolina. The conviction that Northern and Southern interests were at variance was greatly strengthened; a majority of the people were alienated from the general government; and a disposition developed to look to secession as an ultimate necessity.[6] "It has prepared the minds of men for a separation of the States," said James L. Petigru, "and when the question is mooted again it will be distinctly union or disunion."[7]

[3] The classic defense of slavery is (William Harper *et. al.*), *The Pro-slavery Argument, as maintained by the most distinguished writers of the Southern States, containing the several essays, on the subject, of Chancellor Harper, Governor Hammond, Dr. Simms, and Professor Dew* (Charleston, 1852). See also W. S. Jenkins, *Pro-slavery Thought in the Old South* (Chapel Hill, 1933) and for an excellent short summary, Avery Craven, *The Coming of the Civil War* (New York, 1942), Chapter VI.
[4] D. D. Wallace, *The History of South Carolina* (New York, 1934), II, 494.
[5] Chauncey S. Boucher, *The Nullification Controversy in South Carolina* (Chicago, 1916), pp. 3, 14, 61, 78, 233.
[6] David F. Houston, *A Critical Study of Nullification in South Carolina* (New York, 1896), p. 137.
[7] J. L. Petigru to H. S. Legare, July 15, 1833, in James P. Carson, *Life, Letters and Speeches of James Louis Petigru, the Union Man of South Carolina* (Washington, 1920), p. 125.

Secession sentiment steadily developed in the two decades following nullification. Abolitionist literature, anti-slavery petitions before Congress, agitation for and against the annexation of Texas, continued controversy over the tariff and a national bank, "consolidation" in general, kept the state almost continuously stirred and furnished grist for the mill of Robert Barnwell Rhett who emerged from the nullification controvery as the leader of a group working for secession as a thing desirable *per se*. Calhoun, who became virtual political dictator of the state in this period, though friendly to the radical group, was much more conservative. He worked toward Southern political solidarity and hoped that the time might come when a united South, with some help from Northern or Western allies, might effect a thorough reformation of the federal government on the basis of state rights. Sincerely attached to the Union, and ambitious almost to the last for the presidency, he sometimes restrained his more radical followers as in 1844 when he used his influence to check Rhett's so-called Bluffton movement. "I had to act with great delicacy, but at the same time firmness," he said.[8] But, however much he may have deprecated disunion as a calamity to be avoided if possible, he nevertheless schooled South Carolina and the South in the necessity of defending Southern interests by a strict limitation of federal authority and, if need be, through Southern withdrawal from the Union. An increasing number of his followers became convinced that secession was ultimately unavoidable.

The issues brought forward by the Mexican War stirred South Carolina deeply and carried her with what seemed almost complete unanimity to the very brink of secession. The Wilmot Proviso which would have prohibited slavery in any territory acquired in consequence of the war brought a determination in South Carolina that such exclusion should dissolve the Union. Calhoun, instead of restraining the radicals, became active in arousing the people. Denying that Congress had any power over slavery in the territories, he strove to unite the South on a resistance program, and spoke of secession in plainer terms than ever before. "Though the Union is dear to us," he said, "our honor and our liberty are dearer." The state legislature in 1848 unanimously resolved that the time for discussion had passed and that South Carolina stood ready to coöperate with her sister states in resisting the Wilmot Proviso "at any and every hazard."[9]

For a time it seemed that the hoped for coöperation might be forth-

[8] J. C. Calhoun to Francis Wharton, September 17, 1844, in J. F. Jameson (ed.), *Correspondence of John C. Calhoun,* American Historical Association *Report* (1899, Vol. II), p. 616; hereinafter cited *Correspondence of Calhoun.* For the Bluffton movement see C. S. Boucher, "The Annexation of Texas and the Bluffton Movement in South Carolina," *Mississippi Valley Historical Review,* VI (June, 1919), 3-34.
[9] Phillip M. Hamer, *The Secession Movement in South Carolina, 1847-1852* (Allentown, Pa., 1918), pp. 22-23, 29.

4

coming. At the suggestion of Calhoun, Mississippi issued a call for a Southern convention. The South Carolina legislature elected delegates and resolved that the passage of the Wilmot Proviso or the abolition of slavery in the District of Columbia would be tantamount to a dissolution of the Union.[10] But the work of the Nashville Convention (June, 1850) was disappointing to South Carolina, and Rhett, on his return from the convention, began a drive for independent action by South Carolina if other states failed to coöperate.[11]

Meanwhile in Congress an effort was being made through compromise to avert the threatened secession of the Southern states. In January Henry Clay introduced a set of resolutions in which the South was offered the enactment of a drastic fugitive-slave law and the organization of New Mexico and Utah into territories without any mention of slavery; to the North the resolutions promised the admission of California as a free state and the abolition of the slave trade in the District of Columbia.[12] After a memorable debate in which Calhoun made his last great plea for Southern rights, the compromise measures were adopted by Congress. But they were utterly repudiated by South Carolinians. Severely assailed from the first, the passage of the compromise seemed to increase rather than diminish disunion sentiment. The voices of a few unionists such as Benjamin F. Perry, Joel R. Poinsett, and William J. Grayson were as voices crying in the wilderness. Even Christopher G. Memminger who was soon to stand with them was saying at this time that South Carolina should secede alone if no other state would act with her.[13]

In late 1850, however, a line of cleavage began to appear among the secessionists on the question of immediate procedure, a division which became quite clear in the legislature of 1850. Though there were only four or five true unionists, the secessionists were divided. A majority favored calling a convention for immediate secession, alone if necessary, but did not have the required two-thirds majority in the lower house. The minority was more cautious, claiming to stand for secession *ultimately* alone, if necessary, but only after an attempt had been made in a Southern congress to enlist the coöperation of other Southern states. This division between "separate state actionists" and "coöperationists" resulted in a deadlock and a compromise bill calling both a state convention and a Southern congress with elections of delegates to the convention in February, 1851, and to the congress in October.[14]

[10] *Ibid.*, pp. 38-43; C. S. Boucher, *The Secession and Co-operation Movements in South Carolina, 1848-1852*, Washington University *Studies*, V (April, 1918), 84-85; hereinafter cited Boucher, *Secession and Co-operation.*
[11] Hamer, *Secession Movement in S. C.*, pp. 62-63.
[12] The compromise resolutions provided also for the cession by Texas of some disputed territory to New Mexico and for the assumption by the United States of the Texas public debt amounting to about $10,000,000.
[13] Boucher, *Secession and Co-operation*, pp. 93 *et seq.*; Hamer, *Secession Movement in S. C.*, pp. 65-76.
[14] *Ibid.*, pp. 78-81; Boucher, *Secession and Co-operation*, pp. 110-114.

The February elections went overwhelmingly in favor of the separate action secessionists. Of the 169 delegates elected, the *Southern Patriot,* Perry's unionist paper of Greenville, could count only 50 or 60 who were even qualifiedly opposed to secession while the secessionists claimed 127 for separate action, 32 sincere coöperationists, and only 11 "submissionists." Almost immediately, however, there was a reaction. The coöperationists organized to expose the dangers of separate action and soon the state was in the midst of its bitterest factional fight since nullification days. The separate action secessionists, or radicals, over-played their hand in a Southern Rights convention in May by action which many regarded as an attempt to dictate the policies of the state before its people had assembled in convention. The coöperationists, skillfully led by such men as Memminger, Langdon Chevis, James L. Orr, Andrew P. Butler, and Robert W. Barnwell, made rapid gains during the summer. They attracted into their ranks men of various opinions ranging from true resistance men holding out for joint action with at least a few other states to a group of real unionists, mainly in the Greenville area.[15] Meanwhile the resistance program received little encouragement from the other Southern states. Virginia urged South Carolina to desist, and the fall elections in Alabama, Mississippi, and Georgia went against the secessionists. It seemed that the other states of the South would accept the Compromise of 1850 and that no Southern convention would be assembled. Nevertheless the October elections in South Carolina for delegates to the proposed Southern convention were made a test of strength between the parties and a kind of mandate to the state convention which had not yet convened. The results showed a surprising victory for the coöperationists who, by a vote of 25,045 to 17,710, elected candidates in six of the seven congressional districts.[16] Governor John H. Means lamented: "The noble attitude of resistance which I supposed the State about to assume . . . seems to have been delayed or abandoned, judging from the popular voice, as indicated by the results of the late elections."[17] Separate secession was indeed dead.

The state convention which assembled April 26, 1852, though containing a secessionist majority elected more than a year before, was compelled by its recent repudiation to limit its action to an ordinance asserting the right of secession and a resolution declaring

that the frequent violations of the Constitution of the United States by the Federal Government, and its encroachments upon the reserved rights of the sovereign States of this Union, especially in relation to slavery, amply justify this State, so far as any duty or obligation to her confederates is

[15] *Ibid.,* pp. 116-117, 123; Hamer, *Secession Movement in S. C.,* pp. 87-114.
[16] *Ibid.,* pp. 120-123; Wallace, *History of S. C.,* III, 128-129.
[17] *Journal of the Senate of South Carolina Being the Session of 1851* (Columbia, 1851), p. 19. The legislative journals will hereinafter be cited *Senate Journal* and *House Journal.*

involved, in dissolving at once all political connection with her co-States; and that she forbears the exercise of this manifest right of self government from considerations of expediency only.[18]

The more radical disunionists were disgusted. James H. Hammond thought the action "too pitiful for comment" and Rhett resigned his seat in the United States Senate on the ground that he was no longer a proper representative of his state.[19] But Rhett's cause had almost triumphed and succeeding events were yet to bring from other states the coöperation so vainly sought in the crisis of 1850.

The political excitement of 1847-1852 left South Carolina emotionally exhausted. Factional bitterness quickly diminished and for a time the recent political alignments tended to disappear. The radicals were anxious to detach the coöperationists from their erstwhile alliance with the small unionist group in the state and to close the ranks of all true resistance men for possible future emergencies. Governor Means congratulated the state that this had been accomplished by the convention of 1852, and stated his belief that further aggressions of the North, sure to come, would rally sister states and enable the South either to "force our rights to be respected in the Union or take our place as a Southern Confederacy amongst the nations of the earth."[20] Within the state, party division had about ended by the fall of 1852. Elections for the legislature inspired only a small vote, and harmony seemed to prevail as John L. Manning was unanimously elected governor.[21] In 1853, amidst general prosperity, national issues were so dormant that Manning felt justified in omitting from his message to the legislature all discussion of federal relations and referred to the "distinguished head of the Nation" as a fair exponent of the political principles of South Carolina. Seemingly the state had decided to accept under President Pierce the finality of the Compromise of 1850. Certainly the political life of the state was calmer than usual in 1853 and early 1854.[22]

Political strife soon revived, however, as James L. Orr began to organize a party whose program was the abandonment of isolation in national affairs and a close coöperation with the National Democratic party. Associated with him was the consistent unionist, Perry, and

[18] *Journals of the Conventions of the People of South Carolina, held in 1832, 1833, and 1852* (Columbia, 1860), p. 150.

[19] Wallace, *History of S. C.*, III, 131.

[20] *Senate Journal* (1852), pp. 29-30.

[21] C. S. Boucher, *South Carolina and the South on the Eve of Secession, 1852-1860*, Washington University *Studies*, VI (April, 1919), 85; hereinafter cited Boucher, *S. C. and the South*.

[22] *House Journal* (1853), pp. 16, 30. There was, however, a continuation of the old sectional quarrel between the up and low country over removal of glaring inequalities of representation. It centered in the 1850's in an attempt, successful in 1854, to divide Pendleton district to give the up country an additional senator, and in the proposal for popular election of presidential electors, which was agitated until about 1858. Wallace, *History of S. C.*, III, 134-138.

soon Preston S. Brooks, Orr's colleague in Congress after 1853. Francis W. Pickens, a recent secessionist, also associated himself with the group in 1854, as did many of the coöperationists in the struggle of 1850-52. The successor of Rhett in the United States Senate, Josiah J. Evans, also stood with this group of moderates.[23] He wrote in 1854:

I love the Union, and hope it will be perpetual; but at the same time, I love our little State . . . and will stand by its rights when invaded, with my last breath. We have, indeed, been rather too belligerent at times, but I do not think we have lost much of national feeling, and I am sure we have lost nothing of national character.[24]

Evans's statement seems to reflect a rather definite reaction from the extremes of 1850 and probably represents the point of view of most of those affiliated with the National Democratic party in South Carolina. Though they were denounced as nationalists, federalists, and unionists by the State Rights party, the charge in its implications was not altogether just. Some indeed did deny the advantages of disunion and believed that protection of Southern interests should be sought only within the Union. Others were in fact only coöperationists who felt that secession was no longer an immediate issue, and that South Carolina's most practical policy was to influence national affairs as far as possible through the national party. Still others believed that the National Democratic party had proved itself sound on slavery and state rights by its support of the Kansas-Nebraska bill and therefore deserved support. But the radicals made no distinction between these groups. All were bitterly denounced. In the opinion of the State Rights party the National Democratic party was not to be trusted; the South should form a strictly Southern party, nominate only sound Southern men, and if unable to control events in Washington, be organized and prepared to form a separate government.[25]

The struggle between the National and State Rights Democrats was complicated somewhat by the appearance of the Know-Nothing party. Into its ranks went various elements. Some, trusting neither the National Democrats nor the State Rights faction, thought the Know-Nothings offered a truly national organization which might unite the sections. For example, Dr. James H. Thornwell who had been an opponent of disunion in 1832 and 1851 wrote in 1855 that if the Know-Nothings failed, the last hope for the Union was gone.[26] Some secessionists on the other hand seem to have hoped that a great Southern party might be built up under the Know-Nothing name. Still others,

[23] Laura A. White, "The National Democrats in South Carolina, 1852 to 1860," *South Atlantic Quarterly,* XXVIII (October, 1929), 372.
[24] Benjamin F. Perry, *Reminiscences of Public Men* (Philadelphia, 1883), p. 120.
[25] Boucher, *S. C. and the South,* pp. 105, 109, 117-118.
[26] Benjamin F. Palmer, *The Life and Letters of James Henley Thornwell* (Richmond, 1875), pp. 478-479.

fearing immigration as dangerous to slavery, were attracted by the nativist principles of the Know-Nothings. But the party had only a fleeting existence in South Carolina, largely, no doubt, because of its heterogeneous character. It was fought aggressively by the National Democrats and was opposed by the Charleston *Mercury* which feared that the state might be divided into two national parties as in 1840.[27]

The Know-Nothings weakened, Orr proposed that South Carolina participate in the National Democratic convention of 1856 at Cincinnati, and under his influence some forty members of the legislature issued a call for a state convention to choose delegates. The secessionists greeted the proposal with scorn, and characterized the conventionists as cheap politicians, mere office seekers, and spoilsmen who would sacrifice the honor and interests of the state for selfish ambition. They accused the conventionists of sneering at South Carolina's past, and of praising the Union and praying for its preservation. But the National Democrats met in Columbia May 5-6. Delegates from the coastal region were conspicuously absent, only Georgetown and Charleston being represented, but every district of the up country save two was represented. Orr and Pickens, president of the convention, both defended the policy of participating in the national convention against the objections brought by the disunionists. To the contention of the latter that the system of representation in Democratic conventions made possible Northern dictation of candidates and platforms and that Southern interests could only be protected by a strictly Southern party, the conventionists sanely replied that the next contest would be between a Black Republican and the Democratic nominee, and since South Carolina must inevitably support the latter, the wise policy was to have a voice in his selection. Orr denied that the Democratic party was committed to popular sovereignty. He held that its Northern members were divided on the question and that the Kansas-Nebraska act itself left the matter to the courts which would surely decide against the pernicious doctrine; but even if they did not, the South was still much better off than before the Compromise of 1850 and the passage of the Kansas-Nebraska act. The federal government, he said, had ceased to be a "despoiler" of the South and had come to be its protector. In accordance with these ideas the state convention adopted a platform and elected delegates. The platform dodged the question of popular sovereignty but stated that South Carolina's participation in the Cincinnati convention was conditioned on the inclusion in the national platform of a statement that no territory should ever be closed to slavery by Congress and that the fugitive slave law should be permanently continued and enforced.[28]

[27] Boucher, *S. C. and the South*, p. 108; White, "National Democrats in S. C.," *loc. cit.*, pp. 372, 377.
[28] *Proceedings of the Democratic State Convention, held at Columbia 5th and 6th of May, 1856, for the purpose of electing delegates to the Democratic National Convention, to meet in Cincinnati in June* (Columbia, 1856), pp. 5-28.

The course of the National Democrats was regarded by the State Rights party as especially reprehensible in view of the fact that the controversy over Kansas was raging at the very time of the state convention. Now of all times, it was said, Southern men should act only within a strictly Southern party.[29] There was criticism, too, of the choice of Charleston as the next national convention city; it was a mere scheme of the National Democrats, it was said, to increase their prestige and humble the State Rights party. Though Buchanan's nomination was generally acceptable, his tariff record was severely criticized, and Rhett believed that if the tariff were not modified to the level of 1833 the Union should be dissolved. He and others proposed a Southern conference to draw amendments to the Constitution which, if unacceptable to the North, should be followed by conventions of the two sections to divide the national assets and dissolve the Union. This group also demanded that the fall elections to Congress be used to show that South Carolina, by refusing to elect "doughfaces," was not willing to follow the National Democrats.[30]

In the contest between the parties it is probable that the more moderate conventionists represented a majority of the people of the state. The *Darlington Flag* declared:

It is time for us to awake to the full import of the deliberate popular decree promulgated in 1851. South Carolina will not secede from the Union. Nay more than this—we grieve to be compelled to say, but we cannot be blind to the fact—that a great majority of her people, in spite of the wrongs and indignities that we have received, are ardently attached to the Union . . . the overwhelmingly predominant sentiment of the people is in favor of an unreserved union with the Democratic party.[31]

The election of Buchanan gave general satisfaction. Only a few had hoped for John C. Fremont's election as an occasion for disunion and few suggested separate secession in case of Black Republican victory.

[29] South Carolina had had little to do with the passage of the Kansas-Nebraska act but it was highly acceptable to the state. As the New England Emigrant Aid Society sent settlers to Kansas there was much feeling in South Carolina against the "hireling emigrants," and strong editorial and public protest. The legislature of 1855 debated a resolution proposing money and men for Kansas but nothing was done. Unofficial committees were organized, however, for the purpose of sending one hundred men from each district. How many actually went is not clear but well-armed companies are said to have gone from Laurens, Barnwell, Union and the Pee Dee section. Some persons went from Newberry and perhaps from other sections of the state. According to a contemporary estimate between 200 and 300 had gone by July, 1856. This is in line with Professor Wallace's estimate of a total of from 250 to 400. Boucher, *S. C. and the South,* p. 98; Wallace, *History of S. C.,* III, 139; Yates Snowden (ed.), *History of South Carolina* (New York, 1920), II, 644; John A. Chapman, *Annals of Newberry* (Newberry, 1892), p. 371; Charleston *Daily Courier,* July 4, 1856, hereinafter cited *Courier).*

[30] Boucher, *S. C. and the South,* pp. 112-113; Van Deusen, *Economic Bases of Disunion in S. C.,* p. 102.

[31] Quoted by White, "National Democrats in S. C.," *loc. cit.,* p. 377 note.

Although the invitation of Governor Henry A. Wise of Virginia to a Southern governors' conference at Raleigh was accepted, there was slight enthusiasm for it.[32] With Buchanan elected the legislature seemed disposed to await the results of his administration. Resolutions demanding certain amendments to the Constitution were defeated by a vote of 56 to 44 in the House and the feeling seemed to be that Southern interests might be effectively protected within the Union.[33]

The more moderate position of the National Democrats now seemed definitely in the ascendency. Of course, all groups remained alive to Southern rights and interests, and the disunionists lost no opportunity to grumble at anything which seemed unfavorable to the South. Thus the tariff of 1857 was criticized on the ground that it forced the South to pay tribute for the benefit of Northern manufacturers, and the panic of 1857 was blamed on Northern speculation the baneful results of which would not have been felt had no political connection existed between the two sections.[34] Lawrence M. Keitt wrote in the middle of 1857 that "the safety of the South is only in herself."[35] But moderates seemed stronger in their influence. There even occurred a controversy between the Charleston *Courier* and the *Evening News* over the theoretical right of secession.[36] Governor Robert F. W. Allston, in his message to the legislature, defended the Dred Scott decision against the resolutions of Maine and Connecticut but was rather conciliatory when he appealed for charitable judgment of one section by the other. He was willing even that South Carolinians associate themselves with the National Democratic party in nominating conventions so long as they did not pledge the state.[37]

The strength of the moderates was also shown when Rhett received only six votes in the election for United States Senator. The radical James H. Hammond was elected over the National Democratic candidate, F. W. Pickens, but he almost immediately disappointed the ultras by a tendency to ally himself with the moderates. Very soon he was writing Perry that at the time of his election he thought the South to be in a better position than ever before in his time; with abolition somewhat checked, the bank gone, internal improvements given up, and free trade virtually adopted, the South was "on smooth water" and in a position safely to remain in the Union.[38] In the summer of 1858 he returned to South Carolina preaching that the best policy for the South was to remain in the Union and through close coöperation control

[32] *Ibid.*, p. 378.
[33] Boucher, *S. C. and the South*, pp. 115-116.
[34] Van Deusen, *Economic Bases of Disunion in S. C.*, pp. 93-94, 173-174.
[35] *Ibid.*, p. 102.
[36] Boucher, *S. C. and the South*, p. 118; White, "National Democrats in S. C.," *loc. cit.*, p. 379.
[37] *House Journal* (1857), pp. 28-29.
[38] Perry, *Reminiscences of Public Men* (1883), pp. 108-109.

it. The radicals were alarmed at this desertion of their old leader.[39] To them the defeat of the Lecompton constitution was positive proof that the National Democratic party could not be trusted. Orr and Hammond were therefore denounced as rank unionists, while the more radical congressmen, Milledge L. Bonham and John McQueen, were banqueted and praised. The moderates, however, retained their strength. They were unable to elect Orr to the Senate in 1858 but the choice of James Chesnut, Jr. was regarded as a victory for conservatism and a defeat of the "Congo party" which favored the reopening of the slave trade.[40] Pickens wrote Perry from St. Petersburg, "I rejoice to see in our State more reasonable and wiser counsels prevailing than for years."[41]

The hopefulness and what seems to have been the growing influence of the moderates in South Carolina were given a rude shock by the John Brown raid in October, 1859. Undoubtedly the effect of this incident was to drive many conservatives into the camp of the ultras. At the opening of the legislature soon after the raid, Governor William H. Gist's message was frankly disunionist. After reviewing the growth of abolitionism and referring to the Northern acclaim of Brown, he asked:

Can we, then, any longer talk about moderation and conservatism, and statesmanship, and still hug the delusive phantom to our breasts that all is well, and that the Democratic party, upon whom we have too confidently relied, will work out our salvation by platforms and resolutions?

If only the South were united, he said, "we could enforce equality in the Union or maintain our independence out of it." Let South Carolina make every effort to get the coöperation of the South but let her not yield principle, and let her not forget that she is a "sovereign and an equal" with the right to join the family of nations when she willed.[42]

The legislature was equally stirred. No less than sixteen sets of resolutions, all radical, were introduced in the House besides a number in the Senate. One declared that South Carolina was ready to contribute money and men for the defense of the border slave states; another that South Carolina was ready for a Southern confederacy, and that the governor should be given power to call a meeting of the legislature whenever other states indicated a readiness to coöperate to that end; another that "this legislature does not hesitate to declare that this Union, of doubtful value to the South, would be scarcely an atom in the scale

[39] Elizabeth Merritt, *James Henry Hammond, 1807-1864* (Baltimore, 1923), pp. 122-126; White, "National Democrats in S. C.," *loc. cit.,* pp. 379-380. For other optimistic utterances of Hammond and Pickens see Perry, *Reminiscences* (1883), pp. 110-111, 167-170.
[40] Boucher, *S. C. and the South,* pp. 102, 124; White, "National Democrats in S. C.," *loc. cit.,* pp. 380-381. Wallace, *History of S. C.,* III, 145.
[41] Perry, *Reminiscences of Public Men* (1883), p. 177.
[42] *House Journal* (1859), pp. 12-24.

against the perpetual maintenance" of slavery. One looked to the establishment of a committee of public safety and of committees of correspondence. Even Perry, the unionist, offered a resolution stating that the people of South Carolina were prepared to defend the institution of slavery "at any, and every sacrifice of their political relations with the Federal Government and the Northern States, should it be invaded or assailed in any manner or form whatever," and that they felt an "inexpressible scorn and contempt at the infamous, hypocritical sympathy" expressed in the North for John Brown, "a notorious horse thief, assassin and traitor"; and that the general endorsement of John Brown would make it dishonorable in South Carolina to continue in the same government with a people whose social and moral tone "characterizes them as a nation of pirates, savages, assassins and traitors."[43]

From the mass of suggestions a joint resolution, drawn by C. C. Memminger, was finally adopted stating that South Carolina had declined to secede in 1852 on grounds of expediency only; that assaults on slavery and Southern rights had since increased; that South Carolina, still deferring to her sister states, nevertheless felt that a meeting of the slave states should be immediately called; that the governor request the other states to elect delegates; that a special commissioner be appointed to express to Virginia the sympathy of South Carolina and her earnest desire to coöperate in measures of common defense; and finally, that $100,000 be appropriated for military contingencies.[44]

Memminger himself was appointed commissioner to Virginia in the belief that his reputation for conservatism would inspire confidence and render his efforts more effectual. Actually, Memminger was at this time not very conservative, as his corespondence with the secessionist William Porcher Miles of Charleston and others clearly reveals.[45] He wrote: "My own opinion and I think the opinion of our State is that the Union cannot be preserved; and that a sectional Government such as we now have is not worthy of preservation." He added that "new terms" and "fresh constitutional guarantees" might make another Union desirable but he was apparently ready to break up the old.[46] His reception at Richmond was courteous enough but he was disappointed to find that sentiment generally was much more conservative than he had anticipated. In his address of January 19 he made a skillful effort to arouse the Virginians, urging at least a Southern conference to discuss and propose measures which might be demanded as the price of continuing in the Union. He pledged South Carolina's willingness to abide by the decision of such a conference. "If our pace be too fast

[43] *Ibid.*, pp. 42, 53, 57-58, 72.   [44] *Senate Journal* (1859), p. 168.
[45] This correspondence is summarized and the mission well treated in Ollinger Crenshaw, "Christopher G. Memminger's Mission to Virginia, 1860," *The Journal of Southern History*, VIII (August, 1942), 334-349.
[46] Memminger to Miles, January 3, 1860, Miles Papers, Southern Historical Collection, University of North Carolina.

for some, we are content to walk slower; our earnest wish is that all may keep together. We cannot consent to stand still, but would gladly make common cause with all. We are far from expecting or desiring to dictate or lead."[47] But Virginia's reaction was unfavorable. As it became clear to the commissioner that Virginia would not participate in a conference he wrote Miles: "I am brought to the opinion, that we farther South will be compelled to act, and drag after us these divided States."[48] Only Mississippi and Alabama reacted favorably to South Carolina's conference proposal. Mississippi not only accepted the invitation but sent a commission to Virginia in support of Memminger's plea. Alabama took the advanced position of directing her governor to call an election for a state convention should the Republicans elect the President in the fall. On this possibility the South Carolina secessionists now based their hopes.

The significance of the John Brown episode in the development of South Carolina secession sentiment was undoubtedly very great. It weakened the influence of the moderates and strengthened the hands of the radicals. Temporarily it caused even Perry and Pickens to falter in their conservatism and it made secession in late 1860 much less difficult.

Meanwhile the bitter speakership contest in the federal House of Representatives was also contributing to secession sentiment in South Carolina. The radicals seem to have believed that the long desired disunion might come as a result of the election of John Sherman or some other endorser of Helper's *Impending Crisis*. There was even wild talk of ejecting by force an obnoxious speaker and precipitating at Washington a bloody revolution. This course Governor Gist thought unwise but he promised to support it with troops if the South Carolina delegation approved the plan.[49]

[47] Henry D. Capers, *The Life and Times of C. G. Memminger* (Richmond, 1893), pp. 247-278.

[48] Memminger to Miles, January 24, 1860, Miles Papers.

[49] Ollinger Crenshaw, *The Slave States in the Presidential Election of 1860* (Baltimore, 1925), pp. 201-202; hereinafter cited Crenshaw, *Election of 1860*.

CHAPTER II

THE PRESIDENTIAL ELECTION OF 1860

As early as March, 1859, the radical group in South Carolina began a drive to prevent state representation in the National Democratic convention at Charleston. Using the same arguments as in 1856 they insisted that the South's safety lay in a strictly Southern party, and that the South should not allow itself to be dragged along by the "fatal delusions of national partyism, a source of profit to her Southern betrayers and a spoil and mockery to her Northern enemies." The Democratic party was pictured by the *Mercury* as an organization without a creed, divided on every practical issue such as the tariff, internal improvements, Southern slave property, and the right of secession. Such a party could not be depended on to protect the interests of the South.[1]

It is clear that state rights leaders were concerned over the apparent strength of the convention party and fearful that it might even support Stephen A. Douglas at Charleston. Toward the end of March William Porcher Miles wrote various friends asking if Washington rumors of a Douglas party in South Carolina could possibly be true. The replies were not reassuring. Robert N. Gourdin refused to believe the rumors but was afraid they were "founded in truth." Isaac W. Hayne thought there was a "fragment" of the convention party favoring Douglas on a non-committal platform, but did not think it could prevail in the state convention. He mentioned as Douglas men Henry Buist, Thomas Y. Simons, and George Reynolds. Alfred Huger suspected Orr of Douglas affiliations and thought there was a "pigmy race of politicians" willing to "yield to the highest bidder." John Cuningham agreed in thinking there was "much proclivity for Douglas" in Charleston, but was sure that the country was against him and that Orr could not control this opposition. D. H. Hamilton wrote that a Douglas party not only existed in Charleston, but that the events of the convention might even develop a "pretty strong" party favoring him.

They will not show at first, they will play coy, voting for several ballots for Southern Rights Democrats, but when the issue is fairly before the Convention, as to who shall really receive the nomination, I think that you will find that the "eight fire-eaters" will accept the most available candidate. Unfortunately South Carolina will be represented in the Convention by a regular set of "small fry" who are anxious, after swimming in the shallow water of State politics, to try their powers on the "deep" of National politics. . . . Why, they are beginning already to apportion Federal offices here—mine, Conner's and Colcock's have I believe been disposed.[2]

[1] Boucher, *S. C. and the South*, p. 128; Charleston *Mercury*, April 6, 1860.
[2] I. W. Hayne to Miles, April 11, 1860; R. N. Gourdin to Miles, April 4, 1860; John Cuningham to Miles, April 5, 1860; Alfred Huger to Miles, April 4, 1860; D. H. Hamilton to Miles, April 4, 1860, Miles Papers.

It is probable that the Douglas sympathies of the convention party were greatly exaggerated by these opponents of the convention idea. At any rate none openly espoused the Douglas candidacy or defended his squatter sovereignty ideas. South Carolina sentiment generally was so antagonistic to the Little Giant that it is almost inconceivable that South Carolina delegates could have voted for his nomination, though it is quite reasonable to suppose that they might have endorsed him after nomination on the ground that Douglas was better than a Black Republican. Their hope, of course, was that a Southerner such as John C. Breckinridge of Kentucky, Robert M. T. Hunter of Virginia, perhaps Orr himself, might be chosen. As to his own candidacy Orr suggested an endorsement by the state convention but an uninstructed delegation which in the early balloting should vote for some other Southerner in order not to alienate the friends of Douglas.[3]

The efforts of the convention party to assemble a state convention for the nomination of delegates to Charleston met no organized opposition and were highly successful. Only seven districts, five from the low country, were unrepresented when the group gathered in Columbia April 23. The *Conservatist*, in congratulating Newberry District on being unrepresented, claimed that a majority of the people of the state were opposed to the ruinous convention policy and stated that district meetings were so poorly attended in some places that it had been difficult to find enough delegates.[4] It is true that nine districts sent only one delegate each but the National Democrats were highly pleased at the attendance, Orr remarking that the large representation indicated that the propriety of South Carolina participation in national conventions was now definitely settled.[5]

As president of the convention Orr set forth the principles of the party in two addresses in which he argued that only through a strong Democratic party could the election of a Republican President be prevented. Admitting that some Northern Democrats subscribed to the squatter sovereignty principle, he called attention to the fact that even this doctrine was less dangerous than the Republican creed. But the Democratic official platform drawn in 1856 was, he held, no squatter sovereignty platform; rather it meant that slavery could not be excluded from a territory prior to the formation of a state constitution for admission to the Union. He believed that South Carolina delegates would be among friends in Charleston and that there was still good

[3] For correspondence between Orr and his associates regarding his candidacy, see Lillian A. Kibler, *Benjamin F. Perry, South Carolina Unionist* (Durham, 1946), pp. 298-299.

[4] Newberry *Conservatist*, March 13, 20, April 17, 1860.

[5] *Proceedings of the Democratic State Convention of South Carolina, held in Columbia on the 16th and 17th of April, 1860, for the purpose of electing delegates to the Democratic National Convention, to meet in Charleston 23rd April* (Columbia, 1860), pp. 2-3, 5-10; hereinafter cited *Proceedings* (April).

sense and patriotism enough in the North and West to check the fanaticism of others. The approaching campaign was important. "Not only is the maintenance of our principles involved, but the fate of the Government itself." Should the Republicans seize control and attempt to carry out their nefarious purposes it might become necessary for the South to strike for its honor and interest. This being true, it was all the more important for South Carolina to follow a moderate and prudent course in order to have the approval and hearty coöperation of her sister Southern states. Orr's statement may be regarded as representative of the opinions of most members of the convention. Willing to maintain the Union, but believing that the election of a Republican would be sufficient cause for secession of the South, they were of the opinion that every effort should be made through the Democratic party to prevent Republican success.

The platform reflected these views. The Cincinnati platform of 1856 was endorsed as "sound and maintainable," and the Dred Scott decision was approved. The squatter sovereignty interpretation of the Cincinnati platform was denied and Douglas's Freeport Doctrine was repudiated by a resolution declaring that though the people of a territory might adopt a constitution with or without slavery at the time of application for admission to the Union, they could not prior to that time abolish or exclude slavery "either by direct or unfriendly" legislation. But there was no demand made, as in the Alabama platform, for congressional protection of slavery in the territories. James Powell of Chesterfield offered resolutions which were virtually equivalent to the Alabama platform but they were defeated by a vote of 108 to 12. And when Michael P. O'Connor, of Charleston, proposed a somewhat similar resolution demanding that the rights of the South be fully stated in the national platform and pledging South Carolina's "firm and undivided support" to Alabama and other Southern states in working for such a plank, the resolution was defeated 86 to 55.[6] Perry later held that the failure to instruct delegates to withdraw should the platform not include the Southern interpretation of the Cincinnati platform was equivalent to instructions not to withdraw.[7]

After endorsing Orr as a sort of dark horse candidate for the nomination the convention adjourned to meet the scornful comments of its critics. The *Mercury* denounced "coöperationists" who would not coöperate with Alabama, and R. B. Rhett, Jr., telegraphed William Porcher Miles that the convention had been an Orr affair "trimming to keep in with Douglas." The radicals were pleased, however, that the Douglas doctrine of unfriendly legislation had been repudiated.[8]

[6] *Ibid.*, pp. 5-10, 12-14, 18-20.
[7] B. F. Perry, *Biographical Sketches of Eminent American Statesmen, with Speeches, Addresses and Letters* (Philadelphia, 1887), p. 186; hereinafter cited Perry, *Biographical Sketches.*
[8] White, "National Democrats in S. C.," *loc. cit.*, p. 384; R. B. Rhett, Jr., to Miles, April 17, 18, 1860, Miles Papers.

It was unfortunate that the national Democratic convention should have met in Charleston (April 23, 1860). The galleries of the convention hall and the streets of the city were crowded with disunionists. The *Mercury* kept up a constant fire of criticism of Southern coöperation with non-sectional parties. "If the National Democratic party," it declared, "cannot stand the test of principle, matters on which the destiny of the South depends, let us have a sectional party that can. Let the Convention break up." Radical speeches of such men as William Lowndes Yancey were applauded. The Alabama resolutions were printed for the second time. Speeches by Calhoun and others on the dangers to the South of national parties were quoted and endorsed. Clearly the Charleston radicals desired the disruption of the convention, and the *Mercury* was later to claim proudly some of the credit for the accomplishment.[9]

Dissension appeared in the Charleston convention from the first. Besides the personal animosity towards Douglas, who had definitely estranged the South by his opposition to the admission of Kansas under the Lecompton constitution and by his Freeport Doctrine in 1858, there were serious clashes growing out of the presence of contesting delegations from New York and a proposal in effect to discontinue the unit rule except in the case of instructed delegations. Southern members felt that they were unfairly dealt with in both cases. The New York delegation headed by Dean Richmond and committed to Douglas was seated though in a similar case four years before both delegations had been accredited. The new rule to allow uninstructed delegations to divide their votes had the effect, according to the Southern members, of giving to the Douglas group 28 votes which it would otherwise not have received.[10]

It was on the adoption of the platform, however, that the disruption of the convention came. The resolutions committee, with equal state representation, was controlled by the Southern members who made a majority report which included resolutions that neither Congress nor a territorial legislature had power to abolish slavery by direct or indirect legislation and that it was furthermore the duty of Congress to protect slavery in the territories when necessary. This was the position that Jefferson Davis, as spokesman for the South, had taken in his Senate resolutions earlier in the year and the platform for which Alabama had instructed her delegates to insist upon to the point of withdrawal. It was equivalent to the platform of the South Carolina convention except for the additional statement that Congress was duty bound to protect

[9] *Mercury*, April 30, August 28, 1860. For evidence that the radicals were plotting the disruption of the Charleston convention as a step toward disunion see Crenshaw, *Election of 1860*, pp. 203-204.

[10] Dwight L. Dumond, *The Secession Movement, 1860-1861* (New York, 1931), pp. 38-43.

slavery in the territories. The South claimed that it was the Cincinnati platform of 1856 properly interpreted.[11]

The minority report reaffirmed the Cincinnati platform and added a resolution that all rights in regard to property in the territories should be decided by the courts and that the party pledged itself to abide by past and future decisions of the Supreme Court on the matter. From the Southern standpoint this was objectionable because it did not repudiate squatter sovereignty under Douglas's interpretation of the Cincinnati platform and the Dred Scott decision. For the Northern delegates, acceptance of the Southern demands meant political suicide. Neither side would yield.[12]

As the sectional lines drew tighter and feeling mounted, the South Carolina delegates, in caucus, considered the problem of their proper course should other states withdraw. Perry said that he was confident that they had no notion of withdrawing when they entered the convention, though they understood well enough that the issue might be presented. The pressure on them, however, was, as Perry said, very great;[13] and when they sought by telegraph the advice of the South Carolina congressmen the word came back to withdraw. A motion in caucus for this course was withdrawn when Perry refused to be bound by majority action and it was agreed that each delegate should act on his own responsibility. When the Southern platform was defeated in the convention, thirteen of South Carolina's sixteen delegates followed Alabama, Mississippi, and Louisiana out of the hall amidst bursts of enthusiastic cheering on the floor and in the galleries.[14] Their dignified statement was to the effect that since the principles of the state convention had been explicitly denied by the party, they would be acting in bad faith to principles and constituents alike to remain longer in the convention.[15]

Three of the delegates did not sign the statement of withdrawal. One of these, J. P. Reed of Anderson, said later that he refused only because the statement was hastily drawn.[16] Perry and Lemuel Boozer remained in the convention and in the balloting for a nominee cast their votes for R. M. T. Hunter of Virginia, receiving each time the hisses of the gallery for doing so.[17] Perry was greatly disappointed at the with-

[11] *Ibid.*, pp. 44-50.   [12] *Ibid.*

[13] R. B. Rhett wrote: "When they came they had no more idea of going out than of flying. They would not even go to the Southern Caucus. If they had not retired, they would have been mobbed, I believe." Rhett to Miles, May 12, 1860, Miles Papers.

[14] Perry, *Biographical Sketches*, pp. 187-188; Pickens *Keowee Courier*, June 2, 1860, quoting Perry's letter of May 15, 1860; *Mercury*, May 2, 1860.

[15] *Proceedings of the National Democratic Convention, convened at Charleston, S. C., April 23, 1860* (Washington, 1860), pp. 36-37.

[16] Dumond, *Secession Movement*, p. 52. Reed joined the bolters at Saint Andrews Hall and received great applause for his speech stating his reasons for withdrawal. *Keowee Courier*, May 12, 1860.

[17] Perry, *Reminiscences of Public Men* (1883), p. 188.

drawal of his colleagues. While repudiating popular sovereignty, he thought that the demand that Congress protect slavery in the territories was unwise, and even dangerous for the South. The whole quarrel over slavery in the territories, he said, was an abstraction, because soil and climate would determine where slavery would go. He hoped that the convention would endorse the Dred Scott decision, that the bolting delegates would then return, and a united party face the common enemy.[18]

On the evening of their withdrawal, April 30, the seceding delegates met at Saint Andrews Hall with John S. Preston of South Carolina temporary chairman. A permanent organization with James A. Bayard, of Delaware as chairman was effected and a platform drawn for the "Constitutional Democratic" party, the platform being essentially the majority report of the original convention. It was the intention of the bolters to proceed to the nomination of candidates as soon as the "squatter sovereignty convention" should nominate Douglas. The adjournment of that body to Baltimore without naming Douglas, however, caused the bolters to change their plans. Some hoped that the platform might be reconsidered at Baltimore and changed to meet the demands of the South; at least a Southern man might be chosen to give the Cincinnati platform a Southern construction, reunite the party, and perhaps save the Union. They would therefore adjourn to meet at Baltimore. But others, among them James Simons of South Carolina, strongly opposed a reunion of the party, and refused to go to Baltimore. The convention therefore decided to adjourn to meet in Richmond June 11.[19]

The course of the South Carolina delegates at Charleston was generally approved in the state. Among the few who criticized the withdrawal was Orr. In a published letter he argued that the Southern members should have remained in the convention and prevented the nomination of a man obnoxious to the South. Hammond thought it was "silly" to have seceded "on a very distant & improbable issue."[20] At the other extreme, some disunionists, while approving the withdrawal, were half-hearted in their praise and stated that the delegates withdrew only because they were forced by outside opinion; and it was pointed out that the experience at Charleston fully vindicated those who had criticized the convention policy.[21] But there was general agreement that withdrawal was necessary. Nor was there much dis-

---

[18] Convention speech in Perry, *Biographical Sketches*, pp. 145-151.
[19] *Statement of the Proceedings of the Convention of the National Democratic Party, held in Charleston in April, 1860, that led to the withdrawal of certain delegations, and Proceedings of the Delegates that withdrew* (Charleston, 1860), pp. 26-36; Dumond, *Secession Movement*, pp. 57-59.
[20] William Stickney (ed.), *Autobiography of Amos Kendall* (Boston, 1872), p. 573; J. H. Hammond to W. G. Simms, July 10, 1860, Hammond Papers, Library of Congress.
[21] *Conservatist*, May 15, 1860.

agreement on the question of what position the state should assume on the efforts being made by conservatives to reassemble the whole original convention at Baltimore in an attempt to reunite the party. Perry of course worked for this plan and the *Courier* apparently approved it. Alfred Huger urged Miles to consider this course as a means of saving the country from Seward's "gang." Some thought that the Richmond meeting might be postponed on the chance that the Baltimore convention might accept the Southern position.[22] But the overwhelmingly predominant opinion was that South Carolina should accredit delegates to Richmond only. The Greenville *Southern Enterprise,* though hoping that a Southern platform would be adopted at Baltimore and harmony restored, thought it would be the "vilest submission" for the Southern states to re-enter the Douglas convention. Even the suggestion for delaying the convention was severely criticised by the *Mercury.*[23]

Though all agreed that South Carolina should send delegates to Richmond and to Richmond only, there was still a real difference of opinion within the state. Disunionists of the Rhett type, long critical of national conventions, argued that there was no inconsistency in supporting the Richmond convention for it was a sectional, not a national, convention. Called by Southern states, it would be composed of Southern delegates. The fact that some Northern Democrats who agreed with the South would also attend was certainly an objectionable feature, said Rhett, but it was essentially a Southern convention and South Carolina should go to Richmond as it had to Nashville in 1850.[24] This group saw in the Richmond convention an opportunity to further the cause of secession. On the other hand, many had by no means given up either the hope or desire to save the Union and these denied that the Richmond convention would be purely a sectional one. The *South Carolinian* for example, hoped that the Richmond convention would revive the Democratic party as a party of original state rights principles. "Those who imagine they see in it, either with fear or favor, a foreshadow, or rather a design, of disunion are mistaken"; its appeal will be to the states North and South on a platform similar to that rejected at Charleston; let the Southern states endorse the action of their seceding delegates and North Carolina, Tennessee, Maryland, Kentucky, Missouri, California, Oregon, Pennsylvania, New York, and some Northwestern states will fall in line to make it a national party of state rights principles.[25]

[22] White, "National Democrats in S. C.," *loc. cit.,* p. 383; Alfred Huger to W. P. Miles, May 7, 1860, Miles Papers.

[23] *Southern Enterprise,* May 17, 1860; D. L. Dumond, *Southern Editorials on Secession* (New York, 1931), pp. 105-108, quoting *Mercury,* May 23, 1860; *ibid.,* p. xiii.

[24] *Keowee Courier,* June 12, 1860, quoting Rhett's letter of May 10, 1860; *Conservatist,* May 22, 1860.

[25] Dumond, *Southern Editorials on Secession,* pp. 73-74, quoting the Columbia *Daily South Carolinian,* May 6, 1860; hereinafter cited *Carolinian.*

Reflecting the difference of opinion as to the purpose of the Richmond convention was a disagreement between the parties as to who should represent the state in that assembly. Both convention men and radicals wished to control the delegation, and a third group, which according to William Henry Trescot was much larger, was anxious to bring the factions together on a program of coöperation in good faith with the other Southern states. Of this group was Trescot himself. He "would put aside Barker and Reynolds and Simons with one hand and Rhett and Cuningham on the other unless they can get together with us and with themselves." This program required the election of a new state convention. After talking with Theodore G. Barker, the chairman of the state central committee, Trescot feared that the conventionists would insist on merely reassembling the old convention, in which case he thought there would be trouble. He urged Miles and Hammond to join in the harmony movement. "If ever there was an opportunity," he wrote Hammond, "to give practical force to the doctrine you have so ably advocated—if ever there was a chance to teach the South that its battle can be fought in the Union, now is the time."[26]

A degree of coöperation between the parties was temporarily achieved. The state central committee decided against reassembling the April convention and issued a call for election of new delegates. At the request of the anti-convention leaders the call was so framed as to allow the participation of those who had not previously taken part but who now wished to harmonize in the movement to send delegates to Richmond. Pledges were said to have been given by the anti-convention men for friendly coöperation with the National Democrats. As a result of this agreement the State Rights party actively joined in the district meetings and were successful in substituting for old delegates a large number of radical secessionists. Of the 161 delegates to the April convention only 52 were returned to the second convention in May.[27] Much to the chagrin of the conventionists the radicals were in control. D. H. Hamilton wrote Miles on the eve of the convention: "The Union men here are in a great state of excitement at the idea that 'the extreme left' are to get possession of the Convention tomorrow at Columbia— they say So: Car: has never been so divided as she is at present."[28]

[26] W. H. Trescot to W. P. Miles, May 8, 1860, Miles Papers; Trescot to J. H. Hammond, May 12, 1860, Hammond Papers. Hammond wrote about this time that the Richmond convention, by showing the North that the South was in earnest, would have no tendency toward disunion but would have rather the opposite effect. *Keowee Courier*, June 2, 1860. April 15th he had written: "I assure you . . . that unless the slavery question can be wholly eliminated from politics, this government is not worth two years,' perhaps not two months' purchase. . . . While regarding this Union as cramping the South, I will nevertheless sustain it as long as I can." Quoted by J. F. Rhodes, *History of the United States from the Compromise of 1850 to the End of the Roosevelt Administration* (New York, 1928), II, 396.
[27] *Proceedings of the State Democratic Convention held in Columbia, S. C., May 30-31, 1860* (Columbia, 1860), pp. 8-14, 59-61; *Proceedings* (April), pp. 3-4.
[28] D. H. Hamilton to W. P. Miles, May 29, 1860, Miles Papers.

The National Democrats went to the convention, said Samuel Mc-Gowan,

... to find the old Democratic ship in which conservative men had weathered many a storm of ridicule, abuse and opposition, entirely in the possession of a new crew—foremast and mizzen, quarterdeck and all are held by new men ... and what is still more wonderful, we find that their prominent men consist of those who, in times past, have thrown the most broadsides into that same old craft.[29]

Dissension appeared at the outset over organization and procedure. When James M. Gadberry of Union moved that the temporary chairman, C. P. Sullivan of Laurens, appoint a committee to name permanent officers, the low country secessionists demanded that the committee be named by the several delegations. After a sharp debate, ex-Governor John H. Means, an anti-convention man, was chosen chairman by acclamation. A similar division occurred over methods of choosing delegates-at-large. Edmund Rhett proposed that they be nominated by a committee consisting of two delegates from St. Phillips and St. Michaels and one member from each other election district. This would give the parishes control. The opposition wished the committee to be composed of two members from each of the six congressional districts. By a vote of 105 to 63 it was finally decided to choose delegates-at-large from the floor by ballot. This contest was clearly preliminary to the larger issue of whether moderate or ultra men should be sent to Richmond.[30]

The debate over the method of choosing delegates brought forward clearly the question of whether the Charleston delegates should be recommissioned to Richmond or more radical representatives sent. It was on this question that all the old bitterness between the National and State Rights Democrats reappeared. "Madness ruled the hour," said I. W. Hayne. "Nobody seemed sane. Convention men and Anti-Convention men seemed to forget utterly that there was an enemy elsewhere or a purpose to be effected out of South Carolina."[31] A few of the radicals, in the interest of harmony, were willing to let the old delegation serve. W. S. Lyles, of Fairfield, for example, held that though the record of the convention men was to be condemned up to the time of their withdrawal from Charleston, their subsequent record was better and they deserved to be recommissioned and endorsed. This was, moreover, the best policy for the secessionists because other slave states would distrust the Richmond convention should South Carolina send extreme secessionists to it. They would see in it an attempt of South Carolina to precipitate disunion and to force it on the other states. The best way to get secession was to send moderate men and join with other states in one more demand for Southern rights which, if

[29] *Proceedings* (May), p. 51. [30] *Ibid.*, pp. 6, 20-26, 35-36.
[31] I. W. Hayne to J. H. Hammond, June 3, 1860, Hammond Papers.

denied, might drive other states to join South Carolina in forming a Southern confederacy. He feared too that a failure to recommission the old delegates would further divide the state and that many outside of the convention would be driven into a unionist party under the leadership of those who had refused to withdraw at Charleston.[32] But the conciliatory course recommended by Lyles did not appeal to his fellow-secessionists. They were determined to seize control.

The test of strength came on the election of the first delegate-at-large. The National Democrats wished to re-elect the delegates who had served at Charleston but when James Simons withdrew they ran I. W. Hayne who was not a convention man but who consented to run as an independent. The radicals put up R. B. Rhett, long one of the most abusive critics of the convention men. On the first ballot Rhett received a majority of the votes cast, his vote being 84 plus to 68 plus for Hayne.[33] This was a bitter dose for the National Democrats and the signal for an acrimonious quarrel on the floor of the convention. The other delegates-at-large to Charleston, B. H. Wilson, R. B. Boylston, and Samuel McGowan, immediately withdrew their names from the list of candidates saying that they regarded the election of Rhett as a repudiation. Wilson recalled the charge that in withdrawing from Charleston they had merely yielded to outside pressure rather than to patriotism and duty; now the convention by approving their *action* but repudiating the *actors,* was sanctioning the charge. John S. Preston and F. Gaillard refused to stand for re-election from their district and John Wallace withdrew from the convention. Preston regretted that South Carolina should send disunion delegates; the purpose of that convention was solely to reintegrate the party, and anyone going there with the expectation of any steps being taken towards disunion would find himself "most ridiculously out of fashion." The chairman of the state central commitee Theodore G. Barker of Charleston, spoke bitterly of the treatment of his party and resigned the chairmanship.[34]

An attempt to compose the quarrel was made by Hayne who suggested that the radical majority elect any two men named by the National Democrats to serve with Rhett and another of his party as delegates-at-large. In line with this suggestion Alfred P. Aldrich, one of the radicals, nominated McGowan and Boylston but both refused to serve with Rhett on the ground that the delegation should be harmonious.[35] The radicals then proceeded to elect A. C. Garlington, J. I. Middleton, and Armistead Burt by votes which were nearly unani-

[32] *Proceedings* (May), pp. 39-44.
[33] Fifteen and a fraction votes were divided between Garlington, Middleton, McGowan, Barnwell. *Ibid.,* pp. 39, 44-46.
[34] *Ibid.,* pp. 47-62; 70-72.
[35] Perry thought they "evinced unnecessary squeamishness" after following Yancey out at Charleston then to reject the leadership of Rhett. Perry, *Biographical Sketches,* p. 177.

mous due to abstention on the part of the National Democrats. Burt was not friendly to Rhett personally but was careful to declare his radicalism. Anyone who regarded his nomination as a concession to the convention party "was most egregiously mistaken," he said.

I was raised a nullifier of the strictest sect. I was brought up at the feet of Gamaliel, and would be recreant not only to his friendship, but to principle, if I were to apostatize and find myself in the ranks of the National Democracy. . . . from February 1844 I have never doubted, so help me God, that these Southern States would soon have to choose between slavery and the Union.[36]

This was the sentiment no doubt of the whole delegation. Not a single man who served at Charleston was sent to Richmond. The radicals were in the saddle.[37]

The course of the radicals at the state convention left the state for a time badly divided. Some feared that the National Democrats would be permanently alienated from any resistance program. Hayne felt that they might "move off . . . in a *wrong direction* and can never therefore get right." He added: "The older I get the more I feel the force of John Randolph's aphorism that the nonsense of *'principles not men* is like *love without women'*—Rhett! Middleton! Burt! They would ruin any cause."[38] Certainly there was much resentment against the radicals as the convention quarrel was transferred to the newspapers. The *South Carolinian,* for example, was sharply critical of the treatment given the National Democrats and denied a claim that an agreement had been made before the convention to divide the delegation between the two parties.[39] On many sides the claim was made that the Richmond delegation did not by any means properly represent the people of the state, the contention being that the 68 votes for Hayne represented an overwhelming majority of the people.[40] An analysis of the vote does indicate that Rhett's 84 votes represented some 11,000 fewer of the white population of the state than did the 68 votes of Hayne.[41] With the scattered vote taken into account the radical "popular" vote was slightly in excess of that of the moderates. This would seem to indicate that approximately half of the people of South Carolina hoped at the end of May, 1860, that their interest might be protected and at the same time the Union preserved through the agency of a Constitutional Democratic party of state rights principles drawing its support from North

[36] *Proceedings* (May), p. 94.   [37] *Ibid.,* pp. 73-74; 92-95.
[38] I. W. Hayne to J. H. Hammond, June 3, 1860, Hammond Papers.
[39] *Keowee Courier,* June 16, 1860; *ibid.,* June 12, 1860 quoting *Carolinian; cf. Proceedings* (May), p. 69.
[40] *Keowee Courier,* June 9, 1860; *Southern Enterprise,* June 7, 1860; *Proceedings* (May), pp. 59, 71-72.
[41] Hayne 139,102; Rhett 128,208; Garlington 17,306; Middleton, 1,729; McGowan 2,167; Barnwell 1,403. If instead of the census figures for 1860 those for 1850 are used the difference is somewhat greater. *Cf.* Laura A. White, *Robert Barnwell Rhett: Father of Secession* (New York, 1931), p. 167 note.

and West as well as South. The state was still badly divided. Edmund Ruffin, venerable Virginia "fire-eater," and an onlooker at the convention, remarked that he feared there were not many more secessionists in South Carolina than in Virginia.[42] This view was, however, too pessimistic. The disunionists had shattered the political organization of the moderates by seizing control of it, and even the moderates themselves did not, for the most part, propose to submit to a government under Republican control.

The Richmond convention, with ten Southern states in attendance, met June 11, but did nothing. The delegates, except for those of South Carolina and Florida, were accredited to Baltimore as well as to Richmond and after a two-day session proceeded to Baltimore for the final unsuccessful attempt to reunite the party. South Carolina delegates remained at Richmond, impatiently met and adjourned from day to day, and awaited the withdrawal of the Southern states from the Baltimore convention. They continued in Richmond as the Baltimore convention split and as two tickets were nominated. They thus had no part in the nomination of Breckinridge and Lane, though seven states later joined South Carolina at Richmond and ratified the choice.[43]

Numerous public meetings, held for the purpose of endorsing the action of the Richmond convention, evidenced the general satisfaction with which the nomination of Breckinridge and Lane was received in South Carolina.[44] One at Charleston, which Rhett and others addressed, congratulated the South that at last it was united in defense of Southern interests, and looked forward to the approaching election as one which would prove whether the United States government was a "free government under the restraints of a living Constitution, or a sectional despotism under the control of sectional ambition, avarice and fanaticism."[45] Doubtless proof of the latter, by defeat of Breckinridge and Lane, was the result desired for this might rally the South to secession. On the other hand there were many who believed that the nominees were men whom conservatives throughout the Union could and would support to insure the defeat of the Republicans and to preserve the Union.[46]

As the presidential campaign developed through the summer and fall of 1860 there was a clear and rapid swing toward disunion throughout the state. The election of a Republican President was an eventuality which even those who sincerely loved the Union regarded as dangerously imperilling the safety of the South. For some time statements had been openly made that in such a contingency South Carolina should secede. As early as September, 1859, Congressman M. L. Bonham, in antici-

[42] White, *Robert Barnwell Rhett*, p. 166; Crenshaw, *Election of 1860*, p. 209.
[43] Dumond, *Secession Movement*, pp. 75, 77 *et seq.*
[44] *Conservatist*, July 17, 1860.   [45] *Ibid.*
[46] *Southern Enterprise*, June 28, 1860.

pating Republican success in 1860, said: "The electric spark, which conveys that intelligence, ought to be and will be the death signal of this Confederacy, come when it may."[47] Similar views were expressed in the legislature of 1859 and increasingly in the summer of 1860 as division of the Democrats pointed to almost certain Republican victory.

Among the influential leaders of the state who committed themselves to secession long before actual Republican success in November were the governor of the state and every single member of the South Carolina delegation in the federal House of Representatives. Governor Gist favored South Carolina withdrawal even if other Southern states failed to act.[48] Even earlier the old radical L. M. Keitt took the same position arguing that once the Republicans were in office they would use all the power of the government to "cripple and ultimately destroy" the institution of slavery. He insisted that the South should not submit to control by a party which was "stained with treason, hideous with insurrection, and dripping with blood."[49] W. P. Miles and John McQueen were hardly less outspoken. McQueen early lost hope that Lincoln could be defeated and his recommendation was for prompt South Carolina action.[50] Miles in a Charleston speech demanded less talk and more action, and privately he expressed his belief that South Carolina should "break up things generally, which any one State can at any time do."[51] Even the more conservative Congressmen J. D. Ashmore and W. W. Boyce spoke for secession. Ashmore was at first inclined to insist that South Carolina should act only with other states but Boyce, an old cooperationist, came out flat-footedly for separate action. He saw no danger in such a course.

Suppose we have done this. Then only two courses remain to our enemies. First, they must let us alone; secondly, they must attempt to coerce us. . . . Suppose they attempt to coerce us; then the Southern States are compelled to make common cause with us, and we wake up some morning and find the flag of a Southern Confederacy floating over us.[52]

Even more influential than the voices of the congressmen was that of James L. Orr, organizer and leader of the conservatives of the state. In July and August he freely expressed his opinion that it would be impossible to live under Black Republican rule. In defense of this position he wrote Amos Kendall:

[47] *Conservatist,* August 7, 1860. The editor thought Bonham the first, certainly the first congressman, to take this position.
[48] *Courier,* August 25, 1860.
[49] Letter to A. G. Salley and others, *Mercury,* July 20, 1860.
[50] *Courier,* July 16, 1860.
[51] *Courier* July 12, 1860; W. P. Miles to J. H. Hammond, August 5, 1860, Hammond Papers.
[52] Letter of Boyce to D. L. Provence and W. L. Lyles, August 3, 1860, in *Conservatist,* August 13, 1860. For Ashmore, *Keowee Courier,* August 18, 1860; *Courier,* August 25, 1860; J. D. Ashmore to J. H. Hammond, July 10, August 30, 1860, Hammond Papers.

Can it be prudent, safe, or manly in the South to submit to the domination of a party whose declared purpose is to destroy such an amount of property, and subvert our whole social and industrial policy? . . . to allow a Black Republican President to be inaugurated, and put him in possession of the army, the navy, the treasury, the armories and arsenals, the public property, in fact the whole machinery of the government, with its appendants and appurtenances? If the South should think upon this subject as I do, no Black Republican President shall ever execute any law within our borders unless at the point of the bayonet and over the dead bodies of her slain sons.[53]

Orr believed that secession should be coöperative; he would "emphatically reprobate and repudiate" any scheme for separate action by South Carolina but would assent to joint secession by South Carolina, Alabama, and Mississippi since this would give control of portions of the Gulf and Atlantic coasts. He believed, too, that secession might enable the South to obtain from the free states "additional and higher guarantees" for Southern property—that better terms could be made out of the Union than in it. But he professed to be ready to form a Southern Confederacy should the guarantees not be forthcoming. Whatever the reservations of Orr may have been, his influence in the unification of South Carolina on a secession program was very great. A correspondent of the *Mercury* thought that his public statements spoke "more impressively, the conviction of the Southern people" than "any other expression of any other public man."[54] War Governor Andrew G. Magrath later said that when the conservatives Boyce and Orr announced their position "there came to be but one purpose everywhere," everyone feeling that the question had then come to be one of going with the state or opposing it.[55]

The state was of course not as united as Magrath's statement implies. But there can be no doubt that those who opposed secession had become by the end of August a very small minority. And it was increasingly difficult for the minority to maintain its position. Among the few who still spoke for the Union, the most articulate was B. F. Perry. Consistent unionist till the end, he attempted to refute the arguments of Keitt, Boyce, and Orr by denying that the election of Lincoln would constitute a sufficient cause for disunion and all the horrors of civil war. He argued that Lincoln would be a minority President checked by a hostile Congress and moreover pledged to enforce the fugitive slave law. Perry suggested that Lincoln might even exert himself to conciliate the South and that a fair chance should be given him. Should he take the other course and lead an attack on slavery, Perry pledged his help in defending the institution even to the point of secession; but he be-

[53] Stickney, *Autobiography of Kendall*, p. 571. See also *Conservatist*, August 7, 1860; *Courier*, August 13, 1860; J. D. Ashmore to J. H. Hammond, July 10, 1860, Hammond Papers; Rhodes, *History of U. S.*, II, 446.

[54] *Mercury*, August 8, 1860.

[55] Letter of Magrath written from Fort Pulaski in 1865 in the interest of his release. Clipping in Hinson Collection, Charleston Library Society.

lieved that the South should await an overt act of hostility. In any case South Carolina should act only with other states.[56]

How many agreed with Perry is not clear. He apparently had a large following in Greenville and Pickens Districts, and probably the disunionist correspondent of the *Conservatist* was correct when he said that there were large numbers over the state who agreed with Perry but lacked the courage to admit it.[57] The Darlington *Flag* endorsed Perry's position; so did state Senator John P. Zimmerman. The latter not only argued that Lincoln's choice in a fair election was no cause for secession but also insisted that there was no chance of coöperation and that the separate existence of South Carolina would in no way improve her position.[58] A writer in the *South Carolinian* tried to show that slavery would be menaced more by secession than by remaining in the Union.[59] Even as late as November Reverend F. A. Mood wrote that the majority in the upper districts were for from believing that secession was wise.[60]

But the few who spoke against secession were severely criticized. A correspondent of the *Mercury* branded Perry as a traitor to the South, a man who would have been a Tory in the Revolution. "Many Citizens" of Charleston taunted him with a reminder of his statements at the time of the John Brown raid and accused him of inconsistency.[61] The Camden *Journal* regretted that there was even one man in South Carolina who like Perry advocated submission; he was allowing his love for the Union to give courage and support to the enemies of his dearest interests.[62] Even the Greenville *Southern Enterprise* failed to agree with all of Perry's letter, and the Pickens *Keowee Courier,* while criticizing separate secession and describing Rhett as an unsafe leader, disagreed with Perry's contention that Lincoln's election would be no proper cause for secession; South Carolina, it held, must secede with two or more states.[63]

The rapidly growing unity of South Carolina was reflected in the October elections for the legislature. Apparently the only important

[56] Perry's letter to the *Courier,* dated April 13, 1860, was widely copied by other state newspapers and later republished in Perry, *Biographical Sketches,* pp. 171-180.

[57] *Conservatist,* October 2, 1860. R. N. Gourdin wrote August 20 that many Charlestonians agreed with Perry. Crenshaw, *Election of 1860,* p. 221.

[58] *Keowee Courier,* October 6, 1860, quoting Darlington *Southerner.*

[59] Spartanburg *Express,* September 12, 1860, quoting *Carolinian.* Perry in 1863 said he had years before told J. H. Adams that the Union should be saved as a bulwark against abolition; that as soon as secession should remove the outside pressure there would begin an abilitionist movement in the South. B. F. Perry, MSS Journal, June 3, 1863. University of North Carolina Library; hereinafter cited Perry, Journal.

[60] Mood to Hammond, November 2, 1860, Hammond Papers.

[61] Perry, *Biographical Sketches,* p. 180-185 for Perry's reply.

[62] *Conservatist,* September 18, 1860, quoting Camden *Journal.*

[63] *Southern Enterprise,* September 13, 1860; *Keowee Courier,* August 25, September 1, 1860; *Conservatist,* July 12, 1860, quoting *Keowee Courier.*

difference of opinion was, as in 1850, on the question of separate or coöperative action. This issue was, however, not clearly drawn in the election; the candidates were in most places simply required to pledge that they would vote for a convention in case of Lincoln's election. This would only be coöperating with Alabama whose governor had been instructed to call a convention when the presidency went to the Republicans.[64] A drive was nevertheless made against "timid," "oscillating," and "watch-and-wait" politicians. "We must face our enemies at the North and TRAITORS SOUTH," said the radicals. Men should be elected who would see to it that "endeared homes," "patriotic altars," wives and children, would be protected and saved from ruin.[65] James L. Petigru, an opponent of secession under any circumstances, watched the rising feeling with alarm and despaired of the Union. Basing its judgment on the newspapers of the state, the Columbia *Guardian* declared that never in the history of the state had it been so unanimous in its determination.[66] The results of the election did indeed show the legislature almost unanimously pledged to call a convention in the event of Lincoln's election.

There can be no doubt that extremists in South Carolina favored Republican success in order that secession might be carried. As early as May one of them wrote from Beaufort that his candidate was the "most ultra Black Republican" abolitionist to be found, since the election of such a person might force the South to act.[67] The same idea was reflected in a letter from a South Carolina secessionist abroad who expressed fear that Lincoln would be defeated.

> I am sorry to believe that no man can be elected whose elevation would really endanger the Union. Somebody will be elected who will be considered by the North as a concession to the South and by the latter bragged of as a tremendous triumph and so we will go on again for another four years. The people of the South are fickle and vacillating lazy and above all rich. . . . A man will not fight if his belly & pocket are both full and he has to go and look for a row. If we could only have two successive failures of the cotton crop I should feel quite cheerful about Southern rights.[68]

In South Carolina, however, the election of Lincoln was fully expected. Among prominent leaders only Hammond seems to have had any doubts.[69] When the news of Lincoln's election arrived November

[64] Boucher, *S. C. and the South,* p. 100. In some cases, however, candidates were asked to commit themselves on separate action. *Keowee Courier,* September 8, 15, 22, 27, 29, 1860; Spartanburg *Express,* September 5, 1860; Yorkville *Enquirer,* October 4, 1860. For the Charleston contest, see *infra,* p. 51.
[65] *Mercury,* October 6, 1860.
[66] Carson, *Life of Petigru,* p. 357 *et. seq.; Mercury,* September 21, 1860, quoting the *Daily Southern Guardian.*
[67] Crenshaw, *Election of 1860,* p. 211.
[68] C. K. Prioleau to ————————, September 27, 1860, Pettigrew Papers, University of N. C.
[69] For statements of other leaders see Crenshaw, *Election of 1860,* pp. 211-214.

7 there was considerable rejoicing.   In Charleston large crowds broke
into cheers for the Southern Confederacy.   Stores were closed and a
general celebration staged.[70]   "The tea has been thrown overboard—
the revolution of 1860 has been initiated," said the *Mercury* next day.[71]

[70] The Wilmington *Daily Herald* was highly critical of the celebration of
South Carolina.   North Carolina, it said, should not submit to being "dragged
into revolution and anarchy, and all to please South Carolina, who, by her in-
sufferable arrogance, and conceited importance, has been a source of annoyance
and disquietude to the whole country, North and South, for the last thirty years."
Quoted by Dumond, *Southern Editorials*, pp. 225-228.
[71] November 8, 1860.

CHAPTER III

PROPAGANDA ON THE EVE OF SECESSION

Seldom in a great crisis does a political community act with more unity and enthusiasm than did South Carolina in late 1860. The close approach to unanimity is all the more remarkable in view of the fact that the antebellum history of the state was marked by frequent, and often bitter, factional conflicts. During the nullification episode, for example, the state was brought to the verge of civil war, and feeling between the parties continued unabated during the test oath controversy which immediately followed. The crisis of 1850-51 likewise had divided the state into bitterly hostile factions. Less acute were the political disagreements over such issues as the state bank, the Bluffton movement of 1844, the reopening of the foreign slave trade, and the demand of the up country for a larger voice in state government. But division was almost always present. Immediately before secession the radical and moderate parties differed so sharply on the question of South Carolina participation in national nominating conventions that many feared harmonious action would be impossible in the crisis precipitated by Lincoln's election to the presidency. Yet, as later pages will more fully demonstrate, a fusion of the parties did come on the eve of secession to a remarkable degree.

It is not easy to explain fully why South Carolina was so much more united in secession than were other Southern states. It was not merely that South Carolina was more closely identified with the institution of slavery, although part of the explanation may be found here. The percentage of slaves to total population was greater in South Carolina than elsewhere, but the ratio was only slightly lower in Mississippi, and not very much smaller in Louisiana, Alabama, and Georgia. The slave was no more essential to the production of rice and cotton in South Carolina than to the cultivation of similar crops elsewhere. The social danger of Africanization resulting from emancipation was little if any greater in South Carolina than in other parts of the slavery belt.

Nor can it be successfully maintained that secession in South Carolina resulted from a sort of dark lantern conspiracy by a few of her leaders. On the eve of secession there was no dictator in South Carolina politics; there was no all-powerful political ring which could have brought secession through manipulation of the state's political machinery. South Carolinians were traditionally, and actually, highly individualistic in their political opinions and were not easily led by the nose into unpopular ways. Even during the period of John C. Calhoun's greatest influence there were threatened revolts against his leadership, as in the case of Rhett's Bluffton movement of 1844. But in 1860 Calhoun was no more, and the mantle of his leadership had not fallen upon the shoulders of another. Rather, the half dozen years before secession were characterized by confusion in leadership, divided counsel, and party bitterness. Secession came to South Carolina on the crest of a great wave of popular enthusiasm which all but drowned the voices of the few who urged caution. It did not come at the dictation of a handful of leaders.

That secession in South Carolina was essentially an act of the people can hardly be doubted. Nevertheless, the unity at the time of secession must be explained fundamentally in terms of leadership. Probably to a greater extent than in any other Southern state South Carolina had been prepared by her leaders over a period of thirty years for the issues of 1860. Indoctrination in the principles of state sovereignty, education in the necessity of maintaining Southern institutions, warnings of the dangers of control of the federal government by a section hostile to its interests—in a word, the education of the masses in the principles and necessity of secession under certain circumstances—had been carried on with a skill and success hardly inferior to the masterly propaganda of the abolitionists themselves. It was this education, this propaganda,[1] by South Carolina leaders which made secession the almost spontaneous movement that it was. In the following pages an attempt will be made to analyze and evaluate secession propaganda as it existed in late 1860. The agitation in this later period is more or less typical of what had gone before. It was an important factor in bringing unity to South Carolina and may have exerted considerable influence on the secession movement in other Southern states.

Among the most important and obvious agencies of political education was the press. In a section where interest in things political was always great, newspapers were numerous, well-edited, and apparently generally read. In Charleston were two great dailies of more than local importance, the radical *Mercury* and the conservative *Courier*. Columbia could also boast of two dailies, the *Daily Southern Guardian* and the *Daily South Carolinian,* while numerous "country" papers enjoyed considerable weekly circulation.[2] These papers were not all radical in the manner of the Charleston *Mercury* and the Newberry *Conservatist*. Controversies between them were sometimes quite bitter. In the middle of 1860, for example, they reflected the angry feelings of

---

[1] The term "propaganda" as used in this chapter has no sinister meaning.
[2] Among the latter were the Sumter *Watchman,* Clarendon *Banner,* Marion *Star,* Cheraw *Gazette,* Darlington *Flag,* Darlington *Southerner,* Lancaster *Ledger,* Yorkville *Enquirer,* Camden *Journal,* Newberry *Conservatist,* Union *Press,* Edgefield *Advertiser,* Spartanburg *Express,* Spartanburg *Carolina Spartan,* Anderson *Intelligencer,* Pickens *Keowee Courier,* Greenville *Southern Enterprise,* and Greenville *Southern Mountaineer.*

the May convention. But almost without exception their editors were "sound" in the doctrine of secession and in increasing number counselled resistance as the probability of Lincoln's election grew in the summer and fall of 1860. Even in the conservative up country, Perry's contention that the election of Lincoln would be an insufficient cause for secession was denied by such papers as the Spartanburg *Express,* Greenville *Southern Enterprise, Keowee Courier,* and Anderson *Intelligencer.*[3] The Charleston *Courier,* which was probably the most conservative paper in the state, gradually assumed the same position. As early as July 3 it confessed its "firm persuasion, that unless our foes are brought to a sense of their responsibility, unless fanaticism is driven in disgrace, and with the lash, from the pulpits and halls of legislation it has so long desecrated with its foul presence, we may and should apprehend the direst evils." In the end this paper frankly advocated a policy of resistance. Apparently every newspaper in the state agreed that secession was necessary.

It would be difficult to exaggerate the editorial influence of the South Carolina newspapers. Then, as now, however, they were able to mould public opinion in other ways than through editorial columns. In the selection and presentation of news, South Carolina papers were guilty of the charge made against them by Thomas Y. Simons in 1860 when he said:

> While the press of the State in the main, constantly holds up to public attention, as the true types of Northern opinion, the editorials of the New York *Tribune,* and the speeches of Lovejoy, Garrison, Theodore Parker, Wendell Phillips, and their associates, it is seldom that the utterances of the constitutional press and men of the North find a place in their columns.[4]

Continuing, Simons quoted various Northern conservatives to prove his contention that the North as a whole should not be judged by its radicals. Such fair-mindedness, however, was seldom exhibited by the newspapers. The more radical of them, particularly the *Mercury,* lost few opportunities to present to its readers the views of extreme Northern spokesmen, and to use their utterances as texts for editorial sermons on the iniquities of the abolitionists. The *Mercury* was close to the truth when in 1860 it found the explanation of South Carolina "unanimity" in the fact that South Carolina editors and other leaders were truer to "Southern principles" than leaders in other parts of the South.[5]

The South Carolina newspapers influenced public opinion also through the large amount of space which they extended to numerous contributors. The press thus served as a public forum reflecting the

[3] Spartanburg *Express,* September 12, 1860; Keowee *Courier,* September 1, October 20, 1860, quoting Anderson *Intelligencer; Southern Enterprise,* November 15, 1860.

[4] *Speech of Col. Thomas Y. Simons, in favor of South Carolina being represented in the Democratic Convention. . . .* (Charleston, 1860), pp. 7-8.

[5] *Mercury,* August 2, 1860.

extraordinary interest taken in public affairs by antebellum South Carolina. These communications to the press sometimes greatly affected the course of public events, as was the case in the summer of 1860 when the conservative James L. Orr and W. W. Boyce announced their belief that the South should secede on the election of Lincoln. Due to the freedom with which papers opened their columns to secession leaders they became an effective mouthpiece through which warnings were shouted to arouse the masses of the people. The papers also republished many of the most influential pamphlets, speeches, and sermons devoted to the cause of disunion.

Another obvious but important means of inflaming popular passions was the political pamphlet. This was always a popular device in South Carolina. During the thirty years before secession, notably around 1832 and 1850, a pamphlet literature of considerable proportions was published. In the late secession period the number of titles was small, but the pamphlets were widely circulated and seem without exception to have advocated secession. They were very ably written and skillfully designed to "elevate Southern sentiment" and to disseminate "sound and spirited doctrine."[6]

The most notable and influential pamphlets of 1860 were those prepared and distributed by a propaganda organization which called itself "The 1860 Association." This Association was organized by a group of Charleston secessionists in September of 1860 when secession sentiment was already far advanced in South Carolina. But the organizers felt the necessity of guarding against reaction and against probable Northern efforts to "soothe and conciliate the South, by disclaimers and overtures." Specifically the purposes of the Association, as stated in a circular letter of Robert N. Gourdin, chairman of the executive committee, were, first, to conduct correspondence with leading Southerners and by an exchange of information and advice to prepare the South for the impending crisis; second, to prepare, print, and distribute literature designed to awaken the South to its danger and the necessity of resistance; third, to inquire into the defenses of the state and furnish information to the legislature which might aid in the establishment of an effective military organization.[7] According to one of its members an additional purpose was to "spot the traitors to the South, who may require some hemp ere long."[8] The Association had a president, a secretary, and an executive committee of fifteen members with power to appoint other committees to promote the work of the organization. Operating expenses were obtained from initiation fes and from contributions widely solicited through the newspapers and circular letter.

The pamphlets of The 1860 Association seem to have had a wide

[6] *Conservatist,* October 30, 1860.
[7] Circular letter in Hinson Collection, Charleston Library Society.
[8] *Mercury,* October 6, 1860.

circulation in and out of South Carolina. William Tennent, Jr., secretary of the Association, advertised their availability through a standing notice in the *Mercury*[9] and free publicity was given editorially in various papers. The *Conservatist*, for example, urged Southern men to join and support the organization, and printed striking excerpts from the pamphlets. The *Mercury* frequently expressed approval of its work, and the *Courier* in October was also urging on the good work.[10] By November 19, some 166,000 pamphlets had been distributed with the demand from "every quarter" so great that second and third editions were subsequently printed.[11] From Minute Men in Atlanta came an order for 3,000 copies of each pamphlet. Requests were received from Alabama, Florida, Virginia, and no doubt from other states.[12] The number of pamphlets finally distributed is not known but it was very large. Circulation was also increased by the republication in whole or in part of some of them in the newspapers and in *De Bow's Review*.[13]

A brief description of The 1860 Association pamphlets will reveal their own importance and illustrate secession propaganda in general. Tract No. 1 apparently had the greatest circulation and influence. It was entitled *The South Alone Should Govern the South, And African Slavery Should be Controlled By Those Only Who Are Friendly To It*.[14] It was prepared by John Townsend of Saint John's, Colleton, an opponent of nullification in 1832 and of separate secession in 1851, a circumstance which must have increased its significance and influence. Packed into its sixty-three pages is such a wealth of persuasive and inflammatory material that it may be regarded as an almost complete secession handbook. First, was the republication of an address by Townsend on June 7 upon his return from the state Democratic convention which chose delegates to Richmond. Accepting the rupture of the National Democratic party as permanent and the election of a Republican President as certain, Townsend insisted that honor and self-respect demanded Southern action. Urging his audience to face disunion frankly, he exclaimed:

Do not blink it; look it full in the face. Become familiar with it; for the necessities of our condition require it. Let us hear no more of the *sophomoric* sentimentality about "the Union"—"the Glorious Union—cemented with the blood of our fathers, and to be cherished for the memories of the past," etc., etc. Let us brush away these cobwebs, and look at the subject clearly,

[9] *Ibid.*, December-January.
[10] *Conservatist*, September 25, October 30; *Mercury*, September 5, *et. seq*, 1860; *Courier*, September 15, 27, October 29, November 3, 14, 29, 1860.
[11] Circular letter, Hinson Collection.
[12] *Courier*, October 29, November 30, 1860; John K. Young to R. F. W. Allston, February 18, 1861, Allston Collection, South Carolina Historical Society.
[13] *Mercury*, October 23, 31, November 1, 29, 1860; *De Bow's Review*, XXX (January-June, 1861), 67-77, 120-121, 123-124, 249-250.
[14] All 1860 Association pamphlets were published in 1860 by Evans and Cogswell, Charleston, S. C.

36

like practical and sensible men, who have to deal with a great Reality. Let us realize to ourselves this *fact* (calculated, I admit, to sink like a heavy weight upon our hearts) : that *the Union is lost;* that its *spirit* has departed from it; and that for all *beneficent* purposes, for the South, it is no longer worth caring for ![15]

Disunion, Towsend continued, was inevitable sooner or later. That it had not come earlier was due, among other things, to lack of information on the part of the people, and to the false leadership of certain Southern spoilsmen who had proved themselves traitors to the South by holding out delusive hopes of relief. But under abolitionist control of the federal government, insult and degradation would become unbearable, and rebellion would surely come. Why wait until the enemy has seized control of the patronage, the treasury, army, and navy? Townsend skillfully recounted Southern grievances : protective tariffs for the benefit of the rich, incitement of the slave to rebellion, nullification of the fugitive slave law, stealing of slaves, denial of rights in the territories, insults in Congress, armed invasion of the South and the murder of her citizens, declaration of an irrepressible conflict, denial of the right of secession, government by "irresponsible majorities." "In the name of a God of Justice," he asked, "what more or greater wrongs are wanting, to justify a Revolution?" Plausible arguments were advanced to prove that the South as a separate nation would be amply able to protect itself and it would enjoy undreamed-of prosperity if freed from the necessity of paying millions of dollars annually to the North.[16]

The arguments of Townsend were supplemented by no less than nine appendixes which must have been even more effective propaganda than the address. One described the horrors which attended abolition in Santo Domingo and the British West Indies. Another sought to prove that Republicans everywhere were determined to bring these horrors to the South. Liberal and numerous quotations from Northern leaders were skillfully chosen to boil the blood of Southern men. Sumner, for example, was represented as saying that new territories entering the Union must be free in order to form a "belt of fire" about the slave states where slavery must die as "a poisoned rat dies, of rage in its hole." In detail were set forth the plans of John Brown's "Central Association" for revolutionizing the South: war must be made upon the South; slaves must be taught to burn, to kill cattle and horses, and to destroy equipment, build forts, collect arms, etc. Strikes must be fomented on Southern farms. Southern masters must be flogged in the presence of their slaves.[17] What Southerner could read with equanimity the following quotation attributed to Joshua R. Giddings of Ohio?

I look forward to the day when there shall be a *servile insurrection* in the South; when the black man, armed with British bayonets, and led on by

[15] *The South Alone Should Govern the South* p. 8.
[16] *Ibid.,* pp. 3-23.   [17] *Ibid.,* pp. 24-25, 28, 41-46.

British officers, shall assert his freedom, and wage a *war* of *extermination* against his master; when the *torch of the incendiary shall light up the towns* and cities of the South, and *blot out the last vestige of slavery.* And though I may not mock at their calamity, nor laugh when their fear cometh, I shall hail it as the dawn of a political millennium.[18]

To quiet the nerves of "pantalooned" and "petticoated old women" who might fear the great numerical superiority of the North, Townsend argued that although the accidents of the electoral system gave to the Republican fanatics full political control, a majority of the people of the North opposed that party and would not support an attempt to coerce the South. The South should throw off the yoke of political bondage and in doing so free itself from the economic vassalage under which it suffered. Quoting extensively from Thomas Prentice Kettell, *Southern Wealth and Northern Profits,* Townsend estimated that the South paid an annual tribute of $105,000,000 to $231,500,000. With this amount retained, the South was assured of great prosperity and security. The following skillful propaganda was prominently displayed as a preface to Townsend's pamphlet:

MEN OF THE SOUTH
The subject before you, may be disagreeable to contemplate; and the examination of it may be irksome. But it is one, which deeply concerns you.
Time too, is fast hurrying the Question to your hearthstones. It will soon press upon you; and you will not be *allowed* to postpone the Decision.
How then do you decide?
Is it for manly RESISTANCE; to be followed with security and a prosperous end?
Or
Is it for SUBMISSION; and a short and inglorious ease: to be followed with certain ruin?
Say! And after you have made your Decision, write it, upon the doorposts of your habitations, that all who enter may know, what is the fate you have chosen for those whom you cherish within.[19]

Townsend was also author of Tract No. 4 bearing the arresting title, *The Doom of Slavery in the Union: Its Safety Out Of It.* His thesis here was that the Republicans could and would abolish slavery in the states within a short time, one wing of the party attacking by violence and insurrection, the other through constitutional procedure. The violent wing, he claimed, "have sent, and are now sending among our people, fire, and murder, and the sword, and rape, and poison, to desolate our land." Letters and newspaper articles describing conditions in Texas were furnished by Townsend to substantiate these charges. To show how hopeless was the position of the South in the Union and how easy it would be for the Republicans legally to abolish slavery, Townsend drew liberally on the article by "Python" in *De Bow's Re-*

[18] *Ibid.,* p. 47.   [19] *Ibid.,* pp. 47-63, preface.

view.[20] Vividly set forth were the dire results of emancipation to master, non-owner, and slave: "the end of all negro labor; a jubilee of idleness, and a reign of sloth; until famine shall drive them to robbery, or scourge them with pestilence: nine thousand millions of property destroyed . . . in return for negro equality conferred upon the black race: a war of races, the subjugation of one to the other; certain poverty to the whites; degradation, want, expatriation."[21]

As author of two pamphlets and as one of the founders and most active members of The 1860 Association, Townsend was credited with greatly influencing the history of his times. A correspondent of the *Courier* compared his two pamphlets with firebells in the night which aroused the whole South to defiance of Northern aggressors. Another thought that the "remarkable and gratifying unanimity which pervades the State and the South" was in large measure the result of Townsend's efforts. His first pamphlet, said a citizen of Beaufort, had done more good for the cause of the South than any paper ever published.[22]

Tract No. 2 of The 1860 Association included *State Sovereignty and the Doctrine of Coercion,* by William D. Porter, *A Letter from Hon. J. K. Paulding, Former Sec. of Navy,* and *The Right to Secede,* by "States." Porter's article was a reply to the Norfolk speech of Stephen A. Douglas in which Douglas expressed the hope that the next President of the United States would treat disunion as Jackson had in 1832, and in which he pledged his full support to a policy of coercion should secession be attempted. Porter made an extremely able, even scholarly, defense of the right of secession, and a forceful refutation of the legality of coercion. Using the historical approach he found sovereignty residing in the people of the states, the states being not "fractions of a unit, but integers of a multiple." He neatly disposed of the "perpetual Union" obstacle and insisted that delegated power might be reclaimed whether originally granted to a town, state, or federal government. Porter admitted that the laws of the United States must be obeyed so long as a state remained in the Union but skillfully defended the right of withdrawal. This right he found in the reservations made by the ratifying conventions, in the tenth amendment, and in the compact nature of the Union. He used the records of the constitutional convention to refute the doctrine of coercion. Madison, Mason, Martin, and Hamilton were quoted to show that coercion was clearly proposed and firmly rejected by the convention. Forceful in his constitutional argument, Porter was also skillful in emotional appeal.

The Union of these States is a voluntary Union—an association of equals, of their free will and by common accord. A State coerced, would be a subjugated province; no longer a voluntary or an equal member, but

[20] *De Bow's Review,* XXVIII (April, 1860), 367-392.
[21] *The Doom of Slavery in the Union,* pp. 3-39.
[22] *Courier,* November 29, 30, December 3, 1860.

the conquest and the captive of the rest! With her freedom cloven down, and the emblems of her sovereignty trampled under foot and trailing in the dust, her lifeless body would be to the living members of the Union, like the dead body of Hector, dragged in brutal triumph by the victorious chariot of Achilles round the walls of Troy! Better that the last sparkles of her ashes were trodden out, and her name forever lost to history and tradition, than that she should live to swell the triumph of her conquerors! And this to preserve the Union! A union of the living and the dead, bound fast together in loathsome and indissoluble contact! Say rather a union of the *dying* and the *dead,* for the life of all will have received a mortal thrust, their independence a name, their forms of liberty an insulting mockery, and their only privilege that of surviving until the iron heel of one or many despots shall be ready in turn to crush out the miserable remainder of their existence![23]

The Right to Secede likewise set forth the doctrine of secession, and ironically rehearsed the ways in which the compact had been violated. The author indicted the North on every phrase of the preamble to the Constitution. "We the people of the United States" had been interpreted, he said, to mean "We the people of a consolidated nation." "In order to form a more perfect Union" had ben supplanted by a declaration that the South was beyond the pale of civilization and must abolish the institution through which it earned its daily bread. "To establish justice" was made to mean that the South must support the hostile and fanatical North. "Domestic tranquillity" had been insured by the invasion of Virginia, the murder of her citizens, and expression of sympathy for the murderers. "Common defense" was provided by encouragement of rebellion and arming of slaves. The "general welfare" was to be promoted by the sacrifices of the particular interests of fifteen states whose four million slaves were to be freed and their masters placed in bondage. Far from securing the "blessings of liberty to ourselves and our posterity," the South was to be deprived of its property, branded as a public enemy, and, as suggested by Sumner, "driven, like poisoned vermin, to die in our holes." Already in the South,

Whole towns have been laid in ashes. Farms have been desolated. Crops, which were the result of industry and of labor judiciously applied, have been laid waste and destroyed. Fathers and brothers were to be butchered; mothers and daughters, exposed to brutalities, the most atrocious and revolting; children, exterminated; and the first act in the drama requires *us* to become the executioners of slaves.[24]

Thus, he maintained, every condition of the bond between the states had been violated, and no excuse given except that the South had not abandoned slavery, an institution which had been ordained by God, recognized by the Bible and the Constitution, and which clothed the world, converted the heathen, and civilized the barbarian.[25]

Tract No. 3 of The 1860 Association was published under the title,

[23] *State Sovereignty and the Doctrine of Coercion* . . . , pp. 3 *et seq.,* 19.
[24] *Ibid.,* p. 32.   [25] *Ibid.,* pp. 30-36.

To the People of the South. Senator Hammond and the Tribune. The author, apparently a Georgian, took as his pseudonym "Troup," in honor of the fiery and popular Georgia governor of that name. The pamphlet was addressed to the South as a whole but more particularly to the people of Georgia whose attitude in the secession crisis was of special concern to the leaders of South Carolina. Troup presented to his readers two sharply contrasting views of the Southern states and people. On the one hand was the South described in Senator James H. Hammond's well-known "Cotton Is King" speech in which Hammond optimistically canvassed the strength and resources of the South and painted a rosy picture of the prosperity and impregnability of a great Southern Confederacy built on slavery. On the other hand was the South currently ridiculed and caricatured by the New York *Tribune* from whose pages liberal quotations were taken to show the contempt with which the South was regarded in the North. The *Tribune's* mockery of the South and ridicule of Southern strength were presented by such quotations as the following:

The possibility of Disunion on the part of the South is almost too absurd either for discussion or ridicule. In the first place, she does not intend it, in the second place, she hasn't the power to make the attempt, even if she had the will; and, finally, she could not accomplish it if she had both the will and the power to make the attempt. The local police at Washington are quite strong enough to suppress any incipient rebellion at the seat of Government, and a revenue cutter off Charleston bar would be likely to make blue rosettes in South Carolina as scarce as blue roses.[26]

The propaganda value of the mere contrast between Hammond and the *Tribune* is obvious. But Troup elaborated it. With disarming frankness and penetration he took the position that the election of Lincoln was not in itself the sufficient and real cause for the impending secession of the South. Rather, the cause lay "in the incompatibility growing out of two systems of labor, crystallizing about them two forms of civilization—from which have sprung, if not conflicting interests, antipathies at least, instead of sympathies." This fundamental cause, he said, had presented *occasions* for conflict as in 1820, 1832, 1850, and 1860. Out of the same incompatibility had come conflicting interpretations of the Constitution. "The election of Lincoln is but the last developed, cumulative, conclusive *symptom* in the diagnosis of a fatal disease," namely, the development of two civilizations foreign to each other. The South as the weaker of the two people had been forced into the position of colonial vassalage with grievances far greater than those suffered by the thirteen colonies at the time of the Revolution. Against this colonial condition Troup urged his readers to rebel.

The colonial condition is at best one of pupilage, dependence and inferiority, and is degrading to such a people as that described by Senator

[26] *To the People of the South*, p. 21.

Hammond. But when the people who govern are hostile; when the bond of union of the dominant party, of the governing people, is enmity and active antagonism to the mode of labor and social organization of the people governed, then foreign rule assumes its most dangerous form. If, however, political hostility has been intensified into religious hate, and to enmity and antagonism are added scorn and contempt; if the dominant people have been taught to despise, to deride and scoff the weakness of the governed, then their cup of abjectness is full to the brim. . . . Read the annexed articles from the *Tribune* . . . malice and hate are lost in scorn, contempt, ridicule, and derision!

Are we of the South, the people described by Senator Hammond? Or are we the poor, miserable, vaporing, impotent poltroons described by the *Tribune?*

If the former, within forty days the sovereignty of some, at least, of these now subject and derided States, will be asserted, and the flag of Independence floated on the breeze. But if, indeed, we are as impotent as the *Tribune* represents us, in the name of all that is decent, I implore you, my countryman, to submit quietly. If you are incapable of a manly resistance, exhibit the next best proof of manhood, silent endurance. No more threats, no more vauntings, or *prospective platforms*. We can, at least, die with the dignity of martyrs, if we cannot live like heroes. . . .

Shall we, with our fifteen vaunted sovereignties, each A PEOPLE AND A STATE, with the reciprocal duties of allegiance and protection, with whom resistance is not rebellion, and a defeated effort no treason—shall we die and make no sign?

Anything is better than, without one manly effort, to take the fate of prostrate Ireland. . . . Men of the South, "Awake, arise, or be forever fallen!" Our manacles are being forged. Shall we sleep while they are fitted to our limbs, and the rivets clinched?[27]

Running through all 1860 Association literature is a defense of the institution of slavery. While most of the pamphlets emphasized the dangers with which emancipation threatened the owner of slaves, one, Tract No. 5, dealt with the institution from the particular viewpoint of the non-owner. Its full title was *The Interest in Slavery of the Southern Non-slaveholder. The Right of Peaceful Secession. Slavery in the Bible.* The first of these articles was in a limited way an answer to Helper's *Impending Crisis.* It was a letter written by James D. B. De Bow at the request of the Association in which he contended that the non-slaveholder, far from being injured by the institution, had an even greater interest in it than those who owned slaves. He claimed that the institution had produced in the South a larger proportion of property owners than existed anywhere else in the world, and that the two-thirds of the people who did not own slaves profited directly or indirectly from the institution. Because their income came indirectly from agriculture, the merchant and his employees, all mechanics, laborers, doctors, teachers, preachers, and other city dwellers were dependent on slavery for their daily bread. As to the small farmer who produced articles of food, it was the greatest absurdity to claim that he was injured by slave

[27] *Ibid.,* pp. 3-7.

competition, because the slave consumed, but did not produce in large amount, such articles. Certainly white and black did not compete in the field, because tobacco, rice, cotton, and sugar culture was so strenuous that the white cheerfully gave way to the Negro. To prove that slave labor did not reduce wages of the Southern white, De Bow cited statistics showing that bricklayers, carpenters, and ordinary laborers received much higher money wages in Charleston, Nashville, and New Orleans than in Pittsburgh, Chicago, and Lowell, and moreover paid much less for board. Southern laborers had the advantage, too, in that they were not required to work in close and unsanitary factories attending "remorseless" machinery, and were not in degrading competition with foreign pauper labor. In the South the laborer preserved his dignity as a white man and could look forward to the day when he, or certainly his son, would become the owner of slaves and thus relieve wife and children of labor in field and home. These satisfactory conditions would be destroyed by emancipation because ruin would come to the whole population when abolition destroyed the great staple of the South. Worst of all, emancipation would bring racial equality and race war from which the slaveholder might escape through emigration, but which the non-slaveholder, financially unable to escape, must face alone. De Bow arrived at the conclusion that the Southern non-slaveholder had every reason to defend, even unto death if necessary, the slavery regime.[28]

De Bow's article illustrates the earnestness with which the proslavery argument was restated on the eve of secession by The 1860 Association. Most of the arguments of Dew, Hammond, Harper, and other apologists for the institution of slavery may be found somewhere in 1860 Association literature. Hammond's "mud-sill" theories were included in Troup's pamphlet.[29] The Biblical defense was partially set forth in the article, *Slavery in the Bible,* published with De Bow's letter. This article was a long extract from a sermon on "The Character and Influence of Abolitionism" by Henry J. Van Dyke. In it Van Dyke presented a scathing indictment of the abolitionists and placed at their door the responsibility for the strife agitating the country. His text was taken from the sixth chapter of Paul's first letter to Timothy beginning, "Let as many servants as are under the yoke count their own masters worthy of all honour, that the name of God and his doctrine be not blasphemed." He held that abolitionism not only had no foundation in Scripture but also led in multitudes of cases to utter infidelity. The republication of this sermon may have done much to strengthen Southern belief that "if anyone teach differently by affirming that, under the gospel, slaves are not bound to serve their masters, but ought to

[28] *The Interest in Slavery of the Southern Non-slaveholder,* pp. 3-12.
[29] *To the People of the South,* pp. 8-14.

be made free . . . , he is puffed up with pride, and knoweth nothing either of Jewish or Christian revelation."[30]

Although the greatest influence of The 1860 Association was probably exerted through the pamphlets which it distributed, the Association was more than a publication agency. As a group of secessionists, meeting every Thursday at noon in Charleston, it may be regarded as a sort of political club whose purpose was to influence public opinion and political action by whatever means were available. One of its declared purposes was to conduct correspondence with prominent men in various parts of the South. The extent of this activity is not known, but there certainly was a committee of correspondence which functioned in some degree.[31] On occasion, the Association sponsored political rallies, notably a great protest meeting held in Charleston November 9 at a time when the legislature was debating a convention bill.[32] This meeting, merging with another held to welcome a large delegation of Savannah citizens who had arrived to celebrate the completion of the Charleston and Savannah Railroad, made its influence felt by telegraphing resolutions to the legislature and sending a committee to Columbia for the purpose of urging haste.[33] The Association also prepared and published a comprehensive survey of the military resources of the state.[34] These various activities of the Association stamp it as a revolutionary political club. It apparently did not develop a network of affiliated organizations, though there was a "Winyah Association of 1860," and perhaps others.[35] The total influence of the Association seems to have been large enough to justify the prediction of a contemporary when he said: "The labors of the '1860 Association' may not be generally known, and therefore, may not be duly appreciated at the present time, but an intelligent posterity will look back to its patriotic and self-denying exertions" and give due credit.[36]

The propaganda of The 1860 Association was more or less typical of that dispensed through the newspapers and other agencies. Among these should be mentioned the pulpit. The clergy of South Carolina cannot be accused of becoming mere political agitators on the eve of secession, but they did on occasion express in no uncertain terms their approval of the course which South Carolina was about to follow. An excellent opportunity was presented to them when the legislature, "deeply impressed" with the "justice and purity" of the Southern cause, resolved that November 21 should be observed as a day of fasting, humiliation, and prayer. Governor W. H. Gist's proclamation urged

[30] *The Interest in Slavery of the Southern Non-slaveholder,* pp. 17-30.
[31] *Mercury,* November 3, 1860, quoting letter of a Georgia citizen to the committee.
[32] White, *Rhett,* p. 179.   [33] See below, pp. 57-58.
[34] *Suggestions as to Arming the State* (Charleston, 1860). The committee for this project was headed by Gabriel Manigault.
[35] *Courier,* November 15, 1860.   [36] *Ibid.,* December 3, 1860.

44

the people everywhere to pray for "one heart and one mind" in resisting the encroachments on the rights of the state.[37] The day was generally observed in the churches with orthodox state rights sermons, some of them being later published in the newspapers and as pamphlets. Among these secession sermons was one delivered by Reverend Thomas Smyth in the Second Presbyterian Church of Charleston and published under the title, *The Sin and the Curse; or The Union, The True Source of Disunion, and Our Duty in the Present Crisis.*[38] Smyth found the cause of disunion in the Declaration of Independence which set forth Godless ideas of equality. Men were unequal, he contended, in physique, mental ability, emotional reactions, moral taste and judgment, and in their relation to law and government. Since society, government, and parentage were all from God, "these determine every man's rights, responsibilities, and duties, and are to be submitted to, by all men equally and alike as the ordinances of God, and that, too, not only from necessity, but for conscience's sake." Smyth traced the development and consequences of the "aetheistic, revolutionary principle" of equality. It had resulted in a theory of majority rule which had led to majority interpretation of the Bible and the rejection of the idea of its divine inspiration and infallibility. The South, he believed, had a great commission to preserve the word of God against the efforts of those who would make it an abolitionist Bible and God an anti-slavery God.[39] Illustrations of similar utterances of the clergy might be multiplied. Resolutions of the Presbyterian Synod of South Carolina, passed a few days before the election of delegates to the state convention, probably reflected accurately the general attitude of the churches in the crisis. They declared that while it was ordinarily dangerous for ministers to participate in political affairs, the question then at issue was partly religious in that it involved a "duty to God, who gave us our rights; a duty to our ancestors, whose blood and sufferings procured them for us; a duty to our children, whose precious inheritance we may not waste or defile; and a duty to our very slaves, whom men that know them not, nor care for them as we do, would take from our protection." Therefore the synod felt justified in expressing the belief that South Carolinians were "solemnly called on to imitate" their Revolutionary fathers and stand up for their rights.[40] Such sentiments, frequently proclaimed from South Carolina pulpits, were undoubtedly of great importance in the development of secession opinion.

Much more important than pulpit oratory was the speech-making of the politicians. Little need be said concerning this obvious method

[37] *House Journal* (called session, 1860), p. 12; Columbia *Daily South Carolinian,* November 14, 1860.
[38] Charleston, 1860.
[39] Smyth, *The Sin and the Curse,* pp. 3-17.
[40] F. D. Jones and W. H. Mills (eds.), *History of the Presbyterian Church in South Carolina Since 1850* (Columbia, 1926), pp. 75-76.

of arousing the people except to comment on the extent of this kind of activity in 1860. The year was unusual in the opportunities offered to the political orator. This was partly due to the exceptional amount of campaigning for seats in the many political assemblies of 1860. In April there was a meeting of the Democratic state convention, followed by the national Democratic convention in Charleston. New delegates were chosen to a second state convention which met in late May to choose delegates to Richmond. There was a lull in the summer broken somewhat by July 4th celebrations. Then followed a long and exciting campaign ending in the October elections for the legislature which met in extra session early in November. Finally came elections December 6 for convention delegates. The opportunities offered to secession orators in a year thus crowded with political events may be readily appreciated.

As delegates returned from various gatherings, the custom in many places was to hold "ratification" mass meetings at which oratory was unrestrained. To these meetings were often brought the most prominent and popular speakers available, frequently from distant parts of the state. Sometimes three or four members of Congress addressed one meeting. In Pendleton, for example, on one occasion there were Chesnut, Ashmore, Bonham, and Orr.[41] Effective use was made of the services of such former conservatives as A. G. Magrath who became a popular hero after his dramatic resignation from the federal bench early in November.[42]

Various other occasions furnished opportunities for South Carolina speakers to arouse the people. Fourth of July celebrations, a mass meeting in Charleston to celebrate the evacuation of that city during the Revolution, the annual meeting of the South Carolina Agricultural Society in Columbia, reviews of militia companies and battalions, sales days at the district (county) seats, etc., all these brought people together for speeches on the great issue of the day.[43] During convention and legislative sessions every hotel balcony and porch became a rostrum to which prominent men were called by excited crowds for an expression of their views. Especially was this true during the called session of the legislature which considered a convention bill.[44]

In this survey of propaganda agencies several organizations should be mentioned which were not originated for propaganda purposes alone but which were important in the development of secession sentiment. First were the Vigilance Associations and the Committees of Safety whose purpose was to insure the safety of the community against slave disorders fomented by abolitionist agents who were supposedly active

[41] *Keowee Courier,* November 24, 1860.
[42] *Ibid.; Carolina Spartan,* November 29, 1860.
[43] *Courier,* July 6, December 15, 1860; *Mercury,* November 21, 1860; *Daily South Carolinian,* November 14, 1860; *Conservatist,* November 6, 1860.
[44] *Courier,* November 6, 8, 1860; *Conservatist,* November 13, 1860.

in the state. In some cases a Vigilance Committee served as "an active and efficient patrol" to examine and arrest suspects, while a smaller Committee of Safety passed judgment. In other places there was only one committee. If one may judge by the numerous newspaper notices, such committees were organized in practically every community of the state. In some places they were apparently quite active. In Barnwell it was said "that not a suspicious person, or event, escapes their notice, and the offender is brought up with a short turn and is made to feel that eyes are upon him which he cannot elude, and that hands are ready to be laid upon him at any hour of the day or night."[45]

The fear of foreign agents tampering with slaves was an honest one, and must be accounted one of the important motives for secession. Lawrence M. Keitt wrote privately: "Our negroes are being enlisted in politics. With poison and fire how can we stand it? I confess this feature alarms me, more even, than everything in the past."[46] The danger was emphasized by the newspapers and pamphlets which published many reports of poison, fire, and sword in other parts of the South, especially in Texas. Stories were carried of widespread organization of Northern "Wide Awake Clubs" whose purpose was to carry on the work of John Brown. The statement was even made that Charleston was overrun with abolitionist emissaries.[47] It was against these supposed dangers that the Vigilance Committees were established. They were not mere propaganda agencies, but their organization greatly emphasized a danger that was largely imaginary, and added to the sense of insecurity which accompanied the election of Lincoln.

More important than the Vigilance Committees in adding to the excitement of the time were the Minute Men. This was a semi-military organization whose declared purpose was to defend the state should secession lead to war. Although the Minute Men were organized into military companies which did some serious drilling, the military significance of the organization was negligible. Few, if any, companies as such entered the service when war came, though many individual Minute Men must have been among the first volunteers.[48] Essentially the Minute Men were "Southern Rights Associations" agitating for secession. In some cases the military feature was entirely lacking, as in Charleston, where the constitution of the organization listed such activities as public demonstrations for secession but made no reference to military action.[49]

[45] *Mercury*, November 21, 1860. On the Vigilance Associations see also *infra*, pp. 111-112.
[46] L. M. Keitt to J. H. Hammond, September 10, 1860, Hammond Papers.
[47] *Courier*, September 10, 24, October 9, 29, 30, November 6, 1860.
[48] Gregg's first regiment, for example, was said to have been composed largely of Minute Men. *Journal of the Convention of the People of South Carolina, held in 1860, 1861, and 1862, together with the Ordinances, Reports, Resolutions, etc.* (Columbia, 1862), p. 520.
[49] *Courier*, November 12, 1860.

The Minute Men organized on a statewide basis October 3 when "a large meeting of good and true men, of undoubted Southern sentiment" met in Columbia for that purpose.[50] The emblem of the Minute Men, a blue ribbon rosette worn on the side of a cocked hat, became a familiar sight as the organization spread rapidly over the state. Soon the newspapers were full of the doings of the Minute Men. The typical activity was parading by day and by night. In Columbia three hundred marched in a great torchlight procession October 12. A similar demonstration in Newberry featured transparencies proclaiming such sentiments as, "Prepare for the Issue" and "South Carolina is Expected to Lead." During the session of the legislature which considered a convention bill, the Minute Men contributed greatly to the excitement which was kept up night after night. And when the legislature seemed to hesitate to lead the secession movement, they passed resolutions expressing impatience at delay and insisted upon decisive action.[51] In Charleston they announced that they would vote only for convention candidates who favored immediate separate state secession. Hammond heard on "good authority" that the Minute Men of Columbia even warned Lemuel Boozer of Lexington that they would "meet and hang him on the other side of the Congaree" if he dared run for the convention on a coöperationist platform.[52] The chief significance of the Minute Men, however, was in their contribution to secession excitement through their public demonstrations. Because of these activities they must be regarded as one of the important agencies which prepared the way for secession.

Such were the chief propaganda agencies on the eve of secession. It may be observed that the leaders of that period proved themselves masters of the psychology of mass education. They appreciated fully the value of public demonstrations of every kind. Political rallies, mass meetings, spell-binding oratory, torchlight processions, military reviews and parades, fireworks displays, banners, slogans, brass bands, and noise in general were striking features of the South Carolina scene. Skillful appeals were made to such fundamental human emotions as fear, hate, racial prejudice, love, pride, and self-respect. Hate and fear of the abolitionists were not difficult to stir because they had themselves freely furnished the inflammatory materials. It was only necessary to quote, and sometimes to misquote, the more radical Northern agitator to convince the people that the abolitionist was the South's mortal enemy and that abolitionism and Republicanism were synonymous. Good use was made of the art of abuse and ridicule. The horrors of racial equality and race war which emancipation would bring were re-

[50] *Conservatist,* October 16, 1860. General James Jones of Columbia was apparently chosen head of the organization. *Ibid.,* November 6, 1860.
[51] Spartanburg *Express,* October 17, 1860; *Conservatist,* October 16, November 6, 1860; *Courier,* November 10, 1860.
[52] *Ibid.,* November 12, 1860; J. H. Hammond to W. G. Simms, November 10, 1860, Hammond Papers.

peatedly described. The assertion was openly made and apparently believed that Vice-President-elect Hamlin was a mulatto.[53] Even more effective was the appeal to love—love of home, wife, children. A conspicuous feature of secession literature was the call to Southern men to defend Southern womanhood. It was freely charged that the abolitionists had already brought rape as well as fire and sword to parts of the South. Pride was touched by descriptions of the South as a mere economic dependency of the North, and by quotations from Northern sources to show the contempt with which Southern strength and valor were regarded by the North. There was no doubt general agreement with William D. Porter's assertion that the South must move on the election of Lincoln or forever lose caste.[54]

The foregoing description of 1860 propaganda agencies and methods reveals the ability with which South Carolina leaders fired the spirit of the people on the eve of secession. L. W. Spratt, speaking later to the Florida convention said that South Carolina leaders had always been taught that revolution could be precipitated by political action and that they therefore exerted themselves in an effort to stir the people. He believed that if public sentiment, once aroused, had been allowed to subside, the people would have "lost the spirit of adventure, and would have quailed before the shock of this great controversy."[55] Leaders, however, did not allow it to subside. In this way they made South Carolina secession the popular movement that it undoubtedly was. The remarkable unity which finally prevailed is a striking tribute to their leadership.

[53] *Mercury,* November 3, 1860.
[54] W. D. Porter to J. H. Hammond, November 3, 1860, Hammond Papers.
[55] *Mercury,* January 12, 1861.

CHAPTER IV

SOUTH CAROLINA'S DECISION TO LEAD

The decision of South Carolina to lead the secession movement of 1860 was regarded by many contemporaries as the decisive factor in the success of the whole movement. According to this view, delay and apparent hesitation in South Carolina would have had a chilling effect on secession sentiment in other states and would have allowed time for a conservative reaction and possible compromise. If this theory may be accepted as valid—and there is much evidence to sustain it—the special session of the South Carolina legislature which issued the call for convention is worthy of careful study. It was in this legislature that the decision to lead was really made.

As overwhelming as secession sentiment seemed to be in the fall of 1860, unanimity was not complete. Especially significant was the fact that the influential United States Senators James H. Hammond and James Chesnut, Jr., had not yet committed themselves, a fact that caused considerable dissatisfaction and anxiety among the secessionists. Isaac W. Hayne and L. M. Keitt urged Hammond to make a public declaration, and suggested that his failure to do so would imperil his reëlection.[1] But Hammond although invited to speak at many political rallies, consistently refused in cautiously phrased letters which left his position largely undefined. In one of these letters of refusal published in the *Courier*, August 25, he agreed that the election of Lincoln would put the Union at "imminent and instant peril" but professed to believe that Breckinridge and Lane might still be elected. Privately he wrote that if he had the assurance that Georgia and the Gulf states would support the movement he would favor a "complete trial of the experiment of disunion." He doubted, however, that such assurance could be obtained, and he was unalterably opposed to South Carolina leadership unless the clearest proof was given that *all* the cotton states desired it. No reasonable man, he thought, could adopt a program for the state until the election figures were available. Unless these showed the fixed determination of the West and South, secession in South Carolina

---

[1] Hayne stated that he was certain that Rhett and his friends were after Hammond's seat and that Gist also had a clique at work believing that if Hammond stepped aside the malcontent convention men would favor him in preference to Rhett. I. W. Hayne to J. H. Hammond, September 15, 1860; L. M. Keitt to J. H. Hammond, October 23, 1860, Hammond Papers. When a correspondent of the *Mercury* suggested Gist for the Senate should the Union not be dissolved, Gist replied that he was not interested in Hammond's seat and that he would not represent a state submitting to Republican rule. *Carolina Spartan*, November 1, 1860.

would be "the weakest, most impolitic and assuredly abortive movement" that the state had ever made.[2]

Chesnut, too, was unwilling to rush into secession. Absent on vacation in Virginia during the summer, he had been, like Hammond at Redcliffe, somewhat removed from the excitement in South Carolina, and was not stampeded. He was reported by the Washington correspondent of the Philadelphia *Press* as having told someone at White Sulphur Springs that he would not regard the election of Lincoln as a cause for secession.[3] Certainly he was cold to the proposals of many Southern politicians in Virginia that South Carolina secede on the chance of dragging in the other states. Back in South Carolina, he was, by the end of October, more inclined to separate secession but still wished to consult Hammond and other friends before making up his mind.[4]

More important than the silence of Hammond and Chesnut was the fact that many of those who spoke for secession either opposed, or failed to endorse, separate action by South Carolina. Orr, for example, made it quite clear that he would oppose any movement lacking the coöperation of at least Alabama, Mississippi, and Georgia;[5] and Ashmore was at first firmly opposed to separate action.[6] The radicals on the other hand believed that South Carolina should secede immediately and alone if necessary. Here was a difference of opinion which held all the possibilities of factional division and defeat of secession, as in 1851. Recognizing the danger, Robert Barnwell Rhett became strangely moderate in his utterances and the *Mercury* deprecated any agitation of the separate action issue. The moderates agreed that the question was premature, Ashmore remarking that for once in his life he was in agreement with the Rhetts.[7]

The issue between the separate actionists and coöperationists was so fundamental, however, that it could not be completely ignored or suppressed. In the October elections for the legislature, while candidates were generally required simply to pledge that they would vote for a convention in case of Lincoln's election, in some places questionnaires demanded more. In the upper districts most candidates in their replies either insisted that secession should be coöperative or stated that the

---

[2] J. H. Hammond to I. W. Hayne, September 19, 1860; J. H. Hammond to James Chesnut, Jr., October 23, 1860, Hammond Papers.

[3] *Conservatist*, October 30, 1860.

[4] James Chesnut, Jr., to J. H. Hammond, October 17, 27, 1860, Hammond Papers.

[5] *Conservatist*, August 7, 1860. Perry saw in Orr's inclusion of Georgia a condition which he knew could not be fulfilled. Other efforts then and later were made to discount the sincerity of Orr's announcement. Charleston *Courier*, August 10, 1860, quoting New York *Evening Post;* Lillian A. Kibler, "Unionist Sentiment in South Carolina in 1860," *Journal of Southern History*, IV (August, 1938), 353.

[6] J. D. Ashmore to J. H. Hammond, July 10, 1860, Hammond Papers.

[7] *Mercury*, August 10, 1860; J. D. Ashmore to J. H. Hammond, August 30, 1860, Hammond Papers.

question was premature.[8]   In Charleston, protests were made against raising the separate action issue and few candidates replied to the published questionnaires.   There was, however, a real contest between the moderates and radicals indicating that the question was in fact present.   The result of the election was a Charleston delegation divided between separate actionists and coöperationists with the moderates having the advantage.[9]   One observer claimed that not more than four of the twenty men elected favored separate action.[10]   It would be easy, however, to exaggerate the conservatism of the Charleston delegation and to credit it with a unionism which did not exist.   Here, as elsewhere in South Carolina, most moderate, conservative men had concluded that the time for a showdown had come.   Michael P. O'Connor, for example, who was a member of the Charleston delegation and whom historians often include in their lists of the more prominent Charleston unionists, admitted that the entire current of his thoughts had changed.   "The South," he said, "will not, can not in safety to herself, await the overt act."   A month before secession he described the Union as a "dead carcass stinking in the nostrils of the Southern people."[11]

Although secession feeling was running high at the time the South Carolina legislature met in special session on November 5, there was the widest variation of opinion as to the best method of obtaining support of other Southern states, which support all greatly desired and which many demanded as a condition of South Carolina action.   Coöperation through the decision of a Southern congress had been so discredited that few South Carolinians favored it.   Even the coöperationists. thought that each state must act individually under some kind of assurance that it would not be alone.   A correspondent of the *Courier* suggested that a South Carolina convention immediately pass a secession ordinance to go into effect on the day any other state withdrew from the Union or, in the absence of such coöperation, on the day Lincoln assumed the presidency.[12]   Another thought that the South Carolina convention should be delayed until January and that commissioners in the meantime should work for simultaneous secession in other states.[13] Orr, in a speech in Greenville, opposed even the calling of a convention in South Carolina before concerted action had been arranged by commissioners to other states.   Behind these ideas involving delay was the fear of conservative men that the state might be left isolated as in 1832

[8] Yorkville *Enquirer*, October 4, 1860; *Keowee Courier*, September 1, 8, 15, 22, 27, 29, 1860; Spartanburg *Express*, September 5, 1860; *Mercury*, September 11, 1860.

[9] *Courier*, September 14-October 13, 1860.

[10] Kibler, "Unionist Sentiment in South Carolina in 1860," *loc. cit.*, p. 354, quoting Charleston correspondent of the New York *Tribune*.

[11] *Courier*, October 13, November 17, 1860; see *Carolina Spartan*, November 15, 1860, for O'Connor's strong secession stand in the legislature, and *supra*, p. 16 for views in April, 1860.

[12] *Courier*, October 26, 1860.   [13] *Ibid.*, November 5, 1860.

or that hasty action in South Carolina might create resentment and injure the cause of secession in other parts of the South. The radicals, on the other hand, argued that distrust of South Carolina no longer existed, and that immediate separate action was the surest way of obtaining coöperation. In the opinion of the *Mercury*, Orr's plan would lead to "postponement, delay, enervation, feebleness, halting, fainting, paralysis, *submission*—and the downfall of slavery, with the destruction of the South."[14] Serious as these differences were, they were not in any important degree the disagreements of unionists and secessionists but rather lines of cleavage between sincere coöperationists and separate actionists, between those who would have South Carolina lead and those who preferred that South Carolina follow. It was a difference of opinion, however, of great potential importance for the whole secession movement.

On the eve of the meeting of the legislature some shrewd observers believed that there would be a strong disposition not to take the lead even in coöperative secession until the hope of another state's doing so had failed.[15] The drift of opinion was, however, definitely in the other direction. This was due in large part to advice from, and the course of events in, other states. That there was considerable assurance of coöperation is clear. Governor W. H. Gist had sought such assurance from the governors of the cotton states by dispatching a letter to them by his brother, State Rights Gist, on October 5. It was highly desirable, he said, to have a full exchange of views.

It is the desire of South Carolina that some other State should take the lead, or at least move simultaneously with her. . . . If a single State secedes, she will follow her. If no other State takes the lead, South Carolina will secede (in my opinion) alone, if she has any assurance that she will be soon followed by another or other States; otherwise it is doubtful. If you decide to call a convention . . . , I desire to know the day you propose for the meeting, that we may call our convention to meet the same day, if possible. If your State will propose any other remedy, please inform me what it will probably be, and any other information you will be pleased to give me.[16]

The replies to this letter were on the whole very reassuring. Governor John J. Pettus, of Mississippi, wrote that he would call the legislature as soon as Lincoln was elected. He believed that Mississippi would probably want a Southern convention and if it advised secession the state would go out; though Mississippi would not act alone she would follow any other one state. Governor A. B. Moore, of Alabama,

[14] *Mercury*, October 30, 1860.

[15] Henry W. Ravenel, Private Journal, October 29, November 1, 1860, mss., University of South Carolina Library, hereinafter cited Ravenel, Diary; Kibler, "Unionist Sentiment in South Carolina in 1860," *loc cit.*, p. 335, quoting McCarter's Journal; Carson, *Life of Petigru*, pp. 359-360.

[16] W. H. Gist to Thomas O. Moore, October 5, 1860, John G. Nicolay, and John Hay, *Abraham Lincoln, A History* (New York, 1890), II, 306-307.

thought that Lincoln's election would be sufficient cause for secession and that while his state would not act alone, it would secede with two or more states and would certainly support any coerced state; he would call a convention as soon as Lincoln was elected but under the law authorizing the call it could not meet until about February 1. Governor M. S. Perry, of Florida, was sure a convention would be called and that Florida would follow the first seceding state. From Georgia, whose attitude was of particular importance to South Carolina, Governor Joseph E. Brown wrote that his state would favor a Southern convention and be governed by its action; Georgia would not move alone but might be greatly influenced by action of other states. The replies of Governor John W. Ellis of North Carolina and Thomas O. Moore of Louisiana were more discouraging but even those states, it was said, would not consent to coercion of seceding states.[17]

From less official sources also came much encouragement. The *Mercury* claimed "innumerable" assurances that action men in all the Southern states desire that South Carolina act with "promptitude and decision."[18] The conservative J. J. Pettigrew wrote: "We receive numberless letters from the Cotton States urging us to secede alone as under the moral lead of a single State the rest would certainly follow."[19] L. W. Spratt said later in his address to the Florida convention that there was not a public man in the state who had not received scores of urgent letters requesting that South Carolina begin the movement.[20] Many such letters are said to have been read at a caucus held just before the legislature met.[21] There was therefore much to support Governor Gist's statement to the legislature at its initial session, November 5, that the long awaited coöperation seemed near at hand. He requested the legislature to remain in session after choosing presidential electors, await the outcome of the election, and then call a convention of South Carolina. Next day he wrote Governor Pettus: "If your Legislature gives us the least assurance that you will go with us, there will not be the slightest difficulty, and I think we will go out at any rate."[22]

As the legislature stood by for the election results (received November 7) there was much excitement and secession oratory in Columbia. On the evening of the 5th more than a thousand citizens serenaded prominent men. Perhaps the most significant response was that of Senator Chesnut who now declared himself in favor of immediate separate action. He was sure other states would follow, and, discounting the dangers of coercion, he declared that "the man most

[17] *Ibid.*, II, 307-314.   [18] *Mercury*, November 3, 1860.
[19] J. J. Pettigrew to W. S. Pettigrew, October 24, 1860, Pettigrew Papers.
[20] *Mercury*, January 12, 1861.
[21] S. W. Crawford, *The Genesis of the Civil War. The Story of Fort Sumter* (New York, 1887), p. 11; hereinafter cited Crawford, *Fort Sumter.*
[22] *House Journal* (called session, 1860), p. 10; W. H. Gist to J. J. Pettus, November 6, 1860, quoted by Dumond, *Secession Movement*, p. 139.

averse to blood might safely drink every drop shed" in the establishment of a Southern Confederacy. Congressman Bonham also, who had not heretofore been clearly understood to favor separate action, now committed himself to that course.[23] With the exception of Senator Hammond every member of the South Carolina congressional delegation had now spoken. With the hope of bringing him to a similar stand, a group of legislators requested his views in a letter of November 6.[24]

There was much talk of harmony and unanimity as the legislature prepared to consider a convention bill, but sharp differences between moderate and radical secessionists appeared almost at once. At one extreme was legislation proposed on November 7 by R. B. Rhett, Jr., in the House, and Edmund Rhett in the Senate, which looked to a very early convention, the House resolutions fixing November 22 and December 17 as election and meeting dates, respectively, for the convention. It was argued that this would change the question in other states from one of disunion to one of coöperation.[25] Less precipitate was the action proposed in the House bill of Henry Buist of Charleston and in a Senate committee bill which received first reading November 8 and which fixed January 8 and 15 as election and meeting dates.[26] At the conservative extreme were proposals by George A. Trenholm of Charleston in the House, and Henry D. Lesesne in the Senate. Neither of these set definite dates for a convention and both involved delay during which concerted action might be negotiated with other states. Trenholm proposed the election of a commissioner to Georgia instructed to offer the coöperation of South Carolina in secession and to recommend simultaneous conventions to that end. His resolutions provided that the legislature should adjourn after the election of a commissioner, until November 19, and that joint military and finance committees should meanwhile prepare defense legislation. The Lesesne resolutions proposed that the governor be authorized to call a convention as soon as any one Southern state should give assurance of its determination to secede.[27]

The Trenholm resolutions, representing as they do the most conservative position assumed in the legislature, require additional comment. From the standpoint of the radicals they were highly unsatisfactory because they involved delay during which passions might cool and because they might be interpreted in other states as indicating

[23] *Courier*, November 6, 1860; Camden *Weekly Journal*, November 13, 1860, quoting Columbia *Southern Guardian; Conservatist*, November 13, 1860.

[24] A. P. Aldrich and others to J. H. Hammond, November 6, 1860, Hammond Papers.

[25] *Senate Journal* (called session, 1860), p. 14; *House Journal* (called session, 1860), p. 19; *Courier*, November 9, 1860.

[26] *Ibid.*, November 8, 10, 1860; *House Journal* (called session, 1860), pp. 18, 27; *Senate Journal* (called session, 1860), pp. 14-16.

[27] *Ibid.*, pp. 14-15; *House Journal* (called session, 1860), pp. 18-19; *Courier*, November 8, 1860.

lack of determination in South Carolina. It seems clear, however, that the purpose of Trenholm was not to defeat secession through delay, as has sometimes been supposed. His political background was by no means unionist. In 1851 he had been a separate action secessionist. He had not been identified with the later conservative National Democratic party until control of this party was seized by the radicals after the Charleston convention. Indeed, he had been one of those "true" men chosen by the radicals in the hectic May convention to serve as alternate delegate-at-large to Richmond in a group of extremists headed by R. B. Rhett.[28] He himself said, after the adjournment of the legislature, that his objectives in Columbia were, first to produce harmony in the Charleston delegation and in the whole legislature, and second to make sure that if and when a convention was called it should be for the single and determined purpose of carrying South Carolina out of the Union.[29] The record sustains his statement. He was in fact a sincere coöperationist especially anxious, like so many others, to gain the support of Georgia for the secession movement.

The proposals of Rhett, Buist, Trenholm, and Lesesne, however, revealed serious differences of opinion in the Charleston delegation. Almost as soon as this became apparent a caucus was called in which the members for five hours discussed their differences in earnest but friendly fashion. The result was a decision by the caucus that the proper course was to make an unconditional call for a convention with a view to separate action.[30] It is probable that the dates of the Senate bill, January 8 and 15, were agreed upon. Since this decision involved a retreat from the conservative proposals of Trenholm and Lesesne, its importance is obvious. It is to be explained partly by a sincere desire of the Charleston delegation to bring harmony among its members. Another important influence was the dramatic resignation, November 7, of Federal District Judge A. G. Magrath, after the grand jury, of which R. N. Gourdin was foreman, had refused to function.[31] Magrath had not previously expressed his views but in 1850 had vigorously opposed separate action. The resignation created great excitement in Charleston. In Columbia, too, it made a deep impression and furnished additional inspiration for secession orators, including Edmund Ruffin of Virginia, who had just arrived in the city.[32] One observer wrote that from the moment the news of Magrath's resignation was received in

[28] *Courier*, June 5, 1860; *Proceedings* (May), p. 97.

[29] *Courier*, November 17, 1860.

[30] Lesesne's statement in *Courier*, November 16, 1860. The exact time of the caucus cannot be determined but it was probably on the evening of the 8th (Thursday), perhaps early the next day.

[31] See Crawford, *Fort Sumter*, pp. 12-14 for the statements made by Magrath and Gourdin, and for comment on the significance of the resignations.

[32] *Courier*, November 8, 1860; *Mercury*, November 8, 1860; *Conservatist*, November 13, 1860, quoting Columbia *Southern Guardian*.

56

Columbia, all hesitation was ended.[33] Certainly the event must have profoundly influenced the caucus of the Charleston delegation. About the same time came news which seemed to indicate that secession sentiment was rising in Georgia. Governor Brown, it was said, had written Gist announcing his decision to add to his message to the legislature a clause recommending an immediate convention.[34]

The importance of the Charleston caucus was evident when the House met on November 9 and Trenholm modified his resolutions. The amended resolutions retained the proposal for a commissioner to Georgia, but also provided for a South Carolina convention January 15, the date fixed in the Senate bill.[35] The amended resolutions were still unsatisfactory to the more radical separate actionists. They opposed any gesture of coöperation through the sending of a commissioner until South Carolina had made her decision. Martin Witherspoon Gary of Edgefield thought the Trenholm resolutions would defeat speedy secession and throw cold water on the whole movement. W. S. Mullins of Marion insisted that South Carolina had already exhausted the policy of coöperation. "If we wait for coöperation, slavery and State rights will be abandoned, State sovereignty and the cause of Southern rights lost forever," he said. No commissioner should be sent until a pledge to secede had been put in the record.[36] On the other hand, Samuel McGowan of Abbeville, a former National Democrat who had been recently preaching secession in the up country,[37] supported Trenholm. Although opposed "now and forever" to any backward step, he contended that coöperation had long been the settled policy of the state and should not now be abandoned when success seemed certain. He pled that one last effort at coöperation be made in order to refute the false charge that South Carolina was disturbing Southern harmony by a desire to lead. If this effort should fail and the South Carolina convention should decide that secession would bring coöperation, he would then approve and support that action.[38]

As further discussion was postponed in the House, Lesesne of Charleston was speaking on his resolutions in the Senate. He was still of the opinion that it was wiser to seek coöperation before secession than to secede and trust other states to follow. But in accordance with the decision of the Charleston caucus, he moved that his own resolutions be tabled on the ground that only one bill was before the Senate and that some action by South Carolina was necessary. Resolutions by B. H. Wilson, essentially the House resolutions of Trenholm as amended, were also tabled, and the Senate bill for a January convention passed the

[33] Kibler, "Unionist Sentiment in South Carolina in 1860," *loc. cit.*, p. 357, quoting McCarter's Journal.
[34] *Courier*, November 10, 1860.
[35] *House Journal* (called session, 1860), pp. 30-32.
[36] *Courier*, November 10, 1860.   [37] *Ibid.*, November 6, 1860.
[38] *Ibid.*, November 10, 1860.

second reading by a vote of 44 to 1 and was sent to the House. The dissenter was Samuel McAliley of Chester.[39]

That January, instead of an earlier date should have been so over-whelmingly adopted by the Senate is a striking illustration of the great desire of secession leaders to prevent any semblance of division in South Carolina. Many members, probably a good majority of both houses, favored earlier dates but in the interest of harmony late dates were voted by the Senate and were at first accepted by the House committee which considered the Senate bill. As matters stood Friday afternoon, November 9, a late convention was practically assured. That a different decision was finally made was due in part to the pressure of public opinion, especially in Columbia and Charleston, and to news of events in Georgia.

The influence of public sentiment seems to have been felt almost immediately as news reached Columbia of great dissatisfaction in Charleston. The *Mercury* sharply criticised the tendency toward delay and reported general indignation among the people. Certain members of the delegation were impressed by letters from Charleston reporting that they were being referred to as "unionists" and "submissionists."[40] But more important was the fact that within a few hours after the passage of the convention bill by the Senate, highly encouraging news was received from Georgia. According to the reports Brown's recommendation for a convention had been enthusiastically received, and federal officers at Savannah and Milledgeville had already resigned. Even more exciting was the premature information that United States Senator Robert Toombs had tendered his resignation, saying that he did so in order that Georgia might stand with South Carolina for prompt action.[41] The effect of these reports was to convince many in the legislature that an earlier convention was necessary if South Carolina was to keep pace with progress of events.

The Georgia news was also important in stimulating outside pressure upon the legislature. The Columbia Minute Men passed resolutions expressing their impatience at delay and demanding an early convention.[42] In Charleston where a large delegation of Savannah citizens had arrived to celebrate the connection of Charleston and Savannah by rail, enthusiasm was greatly stimulated by the Georgia reports. In great meetings at the Mills House and at Institute Hall the celebration was turned into a grand secession rally. Henry R. Jackson, Judge Miller, F. S. Bartow, John Bilbo, and other Georgia speakers made stirring

[39] *Ibid.*

[40] *Mercury*, November 9, 1860; *Courier*, November 12, 13, 1860.

[41] *Courier*, November 10, 12, 13, 1860; *Conservatist*, November 12, 1860. Toombs really returned to the Senate, served on the compromise committee of thirteen, and made his farewell speech January 7. *Dictionary of American Biography* (New York, 1928-1936), XVIII, 591; hereinafter cited *D. A. B.*

[42] *Courier*, November 10, 1860.

58

addresses in which they promised Georgia coöperation. Resolutions were adopted urging a convention at the "earliest possible moment." A special committee composed of recent United States officials A. G. Magrath, James Conner, and W. F. Colcock was appointed to proceed to Columbia and personally urge haste. At 10:30 that night it sent the following telegram to the Charleston delegation:

The greatest meeting ever held in this city is now assembled in Institute Hall. The meeting has been addresed, among others, by Mr. Jackson, Mr. Bartow and others from Georgia. They have pledged their State, and our people cannot be restrained. They believe that there should be action by the Legislature, in the call for a Convention to be assembled at some early date. The feeling is alike unprecedented and indescribable . . . We expect to be with you by the train tomorrow. . . .[43]

This meeting of Charleston and Savannah citizens was later described by the *Mercury* as the turning point of the whole secession movement. But for this almost accidental incident, it said, the South Carolina convention would have met late, and there would have been no Southern Confederacy.[44] D. H. Hamilton in speaking of the importance of the meeting said that it showed that the people were far ahead of their leaders and that while the latter were temporizing in Columbia the people were rising up and demanding immediate action. "I am told by men who were talking coöperation ten days since," he said, "that it was the most impressive sight, to see the people rising in their strength . . . to hasten the action of the Legislature."[45]

The good news from Georgia and the Charleston action which had been largely inspired by it completely overshadowed cautious advice received about the same time from Senator Hammond. While expressing his willingness to follow his state in whatever course it might take, Hammond strongly opposed taking the leadership unless it was clear that one state would be followed by the others and that others expected South Carolina to start the movement. He himself did not believe that other states would follow South Carolina; they were still prejudiced against her; and he was unwilling for his state to be left isolated as in 1832. He had never believed that the South would break up the Union on the first election of a Republican, nor was the election of Lincoln of itself a justification for disunion, although there had been

[43] *Courier*, November 10, 1860; *Keowee Courier*, November 17, 1860.

[44] *Mercury*, September 26, 1861. The meeting was described as follows: "Impassioned eloquence and burning appeal lifted every heart—a wild storm seemed suddenly to sweep over the minds of men, and riding upon the wings of that storm there came that august spirit which every man at once instantly recognized, as he felt for the first time in his life, that he stood in the presence of the majesty of the *Genius of Revolution.*" *Ibid.*

[45] D. H. Hamilton to D. H. Hamilton, Jr., November 10, 1860, Ruffin-Roulhac-Hamilton Papers, University of North Carolina Library. The remarkable character of the meeting was recalled by the last survivor of the secession convention in an article written in 1901, republished in *The State*, December 18, 1910. See *Senate Journal* (called session, 1860), p. 22, for Charleston resolutions.

ever since 1833 entirely sufficient justification for secession. If, against his advice, South Carolina decided to take the lead, Hammond would insist on two conditions: first, that one or more states were assuredly to follow and, second, that the seceding states adopt without any change whatever the Constitution of the United States. As to the time of secession he thought it made little difference whether it came under Buchanan or after Lincoln took office but since the South was under obligation to Buchanan he should not be put to this extra trial.[46] A. P. Aldrich, on the advice of Gist, Porter, and others, suppressed this conservative letter of Hammond. He explained his action by saying that the letter reached Columbia under circumstances which Hammond did not anticipate and that it would have been unfair to him to publish it. He added that it would have only had the effect of organizing an "ineffectual" opposition to immediate action by the legislature. Hammond was not pleased at the liberty taken by Aldrich but he wrote after secession that a Southern Confederacy had always been the cherished "dream and hope" of his life; that he had taken no part in the movement because he had not believed that it could succeed.[47]

The events of Friday afternoon and night profoundly affected the legislature. The House committee which had been ready to report the Senate bill unchanged now amended it by substituting December 6 and 17 for January 8 and 15 and so reported it on the 10th. Some opposition to the change appeared. W. C. Black of York, although favoring a convention, declared that the people of the larger districts were not "so thoroughly posted up as to the events transpiring around them," and that time was "absolutely necessary" in which to bring them "up to the point." A. W. Thompson of Union agreed, and insisted on the original Senate bill. Winsmith of Spartanburg spoke to his resolutions pointing to coöperative secession. With division thus threatened the House went into committee of the whole. A. P. Aldrich explained the reasons for the changed dates. He argued that the stand of Georgia and the resignation of Toombs gave assurance of the coöperation for which the

[46] J. H. Hammond to A. P. Aldrich and others, November 8, 1860, Hammond Papers.
[47] A. P. Aldrich to J. H. Hammond, November 25, 1860; J. H. Hammond to W. G. Simms, November 10, 1860; J. H. Hammond to M. C. H. Hammond, November 12, 1860; J. H. Hammond to J. D. Ashmore, April 28, 1861, Hammond Papers.
It has been frequently stated that on October 25, 1860, Governor Gist, ex-Governor Adams, Orr, and all of the congressional delegation save one met at Hammond's residence near Augusta and unanimously decided for secession. Apparently later writers have repeated the unsupported statement to this effect in Crawford, *Fort Sumter*, p. 14. The correspondence of Hammond, however, strongly suggests that Hammond attended no such meeting either at his own home or elsewhere. To have done so would have been utterly inconsistent with his views expressed at the time and contrary to his later statement that he had had nothing to do with the secession movement. See also Merritt, *Hammond*, p. 140 note.

state had been working since 1828, and that it was necessary to reassure those who were every hour sending anxious messages to the legislature. John Cuningham of Charleston strongly supported this view. Admitting the propriety of giving time for fair discussion among the people, he was of the opinion that they were now ready or could be brought into line before December 6. But better to lose York District through haste, he said, than Alabama through delay. With Georgia as well as Mississippi, Alabama, and Florida indicating readiness to act, South Carolina coöperationists should be satisfied. "When they invoke us to lead, is there a coöperationist on this floor," he asked, "who will ask us to wait until coöperation is tendered, or will he not tender it by taking the lead?" The position of Aldrich and Cuningham was approved by a vote of 91 to 14 as the committee of the whole reported favorably on the early convention bill. The dissenters now joined the majority as the bill passed the second reading 117 to 0 and was returned to the Senate.[48]

The House amendments for the earlier convention dates received Senate attention in a brief night session of the same day. Apparently there was no debate and the bill passed the third reading by a vote of 42 to 0.[49] Four senators were missing. Of these Wade Hampton had been unable to return from a western trip in time to attend the special session, but according to his own testimony he had already spoken for secession and had freely expressed in Mississippi his opinion that South Carolina would call a convention and secede.[50] Two other senators, Elam Sharpe of Pickens and James W. Harrison of Anderson, had voted for the original bill and were now absent by leave of the Senate. The fourth, Samuel McAliley of Chester, had opposed the original bill and now apparently abstained from voting.[51] Except for the formality of a third reading in the House, Monday the 12th, and ratification in a joint session of the houses on the 13th, the bill for a convention had now completed its course through the legislature.[52] The united action for which men of different shades of opinion had sincerely worked was an accomplished fact. The pressure of public opinion had been of great importance in bringing this about. But one cannot escape the conviction that Georgia, by action taken at the psychological moment, was largely responsible, however unwittingly, for South Carolina's decision to call an early rather than a late convention.

That the call of the convention may properly be regarded as the decision of South Carolina to secede promptly and thus lead the secession

---

[48] *Courier*, November 12, 1860; *House Journal* (called session, 1860), pp. 33-36; White, *Rhett*, p. 181.
[49] *Senate Journal* (called session, 1860), p. 22.
[50] *Courier*, November 26, 1860.
[51] *Senate Journal* (called session, 1860), pp. 21-22, 24-25. McAliley had no leave of absence and participated in Senate business on Monday, November 12.
[52] *Ibid.*, p. 30; *House Journal* (called session, 1860), p. 39.

movement can hardly be doubted. This was the interpretation accepted at the time. Chesnut on the 10th, and Hammond on the 11th, resigned as United States Senators.[53] For South Carolina the Union, except for formalities, had come to an end. Before the formal secession ordinance could be voted in convention there was to come a slight conservative reaction, but there was never any real doubt that the convention would promptly carry South Carolina out of the Union.

The act of the legislature in calling a convention met with general satisfaction. In Columbia excitement was intense as Keitt and others addressed the great crowds which serenaded them. In Charleston also great meetings were held to endorse the legislature's action and to congratulate the returning delegation. Palmetto flags were widely displayed and military companies paraded with enthusiasm.[54] There were similar demonstrations in many places. Henry W. Ravenel, returning from Columbia to Aiken, said he had never seen such excitement and that palmetto flags with one or more stars, or flags bearing the inscription "Separate State Action" were common. He said he had met no single person who did not heartily approve the legislature's action.[55] From Cheraw came reports that great unanimity prevailed in that district which had been opposed to secession in 1852. At a muster of the upper battalion November 15, returning legislators were acclaimed by the people and every militiaman stepped forward when those favoring immediate separate secession were asked to advance five paces. A similar proposal at the muster of the lower battalion received an identical response a few days later. The newspaper correspondent who reported this incident declared that he had yet to learn of a single voter who hesitated.[56] At Abbeville, November 22, A. G. Magrath, M. L. Bonham, Judge David L. Wardlaw, and others addressed a great rally of 2,500 to 3,000 persons on what came to be known as "Secession Hill." Though Wardlaw advised that action be taken only with at least four other states, the meeting adopted immediate secession resolutions.[57] L. M. Keitt said that not a single vote of the 1600 in his congressional district would be for submission.[58] From all parts of the state—

[53] *Senate Journal* (called session, 1860), pp. 21, 27. Hammond wrote: "I heard yesterday that Chesnut & Toombs had resigned—why I know not. But in half an hour Tom was on his way to Augusta with my resignation. . . . I thought Magrath & all those fellows were great asses for resigning & I have done it myself. It is an epidemic and very foolish. It reminds me of the Japanese who when insulted rip up their own bowels. . . . People are wild. The scenes of the French Revolution are being enacted already. Law & Constitution are equally & utterly disregarded." J. H. Hammond to M. C. M. Hammond, November 12, 1860, Hammond Papers.

[54] *Carolinian*, November 14, 1860.

[55] Ravenel, Diary, November 16, 1860.

[56] *Mercury*, November 21, 1860; Wallace, *History of S. C.*, III, 152; *Conservatist*, November 27, 1860.

[57] *Keowee Courier*, November 24, 1860; Wallace, *History of S. C.*, III, 152.

[58] *Mercury*, November 21, 1860.

Pendleton, Union, Greenwood, Newberry, Marion, Spartanburg, Aiken, Anderson—and from South Carolina students at West Point and at the University of Virginia came reports of enthusiastic secession sentiment.[59] Young ladies of Charleston resolved that they would honor all men who were for the revolution but would themselves secede from all who opposed it; they pledged their hearts to the first Garibaldi who appeared. A planter's wife wrote that she would leave the state if men were "too cowardly to protect their women and too mercenary to risk their money."[60] At last, after thirty years, said the *Mercury*, the state was finally convinced of her wrongs and stood united against the common enemy.[61] Even in the stronghold of unionism about Greenville, the people were almost a unit for secession, said the *Southern Enterprise*, and special efforts were being made to convert the reluctant ones there.[62]

[59] *Ibid.*, November 3, 1860; *Keowee Courier*, September 1, October 20, November 24, December 1, 1860; Ravenel, Diary, November 16 *et. seq.*; *Carolina Spartan*, November 22, 29, 1860.

[60] *Mercury*, November 3, 30, 1860.

[61] *Ibid.*, November 21, 1860.

[62] *Southern Enterprise*, November 15, 1860. An address to the people of Greenville district by James C. Furman, W. H. Campbell, and W. M. Thomas, printed in the Greenville *Patriot and Mountaineer*, urged them to make common cause with the rest of the state. All the current arguments were presented, and Baptists were told that the state stood in the same relationship to the federal government as local churches to the association; either state or church might secede at will. *Carolina Spartan*, November 22, 1860.

CHAPTER V

INDEPENDENCE DECLARED

In the December 6 election of delegates to the secession convention voting in most places was light, a fact that has sometimes been interpreted as indicating a strong reaction from the secession enthusiasm so manifest at the time of the passage of the convention bill. That some reaction did occur is clear but it was not of sufficient strength to be important. Actually the light vote must be explained by the absence, in most places, of a contest.

The usual procedure for the nomination of candidates was through mass meetings called for that purpose soon after the convention bill was passed. Leaders urged this procedure in order that all factions might combine to name a fusion ticket and thus present a united front for immediate secession.[1] Under this plan nomination was regarded as equivalent to election, consequently voters in large numbers remained at home on election day. In Newberry District, for example, less than half of those qualified took the trouble to vote;[2] in one place the polls were not even opened. The mass meeting ticket, except for a few scattered votes, was elected without opposition.[3]

In some places more than one ticket did appear. In Greenville a great mass meeting addressed by James C. Furman and others on November 17 passed resolutions for immediate independence and nominated a fusion ticket which was expected to be uncontested. In the days that followed, various speakers including Henry Buist, Memminger, and Magrath of Charleston kept the secession issue prominently before the people. But three days before the election a meeting was held by citizens opposed to separate action and a so-called coöperation ticket nominated consisting of Perry, Chief Justice John Belton O'Neall, Dr. W. A. Mooney, T. C. Bolling, and Dr. James P. Boyce, president of the Baptist Theological Seminary. O'Neall was well known for his anti-secession views but had taken no part in the secession controversy. Not even a resident of Greenville District and eschewing politics, he declined the nomination. Boyce was opposed to secession as a first step but favored a Southern confederacy should proper guarantees not be obtained by the South. Like O'Neall he refused to run, leaving Perry to head a ticket which was at least semi-unionist. Denounced by the

[1] The earliest of these mass meetings was called in Richland for November 15. *Carolinian*, November 14, 1860. See Ashmore's advice to Spartanburg District in *Carolina Spartan*, November 29, 1860.
[2] Chapman, *Annals of Newberry*, p. 373.
[3] *Conservatist*, December 11, 1860.

Southern Enterprise as a "submissionist" slate, it was buried under an avalanche of votes on December 6.[4]

In Spartanburg District the effort to limit nominations to a single ticket also failed, due apparently to local personal jealousies rather than to serious division on the secession issue. At first much harmony seemed to prevail. Representatives returning from the special session of the legislature addressed enthusiastic audiences and spoke for immediate action, although some of them admitted that they had been slow to make up their minds and had favored a January convention until overruled by the majority in Columbia. In a huge mass meeting of November 24 the people met to bear Chesnut and Magrath and to name a fusion ticket. Although the report of the nominating committee was adopted unanimously, there was later some complaint from the Winsmith faction that "steamroller" methods had been used to name a ticket composed of Cannon men only. Several rival lists of nominees now appeared in the newspapers but a number of those listed on the irregular tickets refused to stand and the nominees of the mass meeting were overwhelmingly chosen.[5] Secession itself was apparently not an issue. Only in the rural community of Solitude was there a public protest against undue haste on the part of South Carolina. Resolutions adopted at a meeting in this place expressed the belief that the convention should have been delayed until January or February in order to get more definite assurance of coöperation from other states.[6]

In Charleston, too, old party differences seemed for a time to disappear. Many former coöperationists and old Union men endorsed the action of the legislature in calling an early convention and urged immediate separate action by South Carolina. Richard Yeadon, for example, in a speech of November 15 admitted that hitherto he had been "amongst those rather noted for their devotion to the Union" but that he "worshipped at that political shrine no longer." Separate action, he said, was no longer identified with *isolated* state action; coöperationists therefore could with perfect consistency now support separate secession.[7] H. T. Peake, a former coöperationist, was now ready to "see South Carolina out of this accursed Union."[8] M. P. O'Connor continued to express strong secessionist views; his firmest hope was to live to see a Southern Confederacy; there must be no backward step.[9] J. J. Pope declared that although he had been and still was opposed to the isolation of his state, coöperation and separate action now

[4] Perry received only 225 votes, Mooney 196, and Bolling 190; each of the five regular candidates received more than 1300. Kibler, *Perry*, pp. 337-343; *Courier*, December 10, 1860; John A. Broadus, *Memoir of James Petigru Boyce* (New York, 1893), pp. 183-184.
[5] *Carolina Spartan*, November 22, 29, December 6, 13, 1860.
[6] Spartanburg *Express*, December 5, 1860.
[7] *Courier*, November 17, 1860.
[8] *Ibid.*
[9] *Ibid.*, October 13, November 17, 1860.

amounted to the same thing.[10]   Coffin said: "As slow as I have been to
come to the conviction of the advantages of a separation, I am now convinced that we are *two peoples at heart*."[11]   Theodore G. Barker, speaking for the wholesale merchants, said that they unanimously endorsed
the convention call understanding that it meant "direct, independent,
absolute secession." He had always believed it to be South Carolina's
solemn duty to act only with the other states and to "fight the battle
in the Union" but that with Georgia's assurances, secession had come
to mean coöperation and further delay was dangerous.[12]   Edward
McCrady said that while in 1850 he had counselled delay, in 1860 he
would urge all the haste consistent with the dignity of a sovereign
state.[13]   T. D. Wagner and other conservatives spoke in a similar vein
while Memminger and Magrath were busy preaching secession in the
up country.[14]   Apparently Charleston moderates and radicals had merged
into a single party.

Efforts, however, to bury old party differences in the election of
convention delegates by limiting nominations to a single ticket of
twenty-two names representing the old parties equally, did not succeed.
Although Magrath and others quickly withdrew their names from the
first irregular list which appeared in the newspapers on the ground
that there should be no contest, the *Mercury* soon admitted that the
fusion idea had been misunderstood and that bad feeling existed between the parties.[15]   The whole fusion plan collapsed and soon numerous
tickets appeared in the papers, the number finally reaching twenty-
three.[16]   In the meantime the *Mercury* created deep resentment by daily
classifying the candidates as "explicit" or "not explicit" according to
whether they had satisfactorily replied to a demand that they commit
themselves *both* to *immediate* and *permanent* dissolution of the Union.
Still on the "not explicit" list on election day were such active secessionists as R. N. Gourdin, an active officer of The 1860 Association, and
John Townsend, author of two potent pamphlets of the Association.
Protests were made that the old coöperationists were being proscribed—
that former association with the coöperationist party was still regarded
as a crime not to be forgiven.   The moderates claimed with much truth
that it had been they who had "put forth their mighty arm, and done
the work, for South Carolina and the South" and that the state could
not have been unified for secession except through their efforts.[17]   They
resented bitterly what they regarded as an effort to discriminate against
them.   A few candidates indignantly withdrew their names and some
others refused to publish a statement.   Among the latter were Mem-

[10] *Ibid.*   [11] *Ibid.*
[12] *Ibid.*, November 19, 1860.   [13] *Ibid.*, December 4, 1860.
[14] *Ibid.*, December 4, 15, 1860.
[15] *Courier*, November 14, 1860; *Mercury*, November 14, 15, 1860.
[16] *Mercury* and *Courier*, November 15-December 6, 1860.
[17] *Courier*, December 4, 1860.

66

minger, Edward McCrady, and T. G. Barker, all now good secession-ists.[18] Most candidates, however, gave replies satisfactory to the *Mercury*.

Apparently the *Mercury* sensed a reaction from the earlier enthusiasm and was determined that only extreme men be sent to the convention. There is evidence that some reaction did occur. "Fabius" publicly suggested William J. Grayson as one who might be supported by those who "cannot in blind fury and reckless haste, plunge themselves and the State, they know not whither."[19] H. D. Lesesne said privately that he found numbers of men who were opposed to precipitate action but did not like to speak openly because of the violence of the opposite feeling.[20] Apparently some were suggesting that secession should be delayed until Lincoln took office.[21] But that the overwhelming sentiment of the people was opposed to such caution was indicated by the election returns. Fourteen of those chosen were of the old extreme party. Resentment of the *Mercury's* pre-election campaign was shown, however, by the fact that Townsend and Gourdin, both on the *Mercury's* "not explicit" list, polled a larger vote than Rhett who ran seventh. Magrath, who led, had nearly 1000 more votes than the "father of secession" who complained that an effort had been made to defeat him under "a cloud of falsehoods."[22] For thirty years his name had been almost synonymous with disunion and his long agitation was at last bearing fruit. But as his cause was about to triumph, Rhett's personal popularity was in a state of decline and his leadership widely distrusted. As former moderates like Magrath, Memminger, Chesnut, Orr, and Ashmore spoke at various secession rallies, the services of Rhett were in slight demand.

Except in the places mentioned, the single ticket plan seems to have met with general approval. Occasionally a nominee declined to run, as did John S. Preston who, however, favored secession and even believed that the legislature should have declared it by simple enactment.[23] Ordinarily, however, the nomination was accepted as an honor not to be refused. In almost all cases the candidates were committed to immediate separate action. If their position was not already known, direct inquiry was made, as in the case of Robert W. Barnwell. He replied that though it put "great restraint" upon his feelings and "some vio-

[18] *Mercury,* December 6, 1860.
[19] *Courier,* December 3, 1860. See also *Mercury* (Tri-weekly), December 18, 1860, for protest against undue haste.
[20] Mrs. C. L. Pettigrew to C. L. Pettigrew, November 26, 1860, quoting Lesesne, Pettigrew Papers.
[21] See speech of the former conservative T. Y. Simons denouncing such views in *Courier,* December 15, 1860.
[22] Votes ranging from 102 to 3112 were cast for 47 of the 48 candidates. *Mercury,* December 6, 8, 1860; *Courier,* December 6, 8, 1860; R. B. Rhett to W. P. Miles, December 8, 1860, Miles Papers.
[23] *Carolina Spartan,* November 22, 1860. Preston became a member of the convention on the death of Adams in 1861.

lence" upon his judgment, he would, if elected, vote for secession or resign. Barnwell's reluctance was due to his belief that it would be "in the highest degree mischievous" for South Carolina by precipitate action to try to force the hand of other Southern states. Purely voluntary coöperative secession he favored. A Southern confederacy was in his view something "not to be submitted to as a refuge from evils, but ardently to be desired, and earnestly sought for, as our only source of security and prosperity, the proper and glorious development of the great institution which lay at the basis of our civil polity."[24]

When the convention met December 17, South Carolina was confident that her action would soon be followed by other states. Governor Gist, in his message to the legislature at the end of November, had stated that there was not the least doubt that Georgia, Alabama, Mississippi, Florida, Texas, and Arkansas would immediately follow, and eventually all the South. No longer, he said, was there any jealousy of South Carolina in the resistance states; rather they were urging her to take the lead.[25] Several days before the convention asembled, John A. Elmore and Charles E. Hooker, commissioners from Alabama and Mississippi respectively, arrived in Columbia. They interviewed practically every prominent member of the legislature and the assembling convention, and positively guaranteed secession in their states. Later Governor M. S. Perry of Florida and prominent men from other parts of the South arrived to give their unofficial assurance.[26] From Washington came other encouragement. Early in December a caucus of twenty-six Southern congressmen from eight states met and unanimously decided that immediate action by South Carolina was desirable.[27] Soon thereafter the very encouraging address of the Southern congressmen to their constituents appeared.

The argument is exhausted. All hope of relief in the Union through the agency of committees, Congressional legislation, or constitutional amendment, is extinguished, and we trust the South will not be deceived by appearances or the pretense of new guarantees. In our judgment the Republicans are resolute in the purpose to grant nothing that will or ought to satisfy the South. We are satisfied the honor, safety, and independence

---

[24] *Mercury*, November 21, 1860; *Courier*, November 14, 16, 1860. It is said that Barnwell would have failed to be elected from Beaufort but for the influence of state Senator Edmund Rhett. R. B. Rhett, Jr., "The Confederate Government at Montgomery," R. W. Johnson and C. C. Buell (eds.), *Battles and Leaders of the Civil War* (New York, 1884-1887), I, 104; hereinafter cited Rhett, *Confederate Government*.

[25] *Senate Journal* (1860), p. 23.

[26] Dumond, *Secession Movement*, p. 140; *Convention Journal*, pp. 73, 81.

[27] Represented were North Carolina, South Carolina, Georgia, Florida, Alabama, Mississippi, Texas, Louisiana. *The War of the Rebellion: a Compilation of the Official Records of the Union and Confederate Armies* (Washington, 1880-1901), 1st series, I, 93-94; hereinafter cited *O. R.* with the volume indicated by serial number where one has been assigned.

of the Southern People require the organization of a Southern Confederacy —a result to be obtained only by separate State secession.[28]

This address, published in South Carolina on December 18, was some assurance to the convention that the South would not be tempted by compromises proposed by the House Committee of Thirty-three, scoffingly referred to by the *Mercury* as the "patchwork" or "Crisis" committee.[29] From Washington too, came batches of private letters to members of the convention. W. H. Trescot wrote Governor Pickens and others that R. M. T. Hunter, Jefferson Davis, and David Yulee advised immediate and irrevocable secession to be followed at once by commissioners to Washington. Federal officers in South Carolina, they said, should be notified that after a certain number of days their offices would cease to exist.[30] Davis, John Y. Mason, A. G. Brown, J. L. Pugh, and others wrote emphasizing the importance of unhesitating action.[31] Thus South Carolina was convinced that she would not be left isolated. The conditions for coöperative secession had been fulfilled.

Joseph LeConte thought the secession convention was the "gravest, ablest, and most dignified body of men" he had ever seen together.[32] Of it Dr. James H. Thornwell wrote:

It was a body of sober, grave, and venerable men, selected from every pursuit in life, and distinguished, most of them, in their respective spheres, by every quality which can command confidence and respect. It embraced the wisdom, moderation, and integrity of the bench, the learning and prudence of the bar, and the eloquence and piety of the pulpit. It contained retired planters, scholars, and gentlemen, who had stood aloof from the turmoil and ambition of public life, and were devoting an eloquent leisure . . . to the culture of their minds, and to quiet and unobstrusive schemes of Christian philanthropy. . . . It was a noble body, and all their proceedings were in harmony with their high character. In the midst of intense agitation and excitement, they were calm, cool, collected, and self-possessed. They deliberated without passion, and concluded without rashness.[33]

To speak for her in her most critical hour the state had chosen the best of her talent and character.

Assembling at the Baptist church in Columbia December 17, the convention called D. F. Jamison, delegate from Barnwell, to the chair. If elections meant anything, he said, the state should secede as quickly

[28] *Mercury,* December 18, 1860. The address was signed by thirty senators and representatives from nine Southern states.
[29] *Ibid.,* December 20, 1860.
[30] W. H. Trescot to Governor of South Carolina, December 14, 1860, W. H. Trescot Papers, Library of Congress; Trescot to James Chesnut, Jr., December 16, 1860, mss., University of South Carolina Library.
[31] A. P. Aldrich to J. H. Hammond, December 6, 1860, Hammond Papers. Aldrich stated that there was also conflicting advice from Washington.
[32] William Dallas Armes (ed.), *The Autobiography of Joseph Le Conte* (New York, 1903), p. 180. For sketches of the members see *The State,* December 18, 25, 1910.
[33] J. H. Thornwell, *The State of the Country* (Columbia, 1861), pp. 1-2.

as possible. There was danger of overtures from without the state but he hoped that the door to all further connection with the North was forever closed. No constitutional guarantees could now protect the South; the Constitution having failed in the past to prevent aggression by the North, the South should no longer be duped by paper securities. The greatest honor of his life, he said, would be to sign as chairman of the convention an ordinance of secession.[34]

The danger that some felt in hesitating even for a few days was clearly shown when a resolution was proposed to adjourn to Charleston immediately because of an increasing number of cases of smallpox in the city.[35] Miles opposed the resolution on the ground that it would have a very unhappy and perhaps a disastrous effect in other Southern states. The last statement that Southern congressmen had made to him in Washington, he said, was that much depended on the immediacy of action in South Carolina.[36] Removal to Charleston was agreed to but not before the intentions of the convention were proclaimed in a resolution offered by Chancellor John A. Inglis, and passed unanimously, that South Carolina should "forthwith" secede and that a committee of seven be appointed to draft the ordinance.[37] If any further encouragement were needed for the action, it was supplied by the commissioners from Alabama and Mississippi, both of whom addressed the convention and urged immediate secession. Governor A. B. Moore of Alabama also wired: "Tell the Convention to listen to no propositions of compromise or delay."[38]

[34] *Convention Journal,* pp. 3-4, 9.

[35] The medical committee of the House of Representatives reported three cases as early as November 27. The *Courier* correspondent reported panic conditions two days later although only half dozen cases existed. Additional cases were officially reported December 12, and seven new ones December 14. Some members of the legislature and the students of both colleges left the city. Fourteen new cases had appeared by the 16th and the panic increased. *Courier,* November 27-29, December 13, 15, 17, 1860; *House Journal* (1860), pp. 7, 36; *Senate Journal* (1860), pp. 114, 119; J. F. Williams, *Old and New Columbia* (Columbia, 1929), p. 96. Rumors had it that rags and clothes from infected precincts of New York had been deliberately shipped to Columbia for the specific purpose of contaminating members of the convention and legislature. J. H. Kinsler in *The State,* December 18, 1910.

It has been imagined that the real motive for the desire to adjourn the convention and legislature to Charleston was to place these bodies under the influence of the radicals of that city. There is no doubt, however, that panic conditions existed in Columbia. The fact that the most extreme secessionists opposed the move indicates that the motive was not ulterior.

[36] Since July, Miles had been demanding more action and less talk. "I am chary of seeing the South pass 'resolutions.' They accomplish nothing. In truth, have come to be regarded very much like the cry of 'wolf.' *Let us resolve less and do more.* I am sick at heart of the endless talk and bluster of the South. If we are in earnest let us *act.* Above all, I am weary of these eternal attempts to hold out the olive branch, when we ought rather to be preparing to grasp the sword." From a speech in Charleston quoted by the *Conservatist,* July 24, 1860.

[37] *Mercury,* December 19, 1860; *Convention Journal,* pp. 10-14.

[38] *Ibid.,* pp. 11, 26. The telegram was dated December 17 and was read to the convention on the 19th.

Welcomed on its arrival in Charleston by salvos of artillery, the convention resumed its work first in the hall of the South Carolina Institute and later in Saint Andrews Hall. While the committee to draft an ordinance of secession prepared its report the convention proceeded to the business of making arrangements for the separate existence of South Carolina. A committee headed by C. G. Memminger was appointed to draft a summary of the causes justifying secession, and another, with R. B. Rhett as chairman, to prepare an address to the people of the slaveholding states. Resolutions were introduced and committees appointed looking to the formation of a Southern Confederacy and to the adjustment of matters in connection with the post office, customs, United States property in South Carolina, and other such subjects.

On December 20 the committee on an ordinance of secession made its report. The draft submitted was a brief, dignified statement repealing the act of May 23, 1788, by which South Carolina had ratified the Constitution of the United States, and declaring that the "union now subsisting between South Carolina and other States, under the name of 'The United States of America,' is hereby dissolved."[39] It was quickly adopted by the unanimous vote of the 169 delegates and immediately telegraphed to the South Carolina members of Congress. They at once resigned.[40] It was then decided that the convention should reassemble at 6:45, move in procession to Institute Hall, and there in the presence

[39] Several drafts were offered in the committee consisting of John A. Inglis, R. B. Rhett, James Chesnut, Jr., J. L. Orr, Maxcy Gregg, B. F. Dunkin, and W. F. Hutson. From a statement made at the time by R. B. Rhett to his son R. B. Rhett, Jr., it appears that the draft submitted by J. L. Orr was the one adopted and that Rhett was "chiefly instrumental in pruning and shaping" it into its final clear terse form. The title words, "States united with her under the compact entitled 'The Constitution of the United States,'" were suggested by B. F. Dunkin, according to this statement. *Sunday News,* July 12, 1896. In 1896, Judge Henry McIver, a member of the convention, wrote Mrs. W. C. McGowan that her father, Chancellor F. H. Wardlaw, was undoubtedly the author of the draft. He said that Chancellor Inglis, chairman of the committee, often spoke of his regret that some supposed him to be the author of the draft and asked McIver to correct the error whenever he should meet it, because Chancellor Wardlaw's draft was the one accepted. *Ibid.,* June 28, 1896. Wardlaw was not a member of the committee which drafted the ordinance but it is quite possible that his draft was submitted to the committee by Orr, adopted with Rhett amendments, and given a title suggested by Dunkin. A facsimile of the Wardlaw draft contributed to *The State* of December 18, 1910, by A. S. Salley is consistent with the last statement above.

[40] The letter published in the *Mercury* and dated December 21 was signed by John McQueen, M. L. Bonham, J. D. Ashmore, and W. W. Boyce. L. M. Keitt was reported to have resigned on the 17th. *Mercury,* December 20, 28, 1860, January 8, 1861. The name of W. P. Miles was said to have been omitted by mistake. *Ibid.,* January 8, 1861.

Bonham had resented the November 10th resignation of Chesnut, accusing him of having designs on the governorship. When Bonham in turn was erroneously reported to have resigned a few days later in violation of an agreement among the members of the House delegation to await secession, he was sharply criticized by Ashmore. J. D. Ashmore to W. P. Miles, November 20, 1860, Miles Papers.

of the governor and both houses of the legislature sign the ordinance.[41] News of secession spread quickly through the city. Business was suspended.

The church bells rang out their joyful peals. The artillery salutes were soon heard thundering from the Citadel. New flags were everywhere thrown to the breeze. The volunteers instinctively donned their uniforms, and were seen hurrying to and fro about the streets.[42]

Citizens rushed to the telegraph office to send the glad tidings to absent friends. Old men went shouting down the streets. Within five minutes the *Mercury* was out with an extra publishing the text of the ordinance, and 6,000 copies were quickly purchased by eager citizens.[43]

The scene at Institute Hall that night was one packed with drama. Three thousand people cheered the dignitaries as they marched in. With solemn and reverent attention they heard a prayer by the venerable Dr. John Bachman as he implored divine blessing on the new declaration of independence. As the reading of the ordinance was concluded, a shout that "shook the very building, reverberating, long-continued, rose to Heaven, and ceased only with the loss of breath." With a heavy gold pen presented and engraved for the special occasion, President Jamison affixed his signature and the other members followed suit. The crowd sat through the whole two hours consumed by the ceremony, and after tumultous cheering, dispersed to take part in the celebration outside. Fireworks, brass bands, and parades testified to the general satisfaction. The *Mercury* thanked the abolitionists for ending the Union and began publishing reports of Congress as "Foreign News."[44]

Much has been written on the causes of secession but one who reads the contemporary literature can have no doubt of the fundamental issue in South Carolina. Governor A. G. Magrath made a clear and true statement of the matter in a letter written from Fort Pulaski November 20, 1865.

It is too clear for dispute, that in the revolution to which I have referred, the strong motive power, which carried with it the masses of the people, was the idea, that the right of property in slaves, was about to be questioned & denied, by the power of the political party which had then obtained its ascendancy in the Government of the United States. True with some, other and additional considerations prevailed. Some desired the dissolution of the Union, & were willing to concur in any measures which they supposed would lead to that result. Others had certain political abstract opinions, I use the term in no sense unkindly, which they supposed were to be violated.

[41] *Convention Journal,* pp. 21, 29-32, 39-43, 45. The legislature had also adjourned to Charleston December 17. *Senate Journal* (1860), p. 126.

[42] *Mercury,* December 21, 1860.

[43] *Ibid.* Rhett furnished a copy of the ordinance to the *Mercury* before it was reported to the convention. Having been already printed, the ordinance was on the streets at 1:20 after passage at 1:15 P.M. *Sunday News,* July 12, 1896. For a facsimile of the extra, see Nicolay and Hay, *Lincoln,* III, 14.

[44] *Mercury,* December 21, 22, 23, 1860.

Others had selfish views of their own personal elevation. But with the masses of the people, that idea which was clearly developed, that apprehension which was fully credited, was that which I have stated. In the negro, they had seen the right of property exhibited in its widest signification. . . . To the men who did not own a negro, it was an appeal as strong as it was to him who had many. For the expectation or the hope of having was extinguished. . . .

In addition to this the whole social institutions of the people in the slave-holding States rested as they then supposed upon the stability of the right, which was involved with the ownership of slaves. It was reputed to be the cornerstone of that society which for ages had rested upon it, and which it was supposed would be overthrown at its removal. All of the transactions of life were based upon it; all of the arrangements for the progress of society were made with reference to it; and the civilization, I may say, of the people in the States in which slavery existed, were [sic] regarded as unavoidably connected with it; inseparably dependent upon it. It was thus that the remarkable unanimity was produced in all of these States. No other cause would have produced it. I have said that other considerations attached themselves to it; they were merely incidents to it; of themselves they could never have produced the same result. The question of the sovereignty of the States as exhibited in their power to secede, was an issue; but it was an issue because it was supposed to be the only certain mode by which that interference with the right of property could be avoided, of which such general apprehension existed. The right of property we must remember is the central and is regarded as the most sacred of all rights. . . . It was the apprehension of the invasion of this right of property which . . . was the motive power of the revolution.[45]

Thomas J. Withers, a member of the convention, wrote before secession:

The true question for us is, how shall we sustain African slavery in South Carolina from a series of annoying attacks, attended by incidental consequences that I shrink from depicting, and finally from utter abolition? That is the problem before us—the naked and true point.[46]

Dr. J. H. Thornwell's statement immediately after secession is no less explicit. He indignantly denied that the cause of secession was the belief that the South would be more prosperous as a separate free-trade nation.

The real cause of the intense excitement of the South, is not in vain dreams of national glory in a separate confederacy . . .; it is in the profound conviction that the Constitution, in its relations to slavery, has been virtually repealed; that the new Government has assumed a new and dangerous attitude upon this subject.[47]

Numerous statements to the same effect might be quoted. The modern emphasis on the growth of a distinct Southern nationalism is no doubt well placed. In South Carolina the idea was repeatedly ex-

[45] A. G. Magrath to ———, November 20, 1865, Magrath Papers, University of South Carolina Library.
[46] Quoted by U. R. Brooks, *South Carolina Bench and Bar* (Columbia, 1908), p. 148.
[47] Thornwell, *State of the Country*, p. 9.

pressed in the secession period. For example, Rhett in a speech of November 20, said: "We are two peoples, essentially different in all that makes a people."[48] Jamison in his opening speech to the convention said there was "no common bond of sympathy or interest between the North and South."[49] Likewise, "Troup," in one of the 1860 Association pamphlets, insisted that the cause of secession was the incompatibility of two peoples.[50] Trescot in 1863 thought disunion came as a "natural development of interests, political and economic."[51] Such statements might be multiplied to indicate the presence of a Southern nationalism in South Carolina. But as "Troup" pointed out, this spiritual separation of North and South sprang from "two systems of labor, crystallizing about them two forms of civilization" and causing opposite constructions of the Constitution. The "incompatibility" which manifested itself in quarrels over tariffs and over unequal distribution of federal appropriations were, he thought, fundamentally grounded in the issue of slavery.[52]

The official statements issued by the convention in Memminger's "Declaration of the Immediate Causes which Induce and Justify the Secession of South Carolina" and in Rhett's "Address to the Slaveholding States" differ in the amount of emphasis placed upon slavery as the cause of secession. The "Declaration of Immediate Causes," after defending the right of secession under the compact theory of the Union, justified the exercise of that right almost entirely on the point that Northern states had infringed and abrogated that compact by refusal to abide by their constitutional obligations in regard to slavery. The compact, it said, would not have been entered had no provision been included for the rendition of fugitive slaves. Yet fourteen Northern states had deliberately refused to fulfill this obligation and thirteen states had passed laws nullifying the fugitive slave law. They had denounced slavery as an evil, permitted abolitionist societies, encouraged and assisted thousands of slaves to escape, and incited servile insurrection. Finally, the enemies of slavery had elected a President who proclaimed that slavery must be ultimately extinguished. When this President should gain control of the government, constitutional guarantees would no longer exist, equal rights would have been lost, the power of self-government and self-protection would have disappeared, and the government would have become an enemy. Moreover, all hope of remedy was rendered vain by the fact that the North had "invested a great political error with the sanctions of a more erroneous religious belief."[53]

[48] *Mercury,* November 21, 1860.   [49] *Convention Journal,* p. 4.
[50] *To the People of the South* . . . , p. 3.
[51] The *Mercury* disagreed with Trescot. It held that disunion came as the result of bad statesmanship in the distant past which gave a wrong bias to the government. *Mercury,* October 16, 1863.
[52] *To the People of the South* . . . , pp. 3-4.
[53] *Convention Journal,* pp. 461-466.

Because the Declaration thus baldly placed slavery before the world as the justification of secession, some opposition to it appeared in the convention. Maxcy Gregg thought it was a dishonor to the memory of those who had fought against the tariff, internal improvements, and the bank. Rhett argued that the "dissolution of the Constitution" should be made the basis of the Declaration, and that the cause would be elevated and would receive more sympathy from the world if represented as a defense against taxation and violated freedom, as a contest of free trade against monopoly. But efforts to send the Declaration back to committee were unavailing, and Gregg's motion to table was lost by a vote of 124 to 31. The majority, like Keitt, were willing to rest disunion upon the question of slavery. "It is the great central point from which we are now proceeding," he said. As for the tariff, Keitt pointed out that he and all other Carolina congressmen had voted for the tariff of 1857 and every member of the convention would have done likewise had they been in Congress.[54]

Rhett's views were more apparent in the "Address to the Slaveholding States." He held that the one great evil from which all others had flowed was the overthrow of the Constitution of the United States. The tariff, unequal distributions of appropriations, and attacks on slavery, were only manifestations of a broken faith and a constitution destroyed through construction for Northern aggrandizement at the expense of the weaker South. The sections had grown apart; all identity of feeling, interest, and institutions was gone; they were divided between slaveholding and nonslaveholding, between agricultural and manufacturing and commercial states; their institutions and industrial pursuits had made them totally different peoples. The South was unsafe under a government controlled by a sectional anti-slavery party, and submission to it could only result in emancipation. In thus emphasizing the secondary causes of secession the "Address" was not as sound as the "Declaration" by Memminger, but Rhett's point that a statement which magnified constitutional differences would have a better effect on Europe was well made.[55]

The act of secession made unionism almost nonexistent in South Carolina. "Mr. Petigru alone in South Carolina has not seceded," said Mrs. Chesnut.[56] And there is some evidence that even Petigru may have concluded later that secession had been justifiable.[57] William H.

[54] *Mercury*, December 22, 25, 1860; *Convention Journal*, pp. 75-77.
[55] *Ibid.*, pp. 467-476.
[56] Mary B. Chesnut, *A Diary from Dixie* (New York, 1929), p. 63.
[57] Wilmot G. DeSaussure wrote: "Before his death Mr. Petigru told Mr. William C. Bee that the conduct of the war by the U. S. Government, had changed his opinion so far as to make him believe the war inevitable and just. And in 1862 he brought his grandson Carson to me as Adjutant General to advise with, & in my presence told him that as early as he was old enough to join the army, it was his duty to do so, and that he Mr. P. would use every effort to make him do so." See pencil notation signed "W. G. D." on page 4 of Charleston Library

Russell, the English journalist, agreed that Petigru was almost alone among Charlestonians. There were others, he said, who regretted the dissolution of the Union "such as Mr. [Alfred] Huger, who shed tears in talking of it the other night" but they regarded the fact very much as they would the destruction of any other article which had been valued for its utility and antiquity but which could never be restored.[58] There were of course others besides Petigru who opposed secession. But almost all unionists enthusiastically supported the state once the decision had gone against them. The most active unionist after the election of Lincoln had been B. F. Perry. Defeated for the convention in Greenville, he remarked after secession: "I have been trying to prevent this sad issue for the last thirty years. You are all now going to the devil, and I will go with you. Honor and patriotism require me to stand by my State, right or wrong."[59] He exerted himself to influence his unionist friends and constituents in Greenville and Pickens districts to do likewise, and he proudly claimed in the legislature of 1862 that they had "willingly and nobly" gone with their state.[60] A similar course was followed by General Waddy Thompson who had opposed secession but joined Perry in speaking and working for the cause.[61] The venerable Alfred Huger, a vacillating secessionist, immediately after secession offered his services to Pickens and begged for something to do. He declared: "My whole soul is in this conflict and if I could I would have my entire clan in the field."[62]

Among the other prominent unionists of South Carolina Judge John

Society copy of *Memorial of the Late James L Petigru. Proceedings of the Bar of Charleston, S. C., March 25, 1863* (New York, 1866). Petigru himself seems to have expressed doubt when he wrote: "But when the South has achieved its independence as I have no doubt it will, how will History treat secession? As a deliverance from thralldom; or as an instance of popular passion overruling all regard for the permanent interest of the country." J. L. Petigru to J. J. Pettigrew, October 21, 1862, Pettigrew Papers.

[58] William H. Russell, *My Diary North and South* (Boston, 1863), pp. 136-137.
[59] Perry, *Reminiscences* (1883), pp. 15-16.
[60] *Ibid.; Southern Enterprise*, January 1, 1863. In a speech May 20, 1861, Perry said: "As an old Union man, I give to this Brooks Cavalry my son, two horses and a negro boy, and fifty dollars for the support of necessitous families of soldiers. I hope no secessionist who wore *in peace* his blue cockade . . . will refuse to do less, now that war has come upon us. And furthermore, I tender my own services whenever the occasion requires them." Sumter *Triweekly Watchman*, May 29, 1861. Perry seems, however, never to have given up the belief that the South was guilty of suicidal folly in resorting to secession, and in his diary he continued to grieve that the Union was broken. The North he regarded as "wicked, foolish & fanatical" for waging war for the impossible object of restoring the Union. The war proved, he said, that man was incapable of self-government for any length of time. Perry, Journal, February 10, March 10, May 26, June 2, 13, July 21, August 4, December 22, 1861, *et. seq.*
[61] H. T. Cook, *The Life Work of James Clement Furman* (Greenville, 1926), p. 204.
[62] Alfred Huger to F. W. Pickens, December 27, 1860, Pickens-Bonham Papers; Alfred Huger to J. J. Pettigrew, January 9, 1861, Pettigrew Papers; Alfred Huger to James Chesnut, Jr., November 5, 1861, Chesnut-Manning-Miller Papers.

Belton O'Neall of Newberry, and a number of Charlestonians including ex-Governor William Aiken, George S. Bryan, the bank president Donald McKay, and William J. Grayson should be mentioned. Also unionist was Nicholas Williams of Society Hill.[63] Dr. J. H. Thornwell opposed the earlier disunion movement but strongly defended secession in the crisis of 1860.[64] Robert W. Barnwell seems to have been brought to secession on the very eve of the convention, converted, like Joseph LeConte of South Carolina College, by the "spiritual contagion" which swept over the state.[65]

The women of the state seem to have been quite as enthusiastic for secession as the men. A Charleston woman proudly wrote in her diary, "Secession was born in the hearts of Carolina women."[66] On the other hand a Mrs. Roper, "descended in ideas as well as blood from Henry Laurens of the Revolution," indignantly refused a request that she allow the secession ordinance to be signed on the table erroneously supposed to have been the one used in signing the Declaration of Independence.[67]

Many South Carolinians, in the military service of the United States when war came, proved themselves unionists by refusing to resign to enter the service of the state. Feeling against such men was violent. The *Mercury* thought that such refusal constituted "hideous moral delinquency, ingratitude, dishonor and treachery."[68] A resolution was introduced in the legislature to "record, as infamous" and "false-hearted traitors" the following: Captains William B. Shubrick and Cornelius Stribling, Commanders Percival Drayton, Henry K. Hoff, John S. Missroun, Charles Steedman, Edward Middleton, and Henry Rolando of the Navy; and Henry C. Flagg, John F. Hammond, and C. S. Lovell of the Army.[69] The position of such men was a difficult one. One of

[63] Wallace, *History of S. C.*, III, 158; John A. Chapman, *Annals of Newberry*, p. 360, Perry, *Reminiscences* (1883), p. 16; Chesnut, *Diary*, p. 64; Elizabeth A. Pringle, *Chronicles of Chicora Wood* (New York, 1923), p. 48 note.

[64] Palmer, *Life and Letters of Thornwell*, pp. 485-486, 591-610.

[65] *Supra*, p. 115; *Autobiography of LeConte*, p. 179. LeConte thought that most of the nonsecessionists were a sorry, untrue crowd.

[66] Emma E. Holmes, mss. diary, p. 1, in DeSaussure Papers formerly in possession of Miss Isabelle DeSaussure of Charleston, now at Duke University.

[67] Wallace, *History of S. C.*, III, 158. Another descendent of Laurens, David Ramsey, opposed secession but gave his life in defense of the state at Battery Wagner in 1863. Clement A. Evans (ed.), *Confederate Military History* (Atlanta, 1899), V, 240.

[68] *Mercury*, February 11, 1861.

[69] *House Journal* (1861), p. 253. The resolution did not pass. According to the *Mercury* of December 25, 27, 1860, the Army and Navy list of 1860 included 32 Army and 33 Navy officers from South Carolina. The writer has not determined the exact number of these who refused to resign. C. C. Anderson lists seven who commanded a brigade or more in the Army or who commanded a vessel in the Navy. These were Rear Admiral W. B. Shubrick, Commanders John P. Bankhead and Percival Drayton, Naval Captains Edward Middleton and Charles Steedman, Major General S. A. Hurlbut, Major General J. C. Fremont, and J. S. Missroun, Ordnance Officer of the Boston Navy Yard. C. C. Anderson,

them wrote James Chesnut that he was seventy years old, had no fortune except his commission, and had no assurance that either South Carolina or the Confederacy would even establish a navy. He said that to expect him to resign his position would be the equivalent of expecting every South Carolina citizen to throw all of his property into the treasury of the state.[70]

Another group of South Carolina "unionists" was composed of persons who, in making claims during the reconstruction period for war damages, swore that their sympathy had always been with the North and that they had been "at all times ready and willing to aid and assist the cause of the Union, so far as their means and the circumstances permitted." There were 544 of these persons, of whom 137 were from Marlboro, 106 from Beaufort, 101 from Lancaster, 45 from Charleston, 25 from Georgetown, 22 from Richland, and smaller numbers from most of the other districts of the state. The claims were for amounts ranging from a few dollars up to $400,000. Twenty-two claims were for $10,000 or more, indicating that some of the claimants were persons of property if not in every case, of standing. But one suspects considerable stultification.[71]

The well-nigh complete unity of South Carolina after secession is no more striking than the universal belief that the cause was just. Under a political philosophy which denied that all men were equal, it was believed that the future of republican government itself was involved in the struggle; that only under such a social system as the South enjoyed could constitutional government survive. And since slavery was an institution divinely sanctioned and providentially established in the South for the conversion of the slave, it was believed that the Southern cause was the cause of religion itself.[72] Secession was endorsed by the synod of the Presbyterian church and by the annual conference of the Methodists.[73] Dr. T. L. McBride, in a sermon in Pendleton, defended secession as duty to slaveholder, slave, and religion.[74] The Rev. Thomas

---

Fighting by Southern Federals . . . (New York, 1912), pp. 278, 299, 307, 321, 338, 364, 366. Of the seven officers listed by Anderson neither Fremont nor Hurlbut were South Carolinians in 1860. *D. A. B.,* VII, 19; IX, 425.

[70] W. G. Z. Shubert to James Chesnut, Jr., January 30, 1861, Williams-Chesnut-Manning Papers.

[71] Charleston *News and Courier,* November 24, 1873. The names of the twenty-two large claimants were: from Abbeville, Moses Winstock; from Beaufort, Susan A. Bowers and R. H. Turner; from Charleston, Arthur M. Blake, R. L. David, Michael C. Day, David C. Ebaugh, Edward Middleton, H. A. Middleton, H. Slawson, Jr., John Thomson, M. W. Vennig; from Fairfield, Joseph Freshley; from Georgetown, F. W. Ford, Sidney S. Frazer, John LaBruce, estate of J. D. McGill, E. Jane Reed, Joseh H. Risley, H. W. Tilton; from Richland, Phillip Epstein and Simon Wolf.

[72] *The Relation between the Races at the South* (Charleston, 1861), pp. 3 et. seq.

[73] *Mercury,* December 20, 1860; Jones and Mills, *History of the Presbyterian Church in S. C.,* p. 75.

[74] *Keowee Courier,* January 26, 1861.

Smyth, Presbyterian minister of Charleston, believed that the South had a commission to protect the Bible from the Godless Northern interpretation which would make it an anti-slavery Bible, and God an anti-slavery God.[75] Expressions of confidence in the divine approval of the Southern program is a striking feature of secession literature whether private diary, personal correspondence, or public discourse. One need not question the sincerity of the legislature for appointing on the eve of secession a day of fasting, humiliation, and prayer.[76]

[75] *Supra,* p. 44.
[76] *House Journal* (called session, 1860), pp. 12, 35.

CHAPTER VI

THE REPUBLIC OF SOUTH CAROLINA

South Carolina seceded with the confident expectation that other states would follow and that a Southern Confederacy would be established at an early date. Immediate steps were taken for the realization of this program but until a Confederacy should be established the state was technically an independent nation.[1] It was necessary therefore to reorganize her government to meet the requirements of the new situation. Powers formerly delegated to the federal government must be resumed and machinery created for their execution. A property settlement must be made, if possible, with the government of the United States, and a military establishment created for defense against any attempt which might be made to coerce the state. Congressional law must be reënacted or replaced. New commercial treaties must be negotiated and arrangements made for the collection of such duties at the ports as might be continued. Postal arrangements must be made. These and many other problems incident to the resumption of national sovereignty must be faced, involving in many cases constitutional change and administrative reorganization. And in effecting these changes care must be taken not to estrange the Southern states or incite the United States to hostilities.[2]

To a considerable degree the successful solution of state problems depended upon the choice of a competent executive. A man must be chosen, said W. H. Trescot in a letter to Rhett, whose name and character would "conciliate as well as give confidence to all the men of the State."[3] Rhett was not such a man, however logical his selection might seem to his friends and to himself. Long the leader of those desiring disunion, he had done much to prepare his state for the fateful step. And yet he cannot be regarded as truly representative of his state even after secession. Many conservative men agreed with H. W. Ravenel when he wrote:

Mr. Rhett I hold to the most untrustworthy politician in the State. He is truly devoted to his State & to the South, but he wants judgement, & can never be relied on for statesmanship as a leader.[4]

[1] There were frequent references to South Carolina after secession as the "Palmetto Republic."
[2] The various changes practically effected a new constitution. "This document, beautifully engraved on sheepskin by B. C. Baruc is now in the office of the Secretary of State. The penmanship work on it is remarkable and cost $168." *The State*, May 9, 1901.
[3] Nicolay and Hay, *Lincoln*, II, 317-319.
[4] Ravenel, Diary, June 1, 1860.

80

The *South Carolinian* thought his influence through the *Mercury* did more harm to the resistance movement outside of South Carolina than all the Union papers, and assured Virginia that the party in South Carolina that responded to the *Mercury's* unwise and intemperate criticisms of Virginia was only a small minority, and that the real strength of Rhett was indicated by the small vote he received for senator in 1858 and for governor in 1860.[5]

In electing Francis W. Pickens governor in 1860 the legislature broke a sixteen year old "courteous arrangement" under which the office alternated between up and low country.[6] Pickens had been identified with the moderate National Democratic faction in South Carolina and had at first favored postponing the convention until after Buchanan left office, but his adoption of more extreme views in a speech at Columbia, November 30, just before the election, improved his position as a candidate.[7] On the seventh ballot he was able to muster a bare majority of the votes cast, some of the Rhett faction supporting him in order to defeat the next most prominent candidate, B. J. Johnson.[8] His election was no doubt in the interest of that harmony of which Trescot had spoken but it was not enthusiastically received in the state. He had no little experience in public affairs having served for some time in Congress and recently as ambassador to Russia. His family had been conspicuous since the Revolution and was widely connected. He himself was a cultured planter, a classical scholar, and an orator of ability. But he somehow lacked the ability to draw men close to him and often alienated his associates by what seemed an overbearing manner. Ambitious for conspicuous service to his state, and impulsive by nature, his action was sometimes so bold as to border on rashness while at other times he seemed cautious and hesitant. He was keenly intelligent but was handicapped by an inability to inspire confidence in a crisis which required masterful leadership.[9]

The duties of the governor were considerably enlarged as a result of secession and by an ordinance of December 27. The conduct of foreign relations was placed in his hands, though the convention reserved the right of independent action. He was authorized to make diplomatic appointments and treaties subject to confirmation or ratification by two-thirds of the Senate or by the convention should it be in session. His appointive powers were greatly increased by ordinance

[5] *Mercury*, December 28, 1860, quoting *Carolinian*.
[6] *Carolina Spartan*, October 25, 1860.
[7] *Courier*, November 29, December 1, 3, 1860.
[8] Ravenel, Diary, January 31, 1861. The vote on the seventh ballot was Pickens 83, Johnson 64, scattered 16. *Mercury*, December 15, 1860. Rhett withdrew after the fifth ballot.
[9] Cf. Rhodes, *History of U. S.*, III, 81-82; Crawford, *Fort Sumter*, pp. 79-81; Wallace, *History of S. C.*, III, 153; LeR. F. Youmans, *A Sketch of the Life and Services of Francis W. Pickens of South Carolina* (n.p., n.d.), pp. 1-13.

and by the circumstances of the time. He was given an executive council consisting of the lieutenant governor and four persons appointed by himself with the "advice and consent" of the convention. Like the President of the United States therefore he had an official cabinet, responsible to him. It included A. G. Magrath, Secretary of State; D. F. Jamison, Secretary of War; C. C. Memminger and later Edward Frost and W. G. DeSaussure, Secretary of the Treasury; Lieutenant Governor W. W. Harllee, Postmaster General; and A. C. Garlington, Secretary of Interior. The attorney general was not formally named a member of the cabinet but the holder of this office, I. W. Hayne, might be considered a sixth member of the group.[10]

While the governor was given powers formerly exercised by the President of the United States, congressional authority was transferred to the General Assembly. Temporarily, however, powers over imports and exports, treaties, war, confederacy with other states, citizenship, and treason were reserved to the convention. In the same manner it was declared that judicial powers formerly delegated to the United States had now reverted to the state and should be exercised by such courts as the General Assembly might direct.[11] Under this authority the legislature, by a law of January 28, 1861, gave exclusive original jurisdiction in admiralty and maritime cases to the city court of Charleston and appellate jurisdiction in cases involving over $1,000 to the court of appeals. All other cases were added to the jurisdiction of the regular state courts.[12]

Among the first ordinances of the convention were those striking all references to the United States from the constitution of South Carolina and from the oath required of state officers. Citizenship, expressly denied to Negroes, was defined, and naturalization provided for. The death penalty was decreed for treason which was defined as waging war against the state or giving aid and comfort to her enemies.[13] A national flag was adopted by the legislature, it being finally decided after considerable disagreement to adopt the design of the old state flag.[14]

The collection of duties at the ports was a delicate problem for it involved possible collision with United States authorities. However, the customs service was taken over by the state under a provisional

[10] *Convention Journal,* pp. 22, 30, 52, 137, 243, 758.
[11] *Ibid.,* pp. 762-763, 766.
[12] *Statutes at Large of South Carolina* (Columbia, 1863—), XII, 738-740.
[13] *Convention Journal,* pp. 754, 760-761, 764-765, 770. Citizenship was extended to those who by birth or residence or naturalization were citizens of the state at the time of secession, and who did not establish a foreign residence with intention of expatriation. For the future, all persons born in South Carolina, or of South Carolina fathers abroad, were citizens. Citizens of the United States might establish citizenship in South Carolina by establishing residence within twelve months and taking an oath of allegiance. United States naturalization laws were adopted. *Ibid.,* pp. 764-765.
[14] A. S. Salley, Jr., *The Flag of the State of South Carolina* (Columbia, 1916), pp. 5 *et seq.*

ordinance of December 26 providing for a continuance of the revenue, collection, and navigation laws of the United States except that no duties on imports should be collected on goods from the states of the old Union. In accordance with the ordinance, all officers attached to the customs house at Charleston entered the service of the state on December 27 and W. F. Colcock began collection in the name of South Carolina.[15]

The state also provided for South Carolina registry of vessels if one-third owned by citizens of slaveholding states and commanded by such a citizen. Clearance papers were to be issued in the name of the state.[16]. There was some anxiety over the possibility of the United States government interfering with this program. Colcock wrote Secretary of State Magrath on January 18, 1861, that he understood foreign governments had been notified by the United States that she would regard payments to South Carolina as mispayments and South Carolina clearance papers as invalid. Magrath in a long letter replied that Lewis Cass, the former United States Secretary of State, and ex-Attorney General Jeremiah S. Black, now Secretary of State, had recently held that United States ships in the revolutionary ports of Peru must conform to the decrees of the group in *de facto* control. It could therefore safely be assumed, he said, that the United States would not try to interfere with foreign ships in South Carolina ports. Should the attempt be made, it would place the United States under the necessity of explaining to foreign governments the reasons for changing its rule declared for the protection of its own vessels, and it would then be for the foreign nation to decide whether the explanation was satisfactory. Without regard to the ability of the foreign power to defend itself, South Carolina would regard interference in the same light as if with vessels of South Carolina. As to South Carolina and Southern vessels, Magrath did not believe, he said, that the United States would adopt a policy so "purely mischievous" and so "palpably designed to do evil" as that of seizing such vessels on the high seas for failure to observe United States regulations in a port where no United States customs house existed. Colcock was instructed to report at once any attempted interference with South Carolina vessels.[17] Apparently there was none. The collector

[15] The collector in Georgetown, a Mr. Merriman, was not as loyal to his state. He was said to have written President Buchanan that he would continue to clear vessels in the name of the United States; to have urged him to send a man of war to collect duties; and to have described progress of work on the fortifications at Georgetown. January 7, 1861, Merriman and his deputy, Lopse, were arrested on a charge of treason and held for trial. *Mercury*, January 10, 1861. He was in prison a year and twenty days but in 1862 was in Cincinnati advocating harsh measures for the South and being mentioned as the probable postwar collector at Charleston. Camden *Confederate*, June 6, 1862.
[16] *Convention Journal*, pp. 120-121, 756-757.
[17] *Executive Documents, Number 1. Correspondence with the Collector, 29th. January, 1861* (Charleston, 1861), pp. 3 *et. seq.;* also *Mercury*, February 2, 1861.

of the port of Liverpool assured Charles K. Prioleau of Fraser-Trenholm and Company that vessels cleared by South Carolina would be received on a basis of equality with those of other nations, and Robert Bunch, the British consul at Charleston, coöperated, with the approval of Lord Russell.[18]

The difficulties of establishing a South Carolina postal system were fully appreciated. Nevertheless, the convention on January 5 authorized the legislature to establish postal facilities and to enact postal laws. Governor Pickens had a Post Office and Customs Bureau under W. W. Harllee. The convention, however, continued postmasters in office and Harllee directed them to make their returns to Washington so long as mail was transported under United States contracts and authority. This continued until a Confederate Post Office Department was established, at which time Harllee directed those connected with the service to correspond with the Confederate authorities. Harllee then stepped aside.[19]

Until the Confederacy should be formed South Carolina proposed to conduct foreign relations as an independent nation. Power to conduct foreign affairs was specifically given the governor, and there was a Department of State and a Committee on Foreign Affairs in the South Carolina Senate.[20] Pickens was anxious to send an envoy abroad to establish commercial relations with foreign nations on a free trade basis. It was not his idea, he said, to do anything which would not be to the immediate benefit of other seceding states, nor anything which might embarrass the Confederacy after it should be formed, but he thought it exceedingly important to initiate arrangements which would tend to reopen for South Carolina a flourishing commerce. The proposal for such an envoy met opposition in the legislature and was given up, Magrath said, because of the early meeting at Montgomery and "other considerations of a controlling character."[21] Convention documents were dispatched to foreign governments through their representatives in Washington. Governor Pickens also wrote to Baron Edward de Stoeckl, the Russian minister at Washington, pointing out the advantages to Russia of free trade with the South and expressing the hope that Russia would resist any attempt at a blockade not strictly enforced. Rather strangely, Pickens also suggested that Great Britain might make an attempt to

[18] Fraser-Trenholm and Co. to the Collector of the Port, Liverpool, January 16, 1861, Pickens-Bonham Papers; M. L. Bonham, Jr., *The British Consuls in the Confederacy* (New York, 1911), pp. 20-23.
[19] *Convention Journal*, pp. 553, 755, 766. The appropriation act of January, 1861, contained an item of $30,000 for carriage and delivery of mails. *Statutes at Large*, XII, 719-725.
[20] The foreign affairs committee later became a committee on Confederate relations. *Mercury*, November 27, 1861.
[21] A. G. Magrath to W. G. DeSaussure, January 15, 1861, Pickens-Bonham Papers; "Report of the Secretary of State," March 24, 1861, *Mercury*, April 6, 1861.

recover her sovereignty over the Southern states on the principle that she had acknowledged the independence of the government of the United States composed of thirteen states, and that that government having passed away, sovereignty returned to Great Britain. He hoped that Russia would not submit to such an assumption.[22] Consular agents in South Carolina at the time of secession continued to function through Washington, but the retiring Spanish consul at Charleston was notified that his successor would not be allowed to serve until he had presented his credentials to and had been recognized by the governor.[23]

Meanwhile, there was a diplomatic problem of vital importance, namely, that of conducting negotiations with other Southern states in the interest of completing secession and forming a new confederacy. On December 20, Rhett introduced a resolution in the convention calling for a committee of thirteen to report an ordinance inviting other states to a Southern convention for the purpose of forming a government. On the 26th he proposed an ordinance specifying Montgomery as the place and February 13 as the date for such a conference. This ordinance was tabled by the convention but the report and resolutions adopted December 31 were almost identical except for the omission of a specified time and place. They provided that the South Carolina convention elect a commissioner to each Southern state which called a convention and that these commissioners propose a conference of the states at the earliest possible time before March 4; that they submit the Constitution of the United States as the basis for a provisional constitution to serve until a permanent one could be drafted and ratified; that in the proposed conference voting should be by states, and representation be as in the old Union; that South Carolina's delegates be elected by convention ballot.[24] The plan thus proposed for a conference of the states was followed in detail by the other states.

On January 2 the first commissioners were elected.[25] On the following day they met in Charleston and decided to propose Montgomery as the place and February 4 as the day for the Southern convention.[26]

[22] F. W. Pickens to Edward de Stoeckl, January 1, 1861, F. W. Pickens Papers, Duke University Library.

[23] "Report of the Secretary of State," March 24, 1861, *Mercury*, April 6, 1861.

[24] *Convention Journal*, pp. 41, 92-93, 124, 143, 480.

[25] Commissioners to the several states were to Alabama, A. P. Calhoun; Mississippi, M. L. Bonham who requested that he be excused and whose place was filled by Armistead Burt; Louisiana, John L. Manning; Arkansas, A. C. Spain; Georgia, James L. Orr; Texas, John McQueen; Florida, L. W. Spratt; Virginia, John S. Preston. *Ibid.*, pp. 153-158; Edward McPherson, *The Political History of the United States of America During the Great Rebellion, from November 6, 1860 to July 4, 1864* (New York, 1864), p. 11. Orr was also one of the commissioners to Washington but was sent to Georgia at the request of Howell Cobb. U. B. Phillips (ed.), *The Correspondence of Robert Toombs, Alexander H. Stephens, and Howell Cobb*, American Historical Association *Report*, 1911, II, 529-531.

[26] Montgomery for the place of meeting was first suggested by the *Mercury*, December 24, 1860. Rhett specified Montgomery in the ordinance proposed on

Proceeding to the several states the commissioners, in accordance with instructions, generally urged immediate secession and the sending of delegates to Montgomery. The purpose of proposing such an early convention was, of course, to complete the organization before Lincoln's inauguration. Moreover there was danger of enthusiasm waning if delay was allowed. As Trescot wrote Cobb, the idea was to "weld them together while they are hot."[27]

In the balloting for delegates to Montgomery, Rhett led the ticket with ninety-two votes. Other delegates were Robert W. Barnwell, C. G. Memminger, W. P. Miles, James Chesnut, Jr., L. M. Keitt, T. J. Withers, and W. W. Boyce. The delegation was a strong one but later a subject of complaint because of the overrepresentation of the low country.[28] With the exception of Rhett and Keitt, it was a group which had favored coöperation in 1852.

In the deliberations at Montgomery, the South Carolina delegation played a prominent role. On the second day of the convention, C. G. Memminger of Charleston offered resolutions for a committee on a provisional constitution, and became its chairman. He had already published a plan and probably greatly influenced the Provisional Constitution.[29]

Robert Barnwell Rhett also played a prominent part in the early deliberations at Montgomery but he was greatly disappointed when his views were overruled on a number of important questions, one of which was the purpose of the convention itself. In his view the meeting was simply a constitutional convention to establish at once a permanent government. Ever afraid of attempts to patch up the old Union, he

---

December 26. *Convention Journal*, pp. 92-93. The final choice of Montgomery seems to have been due to the suggestion made by the South Carolina commissioner to Alabama in his address to the Alabama convention January 8, 1861. On the whole subject see Armond J. Gerson, "The Inception of the Montgomery Convention," American Historical Association *Report*, 1910, pp. 179-187.

[27] W. H. Trescot to Howell Cobb, January 14, 1861, *Correspondence of Toombs, Stephens, Cobb*, pp. 529-531. The addresses of the South Carolina commissioners are to be found in the convention journals of the several states and in the contemporary newspapers. Several were published in the *Mercury*, January 12, 14, *et. seq.* Preston's is in pamphlet.

[28] *Courier*, August 9, 1862.

[29] *Journal Confed. Cong.*, I, 19, 22, 24. Barnwell was the other South Carolina member of the committee. The *Plan of a Provisional Government of the Southern Confederacy* published anonymously in Charleston may have been written by Memminger. It provided for the continuation, in large part, of the Constitution of the United States. Under it the Southern senators and representatives who were in Congress at the time of secession would have constituted the Congress of the Confederacy. It also provided for the election by Congress of a commander-in-chief of the army. The biographer of Memminger can find no direct evidence to establish the tradition that Memminger wrote the Provisional Constitution, but he remarks on Memminger's modesty as possibly explaining his failure to claim the credit. He also cites a contributed article in the *Courier* of March 8, 1888, which stated that the draft submitted to the convention was in the handwriting of Memminger. Capers, *Memminger*, p. 304.

saw in the provisional government a danger of reconstruction, but the majority, even his own delegation except Barnwell, opposed his views. Although unable to prevent the establishment of the provisional government, he did succeed in getting a committee appointed for the immediate drafting of a permanent constitution and of this committee he was chairman. Rhett was also chairman of the committee on foreign relations, but failed in his attempt to have commissioners to Europe selected and dispatched by the convention prior to the inauguration of the President.[30]

Rhett's greatest disappointment at Montgomery was that he was given no administrative position in the new government. He no doubt felt entitled to the presidency but he was not supported even by his own delegation. The preferences of the individual members of the South Carolina delegation may not now definitely be determined. Rhett did not call a caucus of the South Carolina delegation on the question and considerable disagreement at first existed. Alexander H. Stephens seems to have inferred from a conversation with Keitt and Chesnut that South Carolina would support Toombs.[31] But Keitt himself, according to Mrs. Chesnut, leaned to Howell Cobb, as did Boyce,[32] and Chesnut became a strong supporter of Jefferson Davis though a majority of the delegation was at first opposed to him.[33] Chesnut was able, however, to persuade his fellow-townsman, Judge Withers, to vote for Davis,[34] and perhaps under the impression that he stood alone, Rhett was persuaded by Barnwell "against his better judgment" to do likewise. Ironically enough it is possible that Rhett's vote was, as Keitt later said, the vote which carried the delegation.[35]

Failing to secure the presidency Rhett set his heart on either the position of Secretary of State or the English mission, but again his

[30] White, *Rhett*, pp. 194-196; Curry, *Civil History*, pp. 63-64; Capers, *Memminger*, p. 304; *Journal Conf. Cong.*, I, 25, 41, 42, 49; Rhett, *Confederate Government*, p. 106.

[31] W. T. Walthall to James Chesnut, Jr., January 29, 1880, referring to a letter of Stephens in *Atlanta Constitution*, January 28, 1880. Chesnut-Manning-Miller Papers.

[32] Chesnut, *Diary*, p. 6.

[33] Keitt's statement in Rhett, *Confederate Government*, pp. 101-102.

[34] Keitt in June, 1861, said that Chesnut "overpersuaded the Judge and those two turned the tide, at least with the South Carolina delegation." Chesnut, *Diary*, p. 68. Withers soon resigned and resumed his judgeship in South Carolina. He is said to have explained his resignation by saying, "Oh, I was tired of seeing Chesnut play rug dog to Jeff Davis." R. W. Winston, *High Stakes and Hair Trigger. The Life of Jefferson Davis* (New York, 1830), p. 179. Cf. T. J. Kirkland and R. M. Kennedy, *Historic Camden* (Columbia, 1905-1926), II, 154-155. Withers was succeeded at Montgomery by James L. Orr.

[35] Rhett, *Confederate Government*, pp. 101-103; White, *Rhett*, p. 194. Mrs. Chesnut said that Barnwell cast the deciding vote. *Diary*, p. 10 note. For the attitude of the South Carolina delegation in the election see also A. L. Aull, "The Making of the Confederate Constitution," *Publications of the Southern History Association*, IX, 272-292; Jefferson Davis, *Rise and Fall of the Confederate Government* (New York, 1881), I, 240-241.

delegation, composed largely of old coöperationists, failed to push his claim. He and his friends made no attempt to conceal their disappointment.[36] President Davis offered the State post to Robert W. Barnwell who refused partly from distrust of his own ability but also because the South Carolina delegation had already recommended C. G. Memminger for Secretary of the Treasury.[37] Davis preferred Toombs for the Treasury post but yielded to the South Carolina delegation and gave Toombs the higher place in the cabinet.[38]

The Provisional Constitutional was criticized in South Carolina because it allowed a continuation of the protective tariff system and because it prohibited slave importations. The *Mercury* regretted that any provisional government was formed at all and appealed for an immediate permanent constitution in which these defects would be remedied. It supposed that the prohibition on the slave trade, which had been opposed at Montgomery by the South Carolina delegation, was a gesture to the border states, but hoped that the permanent constitution would be drawn without regard to any interests except those of the cotton states already out, as it would be very difficult to amend after other states had joined. The *Mercury* did not advocate renewal of the trade but held that the whole question was a matter of policy, not principle, and should be left for legislative decision.[39]

Some objected to the slave clause in the Provisional Constiution because they believed the actual renewal of the trade was necessary for the preservation of the institution itself. Thus L. W. Spratt argued that a slave population at least equal to the white was necessary if slavery continued. Already Virginia, with 1,000,000 whites and only 500,000 slaves, was wavering. For the same reason slavery was being undermined in Tennessee, North Carolina, Maryland, Missouri, and Kentucky. Even in Charleston, he said, there was antagonism between imported free workers and slaves. The slave trade should therefore be kept open as a possibility, to be practiced if necessary. Since the

[36] Montgomery correspondent of the *Mercury*, February 26, 1861; White, *Rhett*, p. 195.

[37] Curry, *Civil Government*, p. 117; Rhodes, *History of U. S.*, III, 182 and note 7; Wallace, *History of S. C.*, III, 169. Rhett and Magrath had also been mentioned for the Treasury. White, *Rhett*, p. 195. R. B. Rhett, Jr., *Confederate Government*, p. 104, states that only Barnwell recommended Memminger for the Treasury.

[38] W. H. Trescot was anxious to have a hand in the organization of the State Department but no use was made of his great ability. *Correspondence of Toombs, Stephens, Cobb*, pp. 529-531. Mrs. Chesnut wrote of Trescot April 2, 1862: "Trescot was very surly; calls himself ex-Secretary of State of the United States; now nothing in particular of South Carolina or the Confederate States. Then he yawned, 'What a bore this war is. I wish it was ended one way or another.' He speaks of going across the border and taking service in Mexico." *Diary*, p. 156.

[39] *Mercury*, February 12, 13, 15, 1861. The South Carolina delegation had tried to defeat the slave trade clause at Montgomery. See Rhett's and Chesnut's resolutions, *Journal Confed. Cong.*, I, 35-36.

contest between the North and South was one between two forms of society, between "slavery" and "democracy," the future of slavery should not be imperiled by a constitutional prohibition of the slave trade.[40]

The permanent Constitution was adopted by the Provisional Congress on March 11. Many of its features had seemed objectionable to the South Carolina delegation but their attempts to remedy what were considered defects were for the most part defeated. Rhett's motion to strike out the constitutional prohibition of the slave trade received the support of no other state. South Carolina stood alone also on a proposal by Boyce and Chesnut specifically to guarantee the right of secession, and on a proposal by Memminger that would have given a state convention the power to force the withdrawal of Confederate troops from the state except in time of war. An effort of the South Carolina delegation to forbid appeals from state courts to the Confederate Supreme Court also failed, as did Keitt's proposal to strike out the clause by which only three-fifths of the slave population was counted for purposes of representation. Defeat also came on a proposal to give state legislatures the exclusive power of choosing presidential electors and on a proposal to withhold from Congress the power to pass a uniform naturalization law. Finally strenuous efforts of the delegation, except Chesnut and Boyce, failed to limit membership in the Confederacy to slaveholding states. All that could be obtained on this subject was a provision requiring a two-thirds vote of both House and Senate voting by states.[41]

Although defeated at Montgomery on most of its efforts to amend the permanent Constitution, the South Carolina delegation originated three notable features of it which marked a departure from the Constitution of the United States. All three came on amendments offered by Rhett. One of these limited the terms of President and Vice-President to six years. Another prohibited bounties and protective tariffs and greatly limited appropriations for internal improvements. The other somewhat changed the process of amendment.[42]

When the permanent Constitution was published in South Carolina it was generally well received. The *Keowee Courier* thought it the "best Constitution yet formed for the government of men" and the *Mercury* believed it a vast improvement over the old United States Constitution.[43] Hammond thought it a masterpiece reforming almost all the abuses of the United States Constitution and embracing all known improvements in government.[44] But while there was general praise for the Constitution

[40] *Mercury*, February 13, 1861.
[41] *Journal Confed. Cong.*, I, 861-862, 866, 873-874, 877, 880, 883-886, 893; White, *Rhett*, pp. 197 et seq.
[42] *Journal Confed. Cong.*, I, 864-865, 875, 891-892; White, *Rhett*, pp. 198, 201.
[43] *Keowee Courier*, March 23, 1861; *Mercury*, March 15, 1861.
[44] J. H. Hammond to W. G. Simms, March 23-24, 1861, Hammond Papers.

as a whole, there appeared a very large amount of opposition to what were regarded as dangerous defects. These were listed by the *Mercury* as being, first, the failure to require choice of presidential electors by the legislature or preferably by the state Senate alone; second, the continuation of the old clause under which only three-fifths of the slave population was counted for purposes of representation; third, the constitutional prohibition of the slave trade; fourth, the failure to prohibit future admission to the Confederacy of nonslaveholding states.[45]   It was on the last of these points that the most general criticism was heard. The Montgomery correspondent of the *Mercury* thought it would allow the reorganization of the Union under the Confederate Constitution and reported that this was really the hope of some of the cabinet and a large number of congressmen.[46]   The *Mercury* held that experience had proved the impossibility of free and slave states living peaceably together, and ran a series of editorials to prove that admission of free states would revive the irrepressible conflict and prove suicidal to the South.[47]   The *Keowee Courier,* the Yorkville *Enquirer,* and Anderson *Intelligencer* agreed that the clause allowing admission of new states by a mere two-thirds vote of Congress was a most serious mistake, and that inclusion of middle or western states would be disastrous to the Southern Confederacy.[48]

The South Carolina convention which had adjourned January 5, reassembled March 26 and proceeded to consider the Confederate Constitution in secret session.[49]   Considerable opposition, on the general grounds already indicated, appeared. Gabriel Manigault of Charleston offered resolutions declaring the document was "imperfect and objectionable" in five particulars.[50]   Resolutions offered by J. Izard Middleton declared that the Confederate Constitution in

> not permitting to us the establishment of the policy of free trade, taking out of our hands . . . the control of our supply of labor, by a positive prohibition, giving us no efficient guaranty of the right and power of self-government at home, mingling, as it does, the National and Federative systems, and permitting the eventual accession of Anti-Slavery communities to our Confederacy by the absence of a constitutional prohibition, cannot be accepted by South Carolina, unless it be amended in all of the particulars above specified.[51]

Rhett wished to instruct the governor to call a convention whenever a nonslaveholding state should be admitted to the Confederacy and

[45] *Mercury*, February 15, 1861.   [46] *Ibid.,* April 4, 1861.
[47] *Ibid.,* March 25-28, April 1, 3, 5, 10, 1861.
[48] *Ibid.,* April 9, 1861; *Keowee Courier,* April 6, 1861.
[49] No stenographic record of the debate on ratification was made and an injunction of secrecy was placed on the members. This injunction was never removed although a committee of the convention in its last session favored removal as soon as the debates in the Montgomery convention were made public. *Convention Journal,* pp. 744-747.
[50] *Ibid.,* p. 207.   [51] *Ibid.,* pp. 214-215.

offered resolutions that South Carolina would not consider herself bound to remain in confederation with nonslaveholding states.[52]

There seems to have been almost unanimous agreement that amendments were needed but a motion to consider amendments before taking the vote on ratification was lost by a vote of 106 to 60. It was decided, however, that after a vote on ratification had been taken amendments would be considered and members later given the opportunity of changing their original vote on ratification. The vote taken April 3 was 138 to 21 in favor of ratification, the minority being for the most part from the low country.[53]

On the day after ratification, debate on amendments was begun. A motion to demand a constitutional convention at once was lost 101 to 44. It was resolved, however, by an overwhelming vote, that as soon as the Confederate States government was securely established and in peaceful operation South Carolina should demand, with two states concurring, a constitutional convention to consider amendments. There were many suggestions as to the amendments then to be proposed. Fifteen members wished the individual states to be allowed to maintain military establishments in time of peace. Twelve thought the right of secession should be specifically written into the Constitution. Twenty wanted to limit congressional power over commerce and to give each state the power to prohibit importation of such persons or things as it wished. The four amendments finally agreed upon were: (1) to repeal the three-fifths clause and to count Negroes in full; (2) to abolish the power of Congress to borrow money; to forbid contracting of debt except for war purposes; and to require that all expenditures in excess of revenues derived from imports (not to exceed 15% ad valorem) should be met from direct taxes laid by the Congress making the appropriation; (3) to repeal the constitutional prohibition of slave importations and give Congress power to prohibit by statute; (4) to prohibit the admission to the Confederate Union of any free state except with the consent of every state legislature. These resolutions, adopted by a vote of 117 to 15, indicate the almost unanimous opinion that amendments were desirable but that agitation for them should be postponed until a more appropriate time.[54]

The ratification of the permanent Constitution on April 3, 1861, formally ended the separate existence which South Carolina had in-

[52] *Ibid.*, pp. 199, 229.

[53] *Ibid.*, pp. 216-221, 236-238, 767. Six negative votes were later changed to the affirmative; three affirmative votes and one negative vote were cast late. The final vote was therefore 147-16. *Ibid.*, pp. 243, 265. Among the most prominent members who voted against ratification were ex-Governor Adams, Maxcy Gregg, Judge Henry McIver, Gabriel Manigault, J. I. Middleton, William Middleton, L. W. Spratt. *Ibid.*, p. 238. Among the effective speakers for ratification were Barnwell and Withers. J. L. Manning to his wife, April 2, 1861, Williams-Chesnut-Manning Papers.

[54] *Convention Journal*, pp. 243-244, 246, 248-249, 253, 255-258, 260-262, 539.

augurated by the ordinance of secession.[55]   The convention immediately repealed those ordinances which had been passed transferring to state agencies certain powers formerly exercised by the United States, and on April 8 adopted a state constitution to conform to the changed situation.   On the same day an ordinance ceded to the Confederate government all forts, navy yards, arsenals, custom houses and other public sites formerly in possession of the United States and lately in the possession of South Carolina.   A resolution was passed expressing "entire confidence" in the experience, patriotism, and ability of President Davis and Vice-President Stephens to "guide the destinies of the new Confederacy."[56]

Before these final steps had been taken, however, "independent" South Carolina had tried unsuccessfully to negotiate a settlement with the United States in regard to the forts.   These efforts will form the subject of the next chapter and will require a return to the period before secession.

[55] The Provisional Constitution was ratified, April 8, in order to validate, so far as South Carolina was concerned, the acts of the Provisional Congress. *Ibid.*, p. 744.

[56] *Ibid.*, pp. 279, 771, 776; *Ordinances and Constitution of the State of South Carolina, with the Constitution of the Provisional Government and of the Confederate States of America* (Charleston, 1861), pp. 37-55.

CHAPTER VII

FORTS DIPLOMACY

While the preparations for a Southern Confederacy were in progress, important negotiations with the United States were being attempted in connection with the federal forts in Charleston harbor.[1] From the point of view of South Carolina it was utterly illogical that these should remain after secession in the possession of the United States, a foreign nation. Even before secession was actually carried, the issue of the forts became a matter of concern. During the summer of 1860 the United States government began the work of repairing and strengthening the harbor fortifications then in use and of completing Fort Sumter which at the time was not occupied by troops. These activities aroused fears that the United States might attempt to use the forts against the seceding state, and resulted in some interruption of the cordial social relations existing between the garrison and the Charleston people.[2] As the work on the forts continued and secession approached, the South Carolina authorities became increasingly anxious to learn the attitude and intentions of the Buchanan administration. The existing garrison was a small one and its position in Fort Moultrie on Sullivan's Island not strong, but reinforcement or transfer of the garrison to Fort Sumter in the middle of the harbor might greatly strengthen the ability of the United States to hold the forts for use against the state.

As early as November 7, Governor Gist requested Thomas F. Drayton to ascertain, while in Washington on other business, what the policy of the administration would be.[3] The governor also kept in touch with W. H. Trescot, the South Carolinian who since June had been Assistant Secretary of State, and in the absence of Lewis Cass, Acting Secretary. The able Assistant Secretary, intimately associated as he was with leading members of the administration and in close touch with the leaders of public opinion in his own state, was in a highly strategic position. He was well aware of the danger of collision at Charleston should any attempt to reinforce be made, and was anxious

[1] The attempt of South Carolina to negotiate is well treated in the standard work by Crawford already cited. The narrative of W. H. Trescot, *American Historical Review*, XIII (April, 1908), 528-556, is indispensable for the earlier negotiations. The documents are to be found in *O. R.*, 1st series, I, VI; *Convention Journal; House Executive Documents*, 2nd session, 36th Congress; *South Carolina Executive Documents*. The defense of President Buchanan is *Mr. Buchanan's Administration on the Eve of the Rebellion* (New York, 1866), hereinafter cited *Buchanan's Administration*. See also P. G. Auchampaugh, *James Buchanan and His Cabinet on the Eve of Secession* (Lancaster, Pa., 1926).

[2] Crawford, *Fort Sumter*, p. 67.

[3] Nicolay and Hay, *Lincoln*, II, 321-322.

to prevent such a misfortune. He used, therefore, whatever influence he could exert in favor of moderate policies both in Washington and South Carolina.

Early in November considerable excitement was aroused in Charleston as a result of an attempt by Colonel John L. Gardner, then in command of Fort Moultrie, to replenish his munitions supply from the United States arsenal in the city. Charleston citizens resented the attempt and a telegram was sent Trescot saying that if the attempted removal was by order of the War Department, the order should be revoked as otherwise collision was certain. Secretary of War John B. Floyd authorized Trescot to say that no such order had been or would be given, and a few days later replaced Gardner with Major Robert Anderson in whose "discretion, coolness, and judgment" Floyd placed great confidence. Meanwhile, on November 9, a state guard for the arsenal was offered by the governor and accepted by the military storekeeper. Its presence and the subsequent appointment of Colonel Benjamin Huger, a Carolinian, to take charge of the arsenal somewhat diminished popular excitement.[4] The arsenal incident indicated that the Secretary of War did not favor a policy of reinforcing the forts.

President Buchanan's cabinet as a whole, however, was badly divided as it considered the problem of Anderson and Fort Moultrie. Trescot wrote Drayton November 19 that the policy of the administration had not been formulated at that time. Knowing the views of Secretaries Floyd, Cobb, and Thompson, however, he felt justified in telling Drayton that South Carolina could assume with confidence that no action to fortify would be taken so long as the Southern members remained in the cabinet.[5] But almost immediately Buchanan, persuaded by Secretaries Cass and Black, called Floyd and informed him of his decision to reinforce. Floyd protested but was successful only to the extent of getting Buchanan to suspend his final decision until General Scott should arrive in Washington.[6]

The Southern members of the cabinet and Trescot, alarmed at Buchanan's decision, consulted as to the best method of dissuading the President. One plan considered was for Trescot to interview Buchanan and attempt to dissuade him; if unsuccessful, Trescot was to announce that he must resign and immediately return to Columbia, in which case South Carolina occupation of the forts must take place within twenty-four hours. This plan was discarded in favor of one under which Governor Gist should be requested to write Buchanan giving assurances that South Carolina would not disturb Anderson so

<hr/>

[4] "Narrative and Letter of William Henry Trescot, concerning the Negotiations between South Carolina and President Buchanan in December, 1860," *American Historical Review*, XIII (April, 1908), 533; hereinafter cited Trescot, "Narrative." Crawford, Fort Sumter, pp. 56-60, 119-121.

[5] Nicolay and Hay, *Lincoln*, II, 322-323; Trescot, "Narrative," *loc. cit.*, p. 534.

[6] *Ibid.*, p. 535; Crawford, *Fort Sumter*, p. 28.

long as no attempt to reinforce was made. In accordance with this plan Trescot wrote Governor Gist, November 26, saying that the President, fearing the forts would be seized, felt obliged to reinforce, and suggested that an assurance from Gist might enable Buchanan to change his decision. Meanwhile Gist would be informed of any reinforcement order.[7]

Gist readily agreed to Trescot's proposal and November 29 wrote that though he was committed to resist any effort to reinforce Anderson he was anxious to avoid a collision. The people of Charleston, he said, had been very impatient for possession of the fort but there would be no attack by the state unless an attempt to reinforce was made or unless the United States refused after secession to evacuate or attempted to interfere with the collection of duties by South Carolina. He expressed the hope that the President would not "light the torch of discord" which could only be quenched in blood.[8]

This letter greatly reassured Buchanan. He, too, was anxious to avoid a collision and he went so far as to request Trescot to carry an advance copy of his annual message to South Carolina in order to clear up possible misunderstanding of it. Trescot agreed to carry the letter but assured the President that there was no hope of South Carolina delaying secession until March 4 as Buchanan desired. The state, he said, would secede immediately and send commissioners. These the President said he could not receive but stated he would refer their communications to Congress, in which case Trescot thought South Carolina would be content to wait a reasonable time for a decision of Congress. On returning from South Carolina, he restated his conviction that South Carolina would use no force until after an attempt to negotiate, unless in the meantime efforts to reinforce the forts were made.[9]

When Trescot returned to Washington (December 9) the South Carolina congressmen had arrived in the capital and on the day before had had the first of their important conversations with the President. In their interview of December 8 they informed the President that the surest way to precipitate a collision would be an attempt to reinforce, but like Trescot, they assured him that there would be no unprovoked attack until after the convention had sent commissioners. Buchanan created the impression on the delegation that he was still undecided on a policy. He asked them, however, for a written memorandum of the substance of their conversation. On December 10, Representatives McQueen, Miles, and Bonham called and submitted a memorandum signed on the 9th by themselves, Boyce, and Keitt in which the dele-

[7] *Ibid.*, pp. 28-31; Trescot, "Narrative," *loc. cit.*, pp. 535-536.
[8] W. H. Gist to W. H. Trescot, November 29, 1860, in Crawford, *Fort Sumter*, pp. 31-32. In a letter of the same date Gist asked Trescot to remain as agent of South Carolina in Washington if he should resign as Assistant Secretary of State. *Ibid.*
[9] *Ibid.*, pp. 33-35; Trescot, "Narrative," *loc. cit.*, pp. 536-538.

gation expressed its "strong convictions that neither the constituted authorities nor any body of the people" would molest the forts prior to an attempt by accredited representatives to negotiate an agreement, "provided that no reinforcement shall be sent into those forts, and their relative military status" be preserved. The President objected to the word "provided" on the ground that it seemed to commit him while the delegation was not authorized to bind the state. The congressmen replied that they "did not so understand it"; that they were expressing their strong belief conditioned on the maintenance of the *status quo*. This seems to have satisfied the President who then stated that it was not his intention to make any change.[10]

According to the account of this interview by Miles and Keitt, when the delegation rose to depart, Buchanan said: "After all, this is a matter of honor among gentlemen. I do not know that any paper or writing is necessary. We understand each other." And when one of the delegation pointed out that they would be put in an embarrassing position should the President change his determination to maintain the *status quo,* Buchanan replied: "Then, I would first return you this paper."[11] Buchanan later denied that any pledge was made to the South Carolina congressmen. Certain it is, however, that his earlier decision to reinforce the forts had been given up. Trescot found Buchanan immediately after the interview much pleased with the situation, saying he regarded the Gist letter of November 29 and the congressmen's memorandum of December 10 a guarantee that South Carolina would not attack. His change of policy brought the immediate resignation of Secretary of State Cass who had insisted on reinforcement. The evidence seems to sustain the view of Trescot, the South Carolina congressmen, and the state authorities that Buchanan was committed by a gentlemen's agreement to maintain the *status quo*.[12]

Such was the situation at the time Pickens succeeded Gist as governor and the convention of South Carolina assembled. Though a satisfactory temporary arrangement had been made, the new governor

[10] "Statement of Miles and Keitt of what transpired between Buchanan and the South Carolina delegation." *O. R.,* 1st series, I, 125-128; also in *Convention Journal,* pp. 498-502.

[11] *O. R.,* 1st series, I, 126. The original memorandum, interestingly enough, is in the Miles Papers. Buchanan's endorsement briefly describes the interview and continues: "Afterward M'Queen & Bonham called, in behalf of the Delegation & gave me the most positive assurance that the forts & public property would not be molested until after Commissioners had been appointed to treat with the Federal Government in relation to the public property & until the decision was known. I informed them that what would be done was a question for Congress & not for the Exec. That if they [the forts] were assailed this would put them completely in the wrong and making [*sic*] them the authors of the Civil War. They gave the same assurances to Messrs Floyd, Thompson & others."

[12] Trescot, "Narrative," *loc. cit.,* p. 539; Crawford, *Fort Sumter,* pp. 42-43. In 1882 Judge Black allowed Crawford to infer that he, Black, believed the pledge had been given. *Ibid.,* p. 25 note; see also pp. 40-41. *Cf.* Auchampaugh, *Buchanan and His Cabinet,* pp. 152-153.

came near upsetting it by almost his first official act. December 17, he addressed a letter to President Buchanan in which he expressed a sincere desire to avoid a collision but stated that he was informed that the forts in the harbor were preparing to turn their guns on the city, that the excitement of the masses under a deep sense of wrong was very great, and that in order to avoid an effusion of blood "which no human power may be able to prevent" it was necessary, first, to discontinue all work on the forts and, second, to allow the occupation of Fort Sumter by a small group of not over twenty-five South Carolina officers and men. "If something of the kind be not done, I cannot answer for the consequences."[13] This letter was dispatched by D. H. Hamilton, and Trescot was requested in a letter of the same date to arrange for him a personal interview with the President and to inform him that a reply within twenty-four hours might be sent by Hamilton or, if the President preferred, by Trescot himself.[14]

Trescot, who from another source had learned of the contents of the Pickens letter, was unsympathetic and disturbed, but on the 20th introduced Hamilton to Buchanan who read the letter and promised a reply next day. Trescot thought the letter ill-advised. He believed that Buchanan would have promised, if requested, not to occupy Fort Sumter but the demand for South Carolina occupation "if persisted in released the President from his pledge to the members of C[ongress] and placed them in a very awkward attitude and in my opinion would lead to exactly what it wanted to avoid."[15] He talked to Senators Davis and Slidell, who agreed, and then invited Bonham and McQueen to join him in a telegraphic request to Pickens for authority to withdraw the letter. The authority was granted. Trescot wrote Pickens: "Its withdrawal was most opportune. It reached here under circumstances which you could not have anticipated." Buchanan, he said, could not have granted the request as he was already being criticized for his pacific course evidenced by his removal of Gardner, his refusal to send reinforcements, his acceptance of Cass's resignation, and his order through the War Department that forty muskets removed from the arsenal on the 17th be immediately restored. Trescot, moreover, quotes Buchanan as saying that he was pledged not to disturb the *status quo* in favor of the United States and that it was unfair for Pickens to ask him to disturb it in favor of the state.[16] Pickens had blundered.

[13] *House Journal* (1861), pp. 167-168.
[14] Trescot, "Narrative," *loc. cit.,* p. 540, note 12.
[15] *Ibid.,* p. 541.
[16] W. H. Trescot to F. W. Pickens, December 21, 1860, *House Journal* (1861), pp. 169-170; Trescot, "Narrative," *loc. cit.,* p. 541. Captain J. G. Foster had obtained forty muskets December 17 for workmen in Fort Sumter. Trescot received a telegram on the 19th saying that unless they were returned immediately "a collision may occur at any moment." Trescot saw Floyd who ordered the restoration made on the 20th. *Ibid.,* p. 539; Crawford, *Fort Sumter,* pp. 77-78; *O. R.,* 1st series, I, 94-103.

A more conciliatory approach to the problem was now made by the convention. On the day after secession this body adopted a resolution that three commissioners, elected by the convention, be sent to Washington to treat with the United States for

... delivery of the forts, magazines, light-houses, and other real estate, with their appurtenances, within the limits of South Carolina, and also for an apportionment of the public debt and for a division of all other property held by the Government of the United States, as agent for the Confederate States, of which South Carolina was recently a member; and generally to negotiate as to all other measures and arrangements proper to be made and adopted in the existing relations of the parties, and for the continuance of peace and amity between this Commonwealth and the Government at Washington.[17]

Robert W. Barnwell was overwhelmingly elected at once and on the next day a third ballot resulted in the choice of J. L. Orr and J. H. Adams.[18] It was a good delegation. Barnwell was a Harvard graduate and had served in both houses of Congress and as president of South Carolina College. Adams was a graduate of Yale and once governor of his state, while Orr had had a long career in Congress. They represented, said Trescot, the minor differences of opinion in the state with "singular accuracy,"[19] Adams being the radical, Orr the old National Democrat, and Barnwell the former unionist. President Buchanan was pleased with the selection and was ready to see them, refer their request to Congress, and meanwhile maintain his pledge in regard to the forts. The commissioners reached Washington on December 26 and conferred with Trescot who agreed to act unofficially with them. An appointment was made with the President for the following day. But that very night Major Anderson by his removal from Moultrie to Sumter complicated the problem almost, if not quite, beyond solution.[20]

The startling news of Anderson's removal reached the commissioners on the 27th as they were preparing for their first interview. Secretary Floyd came in and declared the information was undoubtedly erroneous since such a step was not only without orders but against orders. But the report was at once confirmed by telegrams from South Carolina. Floyd hurried to the War Department and Trescot went to the Senate to see Senators Davis and Hunter who accompanied him to the White House. Buchanan had not heard the news and on receiving it exclaimed, says Trescot, "My God, are calamities never to come singly. I call God to witness—you gentlemen better than anybody know—that this is not only without but against my orders, it is against my policy."[21] He re-

[17] *Convention Journal*, pp. 53-54.
[18] *Ibid.*, pp. 55-56, 59. Magrath on the third ballot received a majority (86) necessary to elect but was two votes behind Orr, and five behind Adams. *Mercury*, December 22, 1860.
[19] Trescot, "Narrative," *loc. cit.*, p. 552.
[20] *Ibid.*, p. 543.
[21] *Ibid.*, p. 544.

fused, after some hesitation, however, immediately to wire orders to Anderson that he should return to Moultrie if the removal had been without attack. He must consult his cabinet.[22]

It can hardly be doubted that Anderson's occupation of Fort Sumter was not only contrary to the expectation and policy of Buchanan and his Secretary of War, but also in violation of the spirit of the understanding with the South Carolina congressmen. On the other hand, Anderson was unaware of the gentlemen's agreement and displayed sound military judgment in transferring his small command to a more defensible position. Moreover, his action was not a violation of his orders liberally construed. On December 11 he had been given verbal instructions through Major D. C. Buell requiring that he "carefully avoid any act which would needlessly tend to provoke aggression" since it was the "studied determination" of the administration to follow a pacific course.

But you are to hold possession of the forts in this harbor, and if attacked you are to defend yourself to the last extremity. The smallness of your force will not permit you, perhaps, to occupy more than one of the three forts, but an attack on or an attempt to take possession of any one of them will be regarded as an act of hostility, and you may then put your command into either of them which you may deem most proper, to increase its power of resistance. You are also authorized to take similar steps whenever you have tangible evidence of a design to proceed to a hostile act.[23]
He believed he had the "tangible evidence."

The importance of Fort Sumter as the key to the harbor situation in Charleston had for some time been realized by both sides. It commanded Fort Moultrie and the entrance to the harbor. From the time Anderson took command he realized that Moultrie was indefensible against a land attack and appreciated fully the advantage of an occupation of Sumter.[24] On the other side, Pickens, from the time of his inauguration, was most anxious to prevent such a move. He was repeatedly urged during the ten days between his inauguration and the time of Anderson's removal to seize Sumter or at least take steps to prevent its occupation by Anderson. This was the purpose of the Hamilton mission to Buchanan. Without waiting for the success or failure of this effort he had proceeded to Charleston on December 18 and arranged for a guard boat to patrol at night the waters between Moultrie and Sumter and prevent by force, if necessary, any attempt of Anderson to change his position.[25] The request that South Carolina be allowed to occupy the fort was, however, withdrawn and Pickens contented himself with what he seems to have regarded as ample precaution against a violation of the *status quo*. Trescot assured him, December 21, that no change would be made.[26]

[22] *Ibid.; Buchanan's Administration,* pp. 180-181.
[23] Crawford, *Fort Sumter,* p. 73; O. R., 1st series I, 89.
[24] *Ibid.,* pp. 74, 78, 105; Crawford, *Fort Sumter,* pp. 60, 62, 92.
[25] *Ibid.,* pp. 88-91; *House Journal* (1861), pp. 21-37.
[26] *Ibid.,* pp. 169-170; Crawford, *Fort Sumter,* pp. 85-86.

Anderson, however, believed that the situation was critical. It had long been openly declared in private and official circles that refusal to evacuate the forts after an attempt by South Carolina to negotiate would lead to an attack. The commissioners were then in Washington, and Anderson, anticipating failure of the mission, believed that an attack might occur even before their return. The nightly appearance of the guard boat, observed and reported, was anything but reassuring. He argued, later, that the establishment of this patrol was sufficient to release his government from any agreement which might have existed. As it turned out, Anderson was able to complete his removal on the evening of the 26th before the guard boat had left the city for its nightly patrol.[27]

The news of Major Anderson's change of position created great resentment and excitement in Charleston. Governor Pickens through his aide-de-camp, Colonel J. J. Pettigrew, immediately charged Anderson with violating the agreement with Buchanan to maintain the *status quo* and demanded his return to Fort Moultrie. Anderson stated that he was unaware of the agreement and defended his action by citing the activity of the guard boat which he feared was transporting troops for an attack on Moultrie from the sandhills north of the fort. He refused to return to his previous position, whereupon Pickens gave orders for the immediate occupation of Castle Pinckney and Fort Moultrie. This was followed on December 29 by a demand for possession of the arsenal and by its surrender under protest the next day. The governor also ordered the erection of batteries on Morris Island and Sullivan's Island to prevent if possible any attempt to reinforce Sumter. Meanwhile, all communication between the fort and Charleston was forbidden.[28]

These events in Charleston harbor complicated enormously the task of the South Carolina commissioners in Washington. Their interview arranged for the 27th was postponed until the following day while Buchanan consulted his cabinet. On the 28th they had a two-hour conference with the President in which they insisted that he was in honor clearly bound to order Anderson's return to Fort Moultrie at once. But he wanted more time to consider the question and would not commit himself.[29] On the same day the commissioners wrote a letter to the President stating their position. It declared that they had been authorized by the convention to treat with the United States government in regard to delivery of the forts and other public property, to arrange for an apportionment of the public debt and generally to negotiate on all matters necessary to the peace and amity between the two governments. They had been ready to begin the negotiations with the

---

[27] *O. R.*, 1st series, I, 105-107; Crawford, *Fort Sumter*, pp. 92, 97-99, 100-101, 105, 127-128; John Johnson, *The Defense of Charleston Harbor Including Fort Sumter and the Adjacent Islands, 1863-1865* (Charleston, 1890), p. 23.
[28] Crawford, *Fort Sumter*, pp. 108-111, 113-118, 122-125, 132, 134.
[29] *Ibid.*, pp. 142, 144, 146-149.

earnest desire to avoid collision and to establish good will and harmony between the two parties. But events of the last twenty-four hours rendered "such an assurance impossible." South Carolina could have at any time during the last sixty days seized all of the forts at Charleston but had relied on the pledge and honor of the President. The violation of the pledges had so altered the situation that they were faced with the necessity of suspending any further discussions until the circumstances of Anderson's removal should be so explained as to remove all doubt as to the spirit in which the negotiations would be conducted. The commissioners requested also that all troops be removed from Charleston harbor; their presence was a "standing menace which renders negotiation impossible," and "threatens speedily to bring to a bloody issue questions which ought to be settled with temperance and judgment."[30]

Buchanan immediately prepared a reply which he submitted next day to his cabinet. While probably not consenting to evacuate or to order Anderson's return to Moultrie,[31] the reply was criticized by Secretaries Black, Holt, and Stanton as conceding too much. On the other hand, Thomas, Thompson, and Floyd objected to it on opposite grounds. Floyd, whose resignation was expected for other reasons, resigned in protest. Black's threat to retire unless the reply was strengthened, led Buchanan to recast it in accordance with Black's suggestions and adopt a new policy in regard to the forts.[32]

The revised reply to the commissioners was delivered December 31. The President stated that he had been willing to met them and transmit to Congress any proposition they might make, and he therefore regretted that they regarded Anderson's removal as rendering negotiations impossible. He reviewed at length the conversations with the South Carolina congressmen and denied that they constituted a pledge on his part. He had acted, however, in accordance with the terms of the alleged pledge; he had not sent reinforcements and had never authorized any change in the relative military status at Charleston; Anderson had clearly acted without authority, unless indeed he had been given "tangible evidence" of a South Carolina "design to proceed to a hostile act." As to the demand that Anderson be ordered back to Moultrie, Buchanan declared that his first impulse had been to issue the order. Before such a step could be taken, however, he had received information that South Carolina had occupied Fort Moultrie and Castle Pinckney, that the South Carolina flag had been raised over the postoffice and customs house in Charleston and that every customs officer had resigned. Under these circumstances he must refuse to withdraw the troops from Charleston; he had never considered withdrawing them. The fact that

---

[30] *O. R.*, 1st series, I, 109-110.

[31] For a discussion of the nature of the draft see Rhodes, *History of U. S.*, III, 117 and note.

[32] *Ibid.*, pp. 117 *et seq.;* Crawford, *Fort Sumter*, pp. 149-156.

Anderson had acted without instructions did not, he said, justify the inference that he was then honor bound to withdraw from the only remaining fort.[33]

This reply of Buchanan made further progress of negotiations practically hopeless. There was, however, one possibility indicated by Buchanan's inference that Anderson could not return to Moultrie because of its occupation by South Carolina. Perhaps the President might consent to order him back if South Carolina offered to restore the seized forts. Senator Hunter, for the commissioners, approached the President with this proposal but it was declined and Hunter reported: "Tell the Comm: it is hopeless. The President has taken this ground—I *can't* repeat what passed between us but if you can get a telegram to Charleston, telegraph at once to your people to sink vessels in the channel of the harbour."[34] An order had indeed been issued on December 31 for the preparation of the *Brooklyn* to reinforce Fort Sumter but it was decided that the courtesy of a few hours should first be allowed to the commissioners for a reply.[35]

The commissioners' letter of January 1, 1861, was apparently not designed or expected to influence Buchanan. Rather it was drafted as a vindication of South Carolina and as proof to the South that all hope for the Union was gone. As propaganda it was an extremely able document. In a lengthy review of recent events it contemptuously accused Buchanan of trying to escape the obligation of his pledge on the ground that South Carolina had seized other United States property before he could act to redeem the pledge; and by his charge that South Carolina had terminated the negotiations by demanding withdrawal as a condition of their continuance. The commissioners denied that withdrawal of all troops had been made a *sine qua non*. They had *demanded* an explanation of Anderson's conduct and had only *urged* withdrawal of troops. As to the seizure by South Carolina of other forts, more than twelve hours had elapsed between the time Buchanan learned of Anderson's removal and the time he received news that South Carolina had seized the forts. He could easily have acted within that period and in any case was obligated to stand by his pledge. By his decision to hold by force what he had obtained through misplaced confidence, and by refusing to disavow Anderson, he had converted a violation of orders into a legitimate act of his own executive authority, and probably rendered civil war inevitable. "If you choose to force this issue upon us, the State of South Carolina will accept it, and relying upon Him who is the God of justice as well as the God of Hosts, will endeavor to perform the great duty which lies before her, hopefully,

[33] *Ibid.*, pp. 156-158; *O. R.*, 1st series, I, 115-118.
[34] Trescot, "Narrative," *loc. cit.*, pp. 546, 553. The South Carolina authorities did decide, January 3, to sink the hulks; it was done January 11. Crawford, *Fort Sumter*, pp. 137, 200-201.
[35] *Ibid.*, p. 171; *O. R.*, 1st series, I, 119.

bravely and thoroughly." After reading this communication to his cabinet, Buchanan returned it to the commissioners with an endorsement that he declined to receive it.[36]

Upon receipt of the commissioners' final letter on January 2, plans were at once renewed for relief of Fort Sumter. It was decided, however, on the advice of General Scott, that men and supplies should be dispatched on a merchant steamer from New York, as it was believed it would have a better chance of secrecy and success than would the *Brooklyn* as originally planned. The necessary preparations were made and the *Star of the West* left New York for Charleston on the afternoon of January 5. After her departure Buchanan learned from Anderson of the erection of the battery on Morris Island which would make it hazardous for an unarmed ship to enter Charleston harbor. This and recent information that Anderson was in no immediate danger led the President to countermand orders for the *Star of the West*—too late, however, to be effective. The *Brooklyn* was ordered on January 7 to escort and protect the *Star of the West,* but the former was unable to overtake the latter ship.[37]

South Carolina authorities had every reason to expect an attempt to reinforce and indeed soon learned that the *Star of the West* had sailed.[38] Preparations against such an expedition had been under way since Anderson's removal to Fort Sumter on December 27. Fort Moultrie was ordered to be ready, and the battery on Morris Island was occupied by Major P. F. Stevens and his Citadel cadets. As an extra precaution, Pickens ordered Colonel John Cuningham to take three hundred well-armed, picked men and on the steamer *Marion* proceed to the bar where he should intercept if possible the *Star of the West.*[39] The feeble effort to reinforce Fort Sumter by the *Star of the West* instead of by a vessel of war as first intended ended in a failure which reflected no credit on the administration. The fire of the Citadel cadets from Morris Island early January 9 did little damage, but Anderson, because of delayed orders, failed to support the reinforcing expedition which, disheartened, returned to New York; the *Brooklyn,* learning from a passing steamer of the failure and being without further orders, likewise turned back.[40]

[36] *Ibid.,* pp. 120-125. The whole correspondence between Buchanan and the commissioners is in *Convention Journal,* pp. 484-497. According to a letter of W. E. Martin to W. P. Miles, May 4, 1861, Miles Papers, W. H. Trescot wrote the letters of the South Carolina commissioners.

[37] Crawford, *Fort Sumter,* pp. 174-176.

[38] Senator L. T. Wigfall wired M. L. Bonham, January 2, "Holt succeeds Floyd. It means war. Cut off supplies from Anderson and take Sumter as soon as possible." *O. R.,* 1st series, I, 252. He wired the commissioners January 6, and Pickens January 8. *Ibid.,* 1st series, I, 253; *ibid.,* serial no. 111, p. 117. Secretary of the Interior wired Judge A. B. Longstreet, January 8. And on the night before, a telegram had been read before the convention. Crawford, *Fort Sumter,* pp. 178-181.

[39] *Ibid.,* pp. 123-125, 138-139.

[40] F. E. Chadwick, *Causes of the Civil War, 1859-1861* (New York, 1906), pp. 222-223; Crawford, *Fort Sumter,* pp. 183-186.

Immediately after the departure of the *Star of the West,* Major Anderson sent an officer to Governor Pickens with a letter demanding a disavowal of the act of firing upon the flag of the United States and declaring that if the act be not disclaimed, he would regard it as an act of war and not permit South Carolina vessels to pass within range of the fort. Pickens replied that evidently Anderson had not learned that South Carolina had seceded, that South Carolina regarded the transfer of Anderson to Sumter as an act of hostility, and the attempt of the *Star of the West* to reinforce as an attempt at coercion which it was plainly the duty of South Carolina to repel; as to the threat to fire on vessels passing within range of Fort Sumter, Anderson must judge his own responsibility. Anderson did not carry out his threat but notified Pickens that he had decided to refer the matter to Washington.[41]

Encouraged by Anderson's retreat and influenced by the popular clamor for Fort Sumter, Governor Pickens attempted through bluff to obtain the fort. Though by no means prepared in a military way to seize it, he sent Secretary of State Magrath and Secretary of War Jamison to Major Anderson January 11, with a demand that the fort be turned over to South Carolina on a pledge from the state to account for the public property received. Magrath forcefully argued acceptance of the proposal and Jamison stated that 20,000 men were ready to come to Charleston and take the fort. Anderson, however, refused the demand, and Pickens would have been in the embarrassing position of having to attack before prepared to do so had not Anderson made the suggestion that should Pickens desire to refer his demand to Washington he would gladly appoint an officer to accompany a state official.[42] Pickens's acceptance of the proposal constituted a kind of truce between the parties which was to continue until the outcome of this second attempt to negotiate.

Pickens selected for the Washington mission his Attorney General, Isaac W. Hayne. He bore a letter demanding evacuation and was instructed to inquire of the President if it was by his order that the attempt to reinforce had been made and if the United States asserted such right. In case the answer was in the affirmative, Hayne was to inform the President that such attempts would be regarded as a declaration of war. Hayne was to pledge the state to adjust any question of property rights but to declare that continued possession of the fort would inevitably lead to a "bloody issue" which in the opinion of the governor could have only one result.[43]

Hayne and Lieutenant Norman J. Hall reached Washington on

---

[41] *Executive Documents No. 2, Correspondence and other Papers relating to Fort Sumter. Including Correspondence of Hon. Isaac W. Hayne with the President* (Charleston, 1861), pp. 3-6, hereinafter cited *Exec. Doc.*; Crawford, *Fort Sumter,* pp. 187-191; *O. R.,* 1st series, I, 134-136.

[42] *Exec. Doc. No. 2,* pp. 7-8; Crawford, *Fort Sumter,* pp. 191-194.

[43] *Ibid.,* p. 195; *Exec. Doc. No. 2,* p. 11.

January 13. Hayne called on the President on the 14th; they agreed that negotiation should be limited to written communications, and Hayne promised to deliver a letter from Pickens the next day. This letter of January 11 was, however, not delivered on the 15th because of the intervention of ten Southern senators who wrote Hayne on January 15, that since their states would share the fortunes of South Carolina they felt justified in asking South Carolina to avoid hostilities if possible. They proposed that Hayne delay the presentation of Pickens's demand until they could attempt an arangement under which South Carolina would promise not to attack and would allow Anderson to receive food, fuel, and water and to enjoy free communication with the President, on the understanding that there would be no effort to reinforce the fort. They hoped that such an arangement might be made to continue until the middle of February at which time the Southern states in convention might devise a "wise, just and peaceable solution of existing difficulties."[44]

Hayne received the proposal of the senators with satisfaction. He had found it generally agreed in Washington that if the demand were presented it would be met by a refusal and followed by another attempt at reinforcement. He wrote Pickens on the 16th that circumstances had wonderfully favored him in effecting the delay which he understood Pickens desired. He would agree to withhold his demand and would perhaps ask for further instructions. Prudence in South Carolina, he said, would prevent all reinforcements and postpone hostilities until a common government could be formed. He therefore advised that Anderson be allowed to obtain fresh meat and vegetables from the city.[45]

Hayne in his reply to the senators agreed to delay his note to Buchanan and to refer the whole matter to Pickens on condition the senators could get an assurance that no hostile act would be permitted in the interval. They submitted their correspondence with Hayne to the President on the 19th. Buchanan refused their proposal in a letter through Secretary of War Holt on the 22nd. The President's policy, said Holt, was one of defense and no reinforcement was planned, but should Anderson request it or should South Carolina resort to an attack, the reinforcement would be made. The President was said to have no authority to dispose of public property and could not evade, even temporarily, his duty to protect it. This letter clearly failed to meet Hayne's conditions. The senators, while admitting on January 23 that the reply was unsatisfactory, nevertheless asserted their confidence that Buchanan would not act until Hayne's mission was ended and urged

[44] *Ibid.*, pp. 11-12; *Buchanan's Administration,* p. 197; Crawford, *Fort Sumter,* pp. 218-220.

[45] I. W. Hayne to F. W. Pickens, January 16, 1861; I. W. Hayne to A. G. Magrath, January 16, 1861, Pickens-Bonham Papers. See also R. N. Gourdin to A. G. Magrath, January 18, 1861, reiterating these ideas. *Ibid.*

him to communicate with Pickens before proceeding further. This Hayne gladly consented to do.[46]

Meanwhile Pickens was well-informed of the trend of events. Hayne by the 22nd had written three and wired five times. Jefferson Davis had written three times and Senator Louis T. Wigfall had written Maxcy Gregg and W. P. Miles. All seemed agreed that Pickens had erred in sending his demand before he was prepared to enforce it, even if he were convinced of the propriety of taking the fort before a provisional Southern government was formed. All counselled delay. But Pickens gave no sign of his reaction. No single letter or telegram had Hayne received by the 22nd. Smarting somewhat under newspaper criticism, he complained that he had a right to know whether his course met the approval of those whom he represented. Defending his course in Washington, he said that "without compromitting in the slightest degree the honor of South Carolina," he had at least postponed an unnecessary collision for which the state was not prepared. Both the President and the senators had procrastinated, he said, and he, himself, had made no effort to hasten proceedings. He believed this was in accordance with the wishes of Pickens as intimated to him before his departure.[47]

Governor Pickens, however, refused to modify his original instructions to Hayne. In a long letter through Secretary of State Magrath he declared that it was indispensably necessary for South Carolina to know the intentions of the government and that while much of the doubt on this point had been removed by the correspondence between the President and the senators, this correspondence confirmed the opinion of the governor that the original demand should be presented. Hayne accordingly on January 31 made his first direct communication as special envoy of South Carolina. Enclosing Pickens's letter of the 11th and reviewing events since his arrival in Washington, he stated that South Carolina could not tolerate the holding of Fort Sumter as a military post. He came, he said, as a legal officer of his state to claim South Carolina's right of eminent domain over all territory within her limits and to guarantee compensation for any property taken.[48]

Buchanan's refusal to surrender Fort Sumter contained in a letter from Holt to Hayne on February 6,[49] closed the mission of Hayne. But before his departure Hayne sent a scorching letter directly to the President in which he took exception to a number of Secretary Holt's statements. The Secretary of War had noted a modification, he said, in South Carolina's original demands and had interpreted Hayne's letter

[46] *Exec. Doc.* No. 2, pp. 15-20; Crawford, *Fort Sumter,* pp. 220-222; *O. R.,* 1st series, I, 149-150.
[47] I. W. Hayne to F. W. Pickens, January 22, 1861, Pickens-Bonham Papers.
[48] *Exec. Doc.* No. 2, pp. 21-28; Crawford, *Fort Sumter,* pp. 222-228.
[49] *O. R.,* 1st series, I, 166-168.

as a mere offer of South Carolina to purchase Fort Sumter. This Hayne repudiated as an "intentional misconstruction." To Holt's point that the possession of Fort Sumter involved "political consideration of a much higher and more imposing character," Hayne replied that any political relations of the United States to anything in South Carolina was not a subject for discussion, for South Carolina had severed all political relations with the United States and was *de facto* a separate nation exercising complete sovereignty over every foot of her territory except Fort Sumter. Hayne ridiculed Holt's contention that the fort was being held, as always, for defense of the people of South Carolina. For one government, he said, to hold a fortress in the territory of a foreign power against her will under the pretense of protecting her citizens was the highest insult one nation could offer another. He pointed out that Sumter had been garrisoned after secession and then secretly, at night. And South Carolina had been prevented from taking it at that time "only because of her misplaced confidence in a Government which deceived her." Insulted by this blistering attack upon his integrity, Buchanan returned the letter to Hayne with a statement that he refused to receive it.[50] Thus, unsuccessfully, ended all attempts of South Carolina to negotiate independently a settlement in regard to the forts.

Governor Pickens, despite his bold front, was no doubt pleased by the delay which the Hayne negotiations afforded. He was between two fires. On the one hand the radicals of South Carolina had from the first demanded that the forts be taken over by the state. Numerous resolutions to this end had been offered (and defeated) in the convention soon after secession.[51] The newspapers continued the agitation. There was considerable chafing at delay during Hayne's mission and criticism of what was called a peace-at-any-price policy. There was a demand that no more commissioners be sent to Washington to be insulted. "It is believed," said an Abbeville correspondent of the *Mercury*, "that our rulers are taking counsel from pretended friends . . . in Washington. We believe these moderate politicians are our deadliest foes."[52] South Carolina, it was said, should not consent to go into a new union until she had herself driven Anderson out.[53] And there were those who believed that a little bloodshed was desirable as a means of consolidating the South and ending all thought of compromise.[54] The *Mercury* was especially insistent that the hated flag of the United States should no longer be allowed to "wave in insolent defiance" in

[50] *Exec. Doc.* No. 2, pp. 36-42; Crawford, *Fort Sumter*, pp. 228-234; *Buchanan's Administration*, pp. 200-205.
[51] *Convention Journal*, pp. 63-66, 82, 90, 110-111, 115, etc.
[52] January 26, 1861.
[53] "Moultrie" in *Mercury*, January 21, 1861.
[54] *Ibid.*, January 18, February 2, 1861; J. H. Hammond to M. C. M. Hammond, February 3, 1861, Hammond Papers.

the harbor of an independent nation.[55] There was severe criticism, too, of the policy of allowing Anderson to receive regularly mail and provisions from the city.[56]

Contrary to the pressure on Pickens from radical South Carolinians was the insistence from other Southern states and from South Carolina conservatives that Sumter should not be attacked. The conservative South Carolina view was expressed by Alfred Huger in a letter to Miles about the time Hayne was consenting to delay in Washington. He appealed to Miles to use his influence in arresting the "madness" of "lavishing Human life upon the unprofitable result" of storming the fort.

Are we not progressing with every breath we inhale? Are we not looking beyond our limits for the triumphant Sympathy which will seal our success? Shall we fly in the face of every feeling that is now favorably manifested to our country and cause? . . . Is not the refusal on the part of Major Anderson to receive reenforcements binding upon us not to molest *him* and his handful of men? Should he not be considered as an object of our care instead of assault? . . . Should not Florida, Alabama, Mississippi & Georgia be consulted before we take a step that will turn mankind against us? And can we not wait until Col. Hayne & Mr. Gourdin shall return? I implore you to raise your voice for the honor & integrity of South Carolina! I do not think of her "safety" tho the consequences would necessarily be fearful, but I do speak for her unsullied name & for her untarnished truth. . . . I am ready to sacrifice anything for the State but her own character and that belongs to posterity.[57]

Voices like Huger's were not very numerous in South Carolina but from outside of the state came many requests for cautious policy. January 13 and 20 Jefferson Davis, a strong candidate for the presidency of the yet unorganized Confederacy, suggested that the presence of Anderson in the harbor touched mainly on a point of pride, and that an attack should be delayed at least a month for both civil and military preparation, after which the South could speak with a voice that all must heed. Delay, he argued, tended to a peaceful solution of all difficulties. Governor Brown of Georgia advised delay until Buchanan was out of office. He believed that an earlier attack would alienate Northern Democrats

[55] *Mercury,* January 16-19, 31, 1861; *Conservatist,* January 26, 1861.

[56] *Mercury,* January 19, 1861. Mail had been withheld from Anderson immediately after his removal from Fort Moultrie but January 9 Pickens issued a permit for its delivery. Crawford, *Fort Sumter,* p. 191. January 13-15 an arrangement was made by which mail was delivered to Fort Johnston by the state and there called for by a boat from Fort Sumter. January 14, Postmaster General Holt wrote Pickens protesting against any interference and threatening to discontinue the Charleston postoffice. Pickens replied through Magrath that mail service to Anderson had been interrupted only when South Carolina felt justified in believing that coercion was about to be attempted. Citing the arrangement already made, he held it was unwise to allow visits from Sumter to the city. Holt's threat, he added, was not worthy of consideration and South Carolina would not in the least be affected by it. *Exec. Doc.* No. 3, pp. 1-12. For the arrangement in regard to provisions, see below, pp. 123-125.

[57] Alfred Huger to W. P. Miles, January 17, 1861, Miles Papers.

who would otherwise stand with the South against Lincoln.[58] Virginia likewise appealed to South Carolina to maintain the *status quo* and urged South Carolina's attendance at her peace conference.[59] The termination of the Hayne mission to Washington further stimulated outside efforts to check rash action in South Carolina. It was feared and rumored that South Carolina would attack at once. John Tyler, of Virginia, sent a number of urgent telegrams during February begging that it not be done.[60] Toombs on February 9 also urged that no attack be made "without the sanction and jurisdiction of our joint Government."[61]

This advice from outside South Carolina must have appealed to the good sense and judgment of Governor Pickens. Essentially conservative, he was anxious to obtain Fort Sumter by peaceful means. Moreover the state was not prepared to enforce a demand for surrender. On the other hand, his personal prestige, which he was anxious to improve, required at least the appearance of a bold and courageous policy. Moreover, he feared a reaction if some step were not taken. Under these circumstances he hesitated between independent South Carolina action and delay until the Confederacy could assume responsibility. He wired Miles February 7:

There is danger ahead unless you give us immediately a strong organized government to take jurisdiction of all military defense. We will soon be forced into a war of sections. Unless you act quickly it will be too late and reaction will commence which will inaugurate confusion & with it the most fatal consequences.[62]

In a communication to Tyler February 9, he said that if the provisional government would "assume the direction of this State in reference to Fort Sumter" her course might be controlled by such direction.[63] To Toombs he wrote that if Congress would by "any public or specific declaration, indicate jurisdiction, either by request or otherwise," he could not hesitate to "abide most cheerfully" by it unless some hostile act required immediate action by South Carolina.[64] On the other hand,

[58] Crawford, *Fort Sumter*, pp. 263-266.
[59] South Carolina's reply to the Virginia proposal was an emphatic refusal to have anything to do with the conference. Resolutions of the legislature stated it was not deemed advisable to coöperate when there was not the slightest desire or intention to promote the object in view; that the separation of the state was final; that South Carolina had no confidence in the pledges of the United States and no interest in its Constitution. *House Journal* (1860), pp. 435-440; *Senate Journal* (1860), pp. 261-262.
[60] *O. R.*, 1st series, I, 253-254, 257; Crawford, *Fort Sumter*, pp. 246-247.
[61] *Ibid.*, p. 266.
[62] Pickens to Miles, February 7, 1861, Miles Papers. The plea was renewed in a telegram of February 8.
[63] Crawford, *Fort Sumter*, pp. 247, 267. On the 7th he wired Tyler that South Carolina would wait as long as was consistent with her rights but no decision could be made until Buchanan's intentions were more fully known. F. W. Pickens to John Tyler, February 7, 1861, Pickens Papers.
[64] Crawford, *Fort Sumter*, p. 267.

when Howell Cobb as president of the Montgomery Congress wired that Congress had by resolution on February 12 assumed control, Pickens replied that South Carolina would not stand idle if action was not immediately taken by Confederate authorities. It had been his "constant, anxious desire" to obtain possession of the forts peaceably, he said, but attempts to negotiate had in every case been met by "positive and unqualified" refusal. South Carolina was convinced that occupation of Sumter was a denial of her independence and thought it necessary and proper for the state to take the fort as soon as preparations were completed, which would be soon. He argued that the best chance of peace lay in an immediate attack, because Lincoln if faced with a *fait accompli* might be more reluctant to declare war than if faced with a "present hostility."[65]

The course of Pickens in this period seems to have been one of reluctance to assume the responsibility of an attack, but by threatening independent action on the part of South Carolina to force the Confederate authorities to meet the demand for possession of Fort Sumter at once. Rumors were abroad that South Carolina was determined to attack without regard to the advice or order of the Montgomery government, and Pickens did little to allay them. When President Davis forwarded resolutions of Congress that the fort should be taken either by negotiations or force at the earliest possible time and that the President be authorized to make the necessary preparations, Pickens replied February 27 that honor and safety required immediate action, that South Carolina was continuing preparations, and that he wished to know if he should proceed when ready or await the order of Davis.[66] About the same time he wired Secretary Memminger:

Received your telegram to-day. But am sure if you do not act immediately and appoint a commander-in-chief to take charge, it will be too late. Act quickly, now, or I shall be compelled to act. Send your Commissioners on to Washington now, right off, and telegraph me, or it will be beyond your control. Things look bad at Washington.[67]

Such was the condition of affairs when Secretary of War Walker notified Pickens March 1 that the Confederacy was taking charge of all military operations and that an officer was being sent to assume command. The Secretary stated that President Davis believed that the fort should be taken at once but not before preparations were complete.[68] On March 6 General Beauregard assumed command.[69] Governor Pickens no doubt breathed a sigh of relief.

[65] Howell Cobb to F. W. Pickens, February 12, 1861, *O. R.*, 1st series, I, 254; F. W. Pickens to Howell Cobb, February 13, 1861, *ibid.*, 254-257; Crawford, *Fort Sumter*, pp. 268-269.
[66] *O. R.*, 1st series, I, 258; Crawford, *Fort Sumter*, pp. 270-271.
[67] *Ibid.*, p. 248.   [68] *Ibid.*, p. 278; *O. R.*, 1st series, I, 258.
[69] Under orders of the Confederate War Department dated March 1, and of the South Carolina War Department dated March 3. *Ibid.*, p. 266. March 20 Beauregard's command was extended, at Pickens's request, over the whole coast from Georgetown to Beaufort. *Ibid.*, p. 277.

CHAPTER VIII

PREPARATIONS FOR WAR

At the time of secession South Carolina was unprepared for the hostilities which soon threatened. Her militia system, organized under a law passed in 1841, was in dire need of reorganization. The law itself was defective and even its meager provisions had not been properly enforced.

The law of 1841 divided the state into five military divisions, and provided for ten brigades and forty-six regiments under the governor as commander-in-chief with an adjutant and inspector general elected by the legislature. All white male citizens sixteen to sixty[1] were made liable to militia duty and those eighteen to forty-five might be called upon for three months' service anywhere within the state, and for two months' service beyond its borders. Companies were required to assemble at least quarterly for drill while regiments must be reviewed at least once a year by the brigade commander and his staff. Once in two years all officers of each brigade were required to encamp for five days' instruction. Men and officers were subject to fines for failure to perform specified duties or for resigning from a militia office, after having accepted it, before the expiration of the term. Company and regimental officers were popularly elected; brigadier generals were chosen by brigade officers and major generals by division officers.[2]

By 1860 this militia organization had become well-nigh worthless. Even volunteer or uniformed companies which were allowed by the law had developed in many cases into mere social clubs and the ordinary militia company was quite without prestige or *esprit de corps*. Without uniforms and frequently with only sticks for arms they feebly fulfilled the technical requirements of the law without contributing to the defensive strength of the state. Much of the inefficiency was due no doubt to officers whose main interest apparently was political advancement rather than military efficiency; at any rate "city companies frittered into social clubs and rural militia musters into picnics." Gossip and electioneering took the place of serious training.[3]

[1] Full exemptions included the lieutenant governor, ordinaries, clerks of court, sheriffs, masters, commissioners, registers in equity, secretary of state, surveyor general, comptroller general, treasurers. Exemption except in time of alarm was allowed members of legislature, clergy, doctors, most school teachers and students, and a few others.

[2] *Statutes at Large*, XI, 191, *et seq.*

[3] Wallace, *History of S. C.*, III, 148-149; Williams, *Columbia*, pp. 44-45; D. A. Dickert, *History of Kershaw's Brigade, with complete roll of companies, biographical sketches, incidents, anecdotes, etc.; with an introduction by Associate Justice Y. J. Pope* (Newberry, 1899), pp. 15-16, hereinafter cited Dickert, *Kershaw's*

Some efforts to improve the militia before 1860 had been made but without success. In 1858 a commission was appointed by the legislature to study the question and report at the next session. Three reports were submitted. The majority recommended a system under which all men under thirty would be trained in regular encampment by battalions and men over thirty exempted by paying a tax till the age of forty-five. The minority report suggested a modified Prussian system under which annual encampment would be required for three years after which one might either serve seven years additional or enter the reserve and pay a tax. A third report suggested a militia of eight regiments raised by volunteering, or if necessary by draft, and supported by a tax on all not volunteering.[4] Either of the three plans would no doubt have vastly improved the South Carolina military organization but nothing was done. The need for reorganization was, however, generally recognized. A committee of The 1860 Association headed by Gabriel Manigault, who had served on the legislative commission, made an independent study of the military condition of the state and printed a pamphlet of suggestions which emphasized the need for reform and pointed out the improvements made elsewhere in arms and tactics. "Taking these things into consideration," the committee wrote, "the people of the Southern States may be pronounced to be . . . unarmed; the militia, as at present organized, and armed, serving only to generate a false security in the midst of danger."[5] Governor Gist in his message of November 5 also called attention to the urgency of reform.[6]

The approach of secession caused some revival of enthusiasm among the volunteer companies and the organization of unofficial military associations in various parts of the state. One type of such organization grew out of the fear that abolitionist emissaries might take advantage of the unsettled condition of affairs and cause serious difficulties with the slave population since the patrol system in connection with the militia had dwindled to a farce. In many places therefore there were organized Committees of Safety or Committees of Vigilance, or both, for the purpose of discharging the duties of an active and efficient patrol.[7] In some places the Vigilance Committee arrested and examined

Brigade; *A Plan to Improve the Present Militia System of South Carolina Submitted at the Session of 1859, by a Portion of the Military Commission, appointed by the Legislature of 1858* (Columbia, 1859), pp. 3-4.

[4] *A Plan to Improve the Present Militia,* pp. 4-27; *Minority Report of the Commission appointed under the Resolution of the Legislature to examine the Militia System of the State and report Amendments thereon* (Columbia, 1859), pp. 3-25. See also *Minutes of the Military Commission at the Meeting in Greenville, S. C., August 4, 1859* (Charleston, 1859).

[5] *Suggestions as to Arming the State,* pp. 5-8.

[6] *House Journal* (called session, 1860), pp. 10-11.

[7] The newspapers are full of notices of Vigilance Associations. *Mercury,* November 21, 1860; Spartanburg *Express,* October 10, 31, 1860; *Keowee Courier,* June 15, 1861; *Conservatist,* October 30, 1860; *Carolina Spartan,* February 7, May 9, 1861; see also Ravenel, Diary, October 22, 1860; Harriet Powe Lynch

the suspects and carried them before a smaller Committee of Safety for punishment.[8] These Vigilance Committees continued into the war period and in many cases meted out punishment to those regarded as public enemies or traitors. Tramps or persons of uncertain appearance, suspected of being "emissaries of John Brown," and natives whose loyalty to the state was questioned were roughly handled, sometimes no doubt unjustly.[9] After the war began there was good chance of almost any outsider being treated as a spy. The most conspicuous case of this kind was that of William Henry Hurlbert, native of Charleston and later editor-in-chief of the New York *World*, who on a visit to his sister in Charleston June 15-18, 1861, was threatened by the Vigilance Association and persuaded by his kinsmen to leave. Feeling against him was so inflamed that during his later imprisonment in Richmond telegrams were sent from Charleston urging that he be returned to that place for punishment.[10]

There were many other cases of threatened or actual violence. For example, at Camden a music master by the name of Devine was tried as a "traitor and spy," narrowly escaped lynching, and was deported beyond Confederate lines.[11] In Anderson a resident dentist was given twenty stripes and driven out.[12] Two men by the name of Hitchings were deported from Bennettsville.[13] A worker on the new State House in Columbia and a prominent business man of the same place were tarred, feathered, and driven from the city.[14] One Jack Couch, jailed by the Flat Shoals Vigilance Association, was seized, whipped, and deported, as was one Dorsey of Pickens and others.[15] The *Mercury* insisted that all foreigners, meaning citizens of the United States, should be arrested,[16] and the Vigilance Association announced that any persons going to a free state without a permit from the association would not be allowed to return.[17]

(ed.), *Reminiscenses & Sketches of Confederate Times, by one who lived through them* (Columbia, 1909, p. 23; hereinafter cited Powe, *Reminiscences.*

[8] E.g., in Barnwell and Bamberg. W. G. Simms and D. F. Jamison were members of the Barnwell committee. *Mercury*, November 21, 1860.

[9] Powe, *Reminiscences*, p. 23.

[10] While he was imprisoned in Richmond, J. L. Petigru wrote a letter in his behalf. Hurlbert was a half-brother of General Stephen A. Hurlbut of the Northern Army. *O. R.*, serial no. 115, pp. 1490 *et seq.; Courier*, September 8, 1862 quoting New York *Tribune; D. A. B.*, IX, 424.

[11] *Carolina Spartan*, June 20, 1861 quoting Camden *Journal; Mercury*, June 21, 1861; Chesnut, *Diary*, p. 60.

[12] *Mercury*, April 2, 1861.

[13] *Conservatist*, October 30, 1860.

[14] Williams, *Columbia*, p. 103; Julian A. Selby, *Memorabilia and Anecdotal Reminiscences of Columbia, S. C., and incidents connected therewith* (Columbia, 1905), p. 131; hereinafter cited Selby, *Memorabilia.*

[15] *Keowee Courier*, April 27, June 15, 1861.

[16] June 4, 1861. The New York *Times* correspondent, "Jasper," had been arrested April 12. *Mercury*, April 13, 1861.

[17] *Mercury*, August 9, 1861.

Besides the Vigilance Associations there was formed also in the months immediately preceding secession a widespread organization of Minute Men whose purpose was partly the maintenance of order, but which also looked to military service in case of the outbreak of war. Leaders from different parts of the state met in Columbia October 3, perfected a statewide organization, and adopted an official badge consisting of a blue rosette about two and one-half inches in diameter with a military button in the center, to be worn on the side of a cocked hat. Thereafter the Minute Men companies spread rapidly over the state and through their drills, parades, torchlight processions, and general activity were an important factor in arousing and maintaining secession sentiment. But while contributing greatly to the popular excitement, the Minute Men were of little military importance since they received little serious training and few companies ever entered the service of the state.[18]

When the legislature met in special session November 5, 1860, some volunteer companies were drilling and many Minute Men were parading but little had been done to improve the military condition of the state. The necessity of preparation was realized, however, and preliminary steps were taken looking to the creation of an armed force. A proposal to float $400,000 of bonds immediately did not pass because of lack of time,[19] but Governor Gist was authorized to draw at once on the $100,000 appropriated by the legislature of 1859,[20] and he was made a member of an Ordnance Board whose duty it should be to purchase and safeguard war equipment and to make a survey through a competent engineer of necessary coast defense.[21] The House and Senate military committees were directed to sit during the recess and report a bill on the first day of the regular session; likewise the finance and the ways and means committees were to prepare a bill for financing the military establishment.[22]

These efforts were resumed in the regular session, and on the day the convention assembled, December 17, the legislature passed a bill providing for an armed military force by engrafting a volunteer system on the existing militia. It authorized and directed the governor to call at once for twelve months one volunteer company of infantry from each

[18] Cf. Convention Journal, p. 520 which states that a large part of Gregg's first regiment were Minute Men; Williams, Columbia, p. 97. Contemporary newspapers are full of the doings of the Minute Men; e.g., Spartanburg Express, October 10, 17, December 5, 1860; Conservatist, October 16 et seq., 1860; Southern Enterprise, November 1, 1860; Mercury, November 21, 1860; see also Ravenel, Diary, October 22, 27, December 1, 1860; Merritt, Hammond, p. 138 and note; G. D. Tillman to J. H. Hammond, October 9, 1860, Hammond Papers. Miss I. D. Martin tells of a company of "Minute Girls" at Columbia Female College. The State, December 18, 1910.
[19] Senate Journal (called session, 1860), pp. 17-18.
[20] House Journal (called session, 1860), pp. 14, 30.
[21] Statutes at Large, XII, 732-734.
[22] Senate Journal (called session, 1860), p. 26.

infantry battalion of the militia and two rifle companies from each infantry brigade, and to resort to draft in any battalion not furnishing its quota within thirty days. He was authorized to receive any volunteer organization when offered as a unit with its full complement of officers and men; one or more cavalry companies from each cavalry regiment in the state; a regiment of artillery from Charleston, and one company of artillery each from Columbia, Georgetown, and Beaufort. All of these forces were to be armed and equipped by the state and organized into battalions, regiments, brigades, and a division under the command of a major general. Election of officers was allowed up to and including colonels of regiments but brigade commanders and the major general were to be appointed by the governor. Any or all of these forces might be called into service at the discretion of the governor for a period not exceeding twelve months. This law was designed to raise about ten thousand men.[23]

A few days after the passage of this law and before it could be put into operation, Major Anderson took Fort Sumter. The immediate need for troops to supplement or relieve the local militia used by Pickens in occupying the remaining forts was realized. The convention therefore on January 1 authorized the governor to enlist, if he desired, such volunteer companies as might tender their services for six months[24] and also to accept existing volunteer companies attached to the regular militia to serve until superseded by the force provided for under the legislative act of December 17.[25] On the day before the arrival of the *Star of the West* Pickens informed the convention that under this authority he had raised a regiment of six months volunteers; he asked confirmation of Maxcy Gregg for colonel, A. H. Gladden for lieutenant colonel, and D. H. Hamilton for major. There thus came into being the 1st (Gregg's)[26] regiment of South Carolina Volunteers. The first two companies reached Charleston January 3, and by February 1 the whole regiment had assembled for the generally understood purpose of taking Fort Sumter.[27]

Besides these volunteers the convention at Pickens's request auth-

[23] *Statutes at Large,* XII, 726-730.

[24] The governor was authorized to appoint field officers with the consent of the Senate.

[25] Officers were to be elected.

[26] There were two regiments designated 1st S. C. Volunteers: Gregg's under the convention resolution of January 1, and Hagood's under the legislature's act of December 17.

[27] A. S. Salley, Jr. (ed), *South Carolina Troops in Confederate Service* (Columbia, 1913-1930), I, 211-212; hereinafter cited Salley, *S. C. Troops; Convention Journal*, pp. 150-151; J. P. Thomas, "The Raising of Troops in South Carolina for State and Confederate Service," *Reports and Resolutions*, 1900, I, 1, 11. This article by Thomas is his third annual report as historian of Confederate records and is built on *Rivers Account of the Raising of Troops in South Carolina for State and Confederate Service, 1861-1865* (Columbia, 1899); hereinafter cited Thomas, *Raising of Troops.*

orized by resolution of December 31 the formation of one, and if necessary two, regiments of 640 regular army troops for twelve months, with company and field officers appointed by the governor with the consent of the Senate.[28] Pickens proceeded under this resolution at once, sending to the Senate, January 19, nominations for the regiment of regulars first commanded by Colonel Richard H. Anderson.[29] Authority for a regular military establishment was somewhat extended by the legislature January 28. Under this act men were to be enlisted for three years to form one regiment of infantry, one battalion of artillery, and one squadron of cavalry.[30] Pickens appointed R. S. Ripley lieutenant colonel of the artillery battalion. It was afterwards increased to a regiment and, practically, the infantry regiment was converted into artillery. Both regiments served in the forts and harbor of Charleston until the end of the war.[31]

It was under these legislative acts of December 17 and January 28 and these convention resolutions of December 31 and January 1 that South Carolina provided the first troops for the war which now so clearly threatened. In the enthusiasm of these first days of independence no difficulty was encountered in raising the comparatively small army for which South Carolina called. Under the act of of December 17, Governor Pickens appointed M. L. Bonham major general in command of the Volunteer Forces of South Carolina and four brigadiers, P. H. Nelson, T. G. Rhett, Samuel McGowan, and A. C. Garlington. On March 6 Adjutant and Inspector General S. R. Gist reported that 104 companies aggregating 8,835 rank and file had been enlisted and organized into ten regiments, four brigades, and one division.[32] Gregg's regiment of six months volunteers numbered 1,059 on March 25 and at the same time the regulars under Brigadier General R. G. M. Dunovant numbered 960. Of these forces 3,027 men were in and about Charleston at the service of General Beauregard.[33]

In the fall of 1860 South Carolina was no better supplied with arms and ammunition than with trained men. An elaborate report by The 1860 Association indicates that there were only 17,000 pounds of pow-

[28] The resolution also authorized Pickens to appoint three or more officers to organize a corps of engineers. A corps of engineers was also authorized by the legislature, January 26. It was to include one major, two captains, four first lieutenants, and ten sergeants, with a bureau in Charleston. *Statutes at Large,* XII, 745.

[29] *Convention Journal,* pp. 123, 137, 140-142; Salley, *S. C. Troops,* I, 1-3.

[30] *Statutes at Large,* XII, 730-732.

[31] Evans, *Confederate Military History,* V, 13.

[32] *O. R.,* Serial no. 126, p. 689.

[33] These first regiments were commanded as follows: first, Maxcy Gregg, and first, Johnson Hagood (see note 26) ; second, J. B. Kershaw; third, J. H. Williams; fourth, J. B. E. Sloan; fifth, Micah Jenkins; sixth, J. H. Rion; seventh, T. G. Bacon; eighth, E. B. Cash; ninth, J. D. Blanding; tenth, A. M. Manigault. The report of Secretary of War Jamison, March 25, 1861, *Convention Journal,* pp. 520-521, describes in detail the location of these forces.

der (chiefly cannon) in the state and only 1,000 shot and shell. Of small arms there were 311 serviceable rifled muskets lately received from the United States and 5,252 muskets, 321 rifles and 457 pistols of old pattern but in good order. This was the total supply of small arms except for 636 percussion muskets at the Citadel. The state had purchased forty-nine pieces of heavy ordnance in 1851-1852, and had fifty pieces of older date and also about sixty field guns.[34] The most serious deficiency was in small arms and powder. At the time of the *Star of the West* incident (January 9) the powder on hand was only enough, according to Secretary of War Jamison, to have kept up fire for three hours.[35]

This deficiency in the implements of war was partially remedied between secession and the outbreak of war in April, 1861. A report of Secretary of War Jamison March 25 showed on hand 240,450 pounds of cannon and 86,900 pounds of rifle and musket powder.[36] Most of this had been acquired by Pickens who purchased in December and January some 300,000 pounds from Hazard's Mills in Connecticut.[37] The urgent need for small arms was relieved when the United States arsenal was seized December 29 with over 22,000 rifles and pistols.[38] Soon thereafter the state purchased 650 Enfields which made the total supply in March more than 28,000.[39]

By seizure and purchase the state also largely increased its supply of heavy ordnance and ordnance supplies. Castle Pinckney's armament when taken December 27 was practically complete, and Anderson had perforce left at Fort Moultrie much that he could not destroy, including sixteen twenty-four-pounders, nineteen thirty-two-pounders, ten eight-inch columbiads, one ten-inch seacoast mortar, four six-pounders, two twelve-pounders, and four twenty-four-pounder howitzers. The arsenal contributed additional heavy ordnance and military stores in general.[40]

[34] *Suggestions as to Arming the State*, pp. 9-12. The 1860 Association made a detailed report of what was urgently needed to equip 87 companies of infantry, 9 companies of artillery, and 20 troops of cavalry. The estimated cost was $384,510. *Ibid.*

[35] *Convention Journal*, p. 519.

[36] *Ibid.* An additional supply was contracted for in August and arrived April 10. Crawford, *Fort Sumter*, p. 422.

[37] *O. R.*, 1st series, VI, 268-269. 2500 pounds of defective powder was obtained from Richmond. *Convention Journal*, p. 519.

[38] *O. R.*, 1st series, I, 130. For an unsuccessful attempt of Governor Gist to purchase through his agent Thomas F. Drayton 10,000 obsolete flint rifles from the War Department with a view to rifling and changing them to percussion muskets, see Nicolay and Hay, *Lincoln*, II, 319-324, and *Buchanan's Administration*, p. 227. Gist also attempted to have South Carolina's 1861 quota of arms advanced at the end of 1860; 646 rifled muskets had been obtained in 1860. *O. R.*, serial no. 122, pp. 5, 28.

[39] The number on hand after seizing those in the arsenal was 27,407. *Report of the Chief of the Department of the Military of South Carolina to His Excellency Governor Pickens* (Columbia, 1862), p. 53, hereinafter cited *Report Chief of Military.* Compare Gist's statement that there were 32,000 small arms in the state, including the arsenal, when his term expired. *Convention Journal*, p. 715.

[40] Evans, *Confederate Military History*, V, 10.

Among the purchases of the state were three nine-inch Dalgren guns and seven ten-inch mortars.[41]

In these early days of preparation individual citizens showed their enthusiasm for the cause through voluntary contributions of money and services.[42] The largest donation was that of Benjamin Mordecai of Charleston for $10,000, but there were numerous others ranging from $5.00 to $2,000. While the total thus received by the state amounted to only $22,275 by March 25,[43] the gifts are good indications of the patriotic fervor which was so characteristic of South Carolina citizens in the period immediately following secession. In addition to cash there were offers of various services. Planters freely offered the labor of their slaves for work in the fortifications, and free Negroes of Charleston, Columbia, and elsewhere tendered their services for this and other tasks. They were in many cases accepted.[44] A most acceptable and effective gift was that of Charles K. Prioleau of the Liverpool branch of John Fraser and Company who shipped in time for use against Fort Sumter an up-to-date rifled cannon inscribed, "Presented to the State of South Carolina by a citizen resident abroad, in commemoration of the 20th December, 1860."[45]

Meanwhile South Carolina continued the preparations necessary for an attack on Fort Sumter. Magrath thought it fortunate that the Hayne mission to Washington had been prolonged by the intervention of the Southern senators. It caused "a delay of great consequence to the State in the preparations of its defenses."[46] At that time South Carolina was utterly unprepared for any formidable naval or military expedition sent in relief of Anderson, and unable to enforce a demand for the evacuation of Fort Sumter. This situation was forcibly described by Brigadier General James Simons in a letter to Pickens January 1 in which he urged the governor to refrain from rashly precipitating hostilities while the state was so impotent, and in which he made some unwelcome suggestions to the governor for organizing defense.[47] By January 5 not a gun had been placed to bear on the fort, and approaches to the harbor were defended by only a few guns in Fort Moultrie and a few on the imperfect earth work on Morris Island. Fort Moultrie, it was said, was tenable for not more than one hour and its

[41] *Convention Journal*, p. 519.
[42] These gifts were acknowledged in the newspapers, e.g., *Mercury*, January 3, 14, 18, 22, 25, 28, 30, February 7, 10, 27, 1861.
[43] *Convention Journal*, p. 526. The amount donated by November was $24,375. *Report of Wilmot G. DeSaussure, Secretary of the Treasury, to His Excellency the Governor* (Charleston, 1861), pp. 1-4.
[44] Pickens message November 5, 1861, *Senate Journal* (1861), pp. 10-25. The *Mercury* of September 5, 1861, reported a donation of $450 from the free Negroes of the city.
[45] Crawford, *Fort Sumter*, p. 397.
[46] Report of Secretary of State Magrath, March 24, 1861, in *Mercury*, April 6, 1861.
[47] Nicolay and Hay, *Lincoln*, III, 118-121.

abandonment was seriously urged by some.[48]   After the *Star of the West* episode, however, when Pickens requested a group of military men to consider and report the most practicable plan for reducing the fort, there was much activity.   In accordance with the plan proposed, batteries on the islands surrounding the fort were strengthened and increased for the purpose of bombarding the fort and making assault easy; guns were placed to command the channel entrances and thus close the harbor.   Four hulks were sunk across the mouth of the harbor on January 11.   Lighthouses and buoys were removed and guard boats stationed at the bar to warn off hostile vessels.   Fort Moultrie was put in order and a number of additional works begun on Sullivan's Island.   The *Star of the West* Battery on Morris Island was greatly strengthened and that at Cummings Point rapidly constructed.   Guns were added at Fort Johnson.   On January 18 construction of a "floating battery" was ordered and the work was immediately begun.   Negroes were worked on the fortifications day and night seven days a week. The harbor was the scene of much activity as vessels carrying troops, munitions, and materials of war distributed them to various points. "Enthusiasm and unanimity of purpose . . . largely compensated for many deficiencies" in experience and materials from which the state suffered in this early period.   On February 12 Governor Pickens wrote Toombs he hoped "to be ready by Friday night" at which time he would be prepared "to take the fort or to silence it."[49]

It would seem that any serious attempt to reinforce Major Anderson would have succeeded at any time up to at least the middle of February. An expedition was being prepared at the time to be sent under Commander Ward of the Navy, but President Buchanan, influenced by the appeals of Virginia and anticipating March 4, decided that it should not be dispatched.   His administration came to an end two days before General Beauregard assumed command in Charleston and began to remedy what were regarded as serious defects in the defenses prepared by South Carolina.   Writing Secretary of War Walker, March 8, he reported that he needed ten days for the construction of essential works.[50]   He was to be afforded more than a month by the indecision of the new administration at Washington.

[48] Report of Secretary of War Jamison, *Convention Journal*, p. 519.
[49] Crawford, *Fort Sumter*, pp. 200-201, 207-211, 267-269.
[50] *Ibid.*, pp. 248-250, 277-278, 306.

CHAPTER IX

THE WAR BEGINS

If South Carolina entertained any hope that the new administration would adopt a conciliatory policy on the question of the forts, it was dispelled by the inaugural address. The President's announcement that he would "hold, occupy, and possess the property and places belonging to the Government" was a specific denial of any intention to evacuate Fort Sumter. His expressed determination to collect duties in the ports of the Confederacy was a denial in practical terms of the right of secession and meant the use of force, if necessary, to preserve the Union. However conciliatory or contradictory the address might have seemed to other readers, to South Carolina it was an announcement of a policy of coercion. As L. T. Wigfall put it in a telegram to Pickens, "Inaugural means war."[1] Only two courses were left the South, said the *Mercury:* an immediate attack on Fort Sumter or a siege for the purpose of starving out the garrison.[2] Almost immediately, however, hope for a peaceful settlement was revived by the failure of the Lincoln administration to adopt the strong measures which the inaugural had seemed to promise.

In the tangled history of the Lincoln administration during the weeks preceding the attack on Fort Sumter there are many points of difficulty for the historian both as to fact and interpretation. The evidence in many places is either so conflicting or incomplete that ample ground is provided for honest difference of conclusion. It is not within the scope of the present narrative to consider in detail the forts policy of President Lincoln, a problem which has received the attention of many competent historians and on which controversy still exists. But its close connection with South Carolina history of the period requires some reference to it. Amidst much that is uncertain two facts seem reasonably clear. The first of these is that after much hesitation in the first days of the new administration a decision was reached for the evacuation of Fort Sumter. The second is that this decision, for reasons not so clear, was toward the end of March reversed, a reversal which led to the dispatch of a relief expedition which precipitated a demand for the surrender of the fort and an attack upon it when the demand was rejected. Behind and beneath these facts were circumstances and forces which somewhat becloud the question of how and on whose immediate responsibility the quarrel between the sections developed into the war of 1861-1865.

[1] *O. R.,* 1st series, I, 261.
[2] March 5, 1861.

The evidence that a decision had been reached to evacuate Fort Sumter seemed overwhelming to South Carolina at the time. Reports of it came from many sources. First, on March 11 the *National Republican* stated definitely that such a decision had been reached two days before.[3] By telegraph the news came to Charleston the same day and caused general rejoicing. One hundred and fifty guns were fired by the harbor batteries in celebration and military activities were noticeably slackened.[4] The only discordant note in the chorus of satisfaction was the fear expressed by the *Mercury* that evacuation might encourage some in the South to consider favorably possible proposals for a reconstruction of the old Union.[5]

The news of March 11 may have been premature but it was soon semi-officially confirmed through the Confederate commissioners, John Forsyth, Martin J. Crawford, and A. B. Roman who had recently arrived in Washington authorized to negotiate a peaceful settlement with the United States. Finding Seward at the head of a party which believed that by avoiding a collision at Fort Sumter the border states and ultimately the seceded states could be saved for the Union, the commissioners decided that the policy of delay, if accompanied by an understanding for the maintenance of the *status quo,* would really profit the Confederacy and should therefore be supported. Learning through R. M. T. Hunter that Seward would be embarrassed by a demand for formal recognition, the commissioners tried to arrange through Hunter an informal interview in which they would agree to postpone their demands for a period of not more than twenty days on the condition that a pledge be given that no reinforcement would be attempted within that time. Their memorandum to this effect was submitted to Seward by Hunter on March 11, but with disappointing results, for Seward on the 12th after consulting the President informed Hunter that he would not be able to see the commissioners. They, therefore, on March 13, sent a note to Seward in which they stated the purpose of their mission and requested that they be received as formal delegates. The Secretary did not at once reply but in a memorandum for the files of the State Department refused the request.[6]

Before the commissioners pressed for a reply to their note, however, the negotiation was extended by the appearance in the affair of Supreme Court Justices John A. Campbell of Alabama and Samuel Nelson of New York. The justices were opposed to coercion on both legal and practical grounds and Justice Nelson presented his arguments in an interview with Seward, Chase, and Bates March 15. Seward was

[3] Rhodes, *History of U. S.,* III, 219. Nicolay and Hay, *Lincoln,* III, 400, say the rumors were purposely spread to prepare the public mind for possible evacuation.
[4] *O. R.,* 1st series, I, 195-196.
[5] *Mercury,* March 12, 1861.
[6] Crawford, *Fort Sumter,* pp. 314-325; Rhodes, *History of U. S.,* III, 215-216.

pleased but indicated that he was embarrassed by the commissioners' demands. Nelson then brought Campbell into a consultation with the Secretary and urged Seward to reply to the commissioners' note and, without extending recognition, assure them that the policy of the government was a peaceful one. To which Seward replied:

I wish I could do it. See Montgomery Blair, see Mr. Bates, see Mr. Lincoln himself; I wish you would: they are all Southern men. Convince them! No; there is not a member of the cabinet who would consent to it. If Jefferson Davis had known the state of things here he would not have sent those commissioners; the evacuation of Sumter is as much as the administration can bear.[7]

Campbell, quite pleased at this announcement of an intention to abandon the fort, got the permission of Seward to pass the information along to the commissioners and to Jefferson Davis himself. "You may say to him," said Seward, "that before that letter reaches him the telegraph will have informed him that Sumter will have been evacuated."[8] Justice Campbell on the same day convinced Commissioner Crawford that the information was authentic. In return for a memorandum in which Justice Campbell stated his confidence that evacuation would take place in five days and that in the meantime no changes would be made in the military status, he received Crawford's consent not to press for a reply to the commissioner's note of March 13. When at the end of five days Sumter had not been evacuated, the justices, pressed by the commissioners, interviewed Seward and received such satisfactory assurances that Campbell on March 21 wrote the commissioners that his confidence was "unabated." On the following day Seward, after seing Lincoln, approved a memorandum drawn by Campbell in which the latter again assured the commissioners that the delay was no cause for apprehension or distrust; Sumter would be evacuated. Further assurance came to the commissioners through the Russian minister whose impressions were based on an interview with Seward March 24.[9]

However slippery Seward's later dealings with the commissioners may have been, it is probable that in the middle of March he was correctly reflecting the administration policy. Rumors of evacuation from other high official circles were common. The *Courier,* for example, quoted General Scott to the effect that evacuation was certain.[10] Similar reports appeared in other papers of the country almost daily.[11] Certain it is that the cabinet was almost unanimous for giving up the fort. In written opinions submitted to Lincoln March 15 only Postmaster General Montgomery Blair was unequivocably opposed to

[7] *Ibid.,* III, 216-217; see also Crawford, *Fort Sumter,* pp. 325-328.
[8] Rhodes, *History of U. S.,* III, 218.
[9] *Ibid.;* Crawford, *Fort Sumter,* pp. 329-334.
[10] March 18, 1861.
[11] Charles W. Ramsdell, "Lincoln and Fort Sumter," *Journal of Southern History,* III (August, 1937), p. 267.

evacuation. Lincoln on the same day informed Francis P. Blair that abandonment of the fort would probably be the outcome.[12]

The trend in Washington was well known in South Carolina, the assurances given by Seward to the justices being passed on to Pickens by the commissioners. Forsyth wired on the 15th that he believed that a messenger had already left Washington with evacuation orders. On the 22nd he again telegraphed that the fort would be abandoned "if there is faith in man."[13] Even more convincing was the information obtained from Ward H. Lamon, an intimate friend of Lincoln, who sought and obtained an interview with Pickens on March 25. Representing himself as a confidential messenger of the President, Lamon told Pickens that he had come to make arrangements for the evacuation, and on a visit to the fort he gave Anderson the impression that his removal would soon be arranged. Lamon even discussed with Pickens the type of vessel to be used in the removal of Sumter's garrison, and immediately after his return to Washington he wrote Pickens that he would come again to Charleston in a few days to withdraw Anderson's command.[14]

Other evidence of an evacuation decision came to Pickens later in 1861 through John W. Lapsley of Selma, Alabama. According to Lapsley's story, there were visiting the White House in mid-March a sister and brother-in-law of Mrs. Lincoln from Cincinnati. Evacuation had been decided upon, a proclamation announcing it had been placed in type, and proofsheets sent to the White House; also proofsheets of another statement in the form of a newspaper release for use in editorial defense of the proclamation. The brother-in-law took a copy of each as souvenirs which ultimately through family connections came into Lapsley's possession and were forwarded to Pickens to be used for propaganda purposes at a point distant enough from Selma to preclude the probability of revealing the White House "thief."[15]

Lincoln's decision to abandon Fort Sumter must have been reached most reluctantly. Letters written before his inauguration indicate that he was opposed to evacuation and was even determined to retake the forts if at the time of inauguration they had been surrendered by Buchanan. To General Scott he sent a confidential message through E. B. Washburne, December 21, 1860, asking him to be prepared for

[12] Crawford, *Fort Sumter*, pp. 347-361, 364. The opinions of the cabinet members are in J. G. Nicolay and John Hay, *Abraham Lincoln; Complete Works* (New York, 1894), II, 11-22. For Chase's willingness to let the South "go in peace" see J. G. Randall, *Lincoln the President, Springfield to Gettysburg* (New York, 1945), I, 320-321.

[13] Pickens-Bonham Papers.

[14] Crawford, *Fort Sumter*, pp. 373-374; O. R., 1st series, I, 218, 221-222, 230, 237, 281-282, 294.

[15] J. W. Lapsley to F. W. Pickens, June 4, July 30, 1861; Lapsley to I. W. Hayne, July 20, 1861. F. W. Pickens Papers. Pickens used the information obtained from Lapsley for a "Secret History" later submitted to the legislature and published in the newspapers. *Mercury*, August 6, 1861.

such action.[16]   And to Senator Lyman Trumbull he wrote December 24 intimating that should Buchanan order evacuation of the forts, he as President-elect might publicly announce his intention to retake them.[17] The South at least was able to detect similar thinking as late as March 4 in the inaugural.   That a contrary decision was reached in so short a time was due to the complexity of the problem which Lincoln faced and his inability at first to find a more satisfactory solution.   Almost inevitably under the existing circumstances he acquiesced in the overwhelming opinion of his political and military advisors.

The problem facing Lincoln was difficult because time *as* a solution and *for* a solution was unexpectedly denied him.   A letter from Major Anderson dated February 28 and referred March 5 to the new administration by Buchanan's Secretary of War, stated that supplies in Fort Sumter were so dangerously short that, unless replenished, surrender would be necessary within a few weeks.[18]   Because the state of Anderson's supplies constitutes an important factor in the situation, a review of South Carolina's course in regard to allowing supplies to reach Anderson is appropriate.

Immediately after the transfer of Anderson's command to Fort Sumter Governor Pickens ordered that no further supplies be allowed to reach the fort.   At this time Anderson reported that he had a year's supply of hospital stores and about four months' supply of provisions, or enough provisions to carry him to about April 26.[19]   About five months' supply was the estimate he gave his Charleston friend, Robert N. Gourdin, about the same time.[20]   His letters in the days immediately following his transfer indicate that he felt perfectly secure, that he had the city of Charleston at his mercy, and that he could certainly hold out until he could be supplied or reinforced.   At this time reinforcement was still perfectly feasible and Anderson seemed to favor and expect it.[21]   By the end of January the situation had changed in two respects.   In the first place, the supply problem had somewhat improved as a result of Governor Pickens's offer of January 19 to send over to the fort a daily supply of fresh meat and vegetables, an offer inspired by the moderate counsel of Southern senators conveyed to Pickens by Hayne in his letter of

[16] John Shipley Tilley, *Lincoln Takes Command* (Chapel Hill, 1941), pp. 105-106; Nicolay and Hay, *Lincoln*, III, 250.

[17] Ramsdell, "Lincoln and Fort Sumter," *loc. cit.*, p. 267.   See also Kenneth M. Stamp, "Lincoln and the Strategy of Defense in the Crisis of 1861," *Journal of Southern History*, XI (August, 1945), 303-304.

[18] The letter has not been preserved but quotations from it and various references to it reveal its essential contents.   See *O. R.*, 1st series, I, 188-189, 191, 197, 202. For an unsuccessful effort to discredit the receipt of such a letter see Tilley, *Lincoln Takes Command*, pp. 306-312.

[19] *O. R.*, 1st series I, 2.

[20] Anderson to Gourdin, December 29, 1860, Crawford, *Fort Sumter*, pp. 128-130.

[21] *Ibid.*; *O. R.*, 1st series, I, 112-113, 114, 120.

January 16. In the second place, Anderson had changed his mind on the question of reinforcement.

Although Anderson refused to accept the proffered supplies as a courtesy, Pickens readily agreed to Anderson's suggestion that he be allowed to purchase "market supplies" from the regular contractor in Charleston. After a slight delay due to the failure of Anderson's order promptly to reach the contractor, the arrangement began to operate smoothly on January 31.[22] Although obviously not in immediate need of staple supplies Anderson raised a question with his friend Gourdin about the possibility of receiving groceries. Apparently at the moment he could find no sound basis of distinction between different classes of food. Neither, apparently, could Pickens when the matter was presented to him by Gourdin. He stated that he was anxious for Anderson to receive his supplies regularly and had no objection to groceries being sent. This information was passed on to Anderson by Gourdin in a letter of February 1.[23]

For some reason Anderson did not profit from the permission thus obtained. Did Pickens on second thought change his mind? Since the basis of the policy of allowing food to reach the fort was a desire to forestall a cry of "starving garrison" as justification for "coercion," it seems probable that South Carolina did not withdraw the permission. Perhaps Anderson hesitated to claim an authorization only indirectly obtained through Gourdin. Perhaps on second thought he found a distinction between foods and felt that some military propriety forbade receiving groceries from the enemy. Another possibility is that Anderson's changed view on the question of reinforcement has some connection with the problem. Apparently favoring and expecting reinforcement in early January, Anderson by the end of the month ventured, in a dispatch of January 30, to express the hope that no attempt to throw in supplies would be made.[24] He does not insist upon the point in subsequent letters due perhaps to a feeling that to have done so would have constituted unwarranted political advice. But his later dispatches report increasing difficulty of reinforcement, and reflect his growing anxiety over the national crisis and his earnest hope that a collision might be avoided. There can be no doubt that Anderson believed that evacuation was politically desirable, and since one of the best practical arguments for such a course was dwindling supplies, it is barely possible that he deliberately neglected the opportunity presented by Pickens of obtaining groceries from the city. And one can hardly suppress the opinion that each report of reduced supplies was meant by Anderson as an indirect appeal for an evacuation order. He made little effort to stretch his staple supplies over a longer period by reduction of daily

[22] *O. R.*, 1st series, I, 144-146, 151-154, 159-160. Cf. Crawford, *Fort Sumter*, pp. 201-203.
[23] *O. R.*, 1st series, I, 160, 162.   [24] *Ibid.*, p. 159.

rations. He did not minimize the difficulty of reinforcement; his report of February 28 expressed the opinion of himself and his fellow officers that it would require a force of 20,000 "good and well-disciplined" men. It was this report that confronted Lincoln on the second day of his administration. The force in Fort Sumter at that time was no "starving garrison." Conceivably men may live and even fight a long time on ample supplies of meat, butter, and vegetables such as Anderson was still receiving, especially if an initial several weeks' supply of staple items are on hand. However, the situation was serious because the ample supply of market supplies might be interrupted by South Carolina if Lincoln within a reasonable time did not give South Carolina possession of the fort.

Faced with Anderson's report of February 28, Lincoln consulted his military advisors. General Scott and Chief Engineer Totten agreed that evacuation seemed inevitable. They believed that reinforcement would require a fleet of vessels requiring four months to assemble and that six or eight months would be consumed in organizing the force stipulated by Anderson. Scott went so far as to submit a draft of an evacuation order. Even Captain Ward of the Navy, who had urged a reinforcement plan on Buchanan, now agreed that reinforcement was infeasible. A contrary view was expressed and defended by G. V. Fox, Assistant Secretary of the Navy, under the sponsorship of Postmaster General Blair, his brother-in-law. Fox believed that small vessels might successfully run the batteries at night and reach the fort with supplies. He defended the plan before the cabinet in the presence of the Army and is said to have convinced the President and some members of the cabinet that the plan was practicable.[25]

The problem, however, was not simply, or even primarily, military. Much more important were the political aspects of reinforcement. The Republican party was already showing signs of disintegration into its heterogeneous elements. An aggressive element in the party insisted on reinforcement which a party of conciliation opposed. The success of the administration and the future of the party were deeply involved. More important still was the question of the effect of reinforcement or evacuation on the fate of the Union. Evacuation might consolidate the "rebellion" and bring foreign recognition of the Confederacy. Reinforcement might alienate the moderate group, lead to secession of the border states, begin a bloody war which the administration could be blamed for initiating, and permanently disrupt the party and the Union.[26] It was on this political problem that Lincoln asked the advice of his cabinet March 15. The almost unanimous agreement that reinforcement was politically unwise seems to have brought a decision to evacuate, and justified Seward, at this stage, in his assurances to the Confederate commissioners.

[25] Nicolay and Hay, *Lincoln*, III, 378-385.
[26] Ramsdell, "Lincoln and Fort Sumter," *loc. cit.*, pp. 269-271.

Lincoln was, however, loathe to issue the evacuation order. Evacuation as the lesser of two evils was still an evil. As Lincoln later put it in his message of July 4, he believed "that the *necessity* under which it was to be done would not be fully understood; that by many it would be construed as a part of a *voluntary* policy; that at home it would discourage the friends of the Union, embolden its adversaries, and go far to insure to the latter a recognition abroad; that, in fact, it would be our national destruction consummated."[27] The President therefore delayed the order. For a little longer at least he could let matters drift while he sought a way out of his dilemma. He must have even considered a "do-nothing" policy under which Anderson would be left to surrender when his staples gave out and market supplies eventually forbidden. But abandonment of Anderson instead of the fort gave little promise of saving either the party or Union.[28]

How long Lincoln drifted cannot be determined. He may have been still fumbling for a solution of his problem when he sent G. V. Fox and Ward H. Lamon to Charleston at almost the same time on apparently quite contradictory errands. Fox was seeking information in support of his plan of reinforcement. Lamon, a few days later, claimed to be an advance agent of evacuation. Both were allowed to visit the fort with the understanding that their missions were pacific.[29] It is hard to reconcile the visits of Fox and Lamon. Perhaps Lincoln was still drifting. Perhaps, as Professor Ramsdell suggests, he had already conceived a plan by which the party and Union might be saved through a war the responsibility for which might be thrown upon the South.[30] At any rate while Lamon was assuring Pickens that evacuation was imminent, the administration was veering toward an opposite course. Although General Scott still advised evacuation, the cabinet when asked for opinions on March 29 was predominantly for reinforcement. On the same day the President directed the Secretaries of War and Navy to prepare an expedition which should be ready to sail by April 6.[31]

Meanwhile South Carolina continued impatiently to desire Fort Sumter, and Governor Pickens, seeing no move towards the fulfillment of Lamon's promises, sent a telegram to the commissioners on March 30 stating the facts of Lamon's visit and expressing his disappointment. The dispatch found its way immediately through Campbell and Seward to President Lincoln. On April 1 Seward reported to Campbell that "the President was concerned about the contents of the telegram—there

[27] Richardson, *Messages and Papers*, VII, p. 3222.

[28] Ramsdell, "Lincoln and Fort Sumter," *loc. cit.*, p. 271.

[29] Fox left the fort more convinced than ever of the feasibility of his plan but Anderson, who still favored evacuation, opposed it as impracticable and likely to begin war.

[30] Ramsdell, "Lincoln and Fort Sumter," *loc. cit.*, pp. 273-274.

[31] Rhodes, *History of U. S.*, III, pp. 221-222; *O. R.*, 1st series, I, 226; Randall, *Lincoln the President*, I, 332-333.

was a point of honor involved; that Lamon had no agency from him, nor title to speak, nor any power to pledge him by any promise or assurance." On the question of reinforcement Seward had two conferences on the same day with Campbell, sandwiching one with Lincoln. At the second he gave Campbell a paper saying, "I am satisfied the government will not undertake to supply Fort Sumter without giving notice to Governor Pickens." This was recognized as less direct than previous pledges, but Seward explained that it did not indicate an intention to reinforce and he convinced Campbell that all was well. Commissioner Crawford wired Seward's memorandum to Pickens on April 1; and added:

My opinion is that the President has not the courage to execute the order agreed upon in Cabinet for the evacuation of the fort, but that he intends to shift the responsibility upon Major Anderson by suffering him to be starved out. Would it not be well to aid in this by cutting off all supplies?

When this telegram was relayed to Montgomery the answer came back that Beauregard should be ready for action, since no trust could be placed in the Washington authorities, and that all communication between the fort and the city should be stopped.[32] Mail and provisions were, however, not yet denied Anderson. On April 4 Lincoln issued definite orders for the Fort Sumter expedition and notified Anderson of its coming. Charleston soon had the information. The widespread rumors caused by the unusual activity in the War and Navy Departments were confirmed on April 6 when South Carolina's Secretary of State Magrath was positively informed by his friend James E. Harvey, newly appointed minister to Portugal, who had the information from Seward.[33] Market supplies on the next day were denied Fort Sumter, leaving Anderson dependent, at last, on his all but exhausted staple supplies. But there were conflicting telegrams from Washington which led Pickens on the 7th to telegraph the commissioners for more light. On the same day Judge Campbell wrote Seward asking that rumors of reinforcement be confirmed or denied and received next day the reply, "Faith as to Sumter fully kept; wait and see. . . ."[34] The commissioners informed Pickens that they were assured no attack would be made on Sumter without notice and they thought that Fort Pickens in Florida would be supplied and Sumter evacuated. That evening (April 8), however, Robert S. Chew, a State Department clerk, read to Pickens and Beauregard the notice which President Lincoln had so carefully and skillfully prepared:

I am directed by the President of the United States to notify you to expect an attempt will be made to supply Fort Sumter with provisions only;

[32] Crawford, *Fort Sumter*, pp. 336-338, 391-393; Rhodes, *History of U. S.*, III, 223.
[33] Nicolay and Hay, *Lincoln*, IV, 31-32; *O. R.*, 1st series, I, 287-288.
[34] Crawford, *Fort Sumter*, pp. 340-341.

and that if such attempt be not resisted, no effort to throw in men, arms, or ammunition will be made without further notice, or in case of an attack upon the Fort.[35]

There is strong evidence to sustain the thesis that President Lincoln, by notifying Governor Pickens of his intention to send supplies, was shrewdly provoking the Confederates to attack Fort Sumter and precipitate the war which he believed was necessary to unite the North and preserve the Union. The evidence is well presented by Professor Ramsdell in his article, "Lincoln and Fort Sumter."[36] In its essentials the thesis is not new. Colored by bitter charges of double dealing and bad faith on the part of the Lincoln administration it was the interpretation set forth by Southern leaders at the time. It was officially proclaimed by Governor Pickens in a "Secret History" dated August 3 and published in the newspapers August 6, 1861. According to Pickens, Lincoln, after having signed an evacuation order, suddenly changed his mind and decided to wage a war of extermination and emancipation, and in order to arouse a war spirt in the North deliberately decided to sacrifice Anderson and Fort Sumter. In support of this view there was published the newspaper release obtained from Lapsley in which Lincoln had defended the evacuation order by saying that there were only two choices before him, namely, evacuation on the one hand, or the sacrifice of Anderson and certain war on the other. Not wanting war, Lincoln, according to the release, had sorrowfully signed the evacuation order. Later, said Pickens, Lincoln deliberately chose war, withdrew his evacuation order, and sent Fox under false pretenses to make arrangements for a "pretended" attempt to supply the fort, his real purpose being to let Anderson perish and thus fire the North to action.[37]

The same general view may be inferred from the account written by two men who were at the time in an excellent position to follow the mental processes of President Lincoln. In their extensive history of the period Nicolay and Hay inadvertently come near expressing what Pickens with very different emphasis and prejudice contended. Lincoln, say these biographers, "adopted a simple but effective policy." He determined to "send bread to Anderson" and "if the rebels fired on that, they would not be able to convince the world that he had begun civil war. . . . To this end he . . . ordered the relief expedition to sail, and sent open notice to Governor Pickens of its coming." They suggest that Lincoln probably did not expect the supplies ever to reach Fort Sumter. In spite of Fox's warning that delay had reduced the chances of success for his expedition, Lincoln nevertheless sent him on saying that "he should best fulfill his duty by making the attempt." Lincoln "foresaw the inevitable rebel attack and the response of an awakened

[35] O. R., 1st series, I, 291.
[36] The Journal of Southern History, III (August, 1937), pp. 259-88.
[37] Mercury, August 6, 1861.

and united North." "Whether the expedition would fail or succeed was a question of minor importance. . . . He was looking through Sumter to the loyal States; beyond the insulted flag to the avenging nation." "When he finally gave the order that the fleet should sail he was master of the situation; master of his Cabinet; master of the moral attitude and issues of the struggle; master of the public opinion which must arise out of the impending conflict; master if the rebels hesitated or repented . . . ; master if they persisted, for he would then command a united North." Lincoln was convinced that the United States was in the right. "But to make the issue sure, he determined that in addition the rebellion should be put in the wrong."[38]

Lincoln himself furnishes what is perhaps the most convincing support of the view that he shrewdly and deliberately maneuvered the South into "firing the first shot." After that shot had been fired and the North had rallied to the President, he wrote to Fox in consolation for his failure to reach Fort Sumter: "You and I both anticipated that the cause of the country would be advanced by making the attempt to provision Fort Sumter, even if it should fail, and it is no small consolation now to feel that our anticipation is justified by the result."[39] And a little later the close personal friend of Lincoln, Orville H. Browning, recorded in his diary Lincoln's private admission:

He told me that the very first thing placed in his hands after the inauguration was a letter from Majr Anderson announcing the impossibility of defending or relieving Sumter. That he called the cabinet together and consulted Genl Scott—that Scott concurred with Anderson, and the cabinet, with the exception of P M Genl Blair were for evaculating the Fort, and all the troubles and anxieties of his life had not equalled those which intervened between this time and the fall of Sumter. He himself conceived the idea, and proposed sending supplies, without an attempt to reinforce giving notice of the fact to Governor Pickens of S. C. The plan succeeded. They attacked Sumpter—it fell, and thus, did more service than it otherwise could.[40]

Whether Lincoln's motives were shrewdly and covertly belligerent, or, as has been cogently argued,[41] entirely pacific, the President's decision

[38] Nicolay and Hay, *Lincoln*, IV, 28, 33, 44-45, 62.

[39] Ramsdell, "Lincoln and Fort Sumter," *loc. cit.*, p. 285.

[40] Ramsdell, "Lincoln and Fort Sumter," *loc. cit.*, pp. 287-288, quoting *Diary of Orville H. Browning*, I, 476.

[41] For refutation of the Ramsdell thesis see David M. Potter, *Lincoln and his Party in the Secession Crisis* (New Haven, 1942), Kenneth M. Stamp, "Lincoln and the Strategy of Defense in the Crisis of 1861," *Journal of Southern History*, XI (August, 1945), 297-323, and Randall, *Lincoln the President*, I, 311-350. In his closely reasoned argument Randall holds that in spite of the preliminary order of March 29 and the more definite order of April 4, Lincoln did not finally commit himself to the Sumter expedition until April 6 when he learned that the earlier orders for reinforcement of Fort Pickens in Florida had not been carried out. Until this time Lincoln might still have been willing to evacuate Sumter if this action could be offset by a show of firmness at Pickens, but the failure at Pickens made it politically impossible for Lincoln to countermand orders for the Sumter expedition. Cf. Craven, *Coming of the Civil War*, pp. 437, 480.

in the face of existing sentiment at Charleston and Montgomery made war almost inevitable. The announcement of an intention to supply Fort Sumter was a signal for greatly increased excitement and activity in and about Charleston. Already on the 7th provisions had been cut off; now Anderson's mail was seized and read.[42] On the 10th orders came from Secretary Walker for Beauregard to demand evacuation of the fort and if refused to proceed to reduce it. The demand, Beauregard replied, would be made on the next day at noon.[43] April 9-11 was a period of great activity as final preparations were made for the attack. There were some 3,700 men about Charleston but Pickens announced that a call for 3,000 more of the twelve months troops would be met by the 10th.[44] Work was pushed on the fortifications; the harbor was alive with guard boats and transports hurrying from place to place and with shipping hastily getting out to sea. New guns were mounted on Morris Island for an expected attack there and buildings were removed on Sullivan's to unmask another battery there. The floating battery was towed into position at the north end of the island, well protected from Sumter's guns. Everywhere things were put in order.[45] "The gage is thrown down," said the *Mercury*, "and we accept the challenge. We will meet the invader, and the God of Battle must decide the issue between the hirelings of Abolition hate and Northern tyranny, and the people of South Carolina defending their freedom and their homes."[46]

The demand for surrender was sent Anderson shortly after noon April 11 through Colonel James Chesnut, Jr., and Captain Stephen D. Lee, aides of Beauregard. After consultation with his officers, Anderson formally refused but casually observed that he would be starved out within a few days unless in the meantime he were battered to pieces. The observation was regarded by Beauregard as of sufficient importance

[42] *Ibid.*, pp. 248, 250, 292. It is said that when the bag of mail was placed before the governor, his cabinet, and Beauregard, on April 9, there was some hesitation about opening the letters. Magrath refused, saying that as federal judge he had sentenced too many people for such an act. Beauregard insisted that it was not his duty. Pickens said, "Well, if you are so fastidious about it, give them to me." But he opened them with nervous fingers. Crawford, *Fort Sumter*, p. 384 and note.

[43] *O. R.*, 1st series, I, 297. When Secretary Walker suggested an earlier demand unless the delay was necessary, Beauregard replied that there was a special reason for it. *Ibid.* The special reason was that a needed shipment of powder was expected; time was also needed for the placement of the gun presented by C. K. Prioleau. Alfred Roman, *The Military Operations of General Beauregard in the War between the States, 1861-1865* (New York, 1884), I, 39.

[44] The report of the Secretary of War had been prematurely published. It indicated the position of every man and gun. This was one reason for the call for more troops. *Mercury*, April 6, 1861; Crawford, *Fort Sumter*, p. 397. There were about 7,000 present at the surrender with about 1,000 taking part in the operations. Rhodes, *History of U. S.*, III, 242 and note; Wallace, *History of S. C.*, III, 167.

[45] Crawford, *Fort Sumter*, pp. 397-399.

[46] *Mercury*, April 9, 1861.

to be referred to Montgomery.[47] In reply Secretary Walker wired that there was no desire to bombard the fort needlessly and that if Anderson would "state the time at which . . . he will evacuate, and agree that in the meantime he will not use his guns against us unless ours should be employed against Fort Sumter, you are authorized thus to avoid the effusion of blood. If this, or its equivalent be refused, reduce the fort. . . ."[48] These terms were carried to the fort by Beauregard's aides soon after midnight, and Anderson after a long consultation agreed to evacuate by noon of April 15 and not to open fire on the South Carolina forces in the meantime "unless compelled to do so by some hostile act against this fort or the flag of my Government," or unless controlling instructions or additional supplies were received prior to the designated time.[49] According to instructions, the aides read this reply of Anderson and, regarding it as unsatisfactory, anounced at 3:20 A.M. on April 12, that the attack upon the fort would begin one hour later.[50] They immediately crossed to Fort Johnson on James Island and gave the necessary orders. At 4:30 the first shot was fired from that point by the battery of Captain George S. James, the lanyard being pulled by Lieutenant Henry S. Farley.[51]

Chesnut, Chisolm, Lee, and Pryor, the aides who received Anderson's conditional promise to evacuate on the 15th, have been criticised for their failure to report back to Beauregard before giving orders for the bombardment of the fort.[52] It is barely possible that had they done so Beauregard might have asked further instructions from Montgomery and a decision to wait might have been reached. But they must have had an understanding with Beauregard as to what would constitute an unsatisfactory reply from Anderson; Beauregard states that they carried out instructions; certainly their decision was well within the orders from Montgomery. Beauregard thought it "manifestly an imperative necessity" to reduce the fort before the fort and fleet could combine against him.[53] It was of course a great advantage to the North that the South fired the first shot and placed herself in the position of the aggressor, and the same impression might not have been created had fire been witheld until the attempt to relieve Anderson was actually made.

[47] O. R., 1st series, I, 13, 59, 301.   [48] Ibid., p. 301.
[49] Ibid., p. 14.   [50] Ibid.
[51] The second shot was from the other battery at Fort Johnson with Lt. W. H. Gibbes of Columbia doing the firing. Edmund Ruffin fired the first shot from Morris Island but not the first against Fort Sumter as often stated. On the whole subject see Robert Lebby, "The First Shot on Fort Sumter," South Carolina Historical and Genealogical Magazine, II (July, 1911), 141-145; Wallace, History of S. C., III, 166 note; O. R., 1st series, I, 30-35, 54, 60, etc; Avery O. Craven, Edmund Ruffin, Southerner; A Study in Secession (New York, 1932), pp. 217, 270 note; hereinafter cited Craven, Ruffin.
[52] Rhodes, History of U. S., III, 236-238.
[53] O. R., 1st series, I, 30-35 (Beauregard's report).

There had been much impatience in Charleston because of the delay, and general satisfaction met the sound of the first gun; "lights flashed from every house," hurrahs rang out as "men *sans* coat and vest, women *sans* crinoline, and children in their night gowns" rushed to the waterfront.[54] "The Battery, the wharves and shipping in the harbor, and every steeple and cupola in the city, were crowded with anxious spectators"[55] as the bombardment continued.

By five o'clock on the morning of the 12th a damaging fire was being poured into Fort Sumter. At seven o'clock the fort responded, first against Stevens Iron Battery[56] at Cummings Point and then against Sullivan's Island, especially Fort Moultrie. Throughout the day the duel continued and by evening it was evident that the Confederate fire was effective. Sumter remained silent during the dark and rainy night of the 12th but received at intervals of fifteen minutes the fire of the Confederate guns. On the 13th the duel was resumed as the relief expedition stood helplessly by. By eight o'clock a fire broke out in the officers' quarters of Sumter and soon spread to the barracks. By noon all the woodwork of the fort was ablaze and the powder magazines so threatened that Anderson with great difficulty removed fifty barrels and closed the magazines. Most of this small supply soon had to be dumped into the sea to escape the advancing flames. The guns of Sumter were now almost quiet as smoke nearly suffocated the men. About 1:30 Sumter's flag was shot down and Beauregard sent three aides with an offer of assistance. At the same time Brigadier General Simons at Cummings Point allowed Colonel L. T. Wigfall with Private Gourdin Young and two Negro oarsmen to proceed to the fort with a request for surrender. The flag was soon restored but Wigfall amidst heavy fire and disregarding an attempt of Fort Moultrie to stop or sink him,[57] proceeded to the fort. Anderson agreed to evacuate on the terms which had been offered on the 11th and ran up a white flag. Wigfall was quite without authority but the same terms were soon officially arranged and on the next day Anderson evacuated with the honors of war. In saluting his flag Anderson had one man killed, one fatally wounded, and several others wounded less severely by the premature firing of a gun and the explosion of nearby loose cartridges. There were no other casualties.[58]

[54] F. G. Fontaine, *Army Letters of "Personne," 1861-1865* (Columbia, 1896), Vol. I, no. 1, p. 29.

[55] *Mercury*, April 13, 1861.

[56] This battery protected by railroad rails set at a forty degree angle was conceived and constructed by Clement H. Stevens, bank cashier and later brigadier general. It was begun in January, 1861, and was built on the principle later used by Eads in constructing sloping-sided gun boats, and by the Confederates in the arming of the *Virginia* (Merrimac). Wallace, *History of S. C.*, III, 166 note.

[57] Lieutenant Colonel R. S. Ripley, in command of the artillery at Fort Moultrie, was quoted as saying that "some d— politician was meddling with what he had no business and he intended to sink him." Young's account in DeSaussure Papers.

[58] Crawford, *Fort Sumter*, pp. 427 *et seq.;* O. R., 1st series, I, 14-15, 16-25, 28, 30-35, *et seq.;* Gourdin Young mss; Abner Doubleday, *Reminiscences of Fort*

The people of Charleston celebrated. Extras of the *Mercury* could not be printed fast enough to meet the demand. Governor Pickens was serenaded and answered those who had criticized him for delay in attacking Sumter by saying that the policy of waiting until the fort could be taken with safety was now vindicated. "Thank God the war is open . . . we will conquer or perish."[59] Next day, Sunday the 15th, a *Te Deum* was celebrated at the Cathedral and other churches held services of thanksgiving. The excitement which continued during the following week-end led a journalist to remark: "The streets of Charleston present some such aspect as those of Paris in the last Revolution."[60]

The war which began at Fort Sumter was probably not expected by the majority of the people of South Carolina. The doctrine of coercion had been denied not only as a right but also as a probability by those who spoke for secession, and there is no reason to believe that they were not for the most part sincere. Armistead Burt of Abbeville, for example, promised to drink all the blood shed in consequence of secession.[61] After the event Hammond admitted that he thought coercion would not be attempted if as many as two states seceded, and he expressed amazement that war should have come after seven states had formed a confederacy.[62] Governor Gist rather boasted that he had predicted war. "I find *my opinion* fully verified," he wrote. "You know I always thought we would have to fight—while many intelligent gentlemen thought otherwise."[63] And the *Mercury,* even after Fort Sumter, for a time insisted that there would be no war. The argument was that attempted coercion would drive all the Southern states out of the Union and convince the North that conquest was impossible.[64] The masses of the people must have been even less aware of the danger of war. Led by public men to believe that disunion could be peaceably effected, they seem to have been carried along on a wave of popular excitement without realizing the consequences. One of their leaders wrote on the eve of secession:

I do not believe the common people understand it, in fact I know they do not understand it; but whoever waited for the common people when a great movement was to be made. We must make the movement and force them to follow.[65]

Sumter and Moultrie in 1860-'61 (New York, 1876), Chapters X, XI; Rhodes, *History of U. S.,* III, 239-242. The South Carolina flag was raised by R. B. Johnson representing Governor Pickens and not by Picken's secretary F. J. Moses, Jr., who claimed the credit. Wallace, *History of S. C.,* III, 167 and note citing Dr. R. B. Johnson in *The State,* December 25, 1906.

[59] *Mercury,* April 15, 16, 1861.

[60] *Ibid.;* Russell, *My Diary North and South,* pp. 98-99.

[61] When reminded later of the statement, Burt said he had qualified it by the condition that the border states secede. *Mercury,* October 26, 1863.

[62] J. H. Hammond to W. D. Porter, June 16, 1861, Hammond Papers.

[63] W. H. Gist to B. T. Watts, May 17, 1861, Watts Papers, University of South Carolina.

[64] *Mercury,* April 4, 17, 20, 1861.

[65] A. P. Aldrich to J. H. Hammond, November 25, 1860, Hammond Papers.

There were of course some who predicted that secession meant war. The unionists and coöperationists argued against separate action secession by pointing out the danger of hostilities, and some secessionists are on record as predicting a conflict. D. H. Hamilton wrote:

I am amused at the coolness with which the Southern States offer to march to the assistance of So Car—they must be sleeping in fancied security—why in less than a year it is more than likely that the whole South will be in a blaze from one end to the other.

And J. J. Pettigrew told the fire-eaters: "Well, the Devil is unchained at last, you have been talking fire a long time, now you must face it."[66] But it was generally believed that the war, if it came, would be a short one. Gist said: "I make another prediction. Two battles will end the war and our independence will be acknowledged."[67]

Under the impression that the war would be short, the Carolinians showed much enthusiasm for it. To William Howard Russell it seemed that they were actually delighted that war had come.[68] Some found satisfaction in the belief that the outbreak of hostilities would prevent any attempt at reconstruction of the old Union, the mere thought of which was extremely distasteful to South Carolina, especially after Fort Sumter.[69] The unionist, W. J. Grayson, wrote: "It would be as rational to believe that France and England may return to the Union of five hundred years ago. . . . Relations, political or social, with the Northern States, are now odious to Southern men."[70] Prominent men told Russell that rather than go back into the old Union they would much prefer to unite with England and be governed by an English prince, statements which led this newspaper man erroneously to report the existence of widespread monarchist sentiment in South Carolina.[71]

[66] D. H. Hamilton to D. H. Hamilton, Jr., November 27, 1860, Ruffin-Roulhac-Hamilton Papers; Mrs. C. L. Pettigrew (quoting J. J. P.) to C. L. Pettigrew, November 7, 1860, Pettigrew Papers. For other predictions of war see Ravenel, Diary, December 18, 1860; Mary D. O'Connor (ed.), *The Life and Letters of M. P. O'Connor* (New York, 1893), pp. 18-19; Palmer, *Life of Thornwell*, pp. 477-478; A. P. Aldrich to J. H. Hammond, December 21, 1860, Hammond Papers.
[67] W. H. Gist to B. T. Watts, May 17, 1861, Watts Papers. J. D. Ashmore wrote: "I suppose that it is hardly reasonable to expect much of a conflict." Ashmore to Hammond, March 21, 1861, Hammond Papers. There were some, however, who warned against this attitude, e.g., "Vinciamus" in *Mercury*, May 30, 1861, and *Mercury* editorials May 30, 31, July 24, 25, 1861.
[68] Russell, *My Diary North and South*, p. 136 (April 24, 1861).
[69] Hammond thought that there was considerable reconstruction sentiment in the state before the shooting began at Fort Sumter. J. H. Hammond to R. M. T. Hunter, November 4, 1861, Hammond Papers. Congressman J. D. Ashmore may be cited as an example of an active secessionist who hoped that after secession a convention of the states might "once more re-organize the Union upon a solid & permanent basis." See Ashmore to Perry, November 19, 1860, in Kibler, *Perry*, p. 340.
[70] (W. J. Grayson), *Remarks on Mr. Motley's Letter in the London Times on the War in America* (Charleston, 1861), p. 4. Ravenel wrote that the very mention of reconstruction "causes the blood to mantle in the cheeks with mingled shame & indignation." Diary, July 8, 1861.
[71] Russell, *My Diary North and South*, pp. 118, 130-131, 134, 147-148. Russell's statement in his letter to the *London Times* (April 30) raised a storm of protest

Enthusiasm in the first months of the war expressed itself in a ready response to calls for troops. Soon after Fort Sumter President Davis called on the state for 8,000 men for the provisional army of the Confederacy, and Governor Pickens urged the troops then in state service to volunteer for Confederate service. The response was excellent. Gregg's first and Kershaw's second regiments left for Virginia April 22 and 25, respectively, carrying regimental colors presented by the ladies of Charleston and Sumter. Hagood's first failed to volunteer, was relieved from duty, and temporarily discharged; but with considerable unanimity the other twelve months state troops entered the Confederate service. There was little difficulty in replacing such companies as did not go in. South Carolina also furnished the legion raised by Wade Hampton under Confederate authority consisting of infantry, artillery, and cavalry. All of these were twelve months troops except Gregg's six months volunteers.[72]

There was a somewhat less eager response to calls for troops for the duration of the war. On June 30 President Davis called on South Carolina for 3,000 men for the duration in addition to those already called for twelve months. They were to be accepted in companies at Lightwood Knot Springs near Columbia and at another camp near Aiken, the field officers to be appointed by the President. On July 1 two fully organized regiments for the duration of the war were called for, making six long term regiments required. Colonel Orr's Regiment of Rifles, the first South Carolina regiment to enlist originally on this basis, was already forming and was designated by Pickens as one of the regiments called for. The other was obtained through the reorganization of Gregg's six months volunteers whose term expired July 1. An arrangement was then made by which the 3,000 men called for in companies

in South Carolina. The *Mercury* called the idea "twaddle and balderdash," but believed the South would prefer a constitutional monarchy to an "irresponsible and vulgar tyranny of an unchecked majority." Its references to a "certain distinguished lawyer of Charleston" as being a monarchist was to J. L. Petigru and drew a letter of protest and denial from Petigru's cousin, J. Johnston Pettigrew. *Mercury*, June 19-22, 1861. For Petigru's own denial see Carson, *Life of Petigru*, p. 382. He wrote Johnston Pettigrew: "I am for the very opposite,—the semi-sovereignty of the U. S. and the quasi sovereignty of the State." J. L. Petigru to J. J. Pettigrew, June 24, 1861, Pettigrew Papers. Hayne said there were not more than fifty monarchists in the state and they could command not more than fifty votes. *Mercury*, June 22, 1861. For other comments see *ibid.*, June 24, 29, 1861; Sumter *Triweekly Watchman*, June 21, 1861; *Keowee Courier*, July 6, 1861; Spartanburg *Express*, June 26, 1861; Chesnut, *Diary*, pp. 64, 66. As the war progressed and discontent developed, there were many doubts expressed as to the feasibility of republican government and some avowals of a preference for monarchy but there was not at any time an appreciable monarchist sentiment in South Carolina. B. M. Palmer, *A Discourse before the General Assembly of South Carolina, on December 10, 1863, appointed by the Legislature as a Day of Fasting Humiliation and Prayer* (Columbia, 1864), p. 8.

[72] *O. R.*, serial no. 127, pp. 413-415; *Mercury* (Triweekly), April 25, 27, 1861; Thomas, "Raising of Troops," pp. 24-28. Much detailed information on the early regiments is to be found in Salley, *S. C. Troops*. Various company, regiment, and brigade histories are listed in the bibliography but there has been less of this work done for South Carolina than for other states.

were allowed to organize as regiments and elect their own field officers. Under this agreement the 12th, 13th, 14th, and 15th South Carolina Volunteers were organized and mustered into Confederate service for the duration of the war.[73]

By November 1 there had been raised for Confederate service eleven regiments for twelve months under the act of December 17, 1860, one regiment for six months under authority of the convention, Hampton's Legion for twelve months under Confederate authority, and six regiments for the duration of war under the calls of President Davis, a total of nineteen regiments, one of which had served its time and disbanded. In addition there was the regiment of infantry and battalion of artillery composing the regular army of the state. Held in reserve were twenty-one companies of cavalry and mounted men in the seacoast parishes raised under a special resolution of the convention, their services limited to ten days after adjournment of the regular session of the legislature.[74]

Of these first troops many early went to Virginia. Gregg's and Kershaw's regiments were soon followed by those of Cash, Bacon, Jenkins, Sloan, and Williams. In July the regiments of Rion and Blanding and the Hampton Legion went, making a total of ten regiments.[75] In the first rush to arms there was no disposition on the part of Governor Pickens to insist on the retention of troops in South Carolina, though Hammond urged it.[76] In the late summer and fall, however, reluctance to part with troops appeared because of a general expectation of an attack on the coast. A request that Hagood's regiment be sent to Virginia was turned down early in September, and a counter request was made that Gregg's regiment be returned to South Carolina.[77] Governor Pickens also requested that no one be allowed to recruit in South Carolina except with his consent.[78] Between July and November South Carolina increased her forces in Virginia by only one regiment.

November 7, 1861, the long expected attack on the coast materialized, with South Carolina ill-prepared to meet it. During the summer a number of warnings had been voiced that large scale preparations were essential, but little had been done.[79] Indeed, a proper defense of the extensive coast of the state was perhaps entirely beyond the resources of South Carolina. The expedition sent against Port Royal was of over-

[73] O. R., serial no. 127, pp. 404, 413, 420-421, 479-480, 487; Thomas, "Raising of Troops," pp. 24, 30-31, 43.
[74] Pickens's message of November 5, 1861, Senate Journal (1861), pp. 10-11.
[75] O. R., serial no. 127, pp. 413, 479, 487.
[76] Hammond said no trust could be put in anybody outside of South Carolina, least of all in Davis. J. H. Hammond to I. W. Hayne, April 21, 1861, Hammond Papers.
[77] O. R., 1st series, VI, 273, 268-269. The request for Gregg's regiment was immediately withdrawn because, Pickens said, "You know the general plans and our resources, and I do not." Ibid., p. 271.
[78] O. R., serial no. 127, p. 624.
[79] Mercury, July 16, 20, 22, August 24, etc., 1861.

whelming strength, the fleet under Commodore Samuel F. DuPont being the largest ever commanded by an American officer to that time, and the convoyed troops under General Thomas W. Sherman numbering about 12,000. Against such a force the weak Forts Walker and Beauregard on the two lips of Port Royal harbor were quite untenable and were easily taken. As a result there soon fell into federal control the greater part of the sea island region of South Carolina which constituted one of the richest portions of the state and of the Confederacy. The great plantations were abandoned and large quantities of cotton and thousands of Negroes fell into the hands of the federals.[80]

The fall of Port Royal threw Charleston into a panic comparable to that of Washington after the battle of Manassas. Rumors of traitors, of the enemy marching to burn the city, of destroyed railroad bridges, and other misfortunes, were widely circulated and many people hurried from the city or sent their valuables to places of greater safety.[81] Criticism of the authorities, especially of Brigadier General Thomas F. Drayton who commanded the forts, was general.[82]

In an attempt to meet the military emergency Governor Pickens on November 11 called for volunteers under a resolution of the legislature which had just been in session for the purpose of choosing presidential electors. These recruits were to enter the Confederate service as troops for special local defense under a Confederate law of August 12, 1861.[83] To receive these and such other state troops as might be transferred to Confederate service and to accept volunteers for the war, General Robert E. Lee who was now in charge of the Department of South Carolina and Georgia, appointed Lieutenant Colonel John S. Preston with headquarters in Columbia. But the results were disappointing. Preston wrote on the 23rd that no troops were coming in "although twenty days have elapsed since 'Carolina's soil is desecrated'—the deep mouthed curse—the fierce shout—the wild rush to arms and vengeance —aren't here."[84] Not a single company had offered for the war December 3 and even recruiting for twelve months service was "very

[80] Daniel Ammen, "Dupont and the Port Royal Expedition," *Battles and Leaders of the Civil War*, I, 674; Wallace, *History of S. C.*, III, 171.

[81] Ravenel, Diary, November 10-15, 1861; Louise — to Mrs. C. L. Pettigrew, November 18, 1861, Pettigrew Papers. Preston wrote, "There is great terror prevailing here and no preparations—neither troops nor defenses. I regard the city in hourly peril. I believe it could be taken in six hours . . . I believe they will have Charleston within thirty days." J. S. Preston to [James Chesnut, Jr], November 14, 1861, William-Chesnut-Manning Papers.

[82] L. G. Young to J. J. Pettigrew (undated), Pettigrew Papers; Holmes, Diary, December 6, 1861. Drayton's brother, Percival Drayton, commanded the *Pocahontas* in the attack on Port Royal. His refusal to resign his commission in the United States Navy was regarded as an unforgivable offense in South Carolina but that he was not permanently estranged from all his family is indicated by the fact that after the war he gave to his brother $27,000 with which to reëstablish himself. *D. A. B.*, V, 445-447.

[83] Pickens's call in Camden *Confederate*, November 29, 1861.

[84] J. S. Preston to James Chesnut, Jr., November 23, 1861, Williams-Chesnut-Manning Papers.

languid," only four companies having been transferred.[85] Lee said that there was no means of defending the state except with her own troops and that if they did not come forward immediately, he feared her suffering would be greatly increased.[86]

To add to the difficulty of the time there was a great scarcity of arms and ammunition. Of the supply obtained before the fall of Fort Sumter Governor Pickens had given much to other states[87] and had used almost all of the remainder in equipping South Carolina troops at home and abroad. As early as July he was writing the Secretary of War for help and his appeals became more urgent in the following months; after Port Royal his requests became almost frantic.[88] About this time there arrived at Savannah through the blockade the steamer *Fingal* bringing a cargo of arms. Half of these were assigned to General Lee for his department, but Governor Pickens was notified that the arms would be placed only in the hands of men enlisting for the duration of the war; and there were few such volunteers in South Carolina at the time.[89]

The need for troops at the end of 1861 led the legislature on December 7 to amend the militia law of 1841 so as to make all persons between eighteen and forty-five liable for twelve months service in or out of the state instead of for three months in and two months out of the state as under the old law. The law authorized the governor to call these troops out at any time provided that, before resorting to draft, an opportunity be given each company to supply its quota by volunteering. The law also attempted to vitalize a militia system which, never efficient, had become utterly disorganized as a result of the volunteering of men and officers during the first months of the war. New elections were ordered for all militia offices, and drill required twice monthly instead of quarterly as before.[90]

Two days after the passage of the law, Governor Pickens called for 12,000 volunteers. "Our State is invaded and Charleston is threatened by land and by sea with large forces," he said, and he warned that if the volunteers were not forthcoming immediately a draft would be resorted to.[91] Before the response to the call could be known, President Jamison reassembled the convention.

[85] *O. R.*, 1st series, VI, p. 335. See also *ibid.*, pp. 337, 339.
[86] *O. R.*, serial no. 111, p. 193.
[87] To Florida had been sent 6,000 arms and 5,000 pounds of powder; to North Carolina 11 heavy cannon and 30,000 pounds of powder; to Lynchburg 1,000 arms and 100,000 cartridges; to Memphis also some cannon and ammunition. *Convention Journal*, pp. 554-560; *O. R.*, serial no. 108, pp. 212-213; *ibid.*, 1st series, VI, 268-269.
[88] *O. R.*, serial no. 127, pp. 479, 624; serial no. 108, pp. 212-213; 1st series, VI, 292, 315, 268-269; serial no. 111, p. 185.
[89] *Ibid.*, 1st series, VI, 318, 340, 346-349, 356-357. Pickens wrote December 13, 1861, "There is great difficulty in enlisting regulars now." *Ibid.*, p. 363.
[90] *Statutes at Large*, XIII, 9-13.
[91] Camden *Confederate*, December 20, 1861.

CHAPTER X

THE EXECUTIVE COUNCIL

In the last days of the second session of the convention (from March 26 to April 10) there had appeared a difference of opinion as to whether or not the convention should adjourn *sine die*. Some held that with the ratification of the Confederate Constitution the convention had completed the work for which it had been assembled and should therefore dissolve; others believed it should adjourn subject to the call of the president in some possible future emergency. It was finally agreed that President Jamison might reconvene the body at any time before January 1, 1862, but in case it should not be assembled by that date, its existence would end. It was under this resolution that Jamison on December 14 issued the call for the meeting of the convention it its third session December 26, 1861.[1]

At the time of Jamison's call conditions seemed much worse than when the convention adjourned. What promised to be a prolonged war had actually come, the coast of the state was blockaded, a considerable portion of the state was occupied by the enemy, and Charleston was thought to be in hourly peril. Volunteering was languid and the need for additional troops was apparent. Scarcity of goods and rising prices were already beginning to pinch. And to add to the misfortunes of the state a great fire of accidental origin had on December 11-12 destroyed a large portion of the city of Charleston.[2]

Under such conditions it was only natural perhaps that President Jamison should have been urged to reassemble that body which included in its membership so many of the state's wisest citizens. Jamison explained his act by saying that the invasion of the state had raised a critical problem of defense and that the occupation of the coast made it imperative to take steps for the protection of a slave population now

---

[1] *Convention Journal*, pp. 241, 284-285.

[2] The fire began at the foot of Hasell Street on the Cooper River and swept from E. Bay across the city to the Ashley at Council Street. For a list of the hundreds of buildings destroyed, including the secession convention halls, see the *Mercury*, December 16, 1861. The estimated loss in immovable property alone was $3,500,000 with $1,500,000 insurance carried mostly by Charleston companies which were ruined. *Ibid.*, December 17, 1861. See also *Charleston Year Book* (1894), p. 295; St. Julien Ravenel, *Charleston, the Place and the People* (New York, 1925), p. 497. Donations poured in from many places. The legislature of Georgia donated $100,000. *S. C. Reports and Resolutions* (1861), 228-229. Congress at the request of President Davis advanced $250,000 on funds due the state. *Journal Confed. Cong.*, I, 566-567, 571. The state legislature appropriated $30,000 for immediate relief and authorized a $1,000,000 building and loan fund. *Reports and Resolutions* (1861), pp. 193-194; *Statutes at Large*, XIII, 24-29. There were many private donations from a number of states, the totals running into large figures. *Mercury*, December 16, 1861-January 29, 1862.

in contact with abolitionism. He added that the absence of the great number of citizens who had entered the army might soon make the election of a regular government impossible.[3] He did not mention that there had developed a widespread lack of confidence in the ability of Governor Pickens to meet the emergency, but he might have given this as the chief explanation.

Murmurings against Governor Pickens had appeared almost immediately after his election. While for a time little was publicly said, considerable dissatisfaction was privately expressed. Ex-Governor John L. Manning wrote as early as December 31, 1860, that the executive department was characterized by "confusion and imbecility." Trescot likewise called attention to the "blunders" of the administration.[4] Late in January, Henry W. Ravenel wrote:

There is great dissatisfaction prevailing in the city [of Charleston] at the course of Gov. Pickens in making appointments to the army & in all his official acts. He is overbearing, haughty & rude, & has given offense in numerous cases. He has caused many resignations & has made himself so unpopular since his election, that were it not for the critical state of affairs now existing, he would be called to account & perhaps impeached. I understand it was with difficulty that a [sic] effort to call an indignation meeting of the people last week was suppressed. . . . Pickens ought never to have been elected Governor.[5]

A little later W. H. Russell reported: "Gov. Pickens is considerably laughed at by his subjects"[6] in Charleston.

It was perhaps inevitable that criticism should appear in the troublous time between secession and Fort Sumter. Governor Pickens was blamed for having allowed Anderson to escape from Fort Moultrie and was charged with causing the war by his failure to take Fort Sumter earlier.[7] He would no doubt have been criticised whatever his course. The same may be said of the criticisms of his appointments, but there was truth in the claim that he favored the upper part of the state, a fact which the low country was quick to resent. By summer of 1861 there was a chorus of protest.[8] However unjust and prejudiced much of the criticism of Governor Pickens may have been, it must be said that his

[3] *Convention Journal,* pp. 302-303.
[4] John L. Manning to wife, December 31, 1860, Williams-Chesnut-Manning Papers; W. H. Trescot to Howell Cobb, January 14, 1861, *Correspondence of Toombs, Stephens, Cobb,* pp. 529-531.
[5] Ravenel, Diary, January 31, 1861. See also January 7.
[6] Russell, *My Diary North and South,* pp. 121-122.
[7] *Mercury,* September 26, 1861, December 1, 1862.
[8] The Marion *Star* said that the Pee Dee section had not only been neglected and wronged but that the appointments were also bad. It mentioned those of Major Smith, Brig. Gen. McGowan, and General Bonham, the latter being, it said, "a crowning act of injustice." Quoted by *Keowee Courier,* March 30, 1861. There was much talk of the appointees being "mere political placemen and kinsmen," and of proscription and favoritism. The men who made the revolution, it was said, were given no consideration. *Mercury,* June 17, August 7, 1861; *Mercury* (Triweekly), August 8, 1861; *O. R.,* 1st series, VI, pp. 363-364.

vanity, egotism, and lack of tact was responsible for no little of it. He did not get along well with his associates and was frequently in controversy with public men. William Gilmore Simms wrote:

Pickens is such an ass that he will drive away from him every decent counsellor. Jamison, Magrath, Frost, all have left him and all, I believe in disgust. He never consulted either in his appointments. . . . Neither that of Bonham, Dunovant, or McGowan would probably have met the approval of his council. . . . His vanity throws him open to the most contemptible advisors. All who will flatter, can rule him. He has caused the most infinite amount of blundering and has offended many. . . . He is at times too flexible to say no, at other times too mulish to say yes though every argument called for it, and all his counsellors. . . . It is a terrible thing that such a man should be Executive at such a moment.[9]

There was a feeling too that the governor had not been sufficiently energetic in preparing for the expected attack on the South Carolina coast. "We are in a state of profound apathy here," wrote J. J. Pettigrew in May, 1861. Pettigrew believed that the enemy with "a little audacity" could take possession of any desired point on the coast.[10] Throughout the summer there were appeals for more active preparation especially in the matter of reorganizing the militia, but little was done to ensure the enrollment and training of persons liable for military duty. The *Mercury* bewailed the "timid and inefficient policy" of the state government and it seemed to John S. Preston after the fall of Port Royal that there was "miserable confusion, ignorance & inefficiency in every department" of state administration.[11] Trescot wrote Miles a month after Port Royal:

I confess I have never seen such perfect, hopeless incapacity. And in this opinion all the members [of the legislature] whom you would respect agree unanimously. Several of them were anxious to pass a resolution expressing the sense of the Legislature that the Convention should be called. . . . There is no leader and everybody seems bewildered. I found a large number who were ready to call the Convention, supersede Pickens and make Orr, or anybody else they could agree on, Governor with extraordinary powers.[12]

Convinced that the governor and legislature were inadequate to the emergency, the convention took drastic action in an attempt to remedy the situation. Governor Pickens was called upon for a detailed report of the number of troops in state and Confederate service, their terms of enlistment and location, and was required to account for all arms which had been under his control.[13] Pickens refused to accept responsibility

[9] W. G. Simms to J. H. Hammond, June 14, 1861, Hammond Papers.
[10] J. J. Pettigrew to his brother, May 13, 1861, Pettigrew Papers.
[11] *Mercury* and correspondents, June 13, July 3, 10, 18, 24, September 19, 26, 1861; J. S. Preston to [James Chesnut, Jr.], November 14, 1861, Williams-Chesnut Manning Papers.
[12] W. H. Trescot to W. P. Miles, December 6, 1861, Miles Papers.
[13] *Convention Journal*, pp. 314-315. The report showed that the state had raised 7,111 men for the war and 20,251 for shorter periods. Of the latter 4,078

for the military reverses of the state. He claimed that control of events had been transferred to the Confederate authorities and that it would therefore be a great wrong to him and an injustice to the state to hold him responsible for the conduct of the war.[14] This defense, however, received little consideration from the convention. Its members were convinced that the executive should be so strengthened as to bring a greater amount of energy and efficiency to the defense of the state.

The method adopted was the creation of an executive council of five persons to consist of the governor, the lieutenant governor, and three others chosen by the convention. To this body was given not only the ordinary executive power heretofore exercised by the governor but also almost unlimited war powers including full control of the military organization of the state, the power to declare martial law, arrest and detain disloyal persons, appropriate private property with compensation, appoint such agents as necessary, and draw money from the treasury for public purposes. The ordinance creating this council did much more than merely give the governor a cabinet of advisers responsible to him. Rather it set up a council of safety of which the governor was simply a member. In fact full power might be exercised in the governor's absence by a quorum consisting of the lieutenant governor and two others. The governor was allowed access to the records of all departments which might be set up by the council and might require written reports from department heads but these heads were responsible to the council as a whole and not to the governor.[15]

The passage of such a drastic ordinance met little opposition either within the convention or out. The vote in convention was an overwhelming 96 to 23, the minority for the most part wishing to leave the council responsible to the governor.[16] Such protests as were made in

though organized were not yet actually in Confederate service. In addition to the above 27,362 men, there were 74 companies raised under the act of December 7, 1861, either in camp or under marching orders for camp. *Ibid.*, pp. 560-567. James Chesnut, Jr., as Chief of the Department of Military, later doubted the absolute accuracy of these figures because of the imperfect methods of keeping the records. *Report of the Chief of the Department of the Military of South Carolina to His Excellency Governor Pickens* (Columbia, 1861), pp. 5, 31; hereinafter cited *Report of Chief of Military.* This report is published also in the *Convention Journal*, pp. 587-648. There was some disagreement between Pickens and Lee as to the number of troops in the Confederate service and under Lee's command. *O. R.*, 1st series, VI, 326, 356-357, 363-364.

[14] *Convention Journal*, p. 554.

[15] *Convention Journal*, pp. 793-796. The earlier cabinet responsible to the governor had been abolished by an ordinance of the convention on April 8, effective as soon as in the governor's opinion public affairs should permit. The ordinance permitted him, however, to retain the lieutenant governor and secretary of the treasury but not beyond the next legislature without the legislature's consent. Pickens approved of this type of council. *Ibid.*, pp. 511, 775; *Mercury*, April 9, 1861.

[16] *Convention Journal*, pp. 306-308, 314, 341-342, 348, 353-355, 362-367, 373. Those voting against the ordinance were about evenly divided between the up and low country. *Ibid.*, p. 367.

the debate did not reach the public because the convention acted in secret session. General Maxcy Gregg, for example, though not able to attend the convention, wrote a strong letter in defense of Governor Pickens but it did not get into print until the following Steptember.[17] A. P. Aldrich carried his opposition to his constituents soon after adjournment, but his speech seems not to have been published till much later. And Aldrich, while opposing the executive council on principle, recommended that it be given a fair trial and applauded if its power was not abused.[18] A few newspapers also expressed doubt as to the wisdom of the ordinance.[19] But so great were the dangers faced by the state in early 1862 that there was little disposition to question the wisdom of the convention's extraordinary action. Nor was there any denial that the persons constituting the council were of the state's very best. Governor Pickens of course voiced his objections. He believed the executive would be greatly weakened and that if military appointments and orders had to be passed upon by the council then "there will be great imbecility in acting as Commander-in-Chief." He intimated that he would resign except for the threatening aspect of public affairs but stated that he would give his support to the ordinance.[20]

The elected members seem to have assumed the leadership from the first meeting of the executive council on January 9. All three, former Senator James Chesnut, Jr., Attorney General I. W. Hayne, and ex-Governor W. H. Gist, were men of known ability and experience in public affairs and enjoyed the confidence of the state. It was on Chesnut's motion that administrative departments were created and rules adopted for conducting them. He became Chief of the Department of the Military with such powers as practically to displace the governor as commander-in-chief.[21] Lieutenant Governor W. W. Harl-

[17] *Mercury*, September 17, 1862. Gregg stated that only distrust of Pickens could explain the proposal to create the council. He argued that if Pickens was inefficient the proper course was to depose him and to appoint the best and wisest man in the state to his place. Division of responsibility among five, he held, would make for inefficiency. Gregg denied, however, that Pickens was incompetent, saying that he had observed him closely from December, 1860, to April, 1861, and that he had been impressed with his energy and wisdom, and could hardly believe that he could have failed so signally between April and December, 1861.

[18] *Mercury*, May 3, 1862.

[19] *Courier*, January 23, 1862, quoting the Edgefield *Advertiser*; *Carolina Spartan*, January 16, 1862.

[20] *Convention Journal*, pp. 385-386.

[21] *Report of Chief of Military*, pp. 3, 29-30. It was the duty of the Chief of Military to examine the amount and condition of all war equipment, estimate needed equipment, and dispose of same; to examine the condition of the army and militia, and to keep records of and make reports on the military forces in the Confederate service and in the militia; to give, through the Adjutant and Inspector General, orders for carrying into effect the resolutions of the council in regard to raising and arming troops, and "to direct the arrangement, transportation, and operation of such troops" until mustered into the Confederate service; to supervise, direct, and give proper orders to the ordnance, quartermaster, and medical departments; to "command all officers and employees in the military

lee and W. H. Gist became heads of the Department of Treasury and Finance, and I. W. Hayne Chief of the Department of Justice and Police. A new department, that of Construction and Manufacture, was a little later created with Gist as its head.[22] Thus began the stormy career of South Carolina's executive council, the source of the greatest political controversy in the Civil War history of the state.

An examination of the work of the executive council will indicate that it accomplished the objects for which it was created. Its most important task, perhaps, was the raising of troops. For this purpose the convention had given the council authority to suspend any part of the confused militia laws which might interfere, and to call into service any portion of the militia in "such manner and under such regulations as may seem most expedient."[23] The occasion for the exercise of this blanket authority appeared almost immediately when President Davis called on February 2 for South Carolina to fill her quota of 18,000 for the war troops. Of this number the state had already furnished about 6,000 according to the Secretary of War.[24] To meet this requisition it would be necessary to enlist at least five new regiments and reënlist enough twelve months troops, whose terms were about to expire, to make the total required. The council acted at once and with vigor. A stirring appeal was made by Chesnut to the twelve months troops in Virginia to "tarnish not the bright crown" gleaming on their brows by leaving the field with the enemy in sight. This was followed by a call, March 5, for 5,000 volunteers with notice that no man would be allowed to enter any organization then in service for less than the war until the five regiments for the war were raised. At the same time notice was given that on March 20 volunteering would end and a system of conscription for the war would be applicable to those between eighteen and forty-five.[25]

The resort to conscription had been decided upon March 3 when the Chief of the Military and the Adjutant and Inspector General had been directed by the council to draft a plan which was adopted by the council on March 6. It required all sheriffs and tax collectors to aid the Adjutant and Inspector General in enrolling those eighteen to forty-

---

service of the State"; and to fill by appointment all vacancies in the military service of the state "heretofore vested by law in the Governor," subject to previous decision of the council.

[22] The establishment and operation of these departments are described in various reports of the departments published in the *Convention Journal*, in pamphlets, and newspapers.

[23] *Convention Journal*, p. 791.

[24] Chesnut thought this number was too small and cited the figures of the Adjutant and Inspector General's report of February 20 which he said gave the number as 9,349. *Report of Chief of Military*, pp. 6-7. Cf. *O.R.*, 1st series, VI, 404-405 which gives 8,153 for the war and 22,754 for shorter terms.

[25] Chesnut's appeal may be found in the *Mercury*, February 18, 1862; and the call for 5,000 volunteers in the Camden *Confederate*, March 7, 1862.

five, with penalties of $50 to $1,000 for failure of enrolling officers to perform their duties. Individuals failing to enroll within ten days were to be penalized by being drafted first. Substitutes were allowed and an exemption list was adopted which increased slightly the number exempt under the militia laws. A notable feature of the new system was the provision that commissioned officers should be appointed by the executive council and not elected as heretofore by the troops.[26]

The stimulus given to volunteering by the announcement of intended conscription was so great that actual draft was not necessary to secure the number of for the war troops then called for.[27] As the deadline of March 20 approached, thousands hastened to volunteer in order to escape the odium of conscription, and the twelve months troops reënlisted with alacrity. By April 28, according to Chesnut's estimate, South Carolina had 21,914 men in Confederate service for the duration of the war, or 4,000 more than the six per cent quota.[28] As an example of the effectiveness of the new system it might be noted that on the day the draft policy was announced every South Carolina College student except three withdrew to enter the service.[29]

The Confederate conscription law which almost immediately followed that of the state, received the support of the executive council. Chesnut wired Davis, "We will give your conscript law a cheerful & prompt support,"[30] and the council announced that it was "induced to waive, for the present, all objections to the measure, and to give it a cheerful and energetic support upon the ground of imperious necessity."[31] To John S. Preston, who was appointed conscript officer for South Carolina, the council offered the rolls recently completed for the state draft and, according to Preston, rendered every possible assistance in enforcing the act.[32] The attitude of the council seems to

[26] For the conscription resolution and the order under it, see *O.R.*, serial no. 127, 973-976; *Mercury*, March 12, 13, 1862. For exemptions, *O.R.*, serial no. 127, 976-977; Camden *Confederate*, March 14, 21, 1862; *Report of Chief of Military*, p. 10.
[27] Except in Charleston where Chesnut said the Adjutant and Inspector General "encountered every species of harrassment and delay." *Report of Chief of Military*, pp. 6-7. "Ladies of Charleston" complained, in the *Mercury* of February 8, that many young men were lounging about the offices of the *Mercury* and *Courier*, and suggested that they should be sent doll babies and hoop skirts on Valentine's day if they had not by then volunteered. For other appeals from ladies see *ibid.*, February 24, 1862; *Courier*, March 4, 1862. L. G. Young wrote from Charleston that only a draft would raise the desired number of troops. L. G. Young to J. J. Pettigrew, February 14, 1862. Pettigrew Papers.
[28] *Report of Chief of Military*, pp. 6-7.
[29] *Report and Resolutions* (1862), pp. 213-216; M. LaBorde, *History of the South Carolina College* (Charleston, 1874), p. 472.
[30] James Chesnut, Jr. to Jefferson Davis, April 20, 1862, Williams-Chesnut-Manning Papers.
[31] Camden *Confederate*, May 2, 1862.
[32] *O. R.*, serial no. 127, pp. 1104, 1107, 1140-1141, 1144, 1153-1154; serial no. 128, pp. 155-156. It should be noted, however, that the council insisted on its own exemption list. See *infra*, pp. 166-167.

146

have been that of the state generally. The *Mercury's* only criticism was that President Davis had prevented the passage of such a law earlier.[33] Other expressions of opposition were conspicuously few.[34] The state seemed, for the moment at least, to be willing to waive in the interest of security, the state rights principles.

The Confederate law claiming the service of men eighteen to thirty-five so disrupted the military organization of the state that the executive council decided upon the organization of two corps of reserves for state defense. The first, for active service anywhere the state required, was composed of men thirty-five to fifty, and the second, for patrol duty and internal defense, was composed of all otherwise exempt from militia duty, all alien residents, and those between sixteen and eighteen and between fifty and sixty-five. Chesnut reported on August 30 that there were ten regiments in the first corps fully organized and officered and that others were being formed.[35] The second Confederate conscription law of September 27, 1862, which extended the draft age to forty-five and actually called for those through the age of forty, again threatened the state military organization since it affected many in the First Corps of Reserves. A temporary arrangement was made by which eight regiments of the First Corps were received into Confederate service for state defense for ninety days, at the end of which time those between thirty-five and forty would remain in Confederate service while the others would be disbanded.[36] Another organization of the militia was necessary, however, and the executive council ordered the formation of companies to include practically all males between sixteen and sixty-five. Drill under pain of court martial was required every two weeks. The order included members of the legislature, doctors, ministers, millers, and others, and exempted only a few groups such as the executive council, judges, and state treasurers. The force as a whole was designed as a district police with access to arms deposited at each court house, but the plan included a scheme for the rapid mobilization and organization of the men between forty and fifty as a reserve force for state defense.[37]

The energetic efforts of the council in raising troops did not prove altogether popular. In fact outright defiance of the council occurred in the fourth division of the militia when a call for volunteers, and then draft, was made for 500 men to defend the approaches to Georgetown

[33] *Mercury,* April 3, 1862, commenting on Davis's request for the law.
[34] The Columbia *South Carolinian* was quoted as saying the act was "fatal to our liberties as a people." Chesnut, *Diary from Dixie,* p. 157. Pickens said the conscript acts were contrary to the spirit of the Consitution and savored of absolute power but intimated that the nature of the war justified them. *Message No. 1 of His Excellency, F. W. Pickens, to the Legislature at the regular session of November, 1862* (Columbia, 1862), p. 5.
[35] *Report of Chief of Military,* pp. 6-7; Camden *Confederate,* May 2, 30, 1862.
[36] *O. R.,* serial no. 111, pp. 261-265; serial no. 128, pp. 156, 176-177.
[37] Camden *Confederate,* November 16, 1862.

which had been abandoned by General John C. Pemberton. Some, said Chesnut, rushed into Confederate service, and some took to concealment; others openly defied the law or refused to obey the orders of General Harllee, while some became predatory outlaws and threatened violence in the vicinity of the few troops which did assemble. Chesnut explained this "unhappy and disgraceful state of affairs" by saying that the call came at a time inconvenient to agriculture; that Georgetown was thought unhealthy at that time of the year; that the best blood had already gone into service and that many who remained loved too well their ease and comfort. But more important, he said, was the fact that some leading men, stimulated by "noxious *pabulum*" supplied by an uninformed press, seized upon the situation to poison the minds of the people against the executive council.

Thus, sir, were ignorance, indolence, selfishness, disaffection, and, to some extent, disappointed ambition, combined, and made, unwittingly, to aid and abet the enemy, and, in like manner, to become the coadjutors of Lincoln and all the hosts of abolition myrmidons.[88]

The council adopted strong measures to meet the resistance. Some were seized and put in prison; others were summoned for court martial. But the council was considerably embarrassed by the strong anti-council sentiment which by this time had developed in the state. On the whole, however, the council proved itself very efficient in the unpopular task of putting men into the field. Chesnut reported 42,973 in Confederate service on August 30, more than one-seventh of the white population of the state.[39]

One of the thorniest problems faced by the executive council was that of furnishing slave labor for the coast and harbor defenses. In the first months of the war planters seem to have offered freely the use of their Negroes, but by the end of 1861 this was no longer the case. That the question contained political dynamite is indicated by the fact that the legislature of 1861 considered the matter in secret session and then withheld from the public its decision to allow the governor and commanding general to obtain the necessary labor by impressment if necessary. Already there was loud complaint of arbitrary power on the part of the military when the council assumed charge of affairs.[40]

[88] *Report of Chief of Military*, pp. 8-9. The fourth division comprised Chesterfield, Darlington, Marlboro, Marion, Williamsburg, Horry, and Georgetown. *Statutes at Large*, XI, 191-192. Many citizens of Marion peitioned the legislature to investigate the charges contained in Chesnut's report. They denied the rush into Confederate service, and said predatory outlaws existed only in the minds of the council. In their indignation they branded Chesnut's references as "untrue in spirit and in detail," "an insolent and malignant slander," a "cruel and wicked attack . . . destitute of truth or decency." Mss South Carolina Historical Commission.
[39] *Report of Chief of Military*, pp. 41-43.
[40] *Mercury*, August 8, 1862.

Believing that sufficient labor could be obtained from the regions immediately threatened, where the Negro was liable to escape anyway and where his work was interrupted by military events, the council at first prevailed upon the military authorities to limit their requisitions to those regions. The authorities complained of insufficient territory, and the council reluctantly agreed to extend the area to include Georgetown, Charleston, Colleton, Beaufort, Williamsburg, Clarendon, Orangeburg, and Barnwell districts.[41] There was considerable complaint in the districts affected and the requisitions were not fully met although the council threatened the use of force.[42] Unwilling to assume the responsibility for the possible fall of Charleston in consequence of an inadequate supply of labor, the council decided upon a state-wide system of impressment of Negroes. That part of the state which had not already been called upon was divided into four districts of approximately equal slave population and each required to furnish successively for one month one-third of all slaves liable to road duty. All sheriffs, road commissioners, and clerks were ordered to coöperate fully with F. S. Holmes, agent in charge of the impressment.[43] The scheme was designed to furnish 3,000 Negroes each month, for four months.

The state-wide impressment was effective but it was not relished by the planters. Memorials and communications begging relief were showered upon the council.[44] James H. Hammond, for example, protested vigorously, saying that the loss of one-third of his force would cost one-half of his crop.[45] A typcial protest was one from Abbeville signed by four members of the convention as well as by the road commissioners. The petitioners said that the chief grounds of objection in their district were that the coast was unhealthy and unsafe, that the Negroes were not properly cared for and were exposed to bad influences; the Negroes were moreover badly needed for pulling fodder. The memorialists hoped that the order would be postponed for a month or two, or that the planters would be allowed to pay fines for noncompliance. It was easy for the council to point out in reply that the dangers to which the Negroes were exposed were much less than those faced by the planters' sons in the ranks, that postponement was possible only if the enemy would agree to postpone his attack, and that experience had shown that labor could not be hired with the money which the planters proposed to pay for exemption. The council promised to reduce the danger of contamination and improper influences to a minimum by appointing a man of character to look after the Negroes while

[41] *Ibid.*
[42] *Courier,* June 20, 1862; Chesnut, *Diary,* p. 180 (June 9).
[43] *Mercury,* August 8, 1862.
[44] *Convention Journal,* p. 678.
[45] He tried to hire free Negroes as substitutes, but although he offered $40 per month he met with little or no success. J. H. Hammond to Pemberton, Ripley, Chesnut, Simms, etc., April 28-July 10, 1862, Hammond Papers.

on duty. But such arguments of the council did not satisfy the planters. Opposition to the impressment of slave labor continued, and no small part of the opposition to the council itself may be attributed to this cause. One opponent of the policy, in explaining a memorial from Clarendon County, charged that the council stood ready to quarter troops in the homes of planters whose Negroes were not furnished. "Can not the people of South Carolina see," he said, "we are drifting into a state of things most certain to end in civil war, if we are not directly restored to the safeguards of our constitutional guarantees?"[46]

A striking feature of the work of the executive council was the energetic and intelligent effort made to obtain war supplies under block-ade conditions. As early as March an agent was sent abroad to pur-chase medical supplies, rifles, and ammunition. Goods were brought through Charleston and Wilmington and other purchases made from privately imported stocks.[47] In order to increase the importation of military supplies the council attempted to prohibit the export of cotton except under bond that the proceeds would be invested in war materials and brought back through the blockade into the Confederacy. The attempt failed because of the opposition of the Confederate government, though the Confederacy itself later adopted a somewhat similar policy.[48]

In addition to the efforts made to import supplies the council made courageous attempts to improve the sources of supply at home. Two important needs were powder and lead. Dr. John LeConte investigated the possibilities of neglected lead mines and the state acquired a prom-ising mine in the Spartanburg District. Skilled labor was brought in from Tennessee and operations were begun.[49] Much lead was also ob-tained through donations. Various banks, churches, colleges, and indi-viduals contributed 66,771 pounds; many churches also gave their bells to be cast into cannon.[50] The scarcity of powder led the council to experiment with the manufacture of the required nitre. In February, Chesnut published a brief statement on how it might be produced and urged all who could to help. Receiving no response he obtained author-ity from the council for manufacture by the state. Dr. W. Hutson Ford, an army surgeon, was made superintendent; and with the help of

[46] *Mercury,* August 22, 1862; B. E. Habersham to J. L. Manning, undated, Chestnut-Manning-Miller Papers.

[47] *Report of Chief of Military,* pp. 6, 18, 22-23, 53; *Report of the Chief of the Department of Treasury and Finance to His Excellency Governor Pickens* (Co-lumbia, 1862), p. 11.

[48] *Convention Journal,* pp. 670-673; Camden *Confederate,* April 11, 1862; *Mer-cury,* April 23, 1862.

[49] *Report of Chief of Military,* p. 24; *Supplemental Report of the Chief of the Department of the Military of South Carolina* (Columbia, 1862), p. 11. The mine was operated through 1863 with indifferent success and sold to the Confederacy. *Report and Resolutions* (1863), pp. 158, 402; *ibid.,* 1864, p. 27.

[50] *Carolina Spartan,* July 31, 1862; *Mercury,* April 11, 24, August 25, 1862; *Courier,* March 27, 1862; Camden *Confederate,* April 11, May 16, 1862.

Dr. Joseph LeConte, he established, on what are now grounds of the state hospital in Columbia, what Chesnut believed was the first saltpetre plantation on the continent. By October 24 a large number of beds were in rapid process of nitrification and were expected to produce when one year old 1,000 pounds of nitre daily, or enough to make 1,333 pounds of powder. The *Courier* referred to the works as the most extensive in the Confederacy.[51]

The council also took steps to establish foundries and workshops for the repair and manufacture of arms. W. H. Gist became the head of a Department of Manufacture and Construction established March 24. He made a thorough investigation of the iron and other resources of the state, obtained machinery and skilled workers from Nashville and Charleston, and established at Greenvile under the superintendency of David Lopez an armory which began the repair of small arms and the manufacture of various kinds of military equipment. Gist thought the "State Works" would be ready to turn out shot and shell by October and cannon soon after.[52]

The council also began the construction of vessels for coast defense. Acting under authority given by the convention and with an appropriation of $300,000, the council appointed a commission to confer with the Confederate naval authorities and build a gunboat.[53] The *Chicora* was completed in October. The state was reimbursed by the Confederate government. In November the commission was pushing the construction of two additional vessels and estimated that one might be completed every ninety days.[54]

In various other ways the executive council exercised its powers for the more efficient prosecution of the war. In the interest of food conservation it prohibited distillation of liquors except under strict license, and finally revoked all licenses to distill except in fulfillment of contracts with the Confederate government.[55] Grog shops were closed in places easily accessible to soldiers.[56] Manufacture of salt was encouraged both through dissemination of information as to methods of production[57] and by appropriating $50,000 for a loan fund to those be-

[51] *Report of Chief of Military*, pp. 24-26; *Supplemental Report of Chief of Military*, p. 11; *Courier*, October 24, 1862.
[52] Gist's report, *Convention Journal*, pp. 712-717, 722; *Reports and Resolutions*, 1863, p. 156.
[53] *Convention Journal*, pp. 789-790.
[54] *Report of Chief of Military*, pp. 26-27; *Supplemental Report of Chief of Military*, p. 12. The cost of the *Chicora* was about $277,000. The commission consisted of J. K. Sass, G. A. Trenholm, C. M. Furman, W. C. Courtenay, and W. B. Heriot. The same commission was continued by the legislature of 1862. *Reports and Resolutions* (1862), p. 378.
[55] Camden *Confederate*, February 28, March 21, 1862; *Mercury*, November 5, 1862.
[56] *Mercury*, March 14, 1862; Camden *Confederate*, March 21, 1862.
[57] John LeConte, *How to Make Salt from Sea-water* (Columbia, 1862), published by the council.

ginning operations.[58] Money was supplied the Charleston and Savannah Railroad with which to purchase rolling stock and construct sidings on a line of great military importance. The council also financed the construction of a bridge over the Ashley River when General Pemberton said that such a bridge was a military necessity to connect the Charleston and Savannah Railroad with the South Carolina and Northeastern.[59] Martial law was proclaimed in and about Charleston at the request of the military authorities.[60] And when General Pemberton, having evacuated Cole's and half of James Island, talked of abandoning Forts Sumter and Moultrie and of defending Charleston in the city itself, the council raised such a storm of protest that Pemberton was finally replaced by Beauregard.[61]

There is little evidence that the council in any way abused the great powers delegated to it by the convention. Though the council received many affidavits and letters charging disloyalty of certain persons, only a few arrests were made and these were soon released. Some were arrested for distilling or selling whiskey on railroad lines but they too were either turned loose or freed on bond.[62] There seems good reason for the declaration of martial law in the zone of war. A passport system established in Columbia was of very short duration and gave little inconvenience. On the whole, it would seem that the council exercised its power with not only considerable energy and wisdom but with restraint as well.

[58] *Convention Journal*, pp. 678-679.

[59] *Ibid.*, pp. 679-682.

[60] *O. R.*, 1st series, XIV, 486-492. A system of police courts was established on the coast under an act of the legislature "to provide for more efficient police regulation" of the seaboard districts. Hayne who kept in close touch with the provost marshals who presided thought they did excellent work. *Convention Journal*, p. 674.

[61] For the council's resolution stating that South Carolina "would prefer a repulse of the enemy with the entire city in ruins to an evacuation or surrender on any terms whatever," see *O. R.*, 1st series, XIV, 510-511. For Pemberton and his inacceptablity in South Carolina see *ibid.*, pp. 503-521, 560-570, 601; *ibid.*, serial no. 111, pp. 247, 255.

[62] *Convention Journal*, pp. 675-676, 683; I. W. Hayne to M. L. Bonham, December 30, 1862, Pickens-Bonham Papers.

CHAPTER XI

ABOLITION OF THE COUNCIL

The effective measures adopted by the executive council for the mobilization of the state's resources for war did violence to the traditional individualism of South Carolina, and at a time when the increasing burdens of war were developing the first clear signs of war weariness. The result was an outcry against the executive council. Finally a political crusade for the restoration of "constitutional" government was waged and the usefulness of the council was largely destroyed. Meanwhile the three elected members whose ability and integrity had been so generally admitted became the objects of a campaign of "misrepresentation and abuse probably unparalleled in the history of the state."[1]

Apparently the first murmurings against the council were from friends of Pickens who resented the reflection cast upon him by the creation of the council. The Edgefield *Advertiser,* published in the home town of Pickens, pretended that the creation of the council was not intended as a slur on the governor. "It would be at once detestable and contemptible," it said, "to seek thus cruelly to wound the reputation of a patriotic public servant."[2] Unpopular measures of the council soon raised up allies for the friends of Pickens. Among the first of these was an order of February 20 that all gold and silver plate in private hands be reported "with a view of hereafter taking and melting such portion thereof as may be necessary to constitute the basis of future circulation to provide means for public defense, if such shall be deemed necessary."[3] This order was recognized as a mistake and withdrawn but a campaign against the council was soon under way. In Edgefield, a mass meeting on April 7 passed resolutions criticising the convention for having created the council and for continuing its own existence. It called upon the Edgefield members of the convention to work for the repeal of the council ordinance and invited other districts to call similar mass meetings.[4] Later in the month, a protest meeting was held in Marion, and in Charleston a petition carrying over seven hundred names called upon the delegates to exert themselves to have the convention reassembled for the purpose of dissolving itself and the council.[5] How much Governor Pickens had to do with initiating the

[1] Laura A. White, "The Fate of Calhoun's Sovereign Convention in South Carolina," *American Historical Review,* XXXIV (July, 1929), 760-761; hereinafter cited White, "Calhoun's Sovereign Convention."
[2] *Courier,* January 23, 1862, quoting the Edgefield *Advertiser.*
[3] Camden *Confederate,* March 7, 1862.   [4] *Carolinian,* April 11, 1862.
[5] *Mercury,* April 29, 1862; *Courier,* May 2, 1862.

movement is not clear.   His antagonistic attitude to the council from
the very first meeting was generally known and in Hayne's opinion was
responsible for early attacks in the Columbia papers.[6]   He seems to
have been kept informed of developments but to have followed the
advice of his friends that he should appear indifferent to the movement and connect himself as little as possible with it.[7]

Once organized the campaign against the executive council rapidly
developed.   Mass meetings were held in only about a dozen districts
of the state[8] but the newspapers with few exceptions waged an unre-
mitting editorial warfare and published hundreds of communications in
denunciation of the council.   They complained that the members of
the council by creating unnecessary offices and by themselves taking
salaries of $2,000 each were putting on the treasury a burden from which
it should be relieved.   There was criticism also of the appointment of
military officers by the council and of the needless closing of the South
Carolina College.[9]   For the most part, however, the objections were on
the general grounds that the council was exercising legislative as well as
executive power; and that it was an arbitrary, irresponsible body which,
meeting in secret sessions, threatened the liberties of the people.   It was
variously referred to as an "Aulic Council," an "odious despotism," a
"Lilliputian Lincolnism," a body of "tyrants" and "usurpers," an "incubus of wrongheadedness and inefficiency," a "snake that ought to be
both scotched and killed."[10]   It was said that the council had accomplished nothing which would not have been possible under a more
regular government, and that the efficiency of the council had been
destroyed by the lack of harmony and friction between its members.
There was some truth in the latter criticism.   Discord between Pickens
and the elected members existed from the first and was publicly aired
when an angry correspondence between Pickens and Hayne found its
way into the newspapers.   Both denied responsibility for the publicity
but the incident was seized upon by the opponents of the council as
proof that five "co-equal dictators" could not fail to "quarrel, snarl at,
and bite one another."[11]

There were comparatively few defenders of the council.   Among the
newspapers the Camden *Confederate* endorsed the work of the council
unreservedly and the Lancaster *Ledger,* though opposed to the council
on principle, thought there was no substantial grievance against it.   The
Mercury's criticism was that the council had failed in energy rather

[6] [I. W. Hayne] to F. W. Pickens, March 5, 1862, F. W. Pickens Papers.
[7] Henry Buist to F. W. Pickens, April 29, 1862, F. W. Pickens Papers.
[8] White, "Calhoun's Sovereign Convention," *loc. cit.,* pp. 761-762.
[9] Correspondents of *Courier,* May 3, July 2, 1862, and Lancaster *Ledger,* September 10, 1862.
[10] *Courier,* May 15, June 16, July 1, 4, August 6, October 14, 1862.
[11] *Ibid.,* August 1, 2, 5, 6, 9, 1862; White, "Calhoun's Sovereign Convention,"
loc. cit., p. 766; I. W. Hayne to F. W. Pickens, March 5, 1862, F. W. Pickens
Papers.

than in aggressiveness and that it had done too little rather than too much. Chiefly interested in its own quarrel with President Davis, the *Mercury* took a minor part in the council controversy. It believed that the council had done good work in raising troops and in calling out labor for the coast. Bitterly denouncing secret sessions of Congress, it defended secret sessions of the council on the ground that the latter was an executive and not a legislative body.[12]

The furious attack on the council as an unconstitutional oligarchy led inevitably to condemnation of the convention which had created it. Indeed one of the most interesting features of the whole controversy was the debate which developed over the abstract, but then quite important question, of the nature and extent of the power vested in a "sovereign convention." Calhoun's theory that sovereignty resided in the people of the state and that they exercised their sovereign power through an elected convention which, once assembled, spoke with a voice which was the voice of the people themselves had long been accepted in South Carolina. According to this theory the convention was not merely a body of delegates representing the people; it *was* the people, and there-fore sovereign. As sovereignty was illimitable, there could be no limit to the authority of the convention. Convenient as this theory had proved as a defense against federal encroachment and as a method of actual secession, it could now only embarrass those who questioned the authority of a council whose powers had been conferred by "the people of South Carolina in convention assembled."[13]

There were many shades of opinion as to the exact status and powers of the convention. Some, unwilling to renounce the old theory, did not deny that the council had been legally created but insisted that by exercising legislative as well as executive powers the council had exceeded its authority and had abused the confidence placed in it by the convention. Even some friends of the council thought it had erred in this respect. Others admitted the complete sovereignty of the convention but held that its ordinance creating the council was an ill-advised action constituting an abuse of its sovereign authority. It was also suggested that while the convention itself was competent to exercise all power it could not legally delegate such unlimited authority to a mere agent, the council.[14]

Many of the council's enemies went further and questioned the funda-

[12] Camden *Confederate*, September 5, 1862; Lancaster *Ledger*, September 10, 1862; *Mercury*, September 2, 6, August 7, 1862. The *Courier* when chided by the *Mercury* for acquiescing in secret sessions of Congress while denouncing secret sessions of the council defended itself by making a distinction between a consti-tutional Confederate government and an unconstitutional, usurping council. *Courier*, August 13, 1862.

[13] An excellent discussion of this phase of the controversy is Miss White's "Calhoun's Sovereign Convention," *loc. cit.*

[14] *Mercury*, September 6, 1862, quoting Lancaster *Ledger*; *Courier*, August 6, 13, 1862 (Civis); White, *loc. cit.*, p. 761, *passim*.

mental theory of convention sovereignty. Quoting the opinion of Chancellor William Harper in 1834 to sustain them, they held that a convention was always limited in power by the act of the legislature which called it. In any event, a convention was only a government-forming or constitution-making body and possessed no governmental power either legislature or executive. In this view, which Chief Justice John Belton O'Neall was represented as endorsing, the convention had accomplished its purpose when it ratified the permanent Confederate Constitution and by continuing its existence had been guilty of usurpation. The *Courier*, most zealous leader of the opposition, even denied that a convention was the people; it was a mere representative body convened on special occasions for the accomplishment of special purposes which were beyond the authority delegated to the legislature. According to this view the convention possessed no sovereign, original power but only derived or delegated power and was fully responsible to the people who alone were sovereign.[15] In its enthusiasm the *Courier* went so far as to question the theory of indivisible and illimitable state sovereignty. Denying any difference between sovereignty and sovereign power, it defined sovereignty as the mere governing power and held that under a system of the separation of powers sovereignty was divided between executive, judicial, and legislative bodies each supreme in its own sphere. Constitution-making sovereignty rested in a convention but was not necessarily of greater importance than legislative sovereignty exercised by the General Asembly. Sovereignty was thus divided. In no agent of the people was it unlimited. And the people themselves were limited by their bill of rights.[16]

These attacks on the sovereignty of the convention drew quick response from the defenders of the council and from some who held no particular brief for that body. The *Mercury*, for example, though lukewarm in its defense of the council, staunchly defended the orthodox theory of the convention and steadily opposed the demand for its dissolution. Apparently it was partly influenced by the belief that the convention might become necessary to defend South Carolina from the usurpations of the Confederate government.[17] Other defenders of the sovereignty of the convention and council insisted that the legislature had not and could not limit the convention by the terms of the act calling it. Indeed there had been no necessity for calling the convention, they said, if the legislature through this power of limitation was itself sovereign. Nor could the convention possibly be guilty of usurpation, for the people could not usurp power from themselves. Even the

[15] *Ibid.*, pp. 762-763 citing *Courier*, February 11, May 1, July 16, August 28, September 6, 1862. See also *Courier*, July 1, 23, August 14, 21, 25, September 8, 11, 20, 1862; *Mercury*, September 3, 1862.

[16] White, Calhoun's Sovereign Convention," *loc. cit.*, pp. 763-764; *Courier*, September 6, 11, 20, October 10, 16, 1862.

[17] *Mercury*, April 29, May 24, August 5, 7, 14, September 2, 1862.

establishment of a monarchy would have been within the convention's power through such an act would perhaps have been an abuse. But there had been no abuse of authority. To the charge that the convention had assumed legislative power the answer was that it had *all* power. To the charge that the convention had encroached upon the executive by creating the council, it was replied that this was necessary because of the "lamentable inertness"' of Governor Pickens after Fort Sumter and the lack of wisdom and foresight displayed by the legislature of 1861. Since it was impossible for either the legislature or the convention to sit continuously, it had been urgently necessary to set up some agency to make the daily decisions required by the emergency.[18] So ran the arguments of the council's friends.

But the people of South Carolina were tired of the council and of the convention which created it. There was talk of calling another convention for the special purpose of dissolving the old one. This, said the *Mercury,* would be revolution and the people who made the revolution of 1860 would not submit to counter-revolution.[19] But President Jamison made no move, on his own responsibility, to reconvene the convention for the purpose of dissolving it, and in spite of urgent requests from those who feared that the situation was becoming dangerous it was difficult to get the required twenty convention members to petition the president to do so. On August 21, however, the twentieth signature was secured and Jamison issued the call for the convention to meet September 9, 1862.[20]

The campaign against the convention and council was at its height when the convention assembled. A few days before the convention met, the anti-convention sentiment in Charleston strikingly expressed itself in the overwhelming election of John Phillips to the seat in the convention vacated by Magrath. Phillips was an outspoken anti-convention man and received 296 of the 310 votes cast. In Lexington a mass meeting adopted anti-convention resolutions with only seven dissenting votes.[21] It was apparent that popular opinion dictated the abolition of the council and dissolution of the convention, but the convention was not stampeded. Dignified and unhurried, it proceeded to examine the record of the council's activity.

[18] *Ibid.,* August 30, September 1, 2, 3, 4, 5, 6, 8 ("South Carolina"), September 4 ("Calhoun"), 1862; *Courier,* August 6, 13, 15, 1862 ("Civis"); Lancaster *Ledger,* September 10, 17, 1862.

[19] Lancaster *Ledger,* September 17, 1862, quoting the *Mercury.*

[20] Jamison was unjustly charged with having postponed the call long after he had received the twenty requests, and he was asked to publish the names and dates. He refused to publish the names but gave the dates. *Courier,* August 18, 19, 30, September 8, 1862. Of the twenty making the requests, ten had voted for the creation of the council, four against, and six had been absent or not voted. One request had been made in April, six in May, two in June, six in July, and five in August. *Convention Journal,* pp. 397-399.

[21] *Mercury,* September 2, 3, 1862; White, "Calhoun's Sovereign Convention," *loc. cit.,* pp. 767-768.

Governor Pickens, in accordance with the convention's request, made a report and transmitted complete records and correspondence bearing on the council's activities. Included were reports from the heads of the departments which set forth the work of each department and constituted as well a defense of the council's record. Hayne's report in large part was in the nature of a legal opinion on the complete sovereignty of the convention and on the legality under the ordinance of each of the council's measures. Incidentally, he was careful to point out that Pickens approved the various decisions of the council and that some of the most unpopular measures, such as the proposal to seize gold and silver plate, had been suggested by him along with other extreme measures not adopted. Among the latter were suggestions for the seizure of half of all cotton, flour, and wheat produced in the state.[22]

The reports and records from the council were submitted to a committee of twenty-one which, through sub-committees, examined them in detail. In its report the committee stated that after careful consideration it had discovered nothing in the proceedings of the governor and council which seemed to require "repeal, modification or animadversion"; that the council had, at a great personal sacrifice and with exclusive regard for the public welfare, discharged its duties with "signal diligence, ability and success." The committee moreover was "deeply impressed with the conviction that the ordinary powers of the Executive would have been entirely inadequate to effect the objects to which the labors of the Council have been directed, and that the establishment of such a body . . . was required by the condition of the country and the exigencies of the times."[23] On the question whether a convention might be limited by the legislature, the committee thought it unnecessary to speak since the convention and council had in every act been well within the scope of the act of the legislature which called it. It was believed that publication of the minutes of the council and the reports of the department heads would "conduce much to the satisfaction of the public mind, and tend to harmonize conflicting views of State policy."[24] The report was adopted without change.

Having placed its stamp of approval upon the work of the council, the convention turned to the future. On the second day of the convention John Phillips had moved the abolition of the council and repeal of all council measures amendatory of acts or resolutions of the legis-

[22] Pickens said that since he had been uninformed of the full intentions of the convention in forming the council he had left the construction of its powers to the elected members. "I acquiesced, and am not responsible for many measures, as original positive measures, but rather as secondary or alternative measures, under the peculiar circumstances of the case." *Convention Journal*, pp. 585-586. The reports of Chesnut, Hayne, Harllee, and Gist are in *ibid.*, pp. 587 *et seq.*

[23] *Ibid.*, pp. 734-735.

[24] *Ibid.*, pp. 736, 739. A motion to strike out of the report the statement concerning the necessity of creating the council was defeated. *Ibid.*, p. 426.

lature, except those which Pickens deemed necessary for the safety of the state. This proposal and a petition from the people of Marlboro that the convention itself dissolve were referred to a committee of seven. The majority report of this committee recommended that an address to the people, explaining why the convention was so long undissolved and why the executive council had been created, be published; that both convention and council expire upon the meeting of the legislature; and that the legislature be empowered to recreate the council with its original powers and to elect its members. A minority report, presented by Phillips, recommended the dissolution of both the council and the convention at once.[25] A number of amendments were offered. One, offered by Hayne, would have continued the council but would have made it responsible to the legislature. Harllee suggested that the council be chosen by the legislature and be made responsible to the governor. An amendment by Inglis proposed that the terms of the members of the council end on the second Monday in December; that their successors be chosen by the legislature should that body decide to continue the council either in original or modified form; and that the convention itself stand dissolved on December 17, exactly two years from the date of its original organization.[26]

There followed an earnest though short debate. Former Governor Richardson represented the small group who attacked the council both on principal and its record. He argued that conventions were mere representative bodies limited to the objects specified in the call of the legislature, and might neither exercise nor delegate legislative powers. The council he held was "impotent for good," having failed to prevent the loss of Georgetown or the abandonment of Cole's Island. It was "omnipotent for evil," having accustomed peaceful and law abiding people to rise up against their rulers. It was expensive, unnecessary, and as capable of abuse as the oligarchy of Venice.[27]

At the other extreme was R. W. Barnwell who thought the council had done its duty and accomplished much good. He was opposed to any compromise. There was still danger, still work to be done; the council and convention should continue unchanged; the convention should not quail before the popular clamor but do its duty regardless of the consequences. With him stood T. D. Wagner who had been one of the twenty calling the convention but who was now convinced by the reports of the department heads that both convention and council should continue. Although J. I. Middleton had voted against the creation of the council he agreed with Barnwell that no change should be made. His people, he said, could not condone the failure of the up country to respond to the call for the defense of Georgetown.[28]

[25] *Mercury,* September 17, 1862; *Convention Journal,* pp. 406-407.
[26] *Ibid.,* pp. 431-434.   [27] *Mercury,* September 18, 1862.
[28] *Ibid.*

The majority of the convention, however, agreed neither with Richardson and Phillips on the one hand nor with Barnwell and Wagner on the other. They believed that the creation of the council had been demanded by the emergency and vindicated by results. Most agreed that it should be continued in some form, though there was a feeling that as a result of the passage of the Confederate conscription acts the situation had so changed as to make it less indispensable. More important than the continuation of the council was some adjustment which would bring an end to the agitation which distracted the state and threatened mischief. The dissolution of the convention seemed the only remedy. To accept Phillips's minority report for immediate dissolution, however, might be construed an acknowledgment of error and the convention voted 99 to 25 against it. Even dissolution as the legislature assembled in accordance with the majority report seemed too undignified. The Inglis amendments, under which the convention would expire December 17 if not reassembled to meet an emergency before that date, were, therefore, adopted. The future of the council was left to the legislature.[29]

The convention adjourned September 17, a few weeks before the October elections for the legislature which would finally decide the council's fate. As early as August it had been suggested that the council be made the issue of the campaign. In Charleston an anti-council ticket was put up with the warning that the odious oligarchy was not yet dethroned and that it would struggle at the next legislature to perpetuate itself and all its iniquities.[30] Public opinion was everywhere so overwhelmingly against the council that there was little contest on the issue. The results of the election did clearly indicate, however, a revulsion against the old leadership. In Charleston, R. B. Rhett, Jr., of the *Mercury* and the old secession radical L. W. Spratt were left at home but Richard Yeadon of the *Courier* was elected; B. F. Perry came back into public life from Greenville and strongly opposed Aldrich for speaker of the house. There were many new faces. Simms wrote from Columbia that there were some ninety-six new members "each eager to fire his pop gun" at the convention and council.[31] It was evident that Governor Pickens and the legislature were ready to take sweet revenge for the indignities forced upon them.

In his opening message Governor Pickens severely arraigned the convention for its "remarkable experiment" in government. It had

[29] *Courier*, November 8, December 4, 1862; *Mercury*, September 18, 1862; *Convention Journal*, pp. 441-450, 798-799.
[30] *Courier*, August 6, 1862; *Mercury*, October 14, 1862. R. B. Rhett, Jr., was curiously enough placed on the anti-council ticket.
[31] White, "Calhoun's Sovereign Convention," *loc. cit.*, pp. 769-770, note 41; *Mercury*, October 15, 1862; W. G. Simms to J. H. Hammond, December 4, 1862, Hammond Papers; *Courier*, November 26, 28, 1862. The final vote for speaker was Aldrich 48, Perry 27, T. N. Dawkins 20.

160

been called, he said, for the sole purpose of ending the old compact and entering a new; this was the only purpose for which it was ever necessary to call a convention in South Carolina because the constitution provided for its own amendment by two successive legislatures; it was against the spirit and genius of the constitution for a convention to amend it on "local points"; it was much less proper for the convention to legislate and even delegate legislative powers. Defending his record in 1861, the governor held that the creation of the council under the pretext of strengthening the executive was not only a gross but a needless violation of the constitution. He recommended that it be immediately abolished and that the governor be given a cabinet responsible to himself.[32]

The legislature needed no urging. It resented the action of the convention in shifting the responsibility for abolishing the council to legislative shoulders, and angrily accepted the invitation not only to abolish the council but also to insult the convention. Trenholm, Simpson Bobo, and W. F. Hutson raised their voices in defense of both but without effect. Perry, though unalterably opposed to the council, expressed regret that such feeling and excitement should appear in the debate, and begged that justice be tempered with mercy, but even his position was far too tame for the great majority in the House.[33] The majority sentiment was expressed in resolutions, offered by William Whaley, which declared that the legislature felt an unabated respect and affection for the constitution; that it still regarded the principle of separation of powers as fundamental and necessary to the continued existence of the constitution; and that all attempts to set aside this principle should be regarded as mischievous and as inevitably tending towards either anarchy or despotism. Conventions should only be called to make important constitutional changes and not to conduct the government either directly or through appointed committees or councils; there was and always must be an essential difference between the power of the people themselves and the powers of any convention of their delegates for whatever purpose assembled. In a final resolution of censure, the legislature declared that it regarded with profound regret any measure which might have been adopted by the late convention at variance with the principles of constitutional government and that the legislature felt obligated to remedy, as far as possible, any mischief or inconvenience that might have resulted from such departure from sound principles. In spite of some objection in the Senate, the last resolution was passed by votes of 25 to 11 and 88 to 15.[34]

[32] *Message No. 1 of His Excellency F. W. Pickens* . . . November, 1862, pp. 22-29.
[33] *Courier*, December 1, 4, 1862. For Perry's speech see the *Southern Enterprise*, January 1, 1863; *Courier*, December 17, 1862.
[34] *House Journal* (1862), pp. 39, 96; *Senate Journal* (1862), p. 100; *Reports and Resolutions* (1862), p. 379.

December 18, 1862, the day after the convention expired by its own ordinance, the legislature abolished the executive council and then declared invalid all its acts, proceedings, resolutions, and orders, except contracts.[35] The legislature also attempted to remedy the "mischief" wrought by the departure from constitutional government. It was especially critical of the military policies of the council. For example, the order of the council disbanding the fourth and tenth regiments of the First Corps of Reserves because of disaffection, was revoked.[36] An investigation was made of the grievances and of the circumstances under which the First Corps of Reserves had been offered to the Confederacy for ninety days' service. It is clear that the legislature felt that the services of the Reserves should not have been offered. Resolutions were adopted, however, which declared that it was inexpedient to discuss the justness of the grievances or the wisdom of forming the First Corps of Reserves and that patriotism required the regiments to waive their grievances and march to active service for the pledged ninety days.[37] An act was soon passed forbidding their service beyond ninety days from the date of enlistment and requiring that field officers appointed by the executive council should be displaced as soon as regimental elections could be held for their successors. This meant the reorganization of the reserve regiments at the very time they were entering Confederate service, and likewise of four volunteer regiments which the *Mercury* described as among the finest in service. The law was not only an untimely and unwise revival of the elective principle but was also of doubtful validity because it applied to troops already mustered into Confederate service. It was criticised by Beauregard and repealed at the request of Governor Bonham.[38]

The legislature, in its hatred of the council, condoned the attitude of those who had resisted the draft for the defense of Georgetown, and at the same time struck at Chesnut who had reported it to the convention. His reference to an uninformed press was heatedly answered by Richard Yeadon who gloried in the fact that he had led the newspaper war against the council. The legislature also adopted resolutions declaring that the section comprising the fourth division of the militia had furnished its full proportion of troops for state and Confederate service; and that if there had been manifested an unwillingness to respond to calls for troops in that, or any other section, it was from no disregard for the sovereignty of the state, nor because "the spirit was

[35] *Statutes at Large,* XIII, 128.
[36] *Ibid.,* pp. 111-112. Pickens said there was so much disaffection in the fourth regiment that Chesnut had recommended a court martial of some of the officers. Pickens suggested a court inquiry. *Courier,* December 6, 1862.
[37] *Courier,* November 29, December 1, 6, 1862; *Mercury,* December 1, 1862; *House Journal* (1862), p. 244.
[38] *Statutes at Large,* XIII, 111-112; *Mercury,* January 8, 1863; *Courier,* January 23, 1863.

wanting," but because of a conviction, common to many citizens, that the extraordinary authority which issued the calls was "unconstitutional and oppressive."[39]

Governor Pickens emerged from the executive council controversy with a popularity greater than he had ever before enjoyed. He had ambitions for the Senate and could no doubt have been elected to Orr's seat if the latter had been willing to accept the governorship. This, however, Orr declined to do.[40] Some of Pickens's friends suggested that his term be prolonged by simply failing to elect a successor, but such a course was immediately denounced as unconstitutional by the strongly pro-Pickens Charleston *Courier*.[41] At the expiration of his term, therefore, Pickens returned to private life.[42]

With Orr eliminated, the race for governor promised to become a general scramble. An unusually large number of men were prominently mentioned. Hammond, because of ill health, declined to be a candidate,[43] and Chesnut was passed over because of his connection with the executive council. There was talk of W. H. Trescot, W. P. Miles, John McQueen, James Simons, and of B. F. Perry who had now returned to the legislature.[44] John S. Preston, who had the promise of support from the influential ex-Governors John P. Richardson and John L. Manning, was a strong candidate. Manning had earlier urged Preston to join the fight against the council which would certainly have been good politics. But Preston frankly defended the council as an emergency agency and in the convention fought for its continuance. Richardson and Manning were displeased, but a few days before the legislature met Manning assured Preston of his continued support. Preston's defense of the council, however, cost him the governorship. Yeadon of the *Courier* thought that he would have had no difficulty in attaining his well-known ambition had his "skirts been clear of this political sin." Sensing the prejudice against Preston, Manning decided to desert his candidate and to stand for the office himself.[45] He had been

[39] *Courier*, December 1, 1862; *Reports and Resolutions* (1862), p. 321.
[40] J. L. Petigru to J. J. Pettigrew, November 30, 1862, Pettigrew Papers; *Courier*, December 4, 1862.
[41] *Courier*, December 8, 1862.
[42] In 1864 two tickets for the legislature in Charleston were headed "F. W. Pickens for Governor" but it was soon pointed out that the constitution required four years between terms and the tickets were abandoned. *Courier*, October 5, 6, 1864.
[43] J. H. Hammond to A. P. Aldrich, November 27, 1862, Hammond Papers.
[44] Jamison, Keitt, John Townsend, and P. C. J. Weston were also mentioned. *Courier*, November 28, 1862; J. L. Petigru to J. J. Pettigrew, November 30, 1862, Pettigrew Papers.
[45] *Courier*, December 5, 1862. An angry correspondence between Manning and Preston followed the election, Preston charging bad faith and Manning pleading his responsibility to defend constitutional government. For the whole incident see Richardson to Preston, July —, 1862; Preston to Richardson July 8, 1862; Preston to Manning, November 30, December 15, 1862; William Whaley to Manning,

urged to run on the ground that after the "manifold blunders" of Pickens and the usurpations of the council, South Carolina needed him again in charge.[46] It was probably not hard to convince himself that Preston's defense of the council had rendered him unavailable.

Manning's expected victory over Preston did not materialize due to the appearance of a dark horse in the person of M. L. Bonham, then a member of the Confederate House.   On the first ballot Bonham led Manning by one vote with Preston a poor third; on the second Bonham was only one short of a majority, and on the third he was elected.[47] Manning complained that he would have been chosen but for the "hostility and personal unkindness of those who, by every consideration of relationship and common gratitude, should have been my fastest friends."   He commented, too, on Bonham's "art of political approaches which even his knowledge of Military Tactics and approaches do not equal."[48]   Plowden C. J. Weston was chosen lieutenant governor.[49]

December 13, 1862; J. J. Williams and T. P. Lockwood to Manning, December 13, 1862; Manning to Preston, December 14, 1862, Williams-Chesnut-Manning Papers.

[46] B. H. Wilson to Manning, September 1, 1862, Chesnut-Manning-Miller Papers.

[47] *Courier*, December 5, 12, 13, 1862; *Mercury*, December 17, 18, 1862; *House Journal* (1862), pp. 191-192. The final vote was Bonham 79, Manning 63, Preston 3, Trescot 6, scattered 7.

[48] Manning to B. T. Watts, January 23, 1863, Watts Papers.

[49] *Senate Journal* (1862), p. 125.

CHAPTER XII

CONSCRIPTION

In Governor Milledge L. Bonham, Edgefield gave her second war governor to South Carolina. After graduating from South Carolina College, he practiced law in his native town and in 1844 was elected to the state legislature. From 1848 to 1857 he was solicitor of his district after which he served in Congress, as the successor of Preston S. Brooks, until the secession of his state in 1860. A former lieutenant colonel in the Mexican War, he was appointed by Governor Pickens as major general and commander-in-chief of the military forces raised by South Carolina immediately after secession. Just after the fall of Fort Sumter he was appointed a Confederate brigadier and served in Virginia until January, 1862, when he resigned in protest against loss of seniority caused by the fact that his original appointment had been superseded by a later one. He then served in the Confederate House of Representatives until his election as governor.[1]

The election of Bonham was generally satisfactory to the state and brought to the office of governor one who was well fitted by political and military experience and by personal qualities to provide the executive leadership in the difficult days of 1863 and 1864. Bred in the South Carolina state rights school and possessing a grievance against the administration at Richmond, he was nevertheless much less disposed than some Southern governors to embarrass the Confederate government by an insistence on the rights of the state. As he said in his farewell message to the legislature in 1864, his aim was not only "to preserve the honor and rights of the State," but also to have South Carolina perform her full duty to the Confederacy.[2] His appointment as brigadier general at the end of his term was a recognition of the coöperation which he gave to the Davis administration.

Bulking large among the problems of Bonham's administration were those intimately connected with the prosecution of the war. Of these the problem of obtaining men for the armies under the Confederate conscription acts was of primary importance. In South Carolina as elsewhere the difficulties of enforcing the draft laws became increasingly apparent in the later years of the war. Such failure as attended conscription in South Carolina was, however, not due in any great degree to obstacles set up by the state authorities. Though second to none in

---

[1] *D. A. B.*, II, 436; Dickert, *Kershaws' Brigade*, pp. 51 *et seq.* For Bonham's defense of his resignation from the army see *Mercury*, March 21, 1862. See also *ibid.*, January 31, February 1, 11, 1862.

[2] *Mercury*, December 2, 1864.

devotion to state rights principles there was a general disposition on the part of South Carolina leaders to waive state rights objections in the interest of harmony and victory. As Professor N. W. Stephenson says, the prevailing view "was that of experienced, disillusioned men who realized from the start that secession had burnt their bridges, and that now they must win the fight or change the whole current of their lives."[3] Some conflict did occur, as will be noted in the following pages, but there did not appear any strong disposition deliberately to withold men from Confederate conscription until the last days of the war when confidence had finally been lost in the ability or willingness of the Confederate government to protect the state from subjugation.

The majority of the South Carolina members of the Confederate Congress opposed the passage of the first conscription law of April 16, 1862. In the Senate, Orr offered an amendment to authorize the President to call on each state for its quota of 600,000 men with the proviso that in states failing to supply their quotas within thirty days he might call out the militia between the ages of 18 and 40 for the duration of the war. This proposal for a sort of conditional draft was rejected and Orr voted against the final passage of the bill. His colleague Barnwell supported it. In the House only W. P. Miles voted for the measure.[4]

Once passed, the constitutionality of the conscription law was immediately upheld by Confederate District Judge A. G. Magrath, his decision being the first of similar ones by state and Confederate courts elsewhere.[5] As has been already shown the executive council raised no protest against conscription and quickly expressed its intention to give cheerful and prompt support to it.[6] The state rolls were offered to the conscription officials and sheriffs were directed to coöperate fully, special pay for such service being allowed them. In explaining the council's attitude, Pickens wrote:

If we submitted to the Confederate law and placed all our military resources under the control of the Confederate authority for the defense of the country, it was sound policy to give the most efficient aid to their officers in bringing men into service.[7]

The legislature which abolished the council continued this policy and authorized the governor to use the militia to assist Confederate agents in arresting deserters and slackers.[8] Other laws were passed from time to time. One of September, 1863, made sheriffs liable to a $1,000

[3] N. W. Stephenson, *The Day of the Confederacy* (New Haven, 1920), p. 75.
[4] *Journal Confed. Cong.*, II, 153-154, V, 219-222, 224, 226, 228. The second conscription act was likewise supported by only Barnwell and Miles. *Ibid.*, II, 321, 335, V, 344-345, 388, 400, 442-443.
[5] A. B. Moore, *Conscription and Conflict in the Confederacy* (New York, 1924), p. 168.
[6] *Supra*, p. 145.
[7] F. W. Pickens to M. L. Bonham, January 21, 1863, Pickens-Bonham Papers.
[8] *Statutes at Large*, XIII, 91.

fine for failing to act after receiving information as to desertion or evasion of conscription.[9]

It is clear that South Carolina officially accepted the policy of conscription and on the whole gave support to its enforcement. There was, however, some conflict between the state and Confederate authorities on the question of exemptions. The state exemption laws were not much more liberal than those of the Confederacy, and probably resulted in only a small number being witheld from draft, but the state was at first quite unyielding in its insistence on the right to exempt. This was made clear immediately after the passage of the first Confederate conscription and exemption laws. The state list of exempted classes differed from the Confederate list mainly in the matter of overseers, whose exemption had been specifically provided for by an ordinance of the convention, and in the case of students over eighteen in the military academy who were included in a list drawn by the the the council March 7, 1862.[10]

In letter of April 30, Chesnut called the attention of the Secretary of War to the fact that the Confederate exemption act did not include overseers. He suggested that in cases where they were exempt under state law they might be assigned to their place without pay. He argued that many volunteers had been able to leave only by employing overseers and that agriculture would suffer greatly if they were taken. They were needed, he said, for protection of women and children. Chesnut also requested exemption for students in the military academy. Secretary Randolph replied on May 13 that he had no authority to exempt overseers but he intimated that Congress would probably act on the matter at its next session.[11] So great, however, was the anxiety on the subject in South Carolina that the council immediately announced that all holding exemptions under the state law would be protected. This position was reasserted June 26 with definite orders to citizens exempt under state law to claim exemption before the enrolling officers and to notify the adjutant and inspector general if the claim were denied by the Confederate officers. Late in July, Chesnut saw the Secretary of War personally and explained that the sovereign convention of South Carolina had demanded the exemption of overseers in certain cases and that the council must therefore insist. Secretary Randolph, while again pointing out his inability to change the law, assured Chesnut there would be no trouble and stated that he would instruct his agents simply to protest, where the state insisted, and to refer the case to Richmond. In accordance with this policy, Commandant of Conscripts John S. Preston announced that individuals claiming exemption under state

[9] *Ibid.*, pp. 153-154.
[10] *Report of Chief of Military*, pp. 10-11; *O. R.*, serial no. 127, pp. 976-977, 1081.
[11] *Ibid.*, serial no. 127, pp. 1106-1107, 1121.

law would not be drafted until their cases were appealed and disposed of.[12]

The issue soon reappeared, however. On August 19 the council felt it necessary to inform Colonel Preston that it still insisted on state exemptions and that public policy demanded that "a countervailing order should issue from the state authority" upon the appearance of any order from him calling into service those exempt by the state. This communication was referred to Richmond and elicited a spirited rebuke from President Davis. It was with profound regret, he said, that he learned of South Carolina's contemplated order to obstruct the operation of the conscription law. South Carolina was claiming the right to relieve "at her pleasure" a portion of her citizens from obedience to a law which was clearly within the scope of the power given Congress to raise armies. If the state could free her citizens from this law then they might be freed from the tax laws, or any other laws, and make a Confederacy impracticable. Strange, he said, was the claim that a state executive could countervail an order of the Confederate executive; certainly he could conceive of no case in which the President might countervail an order of the state executive. And though South Carolina once *nullified* a law of the general government never before had she claimed the right to *modify* one of its orders. He hoped that the rights of citizens would be left for determination by the courts and that South Carolina would not embarrass the conduct of the war by the action proposed. Any conflict between the Confederate and South Carolina executives would have a deplorable effect upon public opinion and should be avoided.[13]

The passage of the liberal Confederate exemption law of October 11, 1862, relieved the conflict insofar as it involved overseers. The new law exempted, for the proper policing of the country, one overseer or owner for each plantation which the state law designated and an additional person for every twenty slaves on two or more plantations within five miles of each other.[14] This liberal law removed South Carolina's objections.

The "twenty-nigger" law, regarded as pure class legislation by many of the people of the South, was so unpopular that it was drastically amended to the overseer's disadvantage May 1, 1863. The new law would have no doubt revived the conflict between state and Confederacy had an effort been made to enforce it strictly. But the Confederate authorities hesitated to apply it in the middle of the crop season and followed a policy of granting temporary exemptions until autumn.[15] There was therefore little conflict between South Carolina

[12] *Report of Chief of Military,* pp. 10-11; *Courier,* July 7, 1862; *Mercury,* June 27, 1862.

[13] *O. R.,* serial no. 128, pp. 73-75.

[14] *Ibid.,* pp. 160-162.

[15] Moore, *Conscription and Conflict,* p. 74; *O. R.,* serial no. 128, pp. 553-554.

and the Confederacy over exemptions throughout the greater part of 1863.

Governor Bonham foresaw the return of trouble as soon as the May law should be strictly applied. He gave as one reason for assembling the legislature in extra session September 21, 1863, the desirability of harmonizing so far as possible the state and Confederate policy in regard to exemptions. He had felt bound to uphold the state law, but he believed the state should conform to the laws of Congress on the subject and so recommended.[16] The legislature, however, failed to take action, possibly for lack of time in the short session.

The failure of the legislature to follow the recommendation of the governor caused immediate trouble. October 1, the day following adjournment, Commandant of Conscripts C. D. Melton, issued orders that overseers and owners hitherto exempt under the law of October 11, 1862, and all persons who had been withheld from draft by claiming exemption under state law, should report to the enrolling officers at once. No overseer would be exempt, he said, except those who were overseers on April 16, 1862, and were employed on a plantation which entitled the owner to claim exemption for an overseer under the law of May 1, namely, plantations of dependents, minors, imbeciles, single women, or men in the field. The privilege of volunteering was offered those who enrolled, indicated their company choice, and went forward by October 26.[17] Thus the issue of exemptions was again joined, for the state law was more liberal than the Confederate law of May 1.[18]

Though Bonham had favored the amendment of the state law to conform to that of the Confederacy, he felt bound to uphold the state's claim. October 4 he issued a proclamation saying that he regarded exemptions under state authority valid in law and that they should be insisted upon. All citizens exempt under state law were ordered therefore to claim the exemption before the enrolling officers and to notify the adjutant and inspector general "to the end that the question may be submitted for the decision of some competent legal tribunal."[19] On October 8 Bonham wrote Secretary of War Seddon saying that the state legislature would no doubt take action at its regular session to remove the conflict. He suggested that the Confederate authorities suspend any further action until the legislature could meet, and added that great inconvenience would result if the overseers were taken off before the end of the year. Seddon replied that Preston, now superintendent of the Bureau of Conscription in Richmond, would visit South Carolina to discuss the whole matter and that he hoped it would result in the removal of the state's objections.[20]

[16] *House Journal* (1863), September session, p. 9.
[17] *O. R.,* serial no. 128, p. 865.
[18] For the South Carolina law see *Statutes at Large,* XIII, 90.
[19] *O. R.,* serial no. 128, p. 866.
[20] *Ibid.,* pp. 864, 867-868, 874.

The mission of Preston to South Carolina was entirely successful. It was agreed, in accordance with Bonham's suggestion, that no action should be taken prior to the meeting of the legislature. When this body assembled, it proceeded to pass a law which gave up all insistence on exemption from Confederate service under state law, declaring that the exemption laws of the state were applicable only to the military forces of South Carolina "and not to troops raised by the laws of the Confederate States."[21]   Under this law of December 17, 1863, little conflict was possible between state and Confederacy over exemptions. There did arise, however, a question as to whether the new Confederate exemption law of February 17, 1864, cancelled overseer exemptions made under the law of May 1, 1863.   The test case involved an overseer for whose exemption the woman owner of a plantation had paid $500 as required by the law of May 1.   Drafted under the subsequent law he was released on a writ of *habeas corpus* by Judge Munro of Greenville on the ground that the exemption involved a contract for one year, a contract not annulled by the subsequent law.   The case was reviewed by the Court of Errors.[22]   Avoiding the question of the *power* of Congress to annul contracts made under the earlier law, the court held that it had not been the *purpose* of Congress to make the law retroactive.[23]

There was some correspondence also between Governor Bonham and Secretary Seddon in connection with Bonham's request that certain soldiers appointed to the state military academy be released from the army.   When Seddon understood that the number was limited by the legislature to six and that the appointments were intended as a reward for peculiar merit, he agreed but expressed the hope that appointments would be made so far as possible from outside of the military service.[24]

The South Carolina law of December, 1863, in giving up all claim to state exemptions, unreservedly placed the military resources of the state at the disposal of the Confederacy.   Moreover, the course of Governor Bonham was quite different from that of some governors, notably Joseph E. Brown of Georgia and Zebulon B. Vance of North Carolina, in the matter of claiming exemption for state officers.   The Confederate laws exempted all such officers certified by the governor as necessary for state administration.   In some states there were great abuses.[25]   But Bonham did not certify insignificant state officers.   He

[21] *Statutes at Large,* XIII, 162-163. It may be noted that Judge D. L. Wardlaw in a letter to Hayne November 19, 1863, submitted an opinion to the effect that South Carolina exemption laws were applicable only to the South Carolina militia. Pickens-Bonham Papers.
[22] The Court of Errors was the court of appeal in constitutional cases and was composed of the justices of the Court of Appeals, the chancellors, and the circuit judges.
[23] *Ex parte* Graham, 13 Richardson (Law), 277.
[24] *O. R.,* serial no. 129, pp. 33, 39, 185, 205.
[25] Moore, *Conscription and Conflict,* pp. 94-96, 249-250, 265-268, 289-292.

170

wrote Vance November 28, 1864, that militia officers, magistrates, deputy clerks, deputy sheriffs, and even the highest officers of the state had gone into Confederate service. He estimated that if South Carolina had claimed exemption for ordinary magistrates and other local officers some 2,500 men would have been withheld from Confederate service.[26] Actually, according to Preston's report, only 233 were exempt from this cause in November, 1864, and only 307 in February, 1865.[27]

At the end of 1864 South Carolina reversed her policy of claiming no exemptions from Confederate service under state law. The explanation is to be found in the rising tide of opposition to the government and policies of President Davis, the refusal of Richmond to send reenforcements, and the conviction that if South Carolina were to be defended from the invasion of Sherman's army she should reserve her remaining resources for her own protection. When the legislature met November 28, 1864, Governor Bonham had just returned from the governors' conference at Augusta and his recommendations reflected discussions looking to more effective defense through closer state cooperation.[28] He asked for authority to use the militia of the state between the ages of 16 and 60 anywhere within the state and those between 16 and 50 outside state limits, and also that all militia forces, all state officers, and all others necessary for the protection of the state be declared exempt from Confederate service.[29]

The legislature responded to Bonham's recommendations by passing laws fully meeting his requests. An act of December 6 dealt with the use and exemption of the militia.[30] Another of December 23 required the governor to claim exemption from Confederate service for certain officers of the state government, the state bank, and state institutions. It authorized but did not require him to claim exemption for various other groups including members of the boards of relief, employees of banks and newspapers, employees of state public works and manufacturies, college teachers, preachers, and such persons as the governor might judge indispensable for the government of the slaves and the protection of citizens and property up to one person per two hundred slaves in any district, in addition to overseers already exempt under Confederate law. The act specifically declared that all persons so required by the governor were exempt from Confederate service.[31]

The reaction of General Preston to this legislation was expressed in a letter of December 29. "It is a matter of pain to me," he said, "that

[26] O. R., serial no. 66, pp. 519-520, serial no. 129, pp. 692-693.
[27] Ibid., pp. 851, 1102. The figures given for North Carolina in November, 1864, were 14,675 and for Georgia 8,229. On the accuracy of these figures see Moore, Conscription and Conflict, pp. 95-96.
[28] For the resolutions of the conference see O. R., serial no. 129, pp. 735-736.
[29] Mercury, November 30, 1864.
[30] Statutes at Large, XIII, 217-218.
[31] Ibid., pp. 216-217.

the first treason to the Confederate States in the form of law has been perpetrated in South Carolina." He believed that the law was designed to prevent the Confederacy from obtaining any further increase in its army from South Carolina "except by express permission of the Governor," and he had no hope that the latter would administer the law in any other spirit than that of hostility to Confederate conscription.[32] The new governor, A. G. Magrath, did in fact soon write the Secretary of War that he "required" the exemption of two soldiers already in Confederate service, for the "proper police of the State." Seddon of course refused to concede this claim for exemption of men in service and Magrath was forced to acquiesce.[33]

As the legislation of December, 1864, indicates, South Carolina adopted at the end of the war an extreme position in regard to exemptions. This legislation must be considered in the light of the fact that Sherman was already in Savannah and ready to wreak vengeance on South Carolina. The state had appealed in vain for reinforcements which Davis and Lee could not supply. In sheer desperation South Carolina determined to control such resources as were left. During the war as a whole the position South Carolina assumed on the matter of exemptions cannot be regarded as seriously embarrassing the operation of conscription. The conflict in 1862 and 1863 was mainly over the exemption of overseers, and during 1864 the claim of the right to exempt was entirely given up. Only in the last months of the war did South Carolina adopt what might be regarded as a policy of obstruction. And in its actual operation the new policy was of little significance because Sherman's invasion, the threat of which had provoked the new law, ended effective conscription in South Carolina. At the time of the invasion the state had a total of 5,839 persons exempt for all causes, a number small in comparison with other Southern states.[34]

Though the attitude of the government of South Carolina and of the public generally was one on the whole favorable to the operation of conscription there was of course evasion on the part of many individuals. This began as early as 1862 and became more serious as the war progressed. First, there were those who by virtue of their wealth were able to hire substitutes allowed under the earlier conscription laws. And when under the second conscription act substitutes between 35 and 45 were made liable to service on their own account and the Secretary of War ruled that their principals were thus made subject to draft, the ruling was challenged in the courts. District Judge Magrath in the case of Leopold Cohen upheld the contention of the principals. He held that though Congress could have cancelled the exemption of Cohen there

[32] *O. R.*, serial no. 129, p. 979.
[33] *Ibid.*, pp. 1004-1005; A. G. Magrath to W. H. Evans, February 10, 1865, A. G. Magrath Correspondence (Letter Book), South Carolina Historical Society.
[34] *O. R.*, serial no. 129, pp. 1102-1103.

was nothing in the act of September 27, 1862, which indicated such an intention.[35] The state courts upheld, however, the constitutionality of the laws passed at the end of 1863 which abolished substitution and specifically declared principals liable.[36] The number of South Carolina persons escaping service by hiring substitutes seems to have been comparatively small. Official reports show that there were only 791 substitutes in the army from South Carolina at the time substitution was abolished. At the same time there were 2,040 from North Carolina, 7,050 from Georgia, and 15,000 from Virginia.[37]

Evasion of conscription was also successfully accomplished by a great number of foreigners who claimed exemption both from state and Confederate service. The *Mercury* complained in 1862 that there were over 600 in Charleston alone who were claiming exemption in spite of the fact that many had long voted in city and state elections and had accumulated property in the city.[38] The fact that they were frequently in business made them liable to the additional charge of profiteering at the expense of soldiers' families. General indignation was expressed at their course and suggestions of boycott were made. The grand jury in the Confederate District Court urged that something be done about the number claiming foreign citizenship, a number so large as to astonish even the foreign consuls at Charleston.[39] One good lady of Charleston almost welcomed the shelling of the city in 1863 because it promised to persuade many foreigners that the time had come to defend their lives and property.[40]

Foreigners found it easier to evade service in the Confederate armies than in the state militia. The Secretary of War ruled that unnaturalized aliens were liable if they had acquired a *domicile* in the United States and the courts held that *domicile* involved an intention to remain in the country. The difficulty of proving an intention to remain in the country made it almost impossible to reach those who tried to evade service.[41] But there was greater difficulty in evading state service. Early in the war the South Carolina Court of Appeals decided, in the case of Ainsley *versus* Timmons, that while mere sojourners were not liable to militia duty, alien residents were liable whether they had established *domicile* or not. The court stated that aliens might depart at any time but so long as they remained they were liable to militia and patrol duty.[42] In spite of this decision, alien residents were for a while able to escape

---

[35] *Courier,* January 31, 1863. [36] *Ibid.,* February 22, 1864.
[37] *O. R.,* serial no. 129, p. 103. [38] *Mercury,* March 21, 1862.
[39] Camden *Confederate,* April 11, 1862; *Mercury,* September 20, 1862; *Courier,* October 17, November 1, 1862.
[40] Holmes, Diary, August —, 1863, DeSaussure Papers.
[41] Moore, *Conscription and Conflict,* pp. 59-61. Judge Magrath, in the case of H. Spincken in July 1863, challenged the ruling of the Secretary of War. Magrath held that a residence of one year was enough to establish liability. Bonham, *British Consuls,* p. 224; *Mercury,* July 3, 1863.
[42] Bonham, *British Consuls,* p. 222 citing *Courier,* December 4, 1861.

service under an order excusing them issued by Governor Pickens in November, 1861. Governor Bonham, however, insisted that alien residents were liable and he refused to be bound by the order of Pickens. In 1863 the acting British consul at Charleston, H. P. Walker, conducted an extended correspondence with Bonham on the subject. The controversy was in connection with the service of aliens in the First Regiment, Charleston Guards. They claimed that they had volunteered for purely local service in Charleston and protested against being detailed for service on the steamboats on duty in the harbor. When neither General Beauregard nor Secretary Walker would give the desired relief, Consul Walker took the matter up with Governor Bonham. Bonham cited the militia law of 1839 and said that the men were liable. Although the consul pointed out that the law of 1839 had been superseded by that of 1841, Bonham, supported by Attorney General Hayne, held to his position and the legislature supported him by passing a law on September 30, 1863, which expressly declared the liability of alien residents.[43]

Those who wished to avoid military service and were neither unnaturalized foreigners nor persons of means sought exemption at the hands of medical boards or by taking refuge in one of the various occupations exempted by law. The *Courier* was amazed to find how much older many citizens were than was generally thought, and how many people outwardly well had incurable diseases.[44] A correspondent of the *Mercury* criticized the medical boards for exempting persons who were able to hunt all day afoot or on horse and then brag of their success.[45]

There were of course various employments which either carried class exemption or made possible the obtaining of a detail and there was no doubt considerable evasion of conscription by persons going into these employments.. The *Courier,* for example, remarked that drugs were being sold by persons who did not know arsenic from soda.[46] The largest single class of exempts and details was that of overseers and agriculturalists, the number reported in February, 1865, being 946.[47] Many of these, perhaps most of them, were necessary to maintain maximum production. Editors, teachers, hospital workers, government contractors, manufacturers, millers, printers, saltmakers, railroad employees, and others were likewise subject to either exemption or detail. Sound policy certainly dictated the use of many of these in civil rather than military employment, but there was from time to time considerable criticism of excessive exemptions and details. The persons involved

[43] Bonham, *British Consuls,* pp. 113 *et seq.;* Pickens-Bonham Papers.
[44] March 22, 1862.
[45] *Mercury,* August 30, 1862; see also *Courier,* March 4, 1863.
[46] *Courier,* December 18, 1862. There were, however, only 53 apothecaries exempted in February, 1865 according to official reports. *O. R.,* serial no. 129, p. 1102.
[47] *O. R.,* serial no. 129, pp. 1102-1104.

were thought by many to be shirking service for individual profits, and the suggestion familiar in modern days was made that they be detailed at soldier's pay. Why, it was asked, should shoemakers be allowed to make $375 per month when the soldier earned only $11.[48] There was criticism of *"overfed, impudent Quartermasters and Railroad Officials,"* and even of preachers whom some proposed to draft.[49]

There was also escape for those who could find employment in public office. "Hundreds of men, or images of men," said the *Courier,* "who could and should be in camp, are dodging duty under sinecure offices or other pretexts."[50] The number thus evading the draft was in South Carolina comparatively small because Bonham refused to certify the lesser state officers as necessary to state administration. But there were small Confederate offices, such as postmasterships, and the more important state offices which did carry exemption. The old unionist, Perry, complained that those most anxious for the war somehow managed to stay out of it.[51] The fact that candidates for the state legislature sometimes valued the office less than the exemption which it carried was so patent in the election of 1864 that in many places candidates were required to state whether they were in the army, whether if already in they intended to remain, and whether if not in the army they would join.[52] In Charleston there were no less than twenty-three tickets for the legislature. Such widespread corruption prevailed, especially in the cities, that the *Courier* remarked that free government could not last ten years under the electoral evils of the time.[53]

In addition to those who escaped service on some legal ground there were of course some who skulked. Many young men, under various pretenses, were journeying from place to place in the country and small towns in 1862 in order to avoid conscription. This practice became more difficult in 1863 but complaint continued that there was a considerable number of slackers.[54] Worse still, actual resistance to the draft developed in 1863 in the northwestern portion of the state.

Reports coming from Spartanburg, Greenville, and Pickens districts in the fall of 1863 were quite alarming. J. D. Ashmore, chief enrolling officer in the section, found when he took charge in June that large numbers of conscripts were refusing to report and that a great number of deserters from the army were coming in. His appeal to them to desist

[48] *Southern Enterprise,* December 17, 1863.
[49] *Ibid.,* August 13, 1863; *Courier,* January 19, 24, 1864. The number of details in South Carolina in February, 1865, was reported as 2,254 and the number exempted at this time was 5,839. *O. R.,* serial no. 129, pp. 1101-1108.
[50] *Courier,* October 18, 1862.
[51] Journal, May 10, 1863. This note runs throughout the journal.
[52] *Mercury,* September 7, 14, 19, October 3, 1864.
[53] *Courier,* October 14, 17, 21, 1864; *Mercury,* October 11, 1864.
[54] *Courier,* July 15, 31, August 5, October 17, 1862; *Mercury,* March 14, June 29, 1863; Charlotte Holmes (ed.), *The Burckmyer Letters, March 1863-June 1865* (Columbia, 1926), p. 240.

from their course excited only "ridicule and contempt." In August, 1863, Ashmore reported conditions "most lamentable and fearful" and beyond his control. The deserters had taken refuge in the mountain sections near the North Carolina line[55] and were armed, defiant, bold, and threatening. Organized in bands of tens, twenties, and thirties, they had a system of spies and signals to warn them of approaching strangers. Sometimes working their farms in common, they travelled from place to place with their threshing machines and swore vengeance on any one who molested them. It was reported that some of them had erected near Gowensville a heavy log building "loopholed and prepared for defense" and that an island in Broad River had been fortified. They were said to be committing serious depredations and threatening even to bring in the "enemy's forces to invade us."[56]

The extent of this disaffection in the three counties named was considerable. Over five hundred deserters were actually reported for arrest and Ashmore thought there were several hundred unreported. "The tone of the people is lost," said Commandant of Conscripts Melton. There was hardly a family that did not have "a husband, a son, a brother, or kinsman, a deserter in the mountains." It was no longer a reproach to be known as a deserter; a great many were ready to "encourage and aid the efforts of those who are avoiding duty, and to refuse information to and thwart and even resist those who seek to make arrests." Even some persons of property and of good social position were in sympathy with the deserters.[57]

Explanation of such serious disaffection is to be found not only in the general discouragement attending Confederate military reverses in the summer of 1863 but also in local conditions. The area was one which had furnished many good companies in the first years of the war but it was a section inhabited mostly by nonslaveholders who were never enthusiastic for secession. As Melton said, the people were "poor, ill-informed and but little identified with our struggle."[58] It was a section in which the absence of the men at the front caused more than the usual amount of suffering. Speculation and extortion flourished, crops failed, and prices soared. Letters written from home giving deplorable pictures of the destitution of families must have put a great strain on the patriotism of even the well-disposed soldier.[59]

[55] In Pickens their chief points of rendezvous were the "mouth of Brass Town Creek, on Tugaloo, the passes west and northwest of Tunnel Hill, Cheohee, bordering the Jocassee Valley and Table Rock." In Greenville they congregated at Caesar's Head, Potts Cave, "Solomons Jaws," Turnpike, Saluda Gap, Howard's Gap, and Hogback Mountain. O. R., serial no. 128, pp. 771-773.
[56] Ibid., pp. 771-774.   [57] Ibid., pp. 769-770.   [58] Ibid.
[59] Many of the deserters were from Evans's brigade which had recently been sent to Charleston after two years of hard campaigning without furlough. Hopes of furlough were destroyed by orders to join the western army. Enroute from Charleston to Jackson many deserted. Melton thought they intended to rejoin their command after a hurried visit home but finding weariness and desertion sentiment there, almost all remained.

Governor Bonham, upon having the disaffection called to his attention, immediately dispatched a company of mounted state troops to correct a condition which was so clearly threatening. He sought and obtained coöperation from Governor Vance of North Carolina.[60] Calling the legislature into extra session September 21, he asked for legislation which would enable him to aid more effectively the Confederate authorities in arresting deserters and enforcing conscription.[61] The legislature responded with an act which made sheriffs liable to a fine of $1,000 for failure to coöperate fully in arresting deserters and evaders. Persons giving encouragement to deserters and evaders or who harbored or concealed them were made liable to a fine of $500 and one year in prison.[62] At the regular session a resolution was adopted approving the proposal of the Confederate government to raise, from men not liable to conscription, a force of six companies of mounted men for twelve months' service against deserters.[63]

The steps taken in 1863 to remedy the situation in northwestern South Carolina were only partially successful. In March, 1864, the *Courier* reported organized gangs of bushwhackers and horse thieves operating around Pendleton and Walhalla, and the *Southern Enterprise* said clans of deserters "in hundreds" were collected together and committing robbery, arson, and even murder in the upper part of Greenville District.[64] Undoubtedly the increasingly bad economic conditions were the chief cause of the disloyalty. An officer, reporting in May, 1864, thought there were few fundamentally disloyal citizens in the section but that the whole region was in a famishing condition. In Pickens District there were, he said, 1,000 persons dependent on public charity and 3,500 more soldiers' wives and children had to be partially supplied. Many were subsisting on bread alone. Similar conditions prevailed in parts of Greenville and Anderson districts.[65]

Some effort was made in 1864 to allay the disaffection but it could not have been very successful. Bonham, in March and April, 1864, wrote Secretary Seddon several times for aid.[66] Chesnut, in command of the South Carolina reserve forces being raised under the conscript law of February 17, 1864, sent a few troops to Greenville and wrote of his intention to send a large force to "make a clean sweep" of the deserters in the mountains,[67] but reports of his success do not appear. The truth is that by 1864 morale had badly weakened in many parts of South Carolina. Chesnut had to send troops not only to Greenville but also to Clarendon and Marion to suppress violence and punish

---

[60] *Ibid.*, pp. 741, 765.
[61] *House Journal* (September session, 1863), p. 9.
[62] *Statutes at Large*, XIII, 153-154.
[63] *Reports and Resolutions* (regular session, 1863), p. 410; *O. R.*, serial no. 128, p. 796.
[64] *Courier*, March 23, June 22, 1864, quoting *Southern Enterprise*.
[65] *O. R.*, serial no. 111, pp. 331-335.   [66] *Ibid.*, p. 327.
[67] *Ibid.*, pp. 336, 342, 360.

marauders.[68] After an unsuccessful expedition into Lexington County
to arrest deserters a conscript officer wrote, "We marched to the different houses & searched them & how the women did curse us was ter-
rific."[69] A woman from Williamsburg wrote that patriotic fervor and
enthusiasm had departed. There was, she said, an almost universal
propensity on the part of the men to avoid service; and the women no
longer frowned them to shame and disgrace but rather assisted them to
escape duty.[70]

In January, 1865, a company of regular troops had to be sent to
St. Matthews to suppress insurrection. On February 1, Governor
Magrath telegraphed General Hardee that deserters were too strong in
Marion County to be dispersed by the militia and requested that Hardee
send a company of regulars to restore order. Disaffection was also
great in Horry District.[71]

The serious disaffection in the mountain counties of South Carolina
in 1863 and 1864 and the general loss of morale because of the well-nigh
complete exhaustion should not be taken as the measure of the loyalty
and devotion of the people of the state to the Confederate cause. There
was no such widespread disaffection as existed in some other states and
the record of South Carolina in the matter of desertions was considerably better than for the Confederacy as a whole. Of a total of 104,428
officers and men deserting, only 3,615 were reported from South
Carolina. The number of deserters returned to the army from the state
between September, 1862, and February, 1865, was 2,514.[72] Evaders
of the draft there were, but it seems safe to say that South Carolina
furnished for the Southern armies more men than she had voters in
1860. The number seems to have been very close to that of the male
population between eighteen and forty-five at the outbreak of war.[73]

[68] *Ibid.*, p. 342.
[69] D. H. Hamilton, Jr., to his wife, August 7, 1864. Ruffin-Roulhac-Hamilton
Papers.
[70] *Mercury*, November 4, 1864.
[71] A. G. Magrath to W. J. Hardee, February 1, 1865, Magrath Correspondence
(Telegraph Book) ; A. G. Magrath to E. B. C. Cash, February 12, 1865, Magrath
Correspondence (Letter Book).
[72] Ella Lonn, *Desertion During the Civil War* (New York, 1928), p. 231,
citing *House Executive Documents,* [39th] Congress, No. 1, IV, part 1, p. 141;
O. R., serial no. 129, p. 1109.
[73] The Bureau of Conscription credited the state with a total of 46,174 conscripts and volunteers in November, 1863. By a highly questionable calculation
it estimated that 13,953 additional men had gone into service, many of them
in North Carolina regiments to which they were drawn by the inducement of a
double bounty which at one time was offered there. This estimate of 60,127 men
by the end of 1863 is too large. *O. R.,* serial no. 129, pp. 99-102. J. P. Thomas,
historian of the Confederate records which were collected by the state after the
war, made a report to the legislature in 1900 in which he gave the number enrolled in Confederate service as 61,608 and the number in state service as 4,944,
a total of 66,552 enrolled of which he said 58,906 were effectives. By making
allowance for men not carried on the rolls, Thomas estimated the total at 71,083
of which 62,838 were effectives. Thomas, *Raising of Troops,* p. 84. An estimate
of approximately 60,000 seems safely conservative for the total of Confederate
and state troops.

CHAPTER XIII

IMPRESSMENT OF NEGROES AND SUPPLIES

One of the most difficult problems connected with the prosecution of the war was that of procuring slave labor for work on coastal defenses. The executive council had wrestled with the problem with some success, as indicated in chapter ten, but had aroused a storm of protest from the planters. The federal threat to Charleston, repulsed at Secessionville in the summer of 1862, was soon renewed. There were also numerous raids inland from the sea islands for the general purpose of cutting the rail connection between Charleston and Savannah. These military operations, particularly those about Charleston, resulted in an almost constant call upon the state for a supply of slave labor to be used in the construction of defensive works. Though Governor Bonham was disposed to coöperate fully in supplying the labor, he met with a strong aversion on the part of planters to the demand for Negroes. The ineffectiveness of legislation on the subject was the despair of the military authorities, leading them to threaten, and at times to practice, impressment on their own authority.

After the abolition of the council, the supply of labor almost ceased. In November, 1862, Governor Pickens recommended, and Beauregard endorsed, a plan for the organization of a permanent force, thus relieving the owners of spasmodic and arbitrary calls made at inconvenient seasons. Pickens believed that 4,000 could be easily recruited from the planters.[1] The plan, however, was not adopted.

A law of December 18, 1862, divided the state into four divisions upon which the governor might make requisitions through a state agent and local road commissioners for as many slaves for thirty days service as needed. Owners were to receive $11 per month per slave, and an attempt was made to insure proper treatment and care of the Negroes while in service. A serious defect of the law was a provision allowing owners to pay $1.00 per day in lieu of furnishing the slave. But a provision which made the law completely inoperative was one suspending its operation until the Confederate government should agree in writing to make compensation for all slaves escaping to, or captured by, the enemy.[2] Secretary of War Seddon notified Governor Bonham, January 8, that he could not pledge his government, that only Congress could authorize such payment.[3] The demand for labor being urgent, the governor, fortified by an opinion from the attorney general, announced that the refusal of the Confederate government to accept the

[1] *Message No. 1 of F. W. Pickens*, November, 1862, pp. 20-21.
[2] *Statutes at Large*, XIII, 92-95.   [3] *O. R.*, serial no. 128, pp. 306-307.

terms of the recent law made it necessary to revert to the act of the executive council. A call was then made on certain districts for the labor desired. There was little response, and when the legislature re-assembled, January 20, one house declared that the call under the council act was illegal.[4]

The act of December 18 was amended February 6 to permit its operation before acceptance of its terms by the Confederate government,[5] but great difficulties were experienced in procuring the Negroes. First, Bonham had trouble in finding a suitable person who would accept the position of state agent.[6] Further delay was caused by the difficulty of meeting the provision of the law which required the appointment of appraisers to assess slaves as they went into service. After the calls went out there was general failure of the planters to respond. They preferred to pay the fine. Meanwhile Bonham was bombarded, on the one hand, by letters from owners protesting against their slaves being kept over time, and on the other, by urgent telegrams from the military calling attention to the imminence of attack and the total inadequacy of the labor supply[7]

The number of slaves requested in this period was about 3,000. The number obtained averaged between November and March only 755 and to maintain even this number it was necessary to retain the Negroes beyond the stipulated thirty days.[8] In April only 380 slaves were obtained from the second division and 370 from the third, although either of these should alone have furnished the number needed for the fortifications. In explaining this failure, W. M. Shannon, state agent, said that some owners were selfish and unpatriotic, many felt that their full duty was performed when they paid the fines, and that others excused themselves with the complaint that slaves were kept beyond the thirty days and when discharged were sent home without sufficient rations and without the tools which they had carried with them.[9] A public meeting in York resolved that the call for May was inopportune and calculated to impair materially all arrangements for a full provision crop, and that if an emergency existed unemployed Negroes near the coast should be used.[10]

One purpose for which the state legislature was called in special

[4] *Mercury*, January 14, 1863; *Southern Enterprise*, January 29, 1863; *House Journal* (1862), pp. 175-176; *Courier*, April 2, 1863.

[5] *Statutes at Large*, XIII, 95. The act also increased the penalty for not meeting requisitions from $1.00 to $1.50.

[6] Colonel W. M. Shannon was finally obtained February 18. *Courier*, April 2, 1863.

[7] *O. R.*, serial no. 111, pp. 282, 284; *Courier*, April 2, 1862; J. P. Nixon, *et al.*, to M. L. Bonham, February 23, 1863; W. G. Harris to M. L. Bonham, February 25, 1863, Pickens-Bonham Papers.

[8] *O. R.*, 1st series, XIV, 827.

[9] *Ibid.*, pp. 912-914. Cf. *ibid.*, serial no. 46, p. 70.

[10] Columbia *Daily Southern Guardian*, April 10, 1863; hereinafter cited *Guardian*.

session on April 3 was to amend the slave labor law. Governor Bonham pointed out that the fine was too light to compel compliance and that the necessity of suing in the courts made collection too slow. Even where the commissioners succeeded in collecting, they had no authority to turn funds over to the state agent for the purpose of hiring substitutes. Without suggesting fundamental changes, Bonham asked that the law be strengthened. The new law was only the old amended to make the fines somewhat more easily collectible and transferable. Although experience had demonstrated its futility, the principle of fines was continued.[11]

Governor Bonham, realizing the weakness of the law, called on two divisions instead of one for May. He wrote Beauregard that he hoped enough labor would be obtained under this call to complete the military works, but the cultivation of the provision crops was important and the planters showed great unwillingness to send their Negroes at that particular season.[12] The unwillingness was immediately and painfully apparent. From the two districts involved for May came only 107 men. In June the number fell to 60. Beauregard reported that during the first six months of 1863 he received an average of only 330 instead of the 3,000 needed.[13]

As July approached and another attack seemed close at hand, there were various protests against such failure. The *Mercury* impatiently condemned the mischievous policy of fines and denounced demagogism in the legislature and want of patriotism among the people. Others pointed out that failure to supply the labor might result in loss not only of the slaves but also of crops, homes, wives, and children.[14]

The enemy occupation of Morris Island July 10, soon followed by the attack on Battery Wagner and the heavy bombardment of Fort Sumter and the city itself, drew sharp attention to the ineffectiveness of the slave labor laws. Beauregard suggested to Governor Bonham that in view of the crisis the patriotism and intelligence of the planters might be successfully appealed to.[15] Bonham, accordingly, called on the planters voluntarily to send as many Negroes as possible. On July 14 he appointed persons in the various parishes to make personal appeals to the planters.[16] Strong support was given the call by some of the press.[17] At the same time, on a request from Beauregard, Mayor Charles McBeth of Charleston ordered the impressment of all free Negroes and slaves in that city.[18] As a result of these measures the number of Negroes obtained in July, either under the regular state call or from volunteering and impressment, rose to 2,850.[19]

[11] *House Journal* (April session, 1863), p. 386; *Statutes at Large*, XIII, 96-97.

[12] *O. R.*, 1st series, XIV, 911-912.   [13] *Ibid.*, serial no. 46, p. 70.
[14] *Mercury*, June 30, July 8, 1863.   [15] *O. R.*, serial no. 47, p. 196.
[16] *Mercury*, July 14, 1863; *Courier*, July 13, 1863.
[17] *Mercury*, July 6, August 7, 1863.   [18] *Ibid.*, July 10, 1863.
[19] *O. R.*, serial no. 47, pp. 525-526.

The supply of labor soon dwindled, however. In August, Bonham urged all who could to allow their volunteered labor to remain beyond the thirty days for which they had been offered and announced that all under the regular call would be retained except in cases where the owners insisted on discharge.[20] Many slaves were withdrawn, however, and Beauregard on the 27th announced that, having relied upon the state and having failed to secure an adequate supply, he was obliged to send agents to impress slave laborers, and hoped that a ready compliance would be given.[21] Bonham, under the circumstances, quickly approved this action.[22] Though the number actually impressed in September was less than 750, the announcement of impressment seems to have been responsible for a good response under the regular state call, which brought in 2,850.[23]

The problem of Negro labor was again considered in a special session of the legislature which met on September 21, 1863. Governor Bonham recommended that fines be abolished and that the governor be authorized to impress the labor necessary to meet the requirements of the military authorites. He asked that service be for two months and that free Negroes as well as slaves be made liable to impressment.[24] The legislature, however, withheld the power of impressment and passed a law increasing the penalty for noncompliance to $200. Though free Negroes were made liable, no increase in the term of service was made.[25] The legislature thus refused to change essentially the old law. In October only 800 and in November only 500 were obtained under the state calls.[26]

Again at the regular session of the legislature, November, 1863, Governor Bonham urged that impressment for sixty days' service, either by the governor or the commanding general, be made legal. The legislature responded with a law abolishing the fine system and directing sheriffs to arrest and deliver those slaves failing to report under call; cost of such process was to be borne by the owner. If slaves were retained beyond the thirty days, the governor was instructed to demand their dismissal unless in his opinion a "peculiar emergency" existed.[27] This law of December 17, 1863, was certainly stronger than its predecessors but its success depended upon its faithful execution by road commissioners and sheriffs. These officers were of course greatly influenced by public opinion which in this case failed to support the slave labor cause. Complaint was earnest and general on all the old sore

[20] *Mercury*, August 10, 17, 1863.
[21] *Ibid.*, August 28, 1863; *O. R.*, serial no. 47, pp. 310, 323, 329.
[22] *Senate Journal* (regular session, 1863), p. 42.
[23] *O. R.*, serial no. 47, pp. 525-526.
[24] *Senate Journal* (September session, 1863), pp. 10-11.
[25] *Statutes at Large*, XIII, 151-153.
[26] *O. R.*, serial no. 47, pp. 525-526. Impressment by Beauregard brought 600 in October and only 60 in November.
[27] *Statutes at Large*, XIII, 168-169.

points: that the Negroes were not well treated, that they were not returned promptly, that the calls interfered with essential agriculture, and that some districts were called upon more frequently than others. State agent Shannon replied that every effort was made to protect the Negroes and that occasional instances of neglect were promptly investigated and remedied. Reports were sent the owners weekly. But there was inevitably considerable sickness and not a few deaths; for a time it was found difficult to obtain proper evidence of death for the validation of death claims.[28] The *Courier* questioned the soundness of the whole slave labor policy. "When," it asked, "did our soldiers decide that it is less patriotic to work than to fight?" It also made the point that if slave labor was to be used it would have been better to hire or even purchase a permanent supply because labor used in thirty-day shifts was inefficient on any kind of project.[29]

Unsupported by strong public opinion, the labor law continued to prove inadequate in 1864. In June, General Sam Jones wrote Bonham that for his district about Charleston he needed 2,000 Negroes but had been furnished only nine by the state agent.[30] In July, he announced impressment to meet his immediate need of 2,500.[31] In November, Bonham told the legislature that not a single division had furnished its quota under the state calls for one-fourth of all road hands. In the summer, he said, he had increased the percentage to one-half and that even then only one division sent the number needed. The failure of the law he attributed to the failure of commissioners and sheriffs to do their duty, and with the courts virtually closed he thought it impossible to compel them to do better. The law was therefore not enforceable and should be supplanted by a system of impressment by the state.[32] December 23, 1864, with Sherman already in Savannah and the Confederate cause hopeless, the legislature at last passed a law providing for impressment of slaves under state authority.

The state was in no small degree finally influenced to authorize impressment by circulars of the bureau of conscription dated September 23 and December 12, 1864. These instructed conscription officers to proceed under a Confederate act of February 17, 1864, to impress for twelve months' service South Carolina's quota of the 20,000 Negroes required for work with the army.[33] The instruction circular ordered the procedure to be in accordance with the state impressment law, where such law existed. Thus threatened by an impressment of slaves through the unpopular bureau of conscription, the legislature hastened to pass a controlling act of its own.

[28] *Mercury,* January 20, February 10, 1864; *Courier,* December 24, 1863. For number of slaves lost see p. 198, note 67.

[29] *Courier,* December 24, 1863.

[30] *O. R.,* serial no. 66, pp. 542-543.   [31] *Courier,* July 20, 1864.

[32] Message of November 28, 1864, in *Mercury,* December 1, 1864.

[33] For the law see *O. R.,* serial no. 129, p. 208; for the circular, *ibid.,* p. 933.

The new law provided that the governor through a state agent and sheriffs might impress up to one-tenth of all male slaves between eighteen and fifty for a period of twelve months, though the owner, if he desired, might make substitutions quarterly. Seemingly every effort was made to make the law effective. If owners failed to deliver slaves when called, the Negroes were to be arrested by the sheriff and in this case the term of service was to be doubled. As an incentive to the performance of duty, sheriffs were allowed $8 per day for their services in addition to the usual fees; in case they failed, they might be prosecuted for a misdemeanor. For the protection of the slaves the state agent was required to inspect slave camps and to report frequently to the governor concerning food, clothing, medical attention, and general treatment. It was specifically stated also that punishment should be administered only by white men and not by other slaves.[34]

In passing its own impressment law South Carolina did not attempt to defeat completely the general purposes of the Confederate law. Rather, it sought to have impressment enforced by state instead of Confederate authority, and to throw safeguards about the Negroes by having discipline, clothing, diet, and general treatment supervised by a state agent instead of Confederate officials. However, it differed from the Confederate scheme also in that it limited the use of the Negroes to work intimately connected with the defense of South Carolina. Under the Confederate law slaves might be used anywhere in the department and for work in munitions factories and hospitals. It also provided a different method of assessing the value of the Negroes.[35] These differences, however, led John S. Preston to write that the law was intended and had the effect of preventing the accession of a single slave to the Confederate service except on such terms as the state wished. This law and an exemption law passed by the same legislature were denounced by him as treason to the Confederacy.[36]

Meanwhile, on December 13, A. G. Magrath was elected governor after a hot race in which the other leading candidates were A. C. Garlington, Samuel McGowan, and J. S. Preston.[37] The well-known state rights views of Magrath caused Preston to fear that little effort would be made to supply labor to the Confederate authorities. At first Preston seemed disposed to proceed with impressment through the bureau of conscription in disregard of the state law. He conferred with Governor Magrath on the subject, however, and sought the opinions

[34] *Statutes at Large*, XIII, 211-214.
[35] *O. R.*, serial no. 129, pp. 1020-1023.
[36] *Ibid.*, p. 979.
[37] On the first ballot the vote was Magrath 55, Garlington 49, Preston 34, McGowan 2, scattered 5. On the succeeding ballots Preston's vote declined, McGowan's reached a high of 23, and Garlington's a high of 53. Magrath was elected on the sixth ballot with a vote of 79. *Courier*, December 15, 16, 1864. Governor Magrath and Lieutenant Governor Robert G. McCaw were inaugurated December 19, 1864. *Carolinian*, December 20, 1864.

of the new state agent, R. B. Johnson, and of C. D. Melton, in charge of conscription for South Carolina. Johnson wrote that he was sure the labor needed could not be obtained through the bureau. The whole question was a sore point, he said, even with loyal and patriotic masters. He added:

So continuous have been the calls for labor for the past three years, so widespread has become the dissatisfaction among the slave-owners with the treatment of their slaves, so imperfect have been the laws to enforce equality in the distribution of the burden, that the well affected are very reluctant to respond to any call, whilst the factious and unpatriotic, the lukewarm and the disaffected, now so numerous, are ready to interpose very possible hindrance to the execution of such impressment. The slaves themselves are very averse to this labor and their owners sympathize with them, feel for them, and are disposed to screen them. All attempts, therefore, to impress by main caption would be futile. The owner has but to wink at evasions by the slaves and the best concocted efforts for arrest are foiled.[38]

C. D. Melton agreed that it would be much better to rely on the state agency, and Preston himself became quite convinced that there was no other way. Otherwise, he said, the labor could not be obtained even with a regiment of cavalry and with bloodhounds in each county.[39]

Steps were promptly taken to put the South Carolina labor law into operation. The law did not have a fair trial, however, for Sherman's invasion of the state and the evacuation of Charleston on February 18 abruptly terminated a problem which throughout the war was a prolific source of dissatisfaction and one cause for the steadily growing criticism of, and opposition to, the administration of President Davis.

Another fertile source of popular dissatisfaction appeared in connection with the impressment of provisions and supplies for the Confederate armies. Under conditions of rising prices which made every producer a speculator in the sense that he wished to hold his produce for higher prices, the military authorities resorted increasingly to impressment although not authorized at first by any specific law. General protest against these extralegal seizures led Congress to pass a law March 26, 1863, authorizing impressment and attempting through various regulations to make it as acceptable as possible to the people.[40]

Before the impressment law was passed there was considerable protest in South Carolina both of the illegality of impressment and of injustices resulting from it. James B. Campbell, a bitter critic of President Davis, thought that nothing was more pernicious "in the whole mismanagement which prevails" than these unlawful seizures of goods.[41] After the passage of the law there was complaint that the commissioners had set prices at little more than half of the market prices and

[38] O. R., serial no. 129, pp. 1018, 1022-1023.
[39] Ibid., pp. 1018-1019, 1024-1025.
[40] O. R., serial no. 128, pp. 469-471.
[41] Courier, April 2, 1863 (letter of March 20, 1863).

that impressments would be unnecessary if the government would efficiently collect the tax in kind which farmers were said to be willing to pay.[42] Impressment agents were accused of abusing their authority and disregarding provisions of the law. Even the *Courier,* staunch defender of the administration, thought there were "gross abuses, oppressing the people, and menacing the towns and villages of the state with starvation."[43]

The general complaint in regard to impressment led Governor Bonham in September, 1863, to call the subject to the attention of the legislature.[44] In response the legislature adopted resolutions declaring that an impressement law could be justified only by necessity and even then should be administered equitably and discreetly. These considerations, it was said, had not ben regarded and the governor was therefore requested to add the legislature's appeal to his own in an attempt to bring reform of the abuses. The resolutions of the legislature were duly forwarded to Secretary Seddon and brought a concilatory reply in which the Secretary stated that every effort was being made to have the limitations of the law strictly enforced. He would be glad, he said, to investigate any specific complaints which might be forwarded to him.[45]

Bonham returned to the subject of impressment in his message to the legislature at its November session. He had hoped, he said, that the irregularities had been corrected but complaints continued to be made. At his suggestion the legislature adopted resolutions requesting South Carolina senators and representatives to work for reform in Richmond. The legislature also requested that the governor himself furnish the people a statement of their rights under the impressment law.[46] In response to the action of the legislature, Orr offered resolutions in the Senate that the Committee on Military Affairs investigate and report a remedy for the "arbitrary, unjust, and needless impressment of provisions."[47]

In submitting a number of specific complaints to Seddon in March, 1864, Governor Bonham said he had made every effort to avoid even the appearance of a conflict with the Confederacy and for that reason had not published the statement requested by the legislature. He argued, however, that since the government was unable to provide depots for all of the tax in kind, impressment was largely unnecessary. He objected especially to many notices issued by Major Trout forbidding

[42] *Mercury,* July 29, 1863; *Courier,* October 10, 12, 1863; *Guardian,* September 2, 1863; *Carolinian* (Triweekly), October 10, 1863.
[43] October 22, November 16, 1863. See also *Carolina Spartan,* December 17, 1862.
[44] *House Journal* (September session, 1863), pp. 9-10.
[45] *O. R.,* serial no. 128, pp. 863, 875-877.
[46] *House Journal* (November session, 1863), pp. 213-214; *O. R.,* serial no. 129, pp. 407-408.
[47] *Journal Conf. Cong.,* III, 453.

citizens to dispose of their surplus supplies. The effect of such notices, Bonham said, had been in many cases to put the poor of the country and the people of the cities in want of the actual necessities of life, for producers were afraid to sell to the needy about them or to carry their produce to market.[48]

Investigation of the complaints forwarded by Governor Bonham revealed that the charges were not well founded. Major Trout was even able to produce statements from a number of citizens to the effect that the impressing agents under his control were creating little dissatisfaction. John M. DeSaussure and G. J. Withers of Camden said they had never heard of any complaints against the officers and that the citizens generally complied rather cheerfully to what they regarded as the needs of the army. One agent reported that it had never been necessary for him to impress because the people complied with his requests to sell. Captain H. W. Conner of Florence said that since he had been in charge he had impressed only once. Major Trout defended the notices complained of by revealing that Senator J. L. Orr had himself drafted the form. The specific charges forwarded by Bonham broke down badly under the investigation. In one case John E. Robertson, of Ridgeway, had complained that two cows with calf had been impressed but the evidence not only showed that Robertson had insisted on the selection of these cattle but also that his loyalty to the Confederacy was highly questionable.[49]

In the middle of 1864 a notable conflict appeared between James H. Hammond and the impressment officers. For his surplus corn Hammond was offered $6 per bushel. He offered to sell 6,000 bushels at $10 per bushel but his offer was refused and impressment ordered. Hammond had already contracted to sell 6,000 bushels to William Gregg of Graniteville and now proceeded to make contracts for the remainder of his 12,000 bushel surplus. He said he could have disposed of 100,000 bushels in ten days. When the impressment officers refused to respect the contracts and wrote out an impressment notice Hammond tore it up in their presence, but finally agreed to appraisal of one lot which a purchaser was willing to release. A price of $10 was fixed but on appeal this was reduced to $5 and Hammond bitterly complained that he was robbed of $12,000. Hammond's attitude was extremely antagonistic to the agents of a government whose President he heartily disliked.[50]

[48] *O. R.*, serial no. 129, pp. 404-405.
[49] He was quoted as saying that "the sooner this damned Government fell to pieces the better it would be for us." *Ibid.*, p. 413. On the whole matter see pp. 402-415.
[50] D. F. Jamison and W. G. Simms were much upset at Hammond's course and urged him to desist. For the whole incident see correspondence between Hammond and Hanckel, Hay, Simms, June 29-August 24, 1864, Hammond Papers; Merritt, *Hammond*, p. 144.

Though Hammond's resistance to impressment officers was by no means typical, the impressment of supplies at less than market prices was a source of great dissatisfaction in South Carolina. Governor Magrath thought it had done more to "weaken the temper of the people, to chill the fervor with which they embraced our cause, than all else which has happened."[51] It was also in no small degree responsible for the increasing discontent with the administration of President Davis. This discontent had reached large proportions in the latter part of the war and will be the subject of a later chapter.

[51] A. G. Magrath to Jefferson Davis, April 10, 1865, Magrath Correspondence (Letter Book).

CHAPTER XIV

STATE FINANCE IN WAR TIME

In spite of greatly increased expenditures for military purposes the war did not present very serious financial difficulties for South Carolina, a fact that may be explained by several favorable circumstances. First of all, South Carolina was, after the prosperous fifties, a rich state with an excellent financial record and a credit position so sound that loans could be made with comparative ease. It should be remembered too that the South Carolina military establishment as distinct from the Confederate forces was comparatively small after the spring of 1861 and therefore necessitated no great outlays in this later period. Moreover much of the large original expense for preparations against Fort Sumter was later assumed by the Confederate government and the state reimbursed; and throughout the war many of the state's expenditures were for general war purposes and therefore chargeable to the Confederate treasury. Finally, the state was fortunate in its ownership of the strong Bank of the State of South Carolina which was ever ready to advance funds for emergency expenditures and in general to render valuable aid to the state in its fiscal operations. Under these conditions, and in spite of a very imperfect tax system which was not reformed in the war years, the state suffered little or no financial embarrassment until collapse came with the fall of the Confederacy.

South Carolina's funded debt October 1, 1860, was $4,046,540.16 representing almost entirely loans authorized in 1838 for the rebuilding of fire-swept Charleston, and in the fifties for aid to the Blue Ridge Railroad and the building of a new state house at Columbia.[1] In addition the state was liable in the amount of $3,035,000 for railroad stock which it had guaranteed,[2] but these liabilities were more than offset by railway stock owned ($2,650,000) and a claim on the Bank of the State for more than $5,000,000 representing bank capital, a sinking fund, and state deposits.[3] The state government was therefore completely solvent on the eve of war and its credit excellent.

From the standpoint of taxation the state was in a less favorable position due to a long established and unfair system of land valuation. Under a law of 1815 which was itself modeled on a law of 1784, land of different types in different parts of the state was arbitrarily classified, valuation for each of ten classes being fixed by law. The valuation

[1] *Reports and Resolutions* (1860), pp. 125-126. The nominal debt of $1,051,-422.09 due to the United States as a result of the distribution of the surplus was not carried as a liability on the books of the state.

[2] This amount had increased by 1865 to $3,722,000. *Ibid.* (1865), pp. 7-8.

[3] Treasury Report, *Mercury,* March 22, 1861.

ranged from twenty cents to $26 per acre with more than 10,000,000 of the state's 17,500,000 acres falling in the twenty cents class and only 1,000,000 acres assessed at one dollar or more. Some of the most valuable cotton land in the state was assessed at twenty cents when its actual value was at least $20. The comptroller general in 1861 estimated that it was easily possible for a 5,000 acre tract worth with improvements $200,000 to escape with a tax of only $8.10. Landed estates worth $10,000 paid into the treasury, he said, less than the tax required for a "superannuated" Negro. Another state official declared that many tracts of land of less than four acres entirely escaped because the tax amounted to less than one cent. On the eve of secession the state was receiving only about $80,000 from land (less than five cents per acre) when a reasonable return without oppression might have been four times this amount.[4]

Although land revenue was inadequate in 1861 it was almost impossible to greatly increase it under the antiquated law without overburdening the more highly valued land. Already glaring inequalities existed. Saint Helena parish with 79,336 acres paid more than Barnwell with over 1,000,000 acres. Five million acres in the low country paid more than the 12,000,000 acres up state. And there was injustice to town because municipal property was assessed on an ad valorem basis while farm land was assessed by law and without regard to improvements. Robert Gourdin showed that in theory at least two men investing $40,000 in identical farms and houses might be required to pay a tax of only sixty cents in one case and $100 in the other. Charleston, he claimed, paid nearly one-fourth of all taxes collected by the state.[5]

Such a sytem of tax assessments in a day when property taxes were chiefly relied upon for state revenue was obviously in need of reform if land taxation was to bear a reasonable proportion of war expenditures. Recommendations for reform were repeatedly made by the governor, comptroller general, treasurer, members of the legislature, and others. The legislature of 1861 did pass a resolution providing for a commission of six persons to "devise and arrange a just, uniform and equitable system of taxation" and to report the plan to the newspapers and to the legislature of 1862, but if such a committee was appointed it failed to make a report. Renewed agitation in 1862 also failed to bring reform. Throughout the war period the revenue from slaves continued to be about four times that from land and about one-half of total revenue.[6]

For the immediate needs of the treasury in 1860 and 1861 South

[4] For contemporary criticism of the tax systems see *ibid.; Reports and Resolutions* (1861), pp. 29-32. For the valuation law, *Statutes at Large,* VI, 7-10.
[5] *Mercury,* November 21, 1861.
[6] *Reports and Resolutions* (1861), p. 344; *House Journal* (1862), pp. 129, 320, 362; Camden *Confederate,* January 23, 1863.

Carolina turned to its bank and to loans. Pickens estimated that about $1,450,000 would be needed for the purchase of arms and the raising of troops called for under acts and resolutions of the legislature and convention.[7] Toward this need there was early made available the $100,000 which had been appropriated at the time of the John Brown raid.[8] The Bank of the State was also ordered to advance $150,000 for the emergency.[9] But for substantial sums a resort was made to loans of which there were three authorized, and two made, in December and January. The first loan was through the issue of 6% state stock under an act of December 22, 1860, to the amount of $400,000, redeemable in four annual installments beginning July, 1862.[10] No difficulty was experienced in floating the loan as the various banks of the state promptly took the loan at par.[11] January 15, 1861, there was authorized a 7% bond issue for $150,000, the proceeds of which were to be used to purchase three small steam vessels for patrol of the coast and inlets.[12] These bonds, however, were never offered for sale but were deposited with the Bank of the State against advances being made.[13] On January 28, 1861, a $675,000 bond issue was provided for in the supply bill for that year. Issued in $50, $100, and $500 denominations these coupon bonds were designed to appeal to the general public.[14] They were for a time advertised in the newspapers, but only $187,000 had been disposed of by March 25. The explanations given by the Secretary of the Treasury were the current low quotations of bank and railway stock, competition with the $15,000,000 Confederate loan, and dislike of the coupon feature. Since the Confederacy meanwhile had somewhat relieved the state treasury by taking over the harbor defenses and by an indication of willingness to reimburse the state for certain earlier expenditures, the bond issue seems not have been pushed.[15] By the end of 1861 only about one half of the issue had been taken and Pickens recommended that the remainder be changed into a form to suit the customer.[16] This was not done, however, and $187,070 still remained unsold a year later when the bonds were withdrawn from sale.[17]

The last war loan came soon after Port Royal fell in November, 1861. On December 21 the legislature authorized $1,800,000 of 7%

[7] *House Journal* (1860), p. 293. $400,000 for arms, $100,000 for a regiment of six months troops, $200,000 for a regiment of twelve months troops, $500,000 for the military force provided for in the act of December 22, 1860, and $150,000 for coast defense. (These figures add to only $1,350,000.)

[8] *Reports and Resolutions* (1860), p. 302.

[9] *Statutes at Large*, XII, 723.

[10] *Ibid.*, p. 813. For reallocation of proceeds see pp. 717-718.

[11] *Convention Journal*, p. 524.

[12] *Statutes at Large*, XII, 805-807.

[13] *Mercury*, November 7, 1861 (Pickens message).

[14] *Statutes at Large*, XII, 718.

[15] *Convention Journal*, p. 524.

[16] *Mercury*, November 7, 1861.

[17] *Reports and Resolutions* (1862), p. 71.

state stock redeemable $100,000 per year beginning July, 1867.[18] As in the case of the earlier $400,000 loan this issue was taken by the banks of the state in proportion to their capital. However, the allotment of the Bank of the State, amounting to $285,290, was not issued, the bank simply making advances against its quota.[19]

Including $350,000 of 6% bonds conditionally authorized early in 1863[20] but never offered, the total for war bond and stock issues authorized during the war period was $3,375,000 but for reasons indicated the amount actually marketed totalled only $2,402,639. All of these loans came within a year and a day of secession and were issued for the expected expenses of 1861 and 1862. During the last two years of the war the state was more than able to meet her obligations from funds advanced by the bank, from reimbursements by the Confederacy, and from taxes. The credit of the state remained good as shown by a market quotation of 127 for South Carolina bonds in 1863[21] and by the reluctance of owners to present them for redemption at maturity.[22]

Meanwhile loans had been somewhat supplemented by increased taxation. In 1860 the total tax revenue for the state was about $600,000 derived mainly from a tax on Negroes with smaller amounts coming from land, city real estate, and business taxes. The rates for 1861 were increased to yield a total of about $800,000.[23] Land taxes were raised from eighty-one cents to $1.30 per $100, city real estate from seventeen cents to twenty-two, and the tax on slaves was upped from ninety cents to $1.26 per head. Similar increases were made in the other schedules, the most important items being taxes on bank stock, money at interest, and a sales tax of twenty-two cents per $100 on general sales except of South Carolina products and unmanufactured products of other slaveholding states. A new feature was a 1% tax on salaries and wages over $500, but its yield was to prove insignificant. Little or no change in these rates were made for 1862, the greatly increased appropriations for war purposes for that year being based on the $1,800,000 loan.[24]

During the first two years of the war period South Carolina spent for military contingencies a total of nearly $3,000,000.[25] This was just about covered by the loans and increased taxation. Since the Confed-

[18] Statutes at Large, XIII, 22-24.
[19] Reports and Resolutions (1862), pp. 71-72.
[20] Statutes at Large, XIII, 80.
[21] Courier, April 2, 1863.
[22] For example, all of the $400,000 loan had matured before the end of 1865 but there was still outstanding $239,200. Reports and Resolutions (1865), p. 10. See also ibid. (1863), p. 72.
[23] Ibid. (1861), p. 28. The report of the comptroller general in 1862 gives the total for 1861 as $913,067.97.
[24] Statutes at Large, XII, 635-637, 715-719, XIII, 1-3.
[25] Report of Wilmot G. DeSaussure, Secretary of the Treasury, November 1, 1861; Pickens Message Number 1, November, 1862, pp. 11-12.

erate government was reimbursing the state during the period, the treasury showed such a good balance at the end of 1862 that no new loans and no increase in tax rates were needed for 1863. Pickens reported December 15 that more than $800,000 was available for "reliable use."[26]

In 1863 increased expenditures were necessary for indirect war costs such as relief for soldiers and their needy families and for slaves lost in public service, but the more strictly military expenditures dropped sharply, the total being only $445,034.08.[27] The chief explanation of such small expenditures is that South Carolina had practically no troops in the active service of the state in 1863. Toward the end of the year the only troops in state service were two companies of mounted rifles.[28] With military expenditures at a minimum no increase in taxes was necessary and the treasury showed a sizable balance at the end of the year.[29]

With Confederate currency depreciating rapidly, and demands for relief of suffering greatly increased, South Carolina tax rates were sharply increased in 1864. On Negroes and land the rates were more

[26] *Mercury*, December 18, 1862. According to the *Report of the Chief of the Department of Treasury and Finance*, August 1, cash in banks and the state treasury totalled $597,500.22.

[27] $373,557.86 for "military expenditures" and $71,476.18 for special military projects. *Reports and Resolutions* (1863), p. 150.

[28] As the year 1863 opened, eight regiments of the First Corps of Reserves organized by the executive council were on ninety-day duty but in temporary Confederate service and paid by the Richmond government. The legislature which abolished the council had resented the offer of these troops, feeling that if the conscription acts were property enforced there would be no need of using the forces of the state over draft age. It forbade any extension of service beyond the ninety days and legislated a new militia organization to replace that built by the council. This left Governor Bonham unable to furnish the troops which Beauregard requested when the federal offensive began along the coast and about Charleston. During the summer Bonham recruited the force of 5,000 troops for six months service in the state called for June 6 by President Davis, but this force also served at Confederate expense when called out September 6. *O. R.*, serial no. 47, p. 143, serial no. 111, pp. 296-297, serial no. 128, pp. 580-582.

In August Bonham tried to organize a small state force of mounted infantry but with slight success. Then, calling the legislature in special session September 21, he called attention to the threatening military situation resulting from the reverses outside the state and from the loss of Morris Island which he believed to be a prelude to a great land and sea attack on Charleston. The state was also open, he said, to raids from Tennessee, and forces were needed to serve against deserters and other disorderly elements in the state. He requested legislation to raise a permanent volunteer force of at least two regiments of infantry (one mounted) and a proportionate force of cavalry and artillery, and to provide a more effective militia organization of all men sixteen to sixty, including aliens, not in Confederate service or otherwise unavailable. The legislature passed the necessary legislation and appropriated $500,000 for equipping the volunteer companies. But efforts to organize the force were not immediately successful. *House Journal* (September session, 1863), pp. 7-10; *Statutes at Large*, XIII, 148-150; *First Annual Report of the Auditor of S. C.*, p. 11; *Reports and Resolutions* (1863), pp. 51, 150.

[29] *Ibid.*, p. 28.

than doubled and business taxes were quadrupled, causing the income from taxes to be almost triple the amount of previous war years. Most of the total of $2,464,623.98 was paid in old currency under an offer of the state to accept it at face value if taxes were paid before April 1, after which date its value was to be reduced one-third by the Confederate act of February 17.[30] There was some complaint that since the state was permitted to exchange depreciated currency for 6% Confederate bonds at any time up to January 1, 1865, the state was making a profit at the taxpayers' expense.[31] The Bank of the State did make a "profit" when it exchanged half of its $3,000,000 supply for new currency and the other half for the bonds.[32]

In addition to the sharp increase in property and business taxes for 1864 South Carolina resorted to a tax in kind for the relief of soldiers' families. From the first days of the war the need for relief was apparent and as inflation came and prices soared the problem became acute. Commendable efforts were made by many individuals and local community organizations to meet the need but these were never adequate. The necessity of state action was recognized as early as 1861 when the legislature gave to a Board of Relief in each election district the authority to levy local taxes up to 40% of the state tax and to distribute the proceeds in cash or purchased goods.[33] Although more than $200,000 was collected and distributed under the law, the results were not satisfactory.[34] The legislature of 1862 appropriated $600,000 apportioned on a white population basis among the districts[35] but the need again exceeded the estimate as the number of needy families rapidly increased.[36]

At the end of 1863 inflation was so great and the suffering among families of soldiers so distressing that the legislature resorted to a tax in kind in addition to a cash appropriation of $500,000. The tax on grain was fixed at 2% of 1863 production as indicated by the returns made to the Confederate government for the similar tax collected by that authority. On manufactured goods of all kinds the tax was 5%.[37]

[30] *Statutes at Large*, XIII, 154-156; *Report of the Comptroller General to the Legislature of South Carolina, November, 1864* (Columbia, 1864), p. 4.
[31] *Mercury*, March 12, 1865.
[32] *Report of the Comptroller General* (1864), p. 4.
[33] *Statutes at Large*, XIII, 13-14.
[34] *Reports and Resolutions* (1862), pp. 38-39. In some cases the need was underestimated and the rate fixed too low to provide funds for the whole year. In Charleston, for example, a levy of 30% of the state tax proved inadequate as the number of claimants jumped from 300 to 1,800 during the year. The law was also fundamentally unsound because it placed the greatest burden on the upper districts which furnished more soldiers but had less taxable property. Sumter *Tri-weekly Watchman*, June 23, November 24, 1862; *Courier*, January 12, 1863; *Pickens Message No. 1*, November, 1862.
[35] *Statutes at Large*, XIII, 119-121.
[36] Although collected funds in some districts were not all spent, in others the Boards of Relief incurred deficits. *Ibid.*, pp. 122-123, 185; *Reports and Resolutions* (1863), pp. 328-329.
[37] *Statutes at Large*, XIII, 164-167.

Apportionment was based on the number of needy persons as reported by the Boards of Relief. Under the law 250,577 bushels of grain were collected and distributed among 55,263 persons. Cloth amounting to 120,706 yards and salt totalling 339,500 pounds was likewise distributed, and the proceeds from sale of other manufactured goods amounting to $391,000 were added to the $500,000 appropriated in cash.[38] The tax in kind was continued, with amendments, until the end of the war.[39]

Although relief expenditures in 1864 ran into large figures, military disbursements were again at a minimum.[40] At the end of the year there was a large accumulation of undrawn appropriations for military purposes and an actual balance in the treasury of $872,354.26. In addition, the state sinking fund was largely in excess of the debt for which it was specifically pledged and the bank showed handsome profits.[41]

With General Sherman marching at will in Georgia and with Richmond rejecting pleas for additional Confederate troops to save South Carolina, the state in late 1864 tried desperately to prepare for its own defense. At Bonham's request, the legislature passed laws designed to withold from the Confederacy the state's remaining man power,[42] and appropriated $2,000,000 for direct military purposes. Various tax rates were again doubled, tripled, or quadrupled to provide the $6,000,000 which the ways and means committee estimated would be the cost of government in 1865.[43] But the Sherman tornado struck before the military appropriation could be spent or any of the taxes collected. The report of the comptroller general of October, 1865, shows only $354,-955.84 spent for military defense but large expenditures for relief and other purposes ran total expenditures to $2,298,753.82. This not only absorbed the substantial balance from 1864 but also made large advances

[38] *Report of the Comptroller General* (1864), pp. 14-22.
[39] The rate for 1865 was 3% on both grain and manufactures and was supplemented by a $450,000 appropriation. *Statutes at Large*, XIII, 205-211.
In spite of the work of the Boards of Relief considerable suffering was experienced throughout the war. Private charity supplemented state relief in many places, notably at Charleston where the Free Market was established in 1862. By the end of the year the Free Market was expending $8,000 per month on some 600 families. In 1864 only about $15,000 of about $120,000 expended was obtained from the Board of Relief, the remainder coming from donations. *Mercury*, March 4, 8, July 30, 1862, April 15, 1863, September 7, 1864.
[40] All men seventeen to fifty were claimed by the Confederacy for service in their respective states under the conscript law of February 17, 1864. Those between seventeen and eighteen and between forty-five and fifty were organized and commanded by General Chesnut under an appointment from President Davis; some were called into active service at Charleston, of course at Confederate expense. *O. R.*, serial no. 111, pp. 329-330, 337-339, 342, 344, 365.
[41] *Report of the Comptroller General* (1864), pp. 5, 26-27, 55.
[42] *Supra*, pp. 170-171.
[43] *Statutes at Large*, XIII, 195-205; *Reports and Resolutions* (1864), p. 25. The reports and resolutions of the legislature of 1864 were mostly lost in the burning of Columbia. A portion is included in *Reports and Resolutions* (1865), which reports the loss, p. 30. Fortunately the report of the comptroller general has survived in pamphlet form.

by the Bank of the State necessary. The State owed the bank at the end of the fiscal year $1,178,789.60.[44]

The Bank of the State had been of great aid throughout the war. Long before 1860 at a time when the bank was under attack, one of the arguments used for its continuance was that it might prove valuable in case of a conflict with the United States.[45] It fully vindicated this expectation. It services were of various kinds. It invested in state bonds; as agent for the state it helped market state securities, paid interest as it fell due, and redeemed bonds when they matured from a sinking fund built from its profits. It was even able to furnish foreign exchange at reasonable rates when it was otherwise almost unobtainable. Exchange for purchase of critical materials for the state military works and for a card factory was thus obtained, and through an arrangement with Baring Brothers of London interest payments on South Carolina bonds held abroad were regularly met.[46] On numerous occasions the bank advanced funds to the state, sometimes with and sometimes without specific collateral, receiving interest on some advances and none on others. A few of the many instances may be mentioned by way of illustration.

Early in 1861 an authorized bond issue of $150,000 was not marketed but simply placed with the bank as security against the advances made for coast defense.[47] About the same time the governor was authorized to request, and the bank to issue, $200,000 in bank notes subject to state draft.[48] Incidentally, this was apparently the only time paper money was issued at state direction, though Pickens in 1862 suggested that the state might save 7% interest on bonds through use of bank notes guaranteed by the state.[49] About this time the notes of the bank were reported at a 30% premium over Confederate currency.[50] Another instance of bank aid was on the eve of the attack on Port Royal in November, 1861, when the request of Pickens for emergency funds was met by an order that the bank advance the $300,000 requested.[51] And when the $1,800,000 loan was authorized at the end of 1861, the $285,290 allot-

<hr>

[44] *Reports and Resolutions* (1865), pp. 20-21. Sherman's march made it impossible to send out the tax books except in some cases in the upper division. In a few of the upper districts small amounts of taxes were collected before the civil government was suspended in May, but the collectors still had in their possession the worthless Confederate notes at the end of the year. *Ibid.*, p. 5.

[45] Wallace, *History of S. C.*, III, 484.

[46] *Reports and Resolutions* (1863), p. 71; *ibid.* (1864), p. 73; *ibid.* (1865), pp. 55-58.

[47] *Mercury*, November 7, 1861.

[48] *Statutes at Large*, XII, 718. Pickens used the authority granted. *Mercury*, November 7, 1861.

[49] Pickens message, November, 1862. A $500,000 issue was authorized early 1863. *Statutes at Large*, XIII, 130.

[50] *Remarks of Mr. Boyce in the House of Representatives of South Carolina, December 9, 1862;* Camden *Confederate*, August 8, 1862.

[51] *Senate Journal* (1861), p. 31; *Mercury*, November 7, 1861.

ment of the bank was not issued but the same advanced.[52] Other substantial advances were made from time to time. In 1864 the report of the president of the bank showed accumulated advances for various purposes: $120,830.61 for cotton, $119,278.49 for the new state house, and $438,504.70 for "sundries."[53] In 1865 the state was almost entirely dependent on the bank for operating expenses, owing it at the end of the year $1,178,789.60.[54] The greatest single accommodation was in connection with the Confederate direct war tax of August 19, 1861. Under the law the state had the option of advancing South Carolina's quota at a discount of 10% and itself collecting the tax from its citizens. Pickens recommended that the state exercise the option and the legislature passed the necessary law.[55] The bank advanced the $1,647,597.43 at 2½% pending the collection of the tax.[56]

The bank could well afford to make such advances to the state because even during the war its profits were substantial. In the year before secession profits amounted to more than $300,000. For the war years 1861-65 total profits were nearly $2,500,000.[57] But the end of the war brought immense loss to the bank due to its holdings in Confederate currency and bonds. President C. M. Furman made the report in 1865 that although the bank had $3,000,000 more in Confederate notes than it owed to its depositors, it could no longer perform the service of financing the business of the country nor could it antici-

[52] *Reports and Resolutions* (1862), pp. 71-72. In October, 1863, the amount advanced lacked $44,374.30 of the total with the stock still not transferred. *Ibid.* (1863), p. 152.

[53] *Reports and Resolutions* (1864), pp. 92-94.

[54] *Ibid.* (1865), pp. 20-21. Compare the annual statement of the Bank of the State, pp. 62-64, which shows somewhat larger accumulated advances to the state.

[55] *Mercury*, November 7, 1861; *Statutes at Large*, XIII, 20-22. The taxpayer was allowed half of the discount of 10% if he paid before August 1.

[56] *Reports and Resolutions* (1862), pp. 71-72. The assumption of the direct tax led to a controversy with the Confederate government when the state withheld $146,547.97 representing assessments in her invaded parishes. Pickens insisted on exemption under a Confederate law of April 19, 1862, regulating collection in invaded districts, and a dispute lasting into 1864 followed. The state made a few collections in some of the invaded parishes and was presented a demand from the Confederate authorities that the money be turned over. But meanwhile the legislature passed a law making refunds to all individuals in certain parishes and to those in certain other areas who were found after investigation to be exempt under the law of Congress. At the same time the legislature directed that claims be made on the Confederacy for any overpayment by South Carolina. The controversy ended with Richmond agreeing to wait for a final settlement until after the investigations were made and state credits determined. State financial reports toward the end of the war carried a claim of $5,447.63 against the Confederacy for overpayment of the war tax. *Ibid.* (1864), pp. 79-82; *O. R.*, serial no. 128, pp. 336-337; *Statutes at Large*, XIII, 109-111; *Report of the Comptroller General* (1864), p. 50.

[57] $233,618.99 in 1861, $300,000 in 1862, $665,523.58 in 1863, $930,495.03 in 1864, and $333,546.61 in 1865. *Reports and Resolutions* (1860), p. 231; (1861), p. 5; (1862), p. 72; (1863), p. 69; (1865), p. 63.

pate tax collections by advancing money to the state as it had customarily done.[58]

Receipts from bonds, taxes, and the Bank of the State were somewhat supplemented by Confederate payments to the state in reimbursement for expenditures made in the common cause. Apparently Pickens and some others in early 1861 insisted that South Carolina as a matter of pride should defray all expense of operations in Charleston harbor.[59] But from the first many felt that reimbursement should be made. It was probably Memminger who inserted in the provisional Confederate Constitution as first reported the statement, later deleted, that "all sums of money expended by any State before the adoption of this constitution, in asserting and maintaining its separation from the late United States, are charged upon this Confederacy, and shall be paid from the treasury."[60]   The South Carolina convention also took a realistic view by authorizing Pickens to subscribe to the Confederate loan up to the sum estimated to represent the value of claims against the Confederacy for arms, etc., furnished by South Carolina provided the Confederacy would agree to an offset.[61]   Soon after Fort Sumter when the Secretary of War was suggesting that now the state might accept reimbursement without offense to her pride,[62] South Carolina was preparing to press her claims.

The legal basis of South Carolina's early claims was a law of Congress March 11, 1861, appropriating money for pay and maintenance of 3,000 twelve months troops "to be called into service at Charleston." The South Carolina Secretary of the Treasury, Judge Frost, and his successor, General DeSaussure, presented substantial claims in May and July. These were at first questioned on the ground that the troops had not been actually mustered into Confederate service and therefore were not covered by the law. Governor Pickens was highly incensed, and wrote Miles:

Because I chose to act liberally, and in devotion to the common interest, and furnished the funds because the Confederate Government was *scarcely organized,* and without funds for immediate and everyday expenses, surely it is not now to be used to cover the common Government from liabilities. . . . if my State is to be eschewed and passed over in her claims, under the contemptible subterfuge that the Troops were under my command . . . then I shall remember it in my future intercourse and shall look rather more to my own State and her local interest.[63]

The technical difficulty was almost immediately removed by a resolution

[58] *Ibid.* (1865), pp. 55-58. After meeting its obligations in full the bank was liquidated in 1870, a year before its charter expired. Horace White, *Money and Banking* (first edition), p. 379.
[59] *O. R.,* 1st series, I, 271; *ibid.,* serial no. 127, p. 250.
[60] *Journal Confed. Cong.,* I, 30, 38.   [61] *Convention Journal,* p. 540.
[62] *O. R.,* serial no. 127, p. 250-251.
[63] Pickens to W. P. Miles, April [May] 9, 1861, Miles Papers.

of Congress May 10 providing repayment to South Carolina for pay of troops in defense of Charleston. Of $1,398,803.17 the Confederacy allowed and paid before November 1, 1861, the sum of $686,774.95, the claims not allowed consisting mainly of those for expenditures made before February 8 when the Confederacy was organized. But South Carolina believed that there were valid claims for earlier expenditures and the legislature of 1861 authorized the governor to appoint an agent to present and adjust claims for expenses in the common defense "from the 20th December, 1860."[64] The executive council in 1862 also adopted a resolution expressing the view that South Carolina's military expenses prior to February 8 were justly chargeable to Confederate treasury and holding that the act of March 11 and the resolution of May 10 were clearly intended to cover South Carolina expenses in the earlier period; and that the intention of Congress was to dispense with the requirements for regular vouchers since most of the disbursements were made before any Confederate officer was present to make or acknowledge requisitions. The council also held that the $250,000 appropriated by Congress December 14, 1861, as an advance to South Carolina, was creditable against these open claims and not against unpaid vouchers already presented. But collections on the 1861 claims were small during 1862, the total reimbursements being increased to only $722,766.33.[65] However, considerable amounts had not yet been passed upon.

In December, 1862, the legislature appointed the very capable James Tupper state auditor of the accounts of various war time enterprises and also gave to him the duty of preparing and presenting South Carolina claims against the Confederacy.[66] He found the Richmond government unwilling to reimburse the state for payment of troops prior to February 8 and after about July 1, 1861, when General Beauregard left Charleston and the Confederate government took over all operations at this point. But Tupper presented new claims (for expenditures other than for pay of troops before February 8 and after July 1) amounting to $774,060.73. This figure did not include a claim for $300,000 advanced by the state for the construction of the gunboat *Chicora* by a special commission at Charleston which was itself negotiating the claim, nor for the loss of slaves in the public service which was held to be a valid claim. At the end of 1863 South Carolina had collected on its 1861 claims a total of $1,131,370.85 and had pending additional active claims amounting to $1,041,493.05.[67] Efforts to collect these and

[64] Report of W. G. DeSaussure, Secretary of the Treasury, November, 1861; *Reports and Resolutions* (1861), pp. 325-326; *First Annual Report of the Auditor of South Carolina*, p. 22.

[65] *Report of the Chief of the Department of Treasury and Finance* (August 1, 1862), pp. 25-26; *ibid.* (November 1), 1862, p. 19.

[66] Claims already presented by DeSaussure were left to him for adjustment. *Reports and Resolutions* (1862), p. 185.

[67] *First Annual Report of the Auditor of S. C.*, pp. 20-25, 95. As noted, the claims pending in late 1863 did not include that for loss of slaves. The writer

other claims continued during the last year of the war. In March, 1865, Governor Magrath, faced with an empty treasury, was still vainly urging Tupper to push the matter.[68]

Other financial relations with the Confederacy were of a more disinterested character. As the notes of the Richmond government depreciated and its credit declined, there was much interest in South Carolina in the problem of how to restore the financial stability of the government. In the legislature of 1862 Dr. J. P. Boyce of Greenville introduced resolutions that the ways and means committee inquire into the expediency of guaranteeing Confederate bonds, and as chairman of that committee reported on December 4 a bill providing for South Carolina endorsement of her share of a $200,000,000 bond issue to be used in retiring depreciated currency. Boyce made a strong speech in support of the bill and it became law on December 18. A few days before (December 12) Governor Pickens transmitted a somewhat similar proposal from Alabama.[69] South Carolina therefore was not the first to offer a guarantee as is sometimes claimed, but her action seems to have been independent of the Alabama suggestion. In January Boyce proposed changes in the South Carolina offer which increased the proposed issue to $500,000,000 and omitted certain provisos that would have given citizens of South Carolina preference in the sale of the bonds endorsed. Under the law as passed February 6, South Carolina would have guaranteed bonds to the amount of more than $34,000,000. The offer was sent to President Davis and to the other states and was placed before Congress March 5 but an insufficient number of states were willing to cooperate in putting the plan into operation.[70]

South Carolina's continued interest in deflationary schemes is attested by the newspapers of 1863 and 1864 which are full of proposals, and by the fact that late in 1864 South Carolina coöperated with Secretary Trenholm in a final unsuccessful effort to float a European loan for reform of the currency. The scheme was proposed to Trenholm in Richmond on December 9, 1864, by B. S. Baruc representing certain Paris bankers. He suggested a 15,000,000 pound loan at 7%, half in gold and the other half in the notes of a bank to be established in South

---

has not determined whether a claim was ever presented on this score but the state would hardly have neglected such an important item. To December, 1863, the state had allowed $236,550 for 156 claims; to December, 1864, $452,150 for 218; between October 1864 and October 1865, $246,000. The state seems therefore to have allowed claims for 450-500 slaves amounting to almost $1,000,000. *Reports and Resolutions* (1863), pp. 350, 360; *ibid.* (1865), pp. 20-21; *First Annual Report of the Auditor of S. C.*, p. 30; *Report of the Auditor of South Carolina on Claims against the State for Slaves Lost in the Public Service* (Columbia, 1864), *passim*.

[68] Magrath Correspondence (Letter Book).

[69] *House Journal* (1862), pp. 68, 109, 157-159; *Remarks of Mr. Boyce in the House of Representatives, December 9, 1862; Statutes at Large*, XIII, 123.

[70] *Southern Enterprise*, February 5, 19, 1863; *Statutes at Large*, XIII, 124; *Reports and Resolutions* (1862), p. 258; *Messages and Papers of the Confederacy*, I, 309.

Carolina, the notes redeemable in coin in Paris and to be used exclusively in buying up Confederate currency at market prices, the bank acting as agent for the government for this purpose and receiving a commission of 1%. Trenholm agreed to the terms and took steps to get the loan authorized by Congress and to get a charter from his own state. Baruc, armed with letters of introduction from Trenholm, proceeded to South Carolina and conferred in great secrecy with Governor Bonham, President Furman of the Bank of the State, and certain legislative leaders who rushed through a charter for the Franco-Carolina Bank, purportedly "for the purpose of establishing a direct commercial intercourse with France, and for advancing means by which the natural resources of the State . . . can be developed, and railroads and water communication within the State improved and extended." The bank's capital of $10,000,000 was to be in gold or silver or foreign exchange, one-twentieth of which was to be raised in South Carolina. Among the directors were T. D. Wagner of John Fraser and Company and J. P. Boyce. Strong objection to granting the highly favorable charter were overcome by the hope that the project might further the interests of the Confederacy.[71]

No statement of reasonable accuracy is possible in regard to the total cost of the war to the government of South Carolina. Figures for total state expenditures as reported by the comptroller general might be given as about $10,000,000, but not all of the expenditures were for war purposes and a considerable amount was returned to the state by the Confederacy; moreover, certain expenditures, such as proceeds of the tax in kind for support of soldiers' families, were not made through the treasury. Nor would the sum of all the appropriation bills during the period be a significant figure because appropriations were not always expended. The funded debt of the state grew from $4,046,540.16 in 1860 to $6,668,280.46, an increase of $2,621,740.30, but while this increase was due largely to war expenditures, it bears little relation to total costs. Any total figure would necessarily include losses due to depreciation of the state's investment in the Bank of the State and in railroad stocks owned and guaranteed, and to wartime destruction of public property. But whatever the correct figure for governmental costs, it was insignificant in comparison with the direct and indirect losses of private citizens, and infinitesimal alongside the cost in human suffering and loss of life.

[71] Duncan F. Kenner was authorized to complete the loan on his early 1865 mission to Europe but the arrangements were never completed. Baruc to Trenholm, December 9, 17, 1864; Trenholm to Baruc, December 13, 1864; Trenholm to Davis, December 15, 1864, January 4, 1865; Trenholm to Fraser, Trenholm and Company, January 5, 1865, Trenholm Papers, Library of Congress; *Statutes at Large*, XIII, 222-225; G. W. Ramsdell (ed.), *Laws and Joint Resolutions of the Last Session of the Confederate Congress, November 7, 1864-March 18, 1865* (Durham, 1941), pp. 13-14.

CHAPTER XV

SOUTH CAROLINA AND THE DAVIS GOVERNMENT

The well-known opposition to the Davis administration on the part of Robert Barnwell Rhett and his mouthpiece, the Charleston *Mercury*, began almost immediately after the organization of the Confederate government. According to Robert W. Barnwell, one of South Carolina's most consistent supporters of President Davis,

The Mercury's influence began this opposition to Jeff Davis before he had time to do wrong. They [*sic*] were offended, not with him so much as with the man who was put into what they considered Barnwell Rhett's rightful place. The latter had howled nullification and secession so long that when he found his ideas taken up by all the Confederate world, he felt he had a vested right to leadership.[1]

Although the feelings of Rhett and his friends were undoubtedly deeply wounded by his failure to become President of the Confederacy which he had been so instrumental in creating, and although they must have resented the failure of President Davis to call Rhett to an important post in the government, the statement of Barnwell was hardly just. Rhett was not a man of such littleness of spirit as to let a personal disappointment lead him into a factious opposition calculated merely to embarrass and undermine his successful rival. His passionate devotion to the cause of Southern independence would not have allowed him to jeopardize in this way the success of the movement so close to his heart. The explanation of Rhett's early opposition is rather to be found in the very enthusiasm with which he worked for the complete and permanent separation of the South from the old Union, and in his egoistic confidence in the infallibility of his own ideas on how success might be obtained. Like most successful crusaders he was prone to feel that those who disagreed with him were traitors to the cause for which he fought.

In the period between secession and the fall of Fort Sumter, Rhett's chief fear and horror was the possible reconstruction of the old Union. Fearing that some of the Southern states had seceded for bargaining purposes only, he fought throughout the period for measures which he hoped would make a restoration of the old Union impossible. He insisted, for example, on a provision in the Confederate Constitution which would exclude free states from the Confederacy. His efforts to have steps taken even before the inauguration of Davis for an alliance with England based on the commercial advantages of free trade, were also in no small degree made with the idea that such an alliance would

[1] Chesnut, *Diary*, p. 104.

make reconstruction forever impossible. These efforts of Rhett, however, failed, and Davis after his inauguration did not empower the Confederate commissioners to Europe to negotiate on a basis of mutual commercial concessions. Rather, President Davis and Congress seemed much more interested in the Washington mission. Rhett feared that they were hoping for a close commercial alliance, if not for some form of political reconciliation.[2] Rhett's horror of reunion, therefore, led him early to question the policies and even the motives of the administration.

Although the Fort Sumter episode temporarily quieted Rhett's fears of reunion he was by no means ready to accept the Davis leadership. He was still determined on the English alliance and as chairman of the Committee on Foreign Affairs worked hard to commit the administration to it. Failing in this he proposed a new policy under which European nations refusing to recognize the Confederacy would be coerced by an official embargo on the export of cotton and tobacco. Again he met defeat. Thus neither his policy of conciliation nor of coercion was adopted and the *Mercury* announced that the administration had no policy.[3]

Rhett early became convinced that the administration was also following an unsound military policy. The *Mercury* began, therefore, on June 1, a campaign to educate the public in the advantages of a policy of offensive warfare hoping that public opinion would influence the administration to abandon its policy of defensive operations. In an editorial on "The War Policy of the South" the *Mercury* stated that the South, though uniformly successful so far, had in every collision of arms been forced to fight. By thus assuming the defensive the South had lost Maryland, endangered Missouri, neutralized Kentucky, and made Virginia the battle field. This was neither wise statesmanship nor good generalship. The South should assume the offensive. Delay was a disadvantage to the South not only from the standpoint of numbers but also in the matter of training because the raw troops of the South, accustomed to horses and arms, were superior to the untrained troops of the North. The war should be carried to Washington and into the states of Ohio and Pennsylvania.[4] The *Mercury* continued:

One or two signal successes will check the war spirit now so rampant in the North, demoralize their troops, and bring them quickly to a knowledge of the folly of their undertaking—will produce a recognition of our independence abroad, followed by peace.[5]

The *Mercury* campaign against the defensive war policy, though implying inefficiency and blundering, was conducted for some weeks in

[2] White, *Rhett*, pp. 191-192, 196-197.
[3] *Ibid.*, pp. 205-206, 209-210.
[4] *Mercury*, June 1, 25, 1861.
[5] *Ibid.*, June 8, 1861.

inoffensive terms. When no attention was paid to it, however, the *Mercury* seems to have concluded that the policy of inaction indicated a desire to make possible, through delay, the reconstruction of the Union.[6] An editorial of July 3 denounced a rumored attempt of R. M. T. Hunter and J. A. Bayard to negotiate a reconciliation. While professing not to believe the rumors the *Mercury* thought that many in the South were thinking along these lines. The transfer of the government from Montgomery to Richmond was "not without reference to this policy on the part of some. And the desire to procrastinate, to avoid preparation for war, and to avoid fighting is also a part of this policy," it said. Thus alarmed by the fear that reconstruction was again a danger, the *Mercury* became more bitter and more personal in its attack on the Davis administration. In an editorial of July 12, it undertook to fix the responsibility of the defensive policy on President Davis. Reviewing the various acts of Congress passed between February 28 and May 11, it stated that the President had been given every power necessary for the successful prosecution of the war. "If our forces are not sufficient . . . Congress is not to blame." From this time on, the entire responsibilty for the defensive policy was attributed to Davis. After Manassas the *Mercury* was especially critical of the failure to follow up the victory by taking Washington, a failure which it held was due entirely to the President. Both Congress and the generals were in favor of a more aggressive policy, it said. When, in September, it was announced that the army would go into winter quarters in Virginia the *Mercury* protested bitterly against such an "absurd, flagitous and fatal policy." The army should bivouac in Washington! In November the invasion of South Carolina and the fall of Port Royal were blamed on the silly policy of defensive war in Virginia.[7]

Rhett thought that the establishment of close commercial ties with the North was only less odious than actual restoration of the old Union. He therefore repudiated what was called commercial reconstruction apparently believing that it might lead to political reunion. After Manassas he seemed especially fearful that peace might be made on the basis of mutual economic concessions. To prevent this he offered a resolution in Congress on July 30 for a 15% discrimination against imports from the United States. Although the resolution failed, a committee was appointed to investigate and report at the next session what, if anything, was necessary to insure the commercial independence of the Confederacy. The *Mercury's* fear of commercial reconstruction was so great that it declared in October that "the present danger of the South is not from Yankee armies, but from the desire and designs entertained by public men of the South for commercial and financial reconstruction."[8]

[6] White, *Rhett*, p. 209.
[7] *Mercury*, July 3, 12, 15, 18, 27, September 5, 6, 12, 27, 28, November 8, 9, 1861.
[8] White, *Rhett*, pp. 214-216.

Although the *Mercury's* chief criticism of the administration in 1861 was for its defensive war policy other complaints were from time to time voiced. The provisional tariff which continued the old tariff of 1857 was criticized and a demand was made for a thorough revision.[9] The direct tax was declared untimely though the principle of the tax was approved. The veto of a law which would have made the African slave trade a high misdemeanor instead of piracy as under the law of the United States was regretted. The War Department was criticized for its appeal to the newspapers to use more discretion in publishing military intelligence; the Commissary Department for the rations served the soldiers; and the Navy Department for its lack of energy.[10] The early failure, as the *Mercury* supposed, to send agents to Europe to procure arms was blamed on Davis personally. Congress had given him ample powers and anyone should have foreseen the need. An agent could have been in Europe within fifteen days of the inauguration and arms could have been received within six weeks, some time before the establishment of the blockade at Charleston on May 11.[11] By September the *Mercury* was refusing to give the Confederate government any credit at all for anything which had been accomplished. It claimed that the army was made by men volunteering and begging to be accepted; all the Confederate government had to do was to accept them and designate a field of action. The states and not the Confederacy had clothed, equipped, and armed them. The Confederate government had been totally incompetent to minister to the necessities of the wounded, sick, and dying soldiers, half of whom, but for other help, would have died from bad food and inadequate medical attention.[12]

Enough has been said to indicate that the *Mercury* had lost all confidence in the administration by the latter part of 1861. It had in fact become rabidly anti-Davis. It denounced the "reckless and partial manner" in which patronage had been dispensed and the evils flowing from incompetent officials. "How much longer is favoritism and folly to sacrifice lives and obstruct our armies?" it asked. "We denounce this matter of personal favoritism. The COUNTRY must be served, not personal predilections."[13] Gradually the *Mercury* came to believe Davis not only incompetent but also a conspirator against constitutional liberty. In an editorial of October 30, 1861, it warned against the tendency of executive power to increase in time of war under pretext

[9] The permanent tariff passed in May, however, was commended. *Mercury*, February 12, 25, May 23, 1861. There was much interest and discussion of Confederate tariff policy in South Carolina. The Charleston Chamber of Commerce, the Charleston Mechanics Society, and the South Carolina Mechanics Association sent lobbyists to Montgomery. *Ibid.*, February 2, 5, 18, March 2, April 27, 29, May 13, 1861.

[10] *Ibid.*, March 6, July 6, August 10, 22, 26, 1861.

[11] *Ibid.*, July 18, September 19, 1861.

[12] *Ibid.*, September 19, 1861.

[13] *Ibid.*, August 6, 21, November 5, 1861.

of military necessity. On November 4 an editorial entitled "Another Usurpation" was highly critical of the appointment by Davis of certain major generals, the claim being that Congress had abolished the office and that Davis by reviving it was usurping authority. "All free government rests upon a faithful enforcement of the laws. The most dangerous source of this violation is the Executive," it said.

In late 1861 the *Mercury* also began its crusade against secret sessions of Congress. The campaign was inspired when Congress, finding the *Mercury* making reference to much that had taken place in secret sessions, passed a resolution of censure against violations of the rule of secrecy. The *Mercury* now began to claim that secret sessions were simply a means of concealing the shortcomings of the administration and that they were tending toward dictatorship and despotism.[14] For the remainder of the war period secret sessions were one of the pet aversions of the *Mercury*.

There were others besides the Rhetts who disliked Davis and his policies. As early as May, 1861, J. J. Pettigrew expressed his fear of a dictatorship.[15] L. M. Keitt, in June, thought "Jeff Davis a failure and his Cabinet a farce."[16] Hammond from the first had a very low opinion of Davis and privately expressed it freely.[17] In September, B. F. Perry and James L. Petigru, the old unionists, agreed that the war would bring a despotism. Petigru went so far as to say that it was a matter of little consequence which side won because liberty would be destroyed in either case.[18] Governor Pickens said to the convention in December that it was useless to disguise the fact that the country was under absolute military control.[19] None of these criticisms of the Confederate government, however, was publicly made, and only here and there was there any open agreement with the *Mercury*. A Cheraw correspondent wrote commending the editor for his fearless attacks on things needing criticism at a time when other papers were pusillanimous; and a friend of Rhett's in Orangeburg congratulated him upon his "independence, unselfishness and courage."[20] Such supporters of the *Mercury* were, however, apparently very few.

The overwhelming sentiment of the people of South Carolina in 1861 was that the *Mercury's* carping criticism was unfortunate. When

[14] White, *Rhett*, p. 217; *Mercury*, August 9, December 27, 1861.
[15] J. J. Pettigrew to C. L. Pettigrew, May 13, 1861, Pettigrew Papers. Pettigrew thought the law allowing the President to accept independent companies and appoint their field officers was dangerous. He said that if he were in North Carolina he would insist that every soldier leaving the state be required to take an oath that his first obedience was to his state.
[16] Chesnut, *Diary*, p. 68.
[17] J. H. Hammond to I. W. Hayne, April 21, 1861; J. H. Hammond to M. C. M. Hammond, August 11, 1861, Hammond Papers.
[18] Perry, Journal, September 18, 1861.
[19] *Convention Journal*, p. 559.
[20] *Mercury*, September 16, 18, 1861.

the Palmetto Guards in Virginia were reported by the *Mercury* to be ready to come home in disgust at the defensive policy of the administration, they indignantly denied the report and expressed confidence in Davis.[21] Henry W. Ravenel, though somewhat worried about the comparative inaction of the armies, thought the criticisms by the *Mercury* were highly reprehensible. The leaders, he thought, were better informed than the general public and should not be judged until the war was over. H. D. Lesesne thought that almost everybody disapproved of the *Mercury's* course and wondered why no one did anything to check the "mischievous print" which to him was a trial "hard to bear patiently."[22] The newspapers apparently without exception refused to follow the *Mercury*. The most prominent of those which came to the defense of the administration was the Charleston *Courier* but various others expressed confidence in the President. The Sumter *Watchman* thought that Davis was generally held in high esteem, and the Spartanburg *Express* "deeply regretted the impatient and impetuous spirit" of his critics. The Camden *Confederate* was content to "repose the most unbounded confidence in the ability and zeal" of Davis and his generals and referred to his annual message as a "model in every particular."[23] The Fairfield *Herald* took issue sharply with the *Mercury's* editorial "Another Usurpation" and called upon the people of the state to repudiate the *Mercury's* course.[24] Official endorsement of President Davis was given by the legislature. In the called session which met to choose presidential electors, Richard Yeadon, of the *Courier,* offered resolutions expressing confidence in the administration and nominating Davis and Stephens for President and Vice-President. More than ten members objected to immediate consideration and Yeadon withdrew the resolutions though he was confident that they would have passed overwhelmingly if there had been time for their consideration.[25] In the regular session resolutions of "full confidence in the ability, integrity and patriotism" of Davis and in the "wisdom and statesmanship" of his administration were passed with only one dissenting vote.[26] The legislature, moreover, elected R. W. Barnwell, strong supporter of Davis, and J. L. Orr, "arch-enemy of the Rhetts," to the Confederate Senate.[27]

The military reverses of February, including the loss of Forts

[21] White, *Rhett,* p. 218.

[22] Ravenel, Diary, June 21, September 13, October 11, 1861; H. D. Lesesne to R. F. W. Allston, September 26, 1861, Allston Papers.

[23] Sumter *Tri-Weekly Watchman,* June 17, 1861; Spartanburg *Express,* October 23, 1861; Camden *Confederate,* November 1, 22, 1861, quoting Fairfield *Herald.*

[24] Spartanburg *Express,* November 20, 1861, quoting Fairfield *Herald.*

[25] *Mercury,* November 9, 10, 11, 1861.

[26] *House Journal* (1861), p. 100; *Senate Journal* (1861), p. 65. The one dissenting vote was probably that of Edmund Rhett. R. B. Rhett, Jr., was a member of the House but must not have voted. White, *Rhett,* p. 219 note 90.

[27] White, *Rhett,* p. 219; *House Journal* (1861), pp. 113, 115, 117, 119.

Henry and Donelson and of Roanoke Island, brought a definite reaction against President Davis in South Carolina. The Columbia *Guardian* became sharply critical, especially of appointments, and insisted that reform was badly needed. The "cup is on the point of overflowing," it said.[28]   Mrs. Chesnut remarked: "In Columbia I do not know a half-dozen men who would not gaily step into Jeff Davis's shoes with a firm conviction that they would do better in every respect than he does."[29]   H. W. Ravenel who had been criticizing the *Mercury* for its attacks, now wondered, "Why is all this neglect of preparation," when every resource of the South is at the disposal of the government? People were asking everywhere, he said, "Has our President done his duty faithfully?"   Ravenel feared Davis was not the "right man in the right place."   He believed that he would not receive the vote of a single state if the election were held again.[30]   James H. Hammond continued to speak bitterly of the President.   "Davis's supreme imbecility has well nigh undone us.   You cannot find a more signal failure in history."[31]   Hammond believed that one more defeat in Virginia would cause Davis to be deposed and a dictator appointed.[32]   Senator Orr wrote General Waddy Thompson censuring the President severely, and Judge O'Neall lamented to Perry that the country was ruined.[33]   William H. Trescot, with his bent for foreign affairs, thought that in the conduct of foreign relations the President had lost a great opportunity.[34] Governor Pickens was correct when he wrote Memminger on April 26 that South Carolina was greatly dissatisfied with the administration. Even Richard Yeadon and Robert W. Barnwell were beginning to doubt the President's ability.[35]

[28] *Mercury,* March 7, 1862, quoting *Guardian.*
[29] Chesnut, *Diary,* p. 140 (March 11).
[30] Ravenel, Diary, March 18, May 5, October 13, 1862.
[31] J. H. Hammond to L. M. Keitt, June 14, 1862, Hammond Papers.
[32] Ravenel, Diary, May 5, 1862.
[33] Perry, Journal, March 23, 1862.
[34] W. H. Trescot to J. J. Pettigrew, September 25, 1862, Pettigrew Papers. Trescot said: "I cannot help thinking . . . that we have altogether wasted our political strength, that we have made this issue too utterly one of bone & muscle and too little of brains. . . . I confess I would like to see Seward defeated as well as McClellan.   I would like to see the political value of this great revolution vindicated to the intellect of the world, as well as commended to its warlike sympthy. . . . I feel it in my brain and blood that we have thrown away in sheer and lamentable ignorance, the opportunity for the greatest diplomatic triumph that history has offered.   Just think of the right to speak to Europe for this great cause—a cause more catholic in its reach than any question which has been debated in the world since William of Orange argued with Louis XIV—a cause entitled to the sympathy of every nation of the world from England with its Magna Charta and its manufacturies to Russia with its serf—a cause which involves [?] every principle for which Europe has been fighting and negotiating for so many centuries—and how has it been handled?"
[35] White, *Rhett,* p. 226.   Barnwell a little later told Perry that Davis was the best man available for the Presidency but that he was not a man of genius or of great talents.   Perry, Journal, August 2, 1862.   Cf. *Courier,* June 6, 1862.

208

In the spring of 1862 when South Carolina as a whole seemed to be turning against the administration, the attacks of the *Mercury* increased in severity. On February 25 editorials of 1861 in which the *Mercury* had urged offensive fighting and had condemned the lack of preparation, were reprinted to show that the criticisms had been pertinent. This was followed by renewed attacks on the "lamentably short-sighted" and "feeble" efforts of the administration to build a well-equipped fighting machine. An appeal was made to the states to make up for the deficiencies of the administration by themselves importing and manufacturing the needed supplies.[36] On February 27 the attack was climaxed by a vitriolic editorial entitled "The President and the Instrumentalities of War" in which the inadequate preparation was attributed solely to the President's "incompetence combined with arrogance and autocracy." The Richmond *Enquirer* came to the defense of the administration but the *Mercury* gave little ground and defended its whole course of "constructive" criticism.[37]

The *Mercury* continued its attacks during April and May. Secret sessions, "crawling diplomacy," and incompetence generally, were almost daily criticized. After the fall of New Orleans the *Mercury* declared that the war was lost unless something be done to end the disasters and suffering which one man, "incompetent" and "perverse," had caused. Congress should assert itself against a President who would not build or buy a navy, or have an army except on his own terms, or send troops where needed, or prepare against the preparations of the enemy. By supporting the executive, Congress was only "intensifying the paralysis he has produced in our affairs." At the end of May the *Mercury* ridiculed a rumor reported by the *Courier* that a movement was on foot to call a convention of the states to depose the President but stated that the "incubus" to the cause would certainly be deposed if a convention of the states for this purpose were permitted by the Constitution.[38]

In Congress, too, South Carolina through her representatives gave evidence in 1862 of the reaction against the administration.[39] When H. S. Foote introduced resolutions which were clearly intended to censure Secretary of War Benjamin for the loss of Forts Henry and Donelson, McQueen was the only member of the South Carolina delegation who voted with the administration.[40] Another resolution of

[36] *Mercury*, February 25, 26, 1862.
[37] *Ibid.*, March 22, 25, 26, 1862.
[38] *Ibid.*, March 28, April 3-4, 16-18, 21-28, May 23, 24, 1862.
[39] In an uneventful election, November 6, 1861, South Carolina chose as representatives in the first Congress W. P. Miles, W. W. Boyce, M. L. Bonham, John McQueen, James Farrow, and Lewis M. Ayer. William D. Simpson on February 5, 1863 took the seat which Bonham vacated to become governor. *O. R.*, serial no. 129, p. 1188. The senators were R. W. Barnwell and James L. Orr.
[40] *Journal Confed. Cong.*, V, 76.

Foote which declared that the defensive policy should be abandoned was supported by Boyce in a long speech. Boyce thought that more energy might be brought into the prosecution of the war if a general-in-chief fully responsible for the conduct of the war, were appointed. For such a post he suggested either Toombs or Beauregard both of whom had been at odds with the President.[41] Ayer showed his anti-Davis leaning when in a prepared speech he fought a bill which would have allowed cabinet members to speak in Congress as the Constitution permitted. He declared that there was already a tendency for the executive to encroach upon the legislative department and that the bill would further increase the executive influence.[42] Every member of the South Carolina delegation except Senator Barnwell and Representative Miles voted against the conscription bills of 1862.[43] Miles was, however, by no means the consistent supporter of the administration in 1862 that Barnwell was. He repudiated a newspaper statement that he was a mouthpiece of the President and at least on one occasion took exception to a remark in a message of the President which he thought cast a reflection on Congress. He also expressed his opposition to the defensive military policy.[44]

On the whole the South Carolina delegation may be regarded as anti-Davis even in 1862. One or two of them were reported to be in favor of deposing the President.[45] In the Senate Barnwell may be regarded as a consistent administration man but his colleague, Orr, was clearly unfriendly to the President. In the House there was no administration supporter to compare with Barnwell in the Senate and a majority was unfriendy to Davis, though Boyce, McQueen, and Miles were somewhat less so than the others.[46]

Criticism of President Davis diminished in the latter part of 1862. This was due in part to the successes of Lee against McClellan and Pope in Virginia and more largely, perhaps, to the all absorbing nature of the executive council controversy in South Carolina. It has been suggested that a prime motive of the *Courier's* crusade against the council may have been to divert attention from the *Mercury's* attacks

[41] *Courier*, February 26, March 4, 1862.
[42] *Ibid.*, March 24, 25, 1862.
[43] *Supra*, p. 165. Miles, in speaking for the second conscription bill, said that he believed that there was a strong desire in South Carolina to have conscription extended. Bonham doubted if this were true but both agreed that South Carolina had given her consent to the first bill in spite of a belief that it was unconstitutional. Orr made a speech against the second bill in the Senate. *Courier*, August 26, 1862; *Mercury*, August 30, 1862.
[44] *Mercury*, March 3, August 26, September 27, 1862; *Courier*, March 3, 1862.
[45] *Courier*, May 24, 1862.
[46] Bonham was no friend of Davis but joined Miles and McQueen in voting for the bill of October 13, 1862, authorizing the President to suspend the writ of *habeas corpus* in any part of the Confederacy whenever he judged it desirable. There was no recorded opposition to the earlier and more limited act of February 27, 1862. *Journal Confed. Cong.*, II, 28, V, 34, 518, 560.

upon the administration.[47] The *Mercury* itself was not entirely diverted. It occasionally restated its objections to secret sessions and it complained of too much censorship of military news. It was especially critical of the interference by Generals Braxton Bragg and Earl Van Dorn with the "freedom of the press" in Alabama. After the Peninsular campaign, the *Mercury* was on the whole less severe in its attacks. It even congratulated the House for some improvement in the matter of secret sessions.[48] But Rhett was by no means converted to the administration. In the last session of the state convention in September, 1862, he introduced anti-administration resolutions and otherwise attacked the Davis government. The resolutions declared that free states should never be admitted to the Confederate union; that the United States should not be given any commercial advantages over other foreign nations; and that since the Constitution gave no power to Congress to establish internal improvements, the recent appropriations for building railroads were usurpations of power contrary to the spirit and letter of the Constitution. The resolutions failed.[49] Rhett also launched an attack on Davis in opposing some resolutions of Gabriel Manigault which proposed that South Carolina prevent agents of the Confederacy from raising troops in South Carolina except through volunteering or state agencies. These resolutions Rhett opposed on the ground that they proposed to throw the state in direct conflict with the Confederacy. He declared that he was in sympathy with the principle of the resolution and would have supported them a year earlier but that the weakness of the administration had made conscription inevitable and necessary to prevent disaster. He insisted that the government was chargeable with weakness, vacillation, and lack of foresight and that reverses were the natural consequence of an inactive and sluggish policy. Against these charges Barnwell defended the administration saying that the South's defeats were caused by disease which had decimated the ranks. Chesnut also came to the defense of Davis.[50] Barnwell and Chesnut were to stand by Davis until the bitter end.

At the beginning of 1863 the *Mercury* was more charitable toward the administration of President Davis than perhaps at any time during the war. The first editorial of the new year declared that the outlook for the Confederacy was bright. "Doubt and discord reign in the councils of our enemies. With us all is confidence, and unity of purpose." It praised President Davis's speech of December 26 before the Mississippi legislature and described his January message to Congress as being "decidedly the ablest and most satisfactory" that he had yet

[47] White, *Rhett*, p. 227.
[48] *Mercury*, June 13, July 25, 26, August 14, 26, 30, September 5, 1862.
[49] *Convention Journal*, pp. 413, 417, 423-425.
[50] *Mercury*, September 16, 23, 1862; *Courier*, October 2, 1862; *Convention Journal*, pp. 412, 417.

delivered.[51] It had only kind words for the new Secretary of War, James A. Seddon, referring to him as "able and energetic" and congratulating him on his determination to enforce the conscription law.[52]

The good humor of the *Mercury* was, however, short-lived. On March 12, in an editorial entitled "A Despotism over the Confederate States Proposed in Congress," it heatedly denounced the bill introduced by Ethelbert Barksdale of Mississippi proposing to give Davis authority to suspend the writ of *habeas corpus*. The bill, it said, would make the people slaves and subjects of the despot Davis. When the Richmond *Enquirer* defended the measure from the attacks of the *Mercury* the later accused the former of inconsistency for railing at the despotism of the United States while proposing to arm Davis with the identical powers exercised by President Lincoln. The *Enquirer* was willing to trust Davis not to abuse his powers and pointed out that he had not done so under the law of October 13, 1862. The *Mercury* replied that it would not trust a Washington with such power; that a "despotism is a despotism" whoever the despot; that if the old law had done no harm, that was proof that it had not been necessary. The *Mercury* even claimed that it had never heard of the October law and took occasion to restate its objections to secret sessions of Congress. During April it returned to the subject of *habeas corpus* again and again.[53]

In the summer and fall of 1863 the *Mercury* became more bitter in its attacks on the administration. It ridiculed the conduct of foreign relations. It declared the tax on slaves and land unconstitutional. It complained of the gross abuse of the appointing power and of the "silly disposition of the troops." After the defeats at Vicksburg and Gettysburg, especially, it was severe in its criticism. Early in the war, it said, when an aggressive policy should have been followed, the army was kept in Virginia. Now when Vicksburg was in danger and Lee should have been kept on the defensive in Virginia while some of his forces were rushed to the West, the administration with great imbecility had sent Lee into Pennsylvania. Nothing could have been more foolish or disastrous. Davis had rightly lost the confidence both of the people and of the army.[54]

Kershaw's Brigade, as in 1861, challenged the *Mercury's* reference to the army and declared that Davis enjoyed its "entire confidence, admiration and respect." The *Mercury* replied that such sentiments were

[51] *Mercury*, January 1, 19, 1863. The *Mercury* regretted, however, that Davis did not follow his denunciation of the paper blockade with an order withdrawing the Confederate commissioners from Europe and dismissing foreign consuls from the Confederacy. *Ibid.*, January 23, February 6, 1863.

[52] *Ibid.*, January 20, February 6, 1863.

[53] *Ibid.*, March 12, April 7, 18, 20, 21, 23, 30, 1863.

[54] *Ibid.*, May 25, June 8, 17, July 30, August 11, 12, November 12, December 19, 23, 24, 28, 1863.

by no means representative of the army as a whole. It then proceeded to review and reiterate its criticism of the mistaken policies of Davis since the beginning of the war. Though the *Mercury* had urged it, the President had failed to build a navy, to import supplies "early and largely," to take the offensive, to accept all twelve month volunteers who offered, to issue letters of marque except to a limited extent, to offer commercial advantages to Europe, to recall our commisioners when rebuffed, to dismiss consuls not accredited to the Confederacy, to retaliate against the brutal warfare of the enemy. The President had been personally responsible for the loss of Fort Donelson, Nashville, and New Orleans in 1862, and for Vicksburg and Gettysburg in 1863. These failures, said the *Mercury*, without mentioning the complication of the finances and the unwise appointments, were enough to convict the President of gross incompetence. The *Mercury* was surprised that the South was not already ruined by the Davis policies.[55]

The anti-Davis group seems to have been much stronger in 1863 than in 1862. The attacks by the *Mercury* were less generally criticized by the press although a few, such as the *Courier* and the Greenville *Enterprise,* still spoke favorably of Davis. Even the *Courier* on occasion complained of government policies. For example, it took the lead in criticizing the compulsory funding act of March, 1863, saying that it was an unconstitutional repudiation which would ruin Confederate credit; the people themselves should repudiate such an "unworthy, discreditable and suicidal" policy.[56] The *Courier* also condemned what it regarded as abuses under the impressment act.[57] The South Carolina delegation in Congress continued to be for the most part unfriendly,[58] and Governor Bonham, though coöperating in his official capacity, was personally unfriendy to Davis. He stated that he had no influence at all with the President.[59]

Although President Davis was increasingly unpopular in 1863, the congressional election indicated that there was no great popular favor

[55] *Ibid.,* September 23, 1863.

[56] *Courier,* June 16, 18, July 2, 1863. The *Mercury* on July 19 reprinted the *Courier* editorial of June 16 with considerable satisfaction. Hammond's view of the funding act was expressed in a letter to Hunter in which he said, "Under the dictation of Memminger . . . a very small potato & fit only for a corner grocery, you have ruined Confederate credit at home & abroad." In speaking of the tax bills before Congress he said, "Some malign influence seems to preside over your Councils. Pardon me, is the majority *always* drunk? The people are beginning to think so." J. H. Hammond to R. M. T. Hunter, April 8, 1863, Hammond Papers.

[57] *Courier,* October 22, November 16, 1863.

[58] Only McQueen voted with Barksdale to suspend the writ of *habeas corpus. Journal Conf. Cong.,* VI, 319. Even Barnwell voted against a bill giving the supreme court appellate jurisdiction over state courts. *Mercury,* March 25, 1863. Barnwell, however, remained loyal to the President but admitted that he was a man of strong prejudice. Perry, *Journal,* June 3, 1863.

[59] M. L. Bonham to Benjamin Rhett, February 9, 1863; M. L. Bonham to R. J. Bacon, February 15, 1863. Pickens-Bonham Papers.

for the President's greatest critic, Barnwell Rhett. Rhett had not been a candidate for Congress in 1861 but after the disasters of 1863 he decided to stand in his old third district. He and his friends seem to have assumed that L. M. Ayer would step gracefully aside for a superior man. This assumption was at once corrected by Ayer in a letter to the *Courier* of September 5. From the first Ayer made the attitude of Rhett and the *Mercury* toward the administration the issue of the campaign. He was himself no Davis man and he frankly stated that he had opposed and would oppose him whenever his judgment directed. If, however, the people of his district desired "to wage war against President Davis at all times, in and out of season, and to create, stimulate and urge on a factious and most mischievous opposition" to the administration, then they should vote for Rhett, not for him. He believed that Davis needed all the support and encouragement possible.[60] While the *Mercury* recounted the sins of the administration Rhett took the stump, and was joined by Ayer in a series of joint debates. There were no reports of the debates but the campaign apparently turned almost entirely on the relation of Rhett and the *Mercury* to the administration. On October 20 Rhett was defeated by a majority of about 500 votes.[61]

Rhett's defeat was clearly not due to any great enthusiasm among his constituents for President Davis. One explanation is to be found perhaps in Ayer's statement that he was elected because he had looked after his sick and wounded constituents. Perhaps many people in their suffering had lost confidence in the wisdom of the man who had so earnestly preached secession. There were claims, too, that at several places in Beaufort and Colleton Districts where Rhett was strongest, the polling places had not been open.[62] The chief explanation, however, seems to be that the people were in about the same position as Ayer; they held no brief for Davis but believed that such carping criticism as that of the *Mercury* was injurious to the Confederate cause which they wished to support.[63]

[60] *Mercury*, September 8, 1863.
[61] White, *Rhett,* pp. 232-234.
[62] *Ibid.,* p. 234.
[63] While South Carolina's greatest critic of Davis was being defeated in the third district, John McQueen, who had generally supported the administration in the House, was being replaced by Colonel James Witherspoon. The defeat of McQueen by a majority of only 135 votes was a political accident; it had not been expected that McQueen could be defeated and the voting was unusually light. In Williamsburg District not a single polling place was open. *Mercury,* November 21, 28, December 3, 1863, February 26, April 22, 1864. Although President Davis was apparently not an issue, one observer saw in the overturn signs of a desire for peace. R. F. W. Allston to Mrs. Allston, November 11, 1863, Allston Papers.

The only other contested election was in the fifth district where Congressman Farrow defeated Reverend James P. Boyce by a vote of 2,755 to 1,610. There is no evidence that the administration was an issue. *Mercury,* November 21, 1863.

A few days after Rhett's defeat President Davis made a three day visit to Charleston. During his stay he made a speech at the city hall, inspected the fortifications, and received all of the formal courtesies which the occasion demanded. In speaking of the successful defense of Fort Sumter and Charleston against the great attacks of 1863, Davis failed to mention the name of Fort Sumter's valiant defender Colonel Alfred Rhett, but did pay a tribute to Major Stephen D. Elliott who had only recently assumed command. He also failed to refer to popular General Beauregard. The general was offended and refused an invitation to dine with the President at the home of ex-Governor William Aiken. The *Courier* reported that the reception of the President in Charleston had been of the "warmest and most cordial" character but there was apparently much less enthusiasm than the *Courier* reported.[64]

By the end of 1863 confidence in President Davis had been considerably impaired in South Carolina but the prevailing view was that the state should maintain an officially correct attitude and coöperate fully with the administration in the prosecution of the war. It was in this spirit that all insistence on exemptions from military service under state law was abandoned. In this spirit the people of the third congressional district refused to endorse the course followed by Rhett and the *Mercury*. It was in this spirit also that the legislature passed resolutions declaring that President Davis was "entitled to the gratitude of the people and the commendation of every enlightened patriot for his unselfish patriotism and untiring devotion to the interests of the whole country"; and that South Carolina tendered him the assurance of "unabated confidence." In the House there was objection to the word "unabated" but a motion by W. S. Mullins to omit the word was defeated 84 to 16.[65] In the Senate, too, an amendment was offered which would have modified the endorsement but the resolutions as originally drawn were passed without a recorded vote.[66]

Of the South Carolina press in 1864 apparently only the *Courier* remained loyal to President Davis and even it occasionally gave evidence of its waning faith in the Richmond government.[67] The news-

[64] *Mercury*, October 31, November 2-5, 1863; *Courier*, November 5, 1863; Roman, *The Military Operations of General Beauregard*, II, 167-168.

[65] *Reports and Resolutions* (regular session, 1863), pp. 457-458; *House Journal* (regular session, 1863), pp. 149-151. Among those voting with Mullins were J. B. Campbell, W. H. Trescot, W. G. DeSaussure, and M. P. O'Connor.

[66] *Senate Journal* (regular session, 1863), p. 83; *Courier*, Dec. 17, 1863.

[67] It could not, for example, see any necessity for the law of February 15, 1864, giving the President power to suspend the writ of *habeas corpus* in certain cases, and it hoped that Davis would not use the power. It condemned "the time and tone and temper" of Governor Brown's vigorous attack on *habeas corpus* and other evils but agreed that the governor was in many respects right in principle. *Courier*, March 16, 1864. It complained, too, of favoritism. Inventions were spurned, it said, unless conceived by West Pointers or Yankees. If the government should want a watch made, a watchmaker would have no chance of employment against a blacksmith, or carpenter, or tinner. *Ibid.*, April 19, 1864.

papers generally became so critical that little difference existed between them and the *Mercury* itself.[68] The latter maintained its hostility throughout the year. It condemned Congress for usurping power at three "vital points": first, in making appropriations for the construction of railroads; second, in passing conscription laws which did not exempt state officers; third, in laying direct taxes on land and slaves without apportionment. Despairing of checking these usurpations during the war, it insisted that a convention must be called for reform as soon as peace was won.[69] Though not denying the power of Congress to suspend the writ of *habeas corpus,* it applauded Brown and Stephens of Georgia for their crusade against the law of February 15 and declared that it would not support such a law if "the Angel Gabriel were our President to administer it."[70] It congratulated the second Congress for its refusal to continue the February law and for its refusal to violate the Constitution by increasing the salary of Davis. Congress was also commended for threatening the impeachment and forcing the resignation of Secretary Memminger. With obvious reference to President Davis, Congress was reminded that by impeachment it could "strike down any portion of the Executive which it deems noxious to the interests of the Confederacy."[71] The state legislature was chided for its failure to assert the rights of the state and for inferentially supporting usurpations by its dumb silence in regard to them.[72] In tiresome repetition all of the sins of Congress and President Davis were paraded down the columns of the *Mercury* during the whole year of 1864.

In the last year of the war it is difficult to discover, outside of the columns of the *Courier,* any South Carolinian speaking kindly words of President Davis. In Congress Barnwell alone remained loyal. Senator Orr had been in opposition to President Davis from the beginning and described him in January, 1864, as a "weak and incompetent President" with "an imbecile cabinet to sustain him."[73] In the House, Miles definitely went into the Davis opposition by 1864. Though never close to the President, Miles, as chairman of the important Committee on Military Affairs, had usually exerted his great influence for the war measures of the administration. Even in early 1864 he voted to leave the whole matter of exemptions to the Secretary of War but his references to Davis in his speech supporting the bill were so unfriendly as to be called an open attack.[74] Miles came to think Davis "so stubborn and so pig-headed" that he could not be influenced except by one of his favorites, among whom, he said, he happened not to be because

---

[68] White, *Rhett,* p. 235.
[69] *Mercury,* March 4, June 8, November 21, 1864.
[70] *Ibid.,* March 24, 25, 30, April 15, 16, 27, 1864.
[71] *Ibid.,* June 27, 28, 29, 1864. See also November 23, 1864.
[72] *Ibid.,* May 20, November 21, 1864.
[73] J. L. Orr to J. H. Hammond, January 3, 1864, Hammond Papers.
[74] *Mercury,* January 11, 26, 1864.

of having opposed him in "one or two acts of tyranny." Thereafter, said Miles, the President lost no opportunity of thwarting him.[75] The other House members were likewise anti-Davis. Boyce and McQueen joined Miles in voting for the very limited *habeas corpus* act of February 15, 1864,[76] but this was apparently the last distinctively administration measure which received South Carolina support. Every member of the delegation, for example, voted against efforts in the last session of Congress to pass another *habeas corpus* law; every member of the House delegation voted for the bill creating the position of general-in-chief for the armies in January, 1865.[77] The whole delegation was reported to have called on the President early in 1865 and demanded a reform in administration.[78]

[75] *Burckmyer Letters,* p. 425.
[76] *Journal Confed. Cong.,* VI, 764.
[77] *Ibid.,* IV, 457-458, 721, VII, 463, 764.
[78] *Mercury,* January 24, 1865. Boyce under somewhat unusual circumstances spoke sympathetically of Davis in October, 1864. *Carolinian,* October 19, 1864.

CHAPTER XVI

DESPAIR AND DEFEAT

The increasing discontent with the Davis administration in 1864 was in no small degree the natural consequence of the disillusionment and suffering which accompanied the steadily waning fortunes of the Confederacy. Disappointment and war burdens also caused a declining confidence in the ultimate success of the South and inspired a peace movement in South Carolina. One suggestion for a negotiated peace came from Senator Orr who in June, 1864, introduced a resolution requesting that negotiations be undertaken. Just what Orr had in mind is not clear, but he probably would have repudiated any idea of peace on the basis of a restoration of the Union. The resolution was defeated by a vote of 14 to 5, Barnwell voting with the majority.[1]

More important than the resolution of Orr was the gesture made by W. W. Boyce. As early as February, 1863, it was rumored that he had been advocating in secret session of the House some form of conciliation with the Northwestern states.[2] When the Democratic convention, meeting at Chicago August 29, 1864, adopted a platform declaring that efforts should be made immediately for a cessation of hostilities and that a convention of the states be employed to restore peace "on the basis of the Federal union of the states,"[3] Boyce addressed an open letter to President Davis urging him to declare his willingness for an armistice and such a convention as the Northern Democrats proposed. In this letter of September 29 Boyce argued that a republic at war inevitably drifted into despotism. This was illustrated, he said, not only by the history of Europe but by the experience of the Confederacy. Under a constitution which undertook to carefully protect individual and state rights the Confederate government had nevertheless in four years come to exercise "every possible power of a national central military despotism." It had conscripted all men seventeen to fifty; illegally laid direct taxes; issued vast quantities of paper money and partially repudiated it; built railroads; established a monopoly on export of staples and forbidden certain imports; suspended the writ of *habeas corpus;* introduced a passport system; in short, had given the President all the powers of a military dictator. Nor would these evils necessarily end with the war; that would depend on the nature of the peace. "A peace without reconciliation carries in its bosom the seeds of new wars." A peace without harmony would be a mere armed

---

[1] *Journal Confed. Cong.,* IV, 143, 211-212.
[2] *Mercury,* February 17, 1863.
[3] McPherson, *Political History of the Great Rebellion,* p. 419.

truce. Such a peace would cause the North to develop great military power and the South would be forced to do likewise. There would then be two opposing military despotisms under which republican institutions would permanently perish. To prevent such an outcome a peace of harmony must be negotiated with the United States. In bringing this to pass a successful military policy was essential but it was not enough; it must be accompanied by a political policy, a political policy which could not succeed if Lincoln, representing the fanaticism of the North, were returned to the White House. The South's only hope for a satisfactory peace, therefore, lay in the victory of the Northern Democratic party which should be encouraged in every possible way. "Fortify that party, if you can by victories, but do not neglect diplomacy." Assure it of the South's willingness to coöperate in a convention of the states, and let the South coöperate even if an amendment of the Constitution be necessary for that purpose. Such a convention would be the "highest acknowledgment" of state rights principles.[4]

Boyce's letter was given to the public on October 13 and brought forth immediate and violent protests. A meeting of Richland citizens was at once called in Columbia to consider the letter, and so many attended, it had to be adjourned from the city hall to the courthouse steps. A committee of sixteen quickly reported a preamble and resolutions repudiating in no uncertain terms the sentiments and opinions of their representative and demanding that he resign his seat. After some discussion as to whether Boyce should be allowed to address the meeting, he was summoned and the resolutions read to him, after which he defended his political life in a very skillful address. J. D. Tradewell, J. D. Pope, W. E. Martin, and others responded with great heat and in unrestrained language after which the resolutions were apdopted by an "overwhelming" vote.[5]

In the course of his remarks Boyce stated that he had always favored a policy of dividing the North by overtures to the Northwest. After the first Battle of Manassas he had urged Davis to propose to Lincoln a treaty giving free trade and the right of navigating the Mississippi. He believed that such an offer would encourage the Northwest to reconcile the dissolution of the Union with their material interests. After the Peninsular campaign he had made a similar suggestion to Secretary of State Benjamin. When the peace party of the North appeared Boyce had believed that some encouragement should be given it but the administration newspapers had greatly weakened it by scornful attacks on the leaders of that party. In the spring of 1864 Boyce stated that he and other congressmen had met together and decided to introduce resolutions asking Davis to propose peace parleys if and when the enemy were defeated at certain points but these resolutions had not met with

[4] *Courier*, October 13, 1864.
[5] *Carolinian*, October 19, 1864. Cf. *Burckmyer Letters*, p. 466.

the approval of those in power.   Finally after the Chicago convention Boyce was convinced that duty required him to write his letter to the President in an attempt to influence public opinion North and South.[6]

There is little direct evidence on which to convict Boyce of the charge that he favored peace at the expense of independence.   In a published letter to J. G. Holmes, Boyce argued that his plan was the best possible one for obtaining Southern independence; and he favored instructing delegates to the proposed convention against any form of reconstruction.[7]   But his motives were widely questioned.   J. D. Pope at the Columbia meeting made much of Boyce's failure unequivocally to repudiate and condemn reunion on any terms whatsover.   The *Mercury* at once assailed the Boyce proposal as a mere reconstruction scheme and denounced Boyce as it had previously condemned the peace movement in Georgia.   The peace party, in the *Mercury's* opinion, was a party of either "the basest treachery or the weakest desperation" and in either case a party of submission.[8]   There were many others who regarded Boyce's letter as a veiled proposal to reënter the old Union.[9] The *Carolinian*, however, was more charitable towards the motives of Boyce.   It believed that he was no submissionist, but rather an earnest Southern patriot of exceptional ability.   For this very reason he was a dangerous man and had identified himself sufficiently with the reconstructionists to make him no longer a proper representative of his people.[10]   The *Courier*, without endorsing Boyce's letter, applauded the *Carolinian's* attitude of respect and spoke highly of Boyce's ability as a thinker and writer.[11]

Whatever may have been the exact price Boyce was willing to pay for peace, his proposal appealed to a very great many who had lost hope of victory and were weary of the war.   A few of these dared to speak for Boyce.   A correspondent of the *Carolinian* said that Boyce had "struck a cord to which the heart of this Confederacy will respond, and does respond, not excluding those 'at the front,' and that is, let diplomacy be tried—fighting has failed to accomplish peace.   He has only anticipated the country by a few months."[12]   After the first outburst of indignation Boyce apparently gained rather than lost support. The meeting of citizens of Fairfield District, for example, passed resolutions repudiating reconstruction but declaring that "all honorable and proper efforts should continue to be made by diplomacy, to put an end to the war" on a Southern independence basis.[13]   Efforts of Boyce's

[6] *Carolinian,* October 19, 1864.
[7] *Mercury,* October 24, 1864.
[8] *Mercury,* October 5, 13, 14, November 5, 7, 1864.
[9] *Carolinian,* October 21, November 5, 1864; *Courier,* October 20, 21, 1864; *Mercury,* October 24, 1864.
[10] *Carolinian,* October 15, 19, 1864.   [11] *Courier,* October 22, 1864.
[12] *Carolinian,* November 2, 1864.   See also November 6.
[13] *Mercury,* November 12, 1864.

220

opponents to assemble meetings in other districts were said to have failed because the people were found to be in agreement with him.[14]

South Carolina for the most part, however, continued to insist that the state should not return to the old Union, and the reëelection of Lincoln convinced her that independence was attainable only through victory. The legislature declared that a convention of states would be unconstitutional and dangerous in the extreme. W. D. Porter apparently voiced the sentiment of the legislature when in a passionate address he insisted that the war should continue till independence was secured.[15]

Although South Carolina was determined that the war should go on, some of the measures proposed by President Davis for prosecuting it raised a storm of protest and helped bring to full maturity the anti-Davis feeling in South Carolina. One of these was his request in his message of November 7 that he be empowered to purchase slaves to be used as cooks and teamsters, and to emancipate them at the end of their service. Though he stated that he was not yet ready to recommend their use as soldiers, his request was clearly designed to test the sentiment of the country on the matter.[16]

The arming of the slaves had already been discussed in South Carolina especially after the conference of governors in Augusta adopted on October 17 a resolution which recommended the use of such portion of the Southern slave population as was necessary. The *Mercury* had immediately assumed that this meant conscription by the Confederate government for military service and attacked the resolution vigorously. When assured that the governors did not so construe their resolution, however, the *Mercury* accepted the explanation and agreed that Governor Bonham could not have supported such a proposal because he did not admit the right of the Confederate authorities to conscript even white citizens.[17]

President Davis's message again aroused the *Mercury*. The idea that the Confederate government could free a slave was as monstrous as it was insulting, the *Mercury* said, and it pointed out that even the United States government had never claimed the right to tamper with slavery in the states. The offer of freedom as a reward to the slave was, moreover, an admission that he would be benefitted thereby and would thus give the lie to the Southern moral defense of the institution.[18] On November 19 the *Mercury* and *Courier* published a long

[14] *Burckmyer Letters*, p. 466.
[15] *Carolinian*, November 29, 30, 1864; *Mercury*, December 7, 1864.
[16] For a detailed treatment of the whole subject see T. R. Hay, "The South and the Arming of the Slaves," *The Mississippi Valley Historical Review*, VI (1919), 34-73.
[17] *Mercury*, November 3, 14, 1864. See also Bonham's message, *ibid.*, December 1, 1864.
[18] *Ibid.*, November 12, 1864.

letter from R. B. Rhett to William Aiken in which Rhett said that nothing since the war began had struck him with "such alarm and despondency" as Davis's claim that the Confederate government might emancipate slaves. And R. B. Rhett, Jr., who had now regained his seat in the legislature, introduced extreme state rights resolutions, one of which declared that slavery was a matter of exclusive state jurisdiction.[19] The definite suggestion of Governor William Smith of Virginia that slaves should be armed, soon followed by General Lee's endorsement of the plan, brought forth a denunciation by the *Mercury* of Virginia's "abolitionism" and Lee's "Federalism."[20]

The *Mercury's* opposition to the Negro troop policy was no doubt representative of state opinion. Miles wrote Lee saying that he had "considerable misgivings" both as to the utility of Negro troops and the effect of the scheme on the political and social system of the South. Anything, he said, was preferable to subjugation by "such a people as this war has revealed the Northern people to be," but he thought it necessary in view of Southern sensitiveness on the subject to proceed cautiously. He suggested that Congress authorize the use of 50,000 or 60,000 Negro sappers and miners as a first measure and the exclusive use of Negroes as cooks and teamsters while more stringent laws on exemption and details were passed to get 50,000 or 75,000 additional whites into the army.[21] Edmund Rhett wrote Miles that the Negro proposal was "breaking down the people's spirits. Men ask what are we fighting for?" He thought the proposal "without a virtue" and extremely dangerous.[22]

There were only a few South Carolinians who openly favored the arming of slaves but fewer still who admitted that the Confederate government could conscript them, much less emancipate them. A correspondent of the *Mercury* argued that companies of Negroes could be effectively used if mixed with white companies, but emancipation of the slave as a reward for his own self-preservation was, he said, inconsistent and inexpedient.[23] As Sherman began his invasion of the state others urged on Governor Magrath the propriety of arming the slaves. The governor himself was apparently willing to use the Negro if it would contribute to the effective defense of the state. He telegraphed Beauregard and Hardee on February 6, 1865, asking their opinion on the problem but the rush of events prevented any definite action being taken by the state.[24]

On the same day that Magrath telegraphed Beauregard the adminis-

[19] *Carolinian*, November 29, 1864.
[20] *Mercury*, December 12, 1864, February 3, 1865.
[21] W. P. Miles to R. E. Lee, October 24, 1864, Miles Papers.
[22] Edmund Rhett to W. P. Miles, January 11, 1865, Miles Papers.
[23] *Mercury*, November 10, 1864.
[24] A. G. Magrath to P. C. T. Beauregard, February 6, 1865; A. G. Magrath to W. J. Hardee, February 6, 1865, Magrath Correspondence (Telegraph Book.)

istration forces began the battle in Congress for the arming of the slaves. Lee on February 18, and Davis on February 21, urged that something be done. On March 13 a bill passed Congress authorizing Davis to call on each state for its quota of 300,000 additional men irrespective of color. The bill did not refer to emancipation and did not provide for conscription by the Confederate government. This compromise measure fully recognizing state rights principles was supported only by Farrow and Simpson from South Carolina. Miles and Witherspoon in the House and both Barnwell and Orr in the Senate voted against it.[25]

President Davis's request, in his message of November 7, 1864, for power to buy and emancipate slaves explains in part the motives of the legislature in passing the slave labor law of December 23, 1864.[26] His request that class exemptions including state officers and newspaper men be abolished and that the classes be made subject to detail by the President likewise aroused much opposition, and helps to explain the reassertion by the state of its right to exempt persons from Confederate conscription laws.[27] To draft state officers was to threaten the very existence of the state. To conscript editors was to silence the watchful sentinels against tyranny. When the legislature assembled it was urged to reassert the rights of the state against the actual and threatened usurpations of the Confederate government.[28] The legislature was in responsive mood. R. B. Rhett, Jr., for example, proposed resolutions in the legislature declaring that any law making state officers subject to conscription was a flagrant usurpation, and that any Confederate law bearing upon the material or personnel of the press was likewise unconstitutional. Though the resolutions were not passed the state exemption law indicated that the legislature was in practical agreement with Rhett on the matter.[29]

The election of Governor Magrath on December 14, 1864, may be regarded as the culmination of the anti-Davis, state rights reaction in South Carolina. He had opposed the earlier secession movements but had taken a leading part in the events of 1860, and in 1864 was fully identified with the extreme state rights point of view. Although as Confederate District Judge he upheld the constitutionality of the sequestration and conscription acts,[30] his decisions in several other cases clashed with the claims of the Richmond government. In the Cohen case, for example, he overruled the contention of the War Department in regard

[25] Hay, "The South and the Arming of the Slaves," loc. cit., pp. 57 et seq.; Journal Confed. Cong., IV, 670, VII, 612, 779.
[26] Supra, pp. 182-183. [27] Supra, pp. 170-171.
[28] Carolinian, November 24, 26, 29, 1864.
[29] Ibid., November 29, 1864; White, Rhett, p. 239.
[30] The Sequestration Cases before the Hon. A. G. Magrath. Report of Cases under the Sequestration Act of the Confederate States, heard in the District Court for the State of South Carolina, in the City of Charleston, October Term, 1861 (Charleston, 1861), pp. 4 et seq.; supra, p. 165.

to the liability to military service of principals whose substitutes had become liable under a subsequent law.[31]   In another case he declared the Confederate war tax unconstitutional insofar as it applied to securities of a state.[32]   His state rights convictions caused him, he said, to become obnoxious to the Richmond authorities, while his own opinion of the Davis government "excluded me from its confidence and deprived me of its favor."[33]

In his inaugural address of December 19 Magrath took extreme state rights ground.   He described the conditions of anarchy and misery which would attend the abolition of slavery and made a stirring plea for the continuation of the struggle until the vile enemy of Southern social and political institutions was defeated.   He asked that South Carolina continue to perform her full duty to the Confederate government, but he insisted that the most effective manner in which to support that government was to maintain the state governments in all the powers which they were intended to exercise.   Abuse of Confederate authority must not be allowed.   Civil liberties guaranteed by the Constitution must be protected because freedom which could not be tolerated in war had no real existence in peace.   He implied that many of the rights of citizens had been ignored and mentioned specifically abuses under the impressment law.   These rights he would attempt to protect; "the honor and independence" of the State of South Carolina he would endeavor to maintain.[34]

At the time of Magrath's inauguration General Sherman was completing his march across Georgia to Savannah and South Carolina was threatened with a similar invasion.   The masses of the people had lost hope.   How to restore confidence and somehow save South Carolina was therefore the problem which presented itself to the state authorities. On December 25 Magrath wrote President Davis that the fall of Savannah had greatly affected the people of South Carolina and that reinforcements were positively necessary; "if you will send us aid, although for the moment it fall short of effective aid, that spirit can be vitalized which . . . supplies the place of numbers."   Help was necessary if Charleston were to be saved, and if Charleston fell, Richmond could not be held.   On the other hand Richmond could fall and Charleston be saved.   Magrath also wrote Barnwell urging him and the other members of the South Carolina delegation to prevail upon the President to send troops and to appoint J. E. Johnston to succeed Beauregard who had been relieved of the command in South Carolina.   He added: "The weight of the war is heavy; it now bears down on all classes; all wish peace.   That wish may become so strong that its gratification will

[31] *Supra*, p. 171.   [32] *Mercury*, April 23, 1862.
[33] A. G. Magrath to [federal authorities], November 8, 1865, Magrath Papers, University of South Carolina.
[34] *Mercury*, December 22, 1864.

be secured even at some sacrifice, perhaps the sacrifice of the principle for which we are contending."[35]

Magrath's alarm became greater when he learned early in January that Beauregard's instructions to General Hardee were to evacuate Charleston rather than lose the garrison. Against this policy Magrath protested bitterly to Hardee. "I tell you now that the retreat from Charleston will be the dead march of the Confederation," he said. "Remember this State has held back not a single man; it has given all without question. Shall not of these it has given for others, be now given back to it for its own defense?" As Sherman crossed into South Carolina Magrath continued to write and telegraph President Davis, Lee, and the South Carolina delegation. He sent a representative to Richmond personally to urge his views. To the very last he insisted with great earnestness that Charleston and Branchville, not Richmond, would determine the fate of the Confederacy. He finally went so far as to urge Hardee to allow himself, against instructions, to be besieged in Charleston. This, he said, would bring the government to see things in the proper light and result in the sending of aid.[36]

It was under these desperate circumstances that Magrath in January, 1865, made his extraordinary proposals to the governors of North Carolina and Georgia. The letters to Vance and Brown were dated January 11, and were borne by W. S. Mullins and W. H. Trescot respectively, both anti-Davis, state rights men. They were instructed to discuss fully with the governors the contents of the letters and report to Magrath at the earliest possible time. The general purpose of Magrath was to arrange a concert between the Carolinas and Georgia, and later Alabama, Mississippi, and Florida, for mutual aid and co-operation in a military and political program which Magrath believed might yet save the Confederacy. The military program looked not only to the pooling of state militia forces when necessary to defend one of the states but also to reform of certain military policies of the Richmond government. By the political program Magrath hoped to force upon the administration the correction of abuses which he believed must be removed if confidence were to be restored and the war spirit rekindled.[37]

Specifically Magrath proposed that the several states agree to remove restrictions which would prevent the sending of their militia to

[35] A. G. Magrath to Jefferson Davis, December 25, 1864; A. G. Magrath to R. W. Barnwell, December 30, 1864, Magrath Correspondence (Letter Book).
[36] A. G. Magrath to Jefferson Davis, January 16, 22, 1865; A. G. Magrath to R. E. Lee, January 16, 1865; A. G. Magrath to W. J. Hardee, January 11, 21, February 5, 1865, Magrath Correspondence (Letter Book).
[37] The proposals of Magrath are contained in the following letters: A. G. Magrath to W. H. Trescot, January 9, 1865; A. G. Magrath to W. S. Mullins, January 9, 1865; A. G. Magrath to J. E. Brown, January 11, 1865; A. G. Magrath to Z. B. Vance, January 11, 1865, Magrath Correspondence (Letter Book).

the rescue of another state, and that they have an understanding that each state might rely upon the others.   Magrath believed that there was yet a large force in each state not subject to conscription and that an agreement to act together would improve the morale of each and make possible the successful defense of any state against a reasonably large enemy force.   Moreover, should Richmond fall and Grant move. into North Carolina, the militia of Virginia would naturally refuse to leave that state.   In such a case the Confederate army would disintegrate and its separate parts falling back upon their states might be a danger instead of a support unless there existed a strong militia organization about which they might rally.

Magrath was anxious to avoid any impression that South Carolina proposed to control any resources on which the Confederacy had a claim. The policy of South Carolina, he said, had been to give whatever it possessed.   But he pointed out that the forces now left to the state were not subject to, or fit for, conscription.   Their better organization would be beneficial to the Confederate government and contribute to the common good.   Although denying that South Carolina wished to control any of the resources which it had given to the Confederate government, Magrath nevertheless believed that the states had a right, and were in duty bound, to protest against unwise and mischievous policies.   He said:

Does not the present condition of our affairs require the interposition of the most active measures to arrest the mischief already experienced and the greater with which we are threatened?   Is it not understood that the powers of the Common Government are exhausted and its policy unfortunate?   Is there any resource left except in the States?   Is there or can there be wrong or insult; is there or can there be anything but right and duty, in the Governors of these States, unitedly if they agree, presenting to the President such changes of policy and of measures as will save the lives, liberties and fortunes of the people of the several States, in and over which they preside?[38]

Magrath believed that demands made on the President should be "distinct" but not offensive, frank but not unkindly.   He was confident they would be heeded.

Among the policies which Magrath proposed for consideration were two which were then exciting much public interest, namely, the powers of the President as military commander and the use of slaves for the purpose of strengthening the armies.   On these Magrath apparently did not reveal his own opinions.   He proposed, however, that the three governors protest against the adoption of a "fatal" policy of abandoning the coast and evacuating the cities.   He also suggested that a demand be made for the assignment of General J. E. Johnston

[38] A. G. Magrath to W. H. Trescot, January 9, 1865, Magrath Correspondence (Letter Book).

to the Carolinas and Georgia and that J. B. Hood's army be transferred to South Carolina. He was confident that the three states acting jointly could obtain Hood's army and that it, with the militia of the three states, could decisively defeat General Sherman. Such a defeat, he argued, would so shatter the morale of the North that peace would speedily come.

Magrath was much concerned about another matter which he feared was pregnant with evil for the Confederacy. This was the talk in North Carolina and Georgia of calling state conventions. This, Magrath believed, was extremely dangerous if attempted in one state and ruinous if tried in several. He therefore instructed his commissioners to urge the governors to use their influence against it. Such a convention would be "Revolution within Revolution," he said. So concerned was Magrath on the subject that he wrote Alexander H. Stephens begging him to use his influence to prevent, or at least postpone, a convention in Georgia. The regular state authorities were fully competent to ascertain and express public opinion, he said, and acting together they could do much to "reform abuses and bring back our Government to that most efficient condition which was designed for it by the Constitution; and which it has only ceased to be because that Constitution has been unheeded and neglected."[39]

The response of Governor Brown was not wholly satisfactory. He was prepared, he said, to render all possible aid to South Carolina but he feared the people would be less willing to help than they would have been had the South Carolina militia gone to the aid of Atlanta. Trescot explained that Bonham had been anxious to send it but that the South Carolina law did not then permit; that the legislature at its next session had, on Bonham's request, unanimously voted to change the law. But Brown was clearly lukewarm. He was also somewhat noncommittal in regard to Hood's army. He believed that it would be necessary for Hood to protect Georgia if, as seemed probable, General Thomas again moved southward. If, however, Thomas turned toward Knoxville Brown would join in a request that Hood be sent to South Carolina. Brown was also indefinite about calling a convention. Though asserting that he did not desire one, he feared the people of Georgia would demand it unless reforms were soon made; he believed that the danger of a convention could be minimized by limiting it to the consideration of certain subjects. On the other suggestions of Magrath, Brown was in full agreement. He thought the restoration of Johnston would have a very wholesome effect and he was in favor of giving Lee supreme command. Brown's chief interest was in the proposal of Magrath that a demand be made for political reform. He was ready and anxious to sign such a demand and suggested that it should insist

[39] A. G. Magrath to A. H. Stephens, January 25, 1865, Magrath Correspondence (Letter Book).

that conscription be abandoned, impressments reduced, and civil rights of the people respected.[40]

Governor Vance of North Carolina concurred in Magrath's suggestion for the interstate use of the militia and promised to renew his request to the legislature that North Carolina restrictions be removed. He feared, however, that the legislature would be very reluctant to act. Vance approved of the proposal in regard to Johnston and frankly stated that the governors should demand the appointment of Lee as supreme military commander. He was opposed to arming the slaves and suggested that the three states try to do something about desertion. Hood, he thought, should be sent to South Carolina. Vance agreed with Magrath also in believing that a state convention would be dangerous. He said he was urging Brown to prevent one in Georgia because he feared the people of North Carolina might be influenced by Georgia's action.[41]

On January 26, Magrath wrote Vance and Brown thanking them for their promises of coöperation and saying that he was now writing to the governors of Alabama, Mississippi, and Florida, and preparing the paper to be presented to the President. Magrath believed that by restoring the Constitution and the dignity of the states, the war could still be won; but it could be won in no other way. Confederate credit was gone. Reckless invasion of personal liberty and property rights had dried up the "openings from which new courage and fresh impulse" could be given to the people. Reliance must be placed in the states; the states as states must fight the war through to victory. Their credit was unimpaired and there were yet enough resources and men. The states must save themselves and thus save the Confederacy.[42]

Magrath wrote Governor T. H. Watts of Alabama on January 30 and dispatched the letter by John L. Manning under instructions dated February 2.[43] By this time, however, the invasion by Sherman's army was well under way and it was too late for Magrath's ideas even to receive a fair trial. By February 10 he had lost hope and was predicting that future generations would assign as the real cause of defeat the patriotic but mistaken policy of the states in yielding to every demand made by the Confederate government. This, he said, was the "fatal heresy" which like a cancer had gradually consumed the substance and exhausted the life of the Confederacy.[44]

In these last days before the Sherman tornado struck South Carolina

[40] J. E. Brown to A. G. Magrath, January 16, 1865; W. H. Trescot to A. G. Magrath, January 21, 1865, Magrath Papers, University of South Carolina.
[41] Z. B. Vance to A. G. Magrath, January 18, 1865; W. S. Mullins to A. G. Magrath, January 24, 1865, Magrath Papers, University of South Carolina.
[42] A. G. Magrath to J. E. Brown, January 26, 1865; A. G. Magrath to Z. B. Vance, January 26, 1865, Magrath Correspondence (Letter Book).
[43] A. G. Magrath to T. H. Watts, January 30, 1865. A. G. Magrath to John L. Manning, February 2, 1865, Magrath Correspondence (Letter Book).
[44] A. G. Magrath to William Whaley, February 10, 1865, Magrath Correspondence (Letter Book).

the *Mercury's* attack reached its climax. Describing the government at Richmond as "a pandemonium of imbecility, laxity, weakness, failure," it declared: "We want no more Jeff Davis' foolery; we want one atom of brains, one spark of nerve." In facetious editorials it cried, "Hurrah! for Jeff Davis, Hurrah!" Finally it openly demanded that the President be replaced. "Can no Lee be raised to Executive power at Richmond?" it asked. "And what is Congress after? Have they forgotten the power to impeach?"[45]

Sherman's march through the state practically ended the political history of South Carolina in the war period. Governor Magrath during the night of February 16 withdrew from Columbia and established headquarters for a few days at Union and then for some time at Spartanburg before returning to Columbia. He can hardly be said to have reorganized the state government. His call for a special meeting of the legislature at Greenville for April 25 brought only a handful of members and no attempt was made to organize, although Magrath addressed them.[46] Until the last, however, Magrath tried to maintain the "honor and independence" of South Carolina. When state troops under the command of Colonel A. D. Goodwyn passed into North Carolina in the retreat before Sherman, he wrote a sharp letter of rebuke to Goodwyn and peremptorily ordered his return to the state. To General Johnston he sent a demand that these troops be released.[47] Magrath finally went so far as to order the seizure of supplies impressed by Confederate officers if requisitions on them for the state militia were not honored.[48]

After the surrender of General Johnston in North Carolina, Magrath used what power and influence he still possessed to maintain order and relieve the suffering of the people. On May 2 he issued a proclamation directing that all Confederate subsistence stores in the state be turned over to state agents to be used in supplying the wants of returning soldiers.[49] The proclamation aroused the ire of General Q. A. Gillmore who pointed out that the supplies were the property of the United States. On May 15 he issued General Order No. 63 charging Magrath with "sundry and divers acts of treason" and warning the people to ignore the pretended claims of Magrath to exercise the functions of governor in South Carolina. Magrath acquiesced under protest. On May 22 he issued his last proclamation. It formally suspended the functions of his office and advised the people to accept a condition which they could not avoid. Magrath declared himself ready to appear anywhere at any time to answer to the charge of treason.

[45] *Mercury,* January 10, 12, 16, 17, 18, February 7, 1865.
[46] The proclamation dated March 27 and the message to the legislature are in Magrath Correspondence (Letter Book).
[47] A. G. Magrath to A. D. Goodwyn, February 25, 1865; A. G. Magrath to J. E. Johnston, March 10, 1865, Magrath Correspondence (Letter Book).
[48] A. G. Magrath to E. B. C. Cash, Magrath Correspondence (Letter Book).
[49] Columbia *Phoenix,* May 4, 1865.

Notified that he might consider himself under arrest upon the arrival in Columbia of the 25th Ohio Regiment, he calmly awaited its appearance. On May 25 he was put in an ambulance and carried to Fort Pulaski where he was soon joined by Secretary of the Treasury, George A. Trenholm.[50]

Commenting on the arrest of Magrath the Columbia *Phoenix* remarked that such an arrest in the capital of South Carolina was conclusive proof of the spiritual and physical collapse of the country. South Carolina was indeed exhausted and disillusioned. "Peaceful" secession had led to war. A "short" conflict enthusiastically, even gaily, entered upon, had developed into a long grim struggle attended by great sorrow and disappointment. An economic system greatly deranged by the war, the blockade, and an unsound currency had produced in numberless cases not only inconvenience and loss but also acute suffering. Invasion had brought humiliation and widespread destruction. Finally peace itself was attended by the overthrow of the social and economic system and by the greatest confusion and uncertainty.

Through it all South Carolina on the whole stood loyally and courageously for the Confederate cause. There were of course many who in war as in peace placed personal gain before the public welfare; such were the speculators and extortioners. There were many who protested against what seemed to them unnecessary burdens forced upon them by impressment of supplies or of Negro labor for the coast defenses. There were some who under various pretenses evaded military service. Finally there were still others, especially in the northwestern part of the state, whose suffering and defeatism led them into actual disloyalty to the cause. But the masses of the people remained firm and determined long after the hope of ultimate victory seemed slim indeed.

Probably no state officially coöperated more fully with the Confederate government. Passionately devoted to state rights principles there was nevertheless a disposition, until the very last months of the war, temporarily to sacrifice these opinions in the interest of harmony and victory. Though questioning the constitutionality of conscription, South Carolina gave to it her unprotesting support. Though she insisted at times on her right to exempt certain classes, especially overseers, her policy in regard to exemptions was until almost the end of the war one of comparative liberality. Only when threatened by invasion and when confidence in the Davis administration had almost completely collapsed did South Carolina reassert her right to control her own resources.

To the end South Carolina maintained a sincere confidence in the

[50] *Ibid.,* May 24, 25, 26, 1865.

230

justice of her cause. Some individuals in fact experienced difficulty in reconciling defeat with their belief in the divine approval of their course.[51] Governor Magrath probably expressed a general thought when, upon vacating his office, he said:

Whatever I have said, I believed to be true; whatever I have done, I believed to be right; and with the consciousness of the rectitude of my purpose, and the integrity of my conduct, I shall not avoid, delay or hinder the closest scrutiny that can be devised.[52]

A few years later William H. Trescot expressed somewhat the same idea when he said, "History will vindicate our motives while she explains our errors."[53] Such indeed is the verdict of history.

[51] See, for example, Ravenel, Diary, 1865.
[52] *Phoenix*, May 24, 1865.
[53] Quoted by Wallace, *History of S. C.*, III, 221.

BIBLIOGRAPHY

I. MANUSCRIPTS

Robert F. W. Allston Papers (South Carolina Historical Society). A large and valuable collection of several thousand items many of which have been published in J. H. Easterby, *The South Carolina Rice Plantation as Revealed in the Letters of Robert F. W. Allston* (Chicago, 1945).

Captain A. H. Boykin Papers (Southern Historical Collection, University of North Carolina). Chiefly military, but of some value for political affairs.

Chesnut-Manning-Miller Papers (South Carolina Historical Society, Charleston, S. C.). A small collection of considerable value.

Isabel DeSaussure Papers (in possession of Miss Isabel DeSaussure of Charleston, S. C.). Includes: a diary of Miss Emma Edwards Holmes (February 13, 1861-April 2, 1862); a narrative of L. G. Wigfall's visit to Major Anderson during the bombardment of Fort Sumter, by L. Gourdin Young who accompanied Wigfall; some family and official letters of Wilmot G. DeSaussure, Adjutant and Inspector General of South Carolina; and some miscellaneous material.

James H. Hammond Papers, 1763-1875 (Library of Congress). Includes correspondence with many public men in the war period.

A. G. Magrath Correspondence (South Carolina Historical Society, Charleston, S. C.). A Letter Book, Telegraph Book, and Order Book of Governor Magrath. Fairly complete.

A. G. Magrath Papers (Southern Historical Collection, University of North Carolina). About 75 letters, 1861-1867, for the most part official.

A. G. Magrath Papers (University of South Carolina). About 50 items including letters from Fort Pulaski during Governor Magrath's imprisonment there.

William Porcher Miles Papers, 1782-1907 (Southern Historical Collection, University of North Carolina). A very large collection, extremely important for secession and war period in South Carolina.

Benjamin F. Perry, Journal, 1832-1863, 2 vols. (Southern Historical Collection, University of North Carolina). Indispensable for Perry.

Pettigrew Family Papers (Southern Historical Collection, University of North Carolina). A large collection, including a considerable number of letters relating to South Carolina.

Francis W. Pickens and Milledge L. Bonham Papers, 1860-1864 (Library of Congress). About 400 items, almost entirely official.

Francis W. Pickens Papers (Duke University). A very useful collection which includes Bonham as well as Pickens official letters.

Henry W. Ravenel, Private Journal, 1859-1883, 11 vols. (University of South Carolina). A diary, faithfully kept by a renowned scientist who followed closely public affairs. About one half of this journal has been published in Arney R. Childs (ed.), *The Private Journal of Henry William Ravenel, 1859-1887* (Columbia, 1947).

Ruffin-Roulhac-Hamilton Papers (Southern Historical Collection, University of North Carolina). Contains many letters of D. H. Hamilton and D. H. Hamilton, Jr., relating to South Carolina.

Major E. P. Smith Papers (University of South Carolina). Several hun-

232

dred letters of a South Carolina legislator; for the most part family letters.

A. Taylor, Autobiography (in possession of A. B. Taylor, Spartanburg, S. C.). One of four volumes covers the war period.

George A. Trenholm Papers (Library of Congress). Two portfolios of correspondence and miscellaneous manuscripts, 1853-1876, of greater economic than political value.

William H. Trescot Papers (Library of Congress). One portfolio of letters and papers, 1851-1867. Includes copies of letters to Governor Pickens in 1860 and Trescot's narrative concerning negotiations between South Carolina and President Buchanan.

Beaufort T. Watts Papers (University of South Carolina). A valuable collection of letters, documents, and miscellaneous material. Watts was secretary to the governors of South Carolina almost continuously from 1834 to 1861.

Williams-Chesnut-Manning Papers (Southern Historical Collection, University of North Carolina). Numerous letters of men prominent in the Civil War period.

II. OFFICIAL RECORDS AND DOCUMENTS

Acts of the General Assembly of South Carolina, 1850-1865.

Acts and Resolutions of the Provisional Congress of the Confederate States of America, 4 vols. Montgomery: Tyler, 1861.

A Plan to Improve the Present Militia System of South Carolina submitted at the Session of 1859, by a Portion of the Military Commission, appointed by the Legislature of 1858. Charleston: Walker, Evans & Company, 1859.

The Correspondence between the Commissioners of the State of So. Ca. to the Government at Washington and the President of the United States; together with the Statement of Messrs. Miles and Keitt. Charleston: Evans and Cogswell, 1861.

Executive Documents, printed by order of the House of Representatives, during the second session of the Thirty-sixth Congress, 1880-'61, IX, no. 61. Washington: Government Printing Office, 1861.

First Annual Report of the Auditor of South Carolina. Columbia: R. W. Gibbes, 1863.

General Orders from Adjutant and Inspector General's Office, from January, 1862 to December, 1863. Columbia: Evans and Cogswell, 1864.

Journal of the Congress of the Confederate States of America, 1861-1865, 7 vols. Senate Document no. 234, 58th Congress, 2nd Session. Washington: Government Printing Office, 1904.

Journals of the Conventions of the People of South Carolina, held in 1832, 1833 and 1852. Columbia: R. W. Gibbes, 1860.

Journal of the Convention of the People of South Carolina, held in 1860, 1861 and 1862 together with the Ordinances, Reports, Resolutions, etc. Columbia: R. W. Gibbes, 1862.

Journals of the House of Representatives of the State of South Carolina. Columbia: State Printer, 1850-1865.

Journal of the Senate of the Confederate States of America (United States Senate Document, 58th Congress, 2nd Session, XVII).

Journals of the Senate of the State of South Carolina. Columbia: State Printer, 1850-1865.

Kennedy, Joseph C. G. (comp.), *Population of the United States in 1860; Compiled from the Original Returns of the Eighth Census, under the direction of the Secretary of the Interior.* Washington: Government Printing Office, 1864.

Minority Report of the Commission appointed under the Resolution of the Legislature, to examine the Militia System of the State and Report Amendments thereon. Columbia: R. W. Gibbes, 1859.

Minutes of the Military Commission at the Meeting in Greenville, S. C., Aug. 4, 1859. Charleston: Walker, Evans & Co., 1859.

Official Records of the Union and Confederate Navies in the War of the Rebellion, 30 vols. Washington: Government Printing Office, 1894-1927.

Ordinances and Constitution of the State of South Carolina, with the Constitution of the Provisional Government and of the Confederate States of America. Charleston: Evans and Cogswell, 1861.

Ramsdell, Charles W. (ed.), *Laws and Joint Resolutions of the Last Session of the Confederate Congress (November 7, 1864-March 18, 1865) together with the Secret Acts of Previous Congresses.* Durham: Duke University Press, 1941.

Richardson, J. S. G. (ed.). *Report of Cases at Law and in Equity, argued and determined in the Court of Appeals and the Court of Errors of South Carolina.* Vol. XIII. Charleston: E. J. Dawson & Company, 1866.

Richardson, James D. (ed.). *Compilation of the Messages and Papers of the Confederacy, including the Diplomatic Correspondence, 1861-1865,* 2 vols. Nashville: United States Publishing Company, 1905.

—— (ed.). *A Compilation of the Messages and Papers of the Presidents,* 20 vols. New York: Bureau of Natural Literature, 1917.

Report of the Auditor of South Carolina on Claims against the State for Slaves lost in the Public Service. Columbia: C. P. Pelham, 1864.

Report of the Chief of the Department of Treasury and Finance to His Excellency Governor Pickens. Columbia: R. W. Gibbes, 1862.

Report of the Chief of the Department of the Military of South Carolina to His Excellency Governor Pickens. Columbia: C. P. Pelham, 1862.

Report of Wilmot G. DeSaussure, Secretary of the Treasury, to His Excellency the Governor. n. p. (1861).

Reports and Resolutions of the General Assembly of the State of South Carolina. Columbia: State Printer, 1850-1866, 1900.

Report of the Comptroller General to the Legislature of South Carolina, November, 1864. Columbia: C. P. Pelham, 1864.

South Carolina Convention Documents, 1860-1862: Report of the Special Committee of Twenty-one on the Communication of His Excellency Governor Pickens, together with the Reports of Heads of Departments, and other Papers. Columbia: R. W. Gibbes, 1862.

South Carolina *Executive Documents,* nos. 1 to 6. Charleston: Evans and Cogswell, 1861.

Supplemental Report of the Chief of the Department of the Military of South Carolina, 1862. Columbia: R. W. Gibbes, 1862.

The Statutes at Large of South Carolina, Vols. XI-XIII. Columbia: State Printer, 1873-1875.

Statutes at Large of the Confederate States of America. Richmond: R. M. Smith, 1863-4.

The Statutes at Large of the Provisional Government of the Confederate States of America, from the Institution of the Government, February 8, 1861 to Its Termination, February 18, 1862, inclusive. Richmond: R. M. Smith, 1864.

The War of the Rebellion: *A Compilation of the Official Records of the Union and Confederate Armies,* 130 vols. Washington: Government Printing Office, 1880-1901.

III. COLLECTED SOURCE MATERIALS

American Annual Encyclopaedia and Register of Important Events, vols. I-V. New York: D. Appleton and Company, 1866-1870.

Ames, Herman V. (ed.). *State Documents on Federal Relations: The States and the United States.* Philadelphia: University of Pennsylvania Press, 1906.

Dumond, Dwight L. (comp.). *Southern Editorials on Secession.* New York: The Century Company, 1931.

Halstead, Murat (comp.). *Caucuses of 1860.* Columbus: Follet, Foster & Company, 1860.

Miller, Marian Mills (comp.). *Great Debates in American History, from the Debates in the British Parliament on the Colonial Stamp Act (1764-1765) to the Debates in Congress at the close of the Taft Administration (1912-1913),* 14 vols. New York: Current Literature Publishing Company, 1913.

Moore, Frank (comp.). *The Rebellion Record: A Diary of American Events, with Documents, Narratives, Illustrative Incidents, Poetry, etc.,* 11 vols. New York: G. P. Putnam, 1861-1868.

McPherson, Edward (comp.). *The Political History of the United States of America during the Great Rebellion from November 6, 1860, to July 4, 1864.* Washington: Philp and Solomons, 1864.

Mrs. A. T. Smythe, *et. al.* (eds.). *South Carolina Women in the Confederacy,* 2 vols. Columbia: The State, 1903-7.

IV. CONTEMPORARY PAMPHLETS

Addresses delivered before the Virginia State Convention by Hon. Fulton Anderson, Commissioner from Mississippi, Hon. Henry L. Benning, Commissioner from Georgia, and Hon. John S. Preston, Commissioner from South Carolina, February, 1861. Richmond: Wyatt M. Elliott, 1861.

Ayer, Lewis M. *Patriotism and State Sovereignty; An Oration delivered before the two Societies of the South Carolina College on the fourth of December, 1858.* Charleston: A. J. Burke, 1859.

Boyce, James P. *Remarks . . . in the House of Representatives of South Carolina, on the 9th December, 1862. . . .* Columbia: R. W. Gibbes, 1862.

De Bow, J. D. B. *The Interest in Slavery of the Southern Non-slave-Holder. The Right of Peaceful Secession. Slavery in the Bible.* Charleston: Evans and Cogswell, 1860.

Central Association for the Relief of the Soldiers of South Carolina. The Plan, and Address, adopted by the Citizens of Columbia, October 20, 1862. Charleston: Evans and Cogswell, 1862.

Dana, W. C. *A Sermon delivered in the Central Presbyterian Church, Charleston, S. C., November 21st 1860, being the Day appointed by the State Authority for Fasting, Humiliation and Prayer.* Charleston: Evans and Cogswell, 1860.

Elliott, James H. *Are These His Doings? A Sermon preached in St. Michael's Church, Charleston, S. C., on the Day of Public Prayer, Wednesday, November 21st, 1860.* Charleston: A. E. Miller, 1860.

Gadsen, Christopher P. *Duty to God not to be Overlooked in Duty to State, a Sermon preached at St. Luke's Church, Charleston, S. C., on the*

Twenty-third Sunday after Trinity, November 11, 1860. Charleston: Evans and Cogswell, 1860.

(Grayson, W. J.) *Remarks on Mr. Motley's Letter in the London Times on the War in America.* Charleston: Evans and Cogswell, 1861.

LeConte, John. *How to Make Salt from Sea-water.* Charleston: Evans and Cogswell, 1862.

(Jones, Ed. C.) *War Finance: A Plan proposing to meet the Government Expenditure During the War, upon a Cotton Basis, while the Crop Remains Unsold and Left upon the Plantations of the South.* Charleston: Evans and Cogswell, [1861].

McKim, James Miller. *The Freedmen of South Carolina, an Address delivered in Sansom Hall, July 9, 1862, together with a Letter from the Same to Stephen Colwell, Esq., Chairman of the Port Royal Relief Committee.* Philadelphia: W. P. Hazaed, 1862.

Memorial of the Late James L. Petigru. Proceedings of the Bar of Charleston, S. C., March 25, 1863. New York: Richardson and Company, 1866.

Nordhoff, Charles. *The Freedmen of South Carolina: Some Account of their Appearance, Character, Condition, and Peculiar Customs.* (1863.)

Official Proceedings of the Democratic National Convention, held in 1860, at Charleston and Baltimore. Cleveland: Plain Dealer Job Office, 1860.

Palmer, B. M. *A Discourse before the General Assembly of South Carolina, on December 10, 1863, appointed by the Legislature as a Day of Fasting, Humiliation and Prayer.* Columbia: C. P. Pelham, 1864.

————. *Address Delivered at the Funeral of Gen. Maxcy Gregg, in the Presbyterian Church, Columbia, S. C., December 20, 1863.* Columbia, 1863.

————. *A Vindication of Secession and the South from the Strictures of Rev. R. J. Breckinridge, D.D., L.L.D., in the Danville Quarterly.* Columbia: Southern Guardian Press, 1861.

Plan of a Provisional Government for the Southern Confederacy. Charleston: Evans and Cogswell, 1861.

Porter, William D. *State Sovereignty and the Doctrine of Coercion; together with a Letter from Hon. J. K. Paulding, Former Sec. of Navy. The Right to Secede by "States."* Charleston: Evans and Cogswell, 1860.

Proceedings of the Democratic State Convention of South Carolina, held at Columbia, 5th and 6th of May, 1856, for the Purpose of Electing Delegates to the Democratic National Convention, to meet in Cincinnati in June. Columbia: R. W. Gibbes, 1856.

Proceedings of the Democratic State Convention of South Carolina, held in Columbia on the 16th and 17th of April, 1860, for the Purpose of Electing Delegates to the Democratic National Convention to meet in Charleston, 23rd April. Columbia: R. W. Gibbes, 1860.

Proceedings of the National Democratic Convention, convened at Charleston, South Carolina, April 23, 1860. Washington: Thomas McGill, 1860.

Proceedings of the State Convention held at Columbia, S. C., May 30-31, 1860. Columbia: Southern Guardian Steam Press.

The Sequestration Cases before the Hon. A. G. Magrath: Report of the Cases under the Sequestration Act of the Confederate States, held in the District Court for the State of South Carolina, in the City of Charleston, October Term, 1861. . . . (Charleston, 1861.)

Remarks on the Policy of Prohibiting the Exportation of Cotton by One of the People. Charleston: Evans and Cogswell, 1861.

Reply to Professor Hodge on the "State of the Country." Charleston: Evans and Cogswell, 1861.

Report of the South Carolina Hospital Aid Association in Virginia, 1861-1862, embracing Report to Legislature, Sketch of Hospitals, Accounts, Lists of Contributors, and Catalogue of Deceased S. C. Soldiers. Richmond: McFarlane and Ferguson, 1862.

(Soldiers Relief Association, Columbia, S. C.). *To the Friends of the Southern Cause at Home.* Columbia: 1864.

Simons, Thomas Y. *Speech in favor of South Carolina being represented in the Democratic Convention, delivered at a Meeting of the Citizens of Charleston, held in Hibernian Hall, February 26, 1860.* Charleston: A. J. Burke, 1860.

Smyth, Thomas. *The Sin and the Curse: or the Union, the True Source of Disunion, and our Duty in the Present Crisis. A Discourse Preached on the Occasion of the Day of Humiliation and Prayer Appointed by the Governor of South Carolina on November 21st, 1860, in the Second Presbyterian Church, Charleston, S. C.* Charleston: Evans and Cogswell, 1860.

Statement of the Proceedings of the Convention of the National Democratic held in Charleston, in April, 1860, that Led to the Withdrawal of Certain Delegations, and Proceedings of the Delegates that Withdrew. Charleston: James and Williams, 1860.

Suggestions as to Arming the State. Charleston: Evans and Cogswell, 1860.

The Battle of Fort Sumter and the First Victory of the Southern Troops, April 13, 1861. Full Accounts of the Bombardment, with Sketches of the Scenes, Incidents, etc. . . . Charleston: Evans and Cogswell, 1861.

The Breckinridge Party a Disunion Party. (1860)

The Relation between the Races at the South. Charleston: Evans and Cogswell, 1861.

Thornwell, James H. *The State of the Country.* Columbia: Southern Guardian Steam Press, 1861.

Townsend, John. *The Doom of Slavery in the Union: Its Safety Out of It.* Charleston: Evans and Cogswell, 1860.

―――. *The South Alone Should Govern the South, and African Slavery Should be Controlled by Those Only, Who are Friendly to It.* Charleston: Evans and Cogswell 1860.

"Troup." *To the People of the South. Senator Hammond and the Tribune.* Charleston: Evans and Cogswell, 1860.

Uniform and Dress of the Officers of the Volunteer Forces Raised under the "Act to Provide an Armed Military Force." Charleston: Evans and Cogswell, 1861.

Winkler Edwin T. *Duties of the Citizen Soldier, A Sermon delivered in the First Baptist Church of Charleston, S. C., . . . January 6th, 1861, before the Moultrie Guards.* Charleston: A. J. Burke, 1861.

V. NEWSPAPERS

Camden *Confederate,* 1861-63, 1864 (broken), 1865 (few copies).

Camden *Weekly Journal,* 1860, 1864 (broken). Also published as the *Journal, Tri-Weekly Journal, Journal and Confederate, Daily Journal.*

Charleston *Daily Courier,* 1859-1865.

Charleston *Mercury,* 1859-1865.

Charleston *News and Courier,* selected copies.

Charleston *Sunday News,* selected copies.

Columbia *Daily South Carolinian,* 1860 (few copies), 1863-1865.

Columbia *Daily Southern Guardian,* 1863-1864.
Columbia *Phoenix,* 1865.
Columbia *State,* selected copies.
Confederate Veteran. Nashville: 1893-1932.
Edgefield *Advertiser,* 1860-1865 (broken).
Greenville *Southern Enterprise,* 1860-1861, 1863.
Lancaster *Ledger,* 1861-1864 (badly broken).
Newberry *Conservatist,* 1860 (badly broken).
Pickens *Keowee Courier,* 1860-1861.
Sumter *Tri-Weekly Watchman,* 1861 (badly broken), 1862-1864.
Spartanburg *Carolina Spartan,* 1860-1864.
Spartanburg *Express,* 1860-1862.
Yorkville *Enquirer,* 1860-1864 (badly broken).

VI. DIARIES, CORRESPONDENCE, AND WRITINGS

(Buchanan, James). *Mr. Buchanan's Administration on the Eve of the Rebellion.* New York: D. Appleton and Company, 1886.
Carson, James Petigru. *Life, Letters and Speeches of James Louis Petigru, The Union Man of South Carolina.* Washington: W. H. Lowdermilk & Co., 1920.
Chesnut, Mary Boykin. *A Diary from Dixie.* New York: Peter Smith, 1929.
Childs, Arney R. *The Private Journal of Henry William Ravenel, 1859-1887.* Columbia: University of South Carolina Press, 1947.
De Fontaine, Felix G. *Army Letters, 1861-1865.* Columbia: War Record Publishing Company, 1896.
The Diary of a Public Man, and a Page of Political Correspondence, Stanton to Buchanan. New Brunswick: Rutgers University Press, 1946.
Elliott, E. N. (ed.). *Cotton Is King, and Pro-Slavery Arguments; Comprising the Writings of Hammond, Harper, Christy, Stringfellow, Hodge, Bledsoe, and Cartwright, on this Important Subject, with an Essay on Slavery in the Light of International Law by the Editor.* Augusta: Pritchard Abbott & Lomis, 1860.
Hammond, James H. *Selections from the Letters and Speeches of the Hon. James H. Hammond of South Carolina.* New York: J. F. Trow Company, 1866.
(Harper, William, et al.). *The Pro-Slavery Argument; as Maintained by the Most Distinguished Writers of the Southern States: Containing the Several Essays on the Subject, of Chancellor Harper, Governor Hammond, Dr. Simms, and Professor Dew.* Charleston: Walker, Richards & Company, 1852.
Holmes, Charlotte R. (ed). *The Burckmyer Letters, March, 1863-June, 1865.* Columbia: The State Company, 1926.
Jameson, J. Franklin (ed.). *Correspondence of John C. Calhoun.* American Historical Association *Report* (1899, II).
Jervey, Susan R., and Ravenel, Charlotte St. J. *Two Diaries from Middle St. John's Berkeley, South Carolina, February-May, 1865.* n. p., St. John's Hunting Club, 1921.
Jones, John Beauchamp. *A Rebel War Clerk's Diary at the Confederate States Capital,* 2 vols. New York: Old Hickory Bookshop, 1935.
Nicolay, John G. and Hay, John. *Abraham Lincoln: Complete Works.* New York: The Century Company, 1920.
Pearson, Elizabeth Ware (ed.). *Letters from Port Royal Written at the Time of the Civil War.* Boston: W. B. Clarke Company, 1906.

Perry, B. F. *Biographical Sketches of Eminent American Statesmen with Speeches, Addresses and Letters.* Philadelphia: Ferree Press, 1887.

Phillips, U. B. (ed.). *The Correspondence of Robert Toombs, Alexander H. Stephens, and Howell Cobb.* American Historical Association *Report* (1911, II).

Rowland, Dunbar (ed.). *Jefferson Davis, Constitutionalist: His Letters, Papers, and Speeches,* 10 vols. Jackson, Mississippi: Department of Archives and History, 1923.

Russell, William Howard. *My Diary North and South.* Boston: T. O. H. P. Burnham, 1863.

————. *Pictures of Southern Life, Social Political, and Military.* New York: James G. Gregory, 1861.

(Trescot, W. H.). "Narrative and Letter of William Henry Trescot, concerning the Negotiations between South Carolina and President Buchanan in December, 1860." *American Historical Review,* XIII (April, 1908), 528-556.

Welsh, Spencer Glascow. *A Confederate Surgeon's Letters to His Wife.* New York: Neale Publishing Company, 1911.

See also Biography.

VII. Autobiographies, Memoirs, and Reminiscences

Adger, John B. *My Life and Times.* Richmond: Presbyterian Committee of Publication, 1899.

Alexander, E. P. *Military Memoirs of a Confederate; a Critical Narrative.* New York: Charles Scribner's Sons, 1907.

Bryce, Mrs. Campbell. *Reminiscences of the Hospitals of Columbia, S. C. During the Four Years of the Civil War.* Philadelphia: J. B. Lippincott, 1897.

Caldwell, James Fitz James. *The History of a Brigade of South Carolinians Known First as "Gregg's" and subsequently as "McGowan's Brigade."* Philadelphia, King and Baird, 1866.

Cardoza, J. N. *Reminiscences of Charleston.* Charleston: Joseph Walker, 1866.

Chapman, John A. *The Annals of Newberry.* Newberry: Aull and Houseal, 1892.

Cowley, Charles. *Leaves from a Lawyers Life Afloat and Ashore.* Boston: Lee and Shepard, 1879.

Coxe, Elizabeth Allen. *Memories of a South Carolina Plantation during the War.* Philadelphia: Privately Printed, 1912.

Davis, Jefferson. *Rise and Fall of the Confederate Government,* 2 vols. New York: D. Appleton and Company, 1881.

DeLeon, Thomas Cooper. *Four Years in Rebel Capitals: an Inside View of Life in the Southern Confederacy, from Birth to Death; from original notes collected in the years 1861 to 1865.* Mobile: The Gossip Printing Company, 1890.

Doubleday, Abner. *Reminiscences of Forts Sumter and Moultrie in 1860-'61.* New York: Harper & Brothers, 1876.

French, Mrs. A. M. *Slavery in South Carolina and the Ex-Slaves; or, the Port Royal Mission.* New York: William French, 1862.

Hagood, Johnson. *Memoirs of the War of Secession, from the Original Manuscripts of Johnson Hagood, Brigadier-General, C. S. A.* Columbia: The State Company, 1910.

Hudson, Joshua Hiliary. *Sketches and Reminiscences.* Columbia: The State Company, 1903.

Johnson, R. V., and Buel, C. C. (eds.). *Battles and Leaders of the Civil War,* 4 vols. New York: Century, 1884-1887.

LeConte, Joseph. *The Autobiography of Joseph LeConte.* New York: D. Appleton & Company, 1903.

(Powe, James H.). *Reminiscences & Sketches of Confederate Times, by One Who Lived Through Them.* Columbia: R. L. Bryan, 1909.

Malet, William Wyndam. *An Errand to the South in the Summer of 1862.* London: Richard Bentley, 1863.

Mixon, Frank M. *Reminiscences of a Private.* Columbia: The State Company, 1910.

McGill, Samuel D. *Narrative of Reminiscences in Williamsburg County.* Columbia: The Bryan Printing Company, 1897.

O'Neall, John Belton. *The Annals of Newberry, Historical, Biographical and Anecdotal.* Charleston, S. C.: Courtenay & Company, 1859.

Perry, Benjamin F. *Reminiscences of Public Men.* Philadelphia: J. D. Avil & Company, 1883.

——. *Reminiscences of Public Men with Speeches and Addresses.* Second series. Greenville: Shannon & Company, 1889.

Porter, A. Toomer. *Led On! Step by Step. Scenes from Clerical, Military, Educational, and Plantation Life in the South, 1828-1898.* New York: G. P. Putnam, 1899.

Pringle, Elizabeth W. Allston. *Chronicles of Chicora Wood.* New York: Charles Scribner's Sons, 1923.

Rhett, R. B., Jr. "The Confederate Government at Montgomery." *Battles and Leaders of the Civil War,* I, 99-110.

Selby, Julian A. *Memorabilia and Anecdotal Reminiscences of Columbia, S. C., and Incidents connected therewith.* Columbia: R. L. Bryan, 1905.

Scott, Edwin J., *Random Recollections of a Long Life, 1806 to 1876.* Columbia: Charles A. Calvo, Jr., 1884.

Sterling, Ada (ed.). *A Belle of the Fifties: Memoirs of Mrs. Clay, of Alabama, covering Social and Political Life in Washington and the South, 1853-66.* New York: Doubleday, Page & Company, 1904.

Stickney, William (ed.). *Autobiography of Amos Kendall.* Boston: Lee and Shepard, 1872.

Whilden, Mary S. *Recollections of the War 1861-1865.* Columbia: The State Company, 1911.

Wright, Mrs. D. Girand. *A Southern Girl in '61, The War-Time Memories of a Confederate Senator's Daughter.* New York: Doubleday, Page & Company, 1905.

VIII. GENERAL WORKS AND SPECIAL STUDIES

Ames, Herman V. *John C. Calhoun and the Secession Movement of 1850. Proceedings* of The American Antiquarian Society, XXVIII (1918), 19-50.

Anderson, Charles Carter. *Fighting by Southern Federals.* New York: Neale Publishing Company, 1912.

Auchampaugh, Philip Gerald. *James Buchanan and His Cabinet on the Eve of Secession.* Lancaster, Pennsylvania: Privately printed, 1926.

Aull, A. L. "The Making of the Constitution." *Publications* of the Southern History Association, IX (1905), 272-292.

Bancroft, Frederic. *Calhoun and the South Carolina Nullification Movement.* Baltimore: Johns Hopkins University Press, 1928.

Bateman, John M. *A Sketch of the History of the Governor's Guards of Columbia, S. C., 1843-1898.* Columbia: R. L. Bryan, 1910.

240

Boddie, William Willis, *History of Williamsburg*. Columbia: The State Company, 1923.

Bonham, Milledge L., Jr. *The British Consuls in the Confederacy*. New York: Longmans Green and Company, 1911.

Boucher, Chauncey Samuel. *Sectionalism, Representation, and the Electoral Question in Ante-bellum South Carolina*. Washington University *Studies*, IV (1917).

————. *South Carolina and the South on the Eve of Secession, 1852 to 1860*. Washington University *Studies*, VI (1919).

————. "The Annexation of Texas and Bluffton Movement in South Carolina." *Mississippi Valley Historical Review*, VI (1919), 3-34.

————. *The Ante-bellum Attitude of South Carolina towards Manufacturing and Agriculture*. Washington University *Studies*, III (1916).

————. *The Nullification Controversy in South Carolina*. Chicago: University of Chicago Press, 1916.

————. *The Secession and Co-operative Movements in South Carolina*. Washington University *Studies*, V (1918).

Brooks, Ulysses Robert (ed.). *Stories of the Confederacy*. Columbia: State, 1912.

Carpenter, J. T. *The South as a Conscious Minority: A Study in Political Thought*. New York: New York University Press, 1930.

Chadwick, F. E. *Causes of the Civil War, 1859-1861*. New York: Harper and Brothers, 1906.

Chandler, J. A. C. *et al.* (eds.). *The South in the Building of the Nation*, 12 vols. Richmond: The Southern Historical Publication Society, 1909-1913.

Charleston Year Book. Charleston, 1880—.

Cole, A. C. *The Irrepressible Conflict 1850-1865*. New York: Macmillan Company, 1934.

Craven, Avery. *The Coming of The Civil War*. New York: Charles Scribners Sons, 1942.

Crawford, Samuel Wylie. *The Genesis of the Civil War, The Story of Fort Sumter, 1860-1861*. New York: C. L. Webster and Company, 1887.

Crenshaw, Ollinger. "Christopher G. Memminger's Mission to Virginia, 1860," *Journal of Southern History*, VIII (August, 1942), 334-349.

————. *The Slave States in the Presidential Election of 1860*. The Johns Hopkins Studies in Historical and Political Science, Series LXIII, no. 3. Baltimore: The Johns Hopkins Press, 1945.

Curry, J. L. M. *Civil History of the Government of the Confederate States with some Personal Reminiscences*. Richmond: B. F. Johnson Publishing Company, 1901.

Dickert, D. Augustus. *History of Kershaw's Brigade*. Newberry: E. H. Aull Company, 1899.

DuBose, Henry K. *The History of Company B, Twenty-first Regiment (Infantry) South Carolina Volunteers, Confederate States Provisional Army*. Columbia: R. L. Bryan Company, 1909.

Dumond, Dwight L. *The Secession Movement, 1860-1861*. New York: Macmillan Company, 1931.

Edwards, W. H. *A Condensed History of the Seventeenth Regiment, S. C. V., C. S. A., from its Organization to the Close of the War*. Columbia: R. L. Bryan, 1908.

Elzas, Barnett A. *Leaves From My Historical Scrapbook*. Charleston, 1907-8.

————. *The Jews of South Carolina from the Earliest Times to the Present Day*. Philadelphia: J. B. Lippincott Company, 1905.

Emlio, Luis Fenollosa. *History of the Fifty-fourth Regiment of Massachusetts Volunteer Infantry, 1863-1865*. Boston: Boston Book Company, 1894.

Evans, Clement A. (ed.). *Confederate Military History*, 12 vols. Atlanta: Confederate Publishing Company, 1899.

Fox, W. F. *Regimental Losses in the American Civil War, 1861-1865*. Albany: Albany Publishing Company, 1889.

Gerson, Armond J. "The Inception of the Montgomery Convention." American Historical Association *Annual Report*, 1910.

Green, Edwin F. *A History of the University of South Carolina*. Columbia: The State Company, 1916.

Hamer, Phillip May, *The Secession Movement in South Carolina, 1847-1852*. Allentown, Pennsylvania: H. R. Haas and Company, 1918.

Hay, T. R. "The South and the Arming of the Slaves." *The Mississippi Valley Historical Review*, VI (1919), 34-73.

Hennig, Helen Kohn (ed.). Columbia: *Capital City of South Carolina 1786-1936*. Columbia: R. L. Bryan Company, 1936.

Hesseltine, William Best. *Civil War Prisons, A Study in War Psychology*. Columbus: Ohio State University, 1930.

Hosmer, James K. *The Appeal to Arms, 1861-1863*. New York: Harper and Brothers, 1907.

————. *The Outcome of the Civil War, 1863-1865*. New York: Harper and Brothers, 1907.

Houston, David F. *A Critical Study of Nullification in South Carolina*. New York: Longmans Green and Company, 1896.

Hoyt, James A. *The Palmetto Riflemen; Co. B., Fourth Regiment S. C. Vol., Co. C., Palmetto Sharpshooters*. Greenville: Hoyt and Keys, 1886.

Izlar, William V. *A Sketch of the War Record of the Edisto Rifles, 1861-1865*. Columbia: The State Company, 1914.

Jenkins, William S. *Pro-slavery Thought in the Old South*. Chapel Hill: University of North Carolina Press, 1935.

Jervey, Theodore D. "Charleston During the Civil War." American Historical Association *Annual Report*, 1913, I, 169-176.

Johnson, Guion Griffis. *A Social History of the Sea Islands with special reference to St. Helena Island, South Carolina*. Chapel Hill: University of North Carolina Press, 1930.

Johnson, John. *The Defense of Charleston Harbor, including Fort Sumter and the Adjacent Islands, 1863-1865*. Charleston: Walker, Evans and Cogswell, 1890.

Jones, F. D., and Mills, W. H. (eds.). *History of the Presbyterian Church in South Carolina Since 1850*. Columbia: R. L. Bryan, 1926.

Kibler, Lillian A. "Unionist Sentiment in South Carolina in 1860," *The Journal of Southern History*, IV (August, 1938), 346-366.

King, William L. *The Newspaper Press of Charleston, S. C., a Chronological and Biographical History, Embracing a Period of One Hundred and Forty Years*. Charleston: Edward Perry, 1872.

Kirkland, Thomas J., and Kennedy, Robert M. *Historic Camden*, 2 vols. Columbia: The State Company, 1905, 1926.

LaBorde, Maximilian. *History of the South Carolina College*. Charleston: Walker, Evans and Cogswell, 1874.

Lebby, Robert, "The First Shot on Fort Sumter," *South Carolina Historical and Genealogical Magazine*, XII (July, 1911), 141-145.

Lesesne, J. Mauldin. "The South Carolina State House," *South Carolina Education,* XVI (April-May 1935), 288-291.

Lonn, Ella. *Desertion During the Civil War.* New York: The Century Company, 1928.

———. *Salt as a Factor in the Confederacy.* New York: Walter Neale, 1933.

Moore, Albert Burton. *Conscription and Conflict in the Confederacy.* New York: Macmillan Company, 1924.

Murray, J. Ogden. *The Immortal Six Hundred, A Story of Cruelty to Confederate Prisoners of War.* Roanoke: Stone Printing Company, 1911.

Owsley, Frank L. *King Cotton Diplomacy.* Chicago: University of Chicago Press, 1931.

———. *State Rights in the Confederacy.* Chicago: University of Chicago Press, 1925.

Potter, David M. *Lincoln and His Party in the Secession Crisis.* New Haven: Yale University Press, 1942.

Ramsdell, Charles W. "The Changing Interpretation of the Civil War," *The Journal of Southern History,* III (February, 1937).

———. "Lincoln and Fort Sumter," *The Journal of Southern History,* III (August, 1937), 259-88.

Randall, J. G. *The Civil War and Reconstruction.* New York: D. C. Heath and Company, 1937.

———. *Lincoln the President: Springfield to Gettysburg,* 2 vols. New York: Dodd, Mead and Company, 1945.

Ravenel, St. Julien. *Charleston, the Place and the People.* New York: The Macmillan Company, 1894.

Reid, J. W. *History of the Fourth Regiment of South Carolina Volunteers, from the Commencement of the War until Lee's Surrender.* Greenville: Shannon and Company, 1892.

Rhodes, James Ford. *History of the United States from the Compromise of 1850 to the End of the Roosevelt Administration,* 9 vols. New York: Macmillan Company, 1928.

(Rivers, William J.). *Rivers' Account of the Raising of Troops in South Carolina for State and Confederate Service, 1861-1865.* Columbia: R. L. Bryan, 1899.

Robinson, William Morrison, Jr. *The Confederate Privateers.* New Haven: Yale Press, 1928.

———. "Prohibition in the Confederacy," *American Historical Review,* XXXVII, no. 1 (October, 1931), 50-58.

Ropes, John C., and Livermore, W. R. *The Story of the Civil War; A Concise Account of the War in the United States of America between 1861 and 1865,* 3 vols. in 4. New York: G. P. Putnam's Sons, 1894-1913.

Russel, Robert R. *Economic Aspects of Southern Sectionalism, 1840-1861.* Urbana, Illinois: The University of Illinois Press, 1924.

Salley, A. S., Jr. (ed.). *South Carolina Troops in Confederate Service,* 3 vols. Columbia: R. L. Bryan, 1913-1930.

———. *The Flag of the State of South Carolina.* Columbia: South Carolina Historical Commission, 1915.

———. *The Methods of Raising Taxes in South Carolina prior to 1868.* Columbia: State Company, 1925.

Scharf, John Thomas. *History of the Confederate States Navy.* Atlanta: W. H. Shepard and Company, 1887.

Schwab, John Christopher. *The Confederate States of America, 1861-1865;
a Financial and Industrial History of the South During the Civil War.*
New York: Charles Scribner's Sons, 1901.

Sellers, W. W. *A History of Marion County, South Carolina, from the
Earliest Times to the Present, 1901.* Columbia: R. L. Bryan, 1902.

Simkins, F. B., and Patton, J. W. *The Women of the Confederacy.* Richmond: Garrett and Massie, 1936.

Snowden, Yates (ed.). *History of South Carolina,* 5 vols. Chicago: Lewis
Publishing Company, 1920.

——. *War-time Publications (1860-1865) from the Press of Walker,
Evans & Cogswell Co., Charleston, S. C.* Charleston: Walker, Evans &
Cogswell, 1922.

Spaulding, Oliver L., Jr. "The Bombardment of Fort Sumter, 1861,"
American Historical Association *Annual Report,* 1913, I, 179-203.

Stamp, Kenneth M. "Lincoln and the Strategy of Defense in the Crisis of
1861," *Journal of Southern History,* XI (August, 1945), 297-323.

Stephenson, N. W. *The Day of the Confederacy.* New Haven: Yale University Press, 1920.

——. "The Question of Arming the Slaves," *American Historical Review,* XVIII (1913), 295-308.

Stephenson, N. W. "Southern Nationalism in South Carolina in 1851."
American Historical Review, XXXVI (1931), 314-335.

Tatum, Georgia Lee. *Disloyalty in the Confederacy.* Chapel Hill: University of North Carolina Press, 1934.

Thomas, John P. *The History of the South Carolina Military Academy.*
Charleston: Walker, Evans and Cogswell, 1893.

——. "The Raising of Troops in South Carolina for State and Confederate Service." *Reports and Resolutions,* 1900, I, 7-86.

Tilley, John S. *Lincoln Takes Command.* Chapel Hill: University of
North Carolina Press, 1941.

Van Deusen, John George. *Economic Bases of Disunion in South Carolina.*
New York: Columbia University Press, 1928.

Walker, Cornelius Irvine. *Rolls and Historical Sketch of the Ninth Regiment, South Carolina Volunteers, in the Army of the Confederate States.*
Charleston: Walker, Evans and Cogswell, 1881.

Wallace, David Duncan. *The History of South Carolina.* 3 vols. New
York: The American Historical Society, 1934.

Way, William. *History of the New England Society of Charleston, South
Carolina for One Hundred Years, 1819-1919.* Chicago: University of
Chicago Press, 1920.

Wells, E. L. *Hampton and His Cavalry in '64.* Richmond: B. J. Johnson
Publishing Company, 1899.

White, Laura A. "The Fate of Calhoun's Sovereign Convention in South
Carolina." *American Historical Review,* XXXIV (1929), 757-771.

——. "The National Democrats in South Carolina, 1852 to 1860."
South Atlantic Quarterly, XXVIII (1929), 370-389.

White, Horace. *Money and Banking,* 1st edition. Boston: Ginn & Company.

Williams, J. F. *Old and New Columbia.* Columbia: Epworth Orphanage
Press, 1929.

IX. BIOGRAPHY

Bachman, C. L. *John Bachman, D. D., L.L.D., Ph.D., The Pastor of St.
John's Lutheran Church, Charleston.* Charleston: Walker, Evans and
Cogswell, 1888.

Broadus, John A. *Memoir of James Petigru Boyce, D.D., L.L.D., Late President of the Southern Baptist Theological Seminary, Louisville, Ky.* New York: A. C. Armstrong and Company, 1893.

Brooks, U. R. *South Carolina Bench and Bar.* Columbia: The State Company, 1908.

Capers, Henry D. *The Life and Times of C. G. Memminger.* Richmond: Everett Waddey and Company, 1893.

Capers, Walter B. *The Soldier-Bishop Ellison Capers.* New York: Neale Publishing Company, 1912.

Claiborne, John F. H. *Life and Correspondence of John A. Quitman, Major-General, U.S.A., and Governor of the State of Mississippi,* 2 vols. New York: Harper & Brothers, 1860.

Cook, Harvey Tolliver. *The Life Work of James Clement Furman.* Greenville. n. p., 1926.

Craven, Avery O. *Edmund Ruffin, Southerner; a Study in Secession.* New York: D. Appleton and Company, 1932.

Cyclopaedia of Eminent and Representative Men of the Carolinas of the Nineteenth Century, 2 vols. Madison, Wisconsin: Brant and Fuller, 1892.

Daly, Louise Haskell. *Alexander Chevis Haskell, The Portrait of a Man.* Norwood, Massachusetts: Plimpton Press, 1904.

Fraser, Jessie Melville. *Louisa C. McCord.* University of South Carolina *Bulletin,* no. 91 (1920).

Grayson, William J. *James Louis Petigru.* New York: Harper and Brothers, 1866.

Jervey, Theodore D. *Robert Y. Hayne and His Times.* New York: Macmillan Company, 1909.

Johnson, Allen and Malone, Dumas (eds.). *Dictionary of American Biography,* 20 vols. New York: Charles Scribner's Sons, 1828-1936.

Johnson, Thomas Cary. *The Life and Letters of Benjamin Morgan Palmer.* Richmond: Presbyterian Committee of Publication, 1906.

Kibler, Lillian A. *Benjamin F. Perry, South Carolina Unionist.* Durham: Duke University Press, 1946.

Malone, Dumas. *The Public Life of Thomas Cooper, 1783-1837.* New Haven: Yale University Press, 1926.

Meigs, William M. *The Life of John Caldwell Calhoun.* 2 vols. New York: Neale Publishing Company, 1917.

Merritt, Elizabeth. *James Henry Hammond, 1807-1864.* Baltimore: Johns Hopkins University Press. 1923.

Mitchell, Broadus. *William Gregg, Factory Master of the Old South.* Chapel Hill: University of North Carolina Press, 1928.

Nicolay, John G., and Hay, John. *Abraham Lincoln, a History.* 10 vols. New York: The Century Company, 1890.

O'Connor, Mary Doline. *The Life and Letters of M. P. O'Connor.* New York: Dempsey and Carroll, 1893.

O'Neall, John Belton. *Biographical Sketches of the Bench and Bar of South Carolina.* 2 vols. Charleston: S. G. Courtenay and Company, 1859.

Palmer, Benjamin Morgan. *The Life and Letters of James Henley Thornwell.* Richmond: Whittit and Shepperson, 1875.

Rippy, J. Fred. *Joel R. Poinsett: Versatile American.* Durham: Duke University Press, 1935.

Roman, Alfred. *The Military Operations of General Beauregard in the War between the States, 1861-1865; including a brief sketch and a narrative of his services in the War with Mexico, 1846-1848.* 2 vols. New York: Harper and Brothers, 1884.

Stevens, Hazard. *Life of Isaac Ingalls Stevens.* 2 vols. Boston and New York: Houghton Mifflin and Company, 1900.

Thomas, John P. *Career and Character of General Micah Jenkins, C.S.A.* Columbia: The State Company, 1903.

Trent, W. P. *William Gilmore Simms.* New York: Houghton Mifflin and Company, 1892.

Trescot, William H. *Memorial of the Life of J. Johnston Pettigrew, Brigadier-General of the Confederate States Army.* Charleston: J. Russel, 1870.

Walker, C. Irvine. *The Life of Lieutenant General Richard Heron Anderson of the Confederate States Army.* Charleston: The Art Publishing Company, 1917.

White, Laura A. *Robert Barnwell Rhett: Father of Secession.* New York: The Century Company, 1931.

Wiese, E. Robert. *Life and Times of Samuel Preston Moore, Surgeon-General of the Confederate States of America.* Reprinted from *The Southern Medical Journal,* XXIII (1930).

Winston, Robert W. *High Stakes and Fair Trigger, The Life of Jefferson Davis.* New York: Henry Holt and Company, 1930.

Youmans, LeR. F. *A Sketch of the Life and Services of Francis W. Pickens of South Carolina,* n. p., n.d.

————. *Sketch of the Life of Governor A. G. Magrath.* Charleston: 1896.

INDEX

Abbeville, secession meeting, 61

Abolitionists, mentioned, 1, 3, 32–33, 36, 42, 45–48, 111, 140

Adams, John H., in secession movement, 59 n., 90 n.; commissioner to Washington, 97 and n.; death, 66 n.

Address to the Slaveholding States, 74

Aiken, William, opposes secession, 76; entertains Davis, 214; mentioned, 221

Ainsley *versus* Timmons, 172

Alabama, defeats secessionists 1851, 5; and election 1860, 13, 16–17; commissioner to South Carolina, 67, 69; proposes guarantee Confederate bonds, 199

Aldrich, A. P., as secession leader, 23, 59–60; opposes Executive Council, 143; re-elected speaker, 159 and n.

Aliens, and conscription laws, 172–173

Allston, R. F. W., 10

American Heritage Pictorial History of the Civil War (Catton), ix–x

Anderson, Richard H., appointed colonel, 115

Anderson, Robert, x; assigned to Charleston forts, 93; and removal to Fort Sumter, 97–102, 114; and *Star of West* expedition, 102–103; and Lamon's visit, 122; and problem of supplies, 123 ff.; and question of reinforcement, 123–129; surrender, 130–132; mentioned, 104–107, 117–118. *See also* forts, Fort Moultrie, Fort Sumter

Anderson *Intelligencer,* 33, 89

Arms and ammunition, supply 1860, 115–116; increased 115 ff.; scarcity 1861, 138; imported, 138, 149; manufactured, 149–150

Army of Northern Virginia, xi

Army of Tennessee, xii

Ashmore, John D., advocates secession, 26, 45, 50, 66; on reunion, 134 n.; resigns United States Congress, 70 n.; predicts short war, 134 n.; conscription officer, 174–175

Association of 1860, organized 34; pamphlets, 34–43, 73; political club, 43; military survey, 43, 111, 115, 116 n.; Winyah Association, 43; mentioned, 65

Augusta, Georgia, governors conference 1864, 170, 220

Ayer, Lewis M., member Confederate Congress, 208 n., 209, 213

Bachman, Rev. John, 71

Bacon, Thomas G., Colonel, 7th South Carolina Volunteers, 115 n., 136

Baltimore National Democratic Convention, 19–20, 25

Bankhead, John P., 76 n.

Bank of the State of South Carolina, 188, 190–191, 195–197, 200

Baring Brothers, London bankers, 195

Barker, Theodore G., National Democrat, 21, 23; secessionist, 95–96

Barksdale, Ethelbert, 211

Barnwell, Robert W., coöperationist 1850, 5; candidate Richmond convention, 23 n., 24 n.; supports secession, 66–67, 76; commissioner to Washington, 97–102; in Montgomery convention, 85 and n., 86, 87 n.; offered cabinet post, 87; in secession convention, 90 n., 158–159; in Confederate Senate, 165 and n., 201, 206–207 and n., 209–210, 212 n., 215, 217, 223

Bartow, F. S., pledges Georgia, 57–58
Baruc, B. C., 79 n., 199–200
Bates, Edward, 120–121
Battery Wagner, Battle of, xiv
Bayard, James A., 19, 203
Beaufort, Federal occupation of, xii, xiv
Beauregard, P. G. T., and fall of Fort Sumter, 109 and n., 115, 130 and n., 131–132; replaces Pemberton, 151; on reserves law, 161; on foreigners, 173; and slave labor for defenses, 178, 180; leaves Charleston, 198; suggested for general-in-chief, 209; offended by Davis, 214; on arming slaves, 221; relieved South Carolina command, 223; plan to evacuate Charleston, 224
Bee, William C., on Petigru, 74 n.
Benjamin, Judah P., 218
Bilbo, John, pledges Georgia, 57
Black, Jeremiah S., and Charleston forts, 82, 93, 95 n., 100
Black, W. C., 59
Blair, Montgomery, 121, 125
Blake, Arthur M., 77 n.
Blanding, J. D., Colonel, 9th South Carolina Volunteers, 115 n., 136
Blue Ridge Railroad, 188
Bluffton Movement, 3, 31
Bobo, Simpson, 160
Boiling, T. C., defeated for secession convention, 63, 64 n.
Bonham, Milledge L., xiii; sketch, 164; advocates secession, 11, 25, 45, 54, 61; forts agreement with Buchanan, 94–95 and n.; and Hamilton mission, 96; resigns U. S. Congress, 70 n.; commissioner to Mississippi, 84 n.; Major General, South Carolina forces, 115; appointment criticized, 140 n., 141; and Wigfall, 102 n.; Confederate brigadier, 164 and n.; member Confederate Congress, 208 n., 209 n.; elected governor, 163 and n.; and Confederate conscription, 164–170, 194; measures against deserters, 176, 192 n.; on

reserve corps, 161; on use of militia outside state, 170, 226; on foreigners, 173, 192 n.; raises troops, 192 n.; and slave labor for defenses, 178–182; and Franco-Carolina Bank, 200; on Davis, 212; at governors' conference, 170, 220; and impressment, 185–186
Boozer, Lemuel, 18, 47
Bowers, Susan A., 77 n.
Boyce, James P., nominated for secession convention, 63; proposes guarantee Confederate bonds, 199; bank director, 220; defeated for Congress, 213 n.
Boyce, William W., advocates secession, 26–27; forts agreement with Buchanan, 94–95; resigns U. S. Congress, 70 n.; in Montgomery convention, 85–86, 88; member Confederate Congress, 208 n., 209, 216 and n.; peace proposal, 217–220
Boylston, R. B., 23
Breckinridge, John C., 15, 25, 49
Brooklyn, and *Star of the West,* 102
Brooks, Preston S., 7, 164
Brown, John, 11–12, 13, 36, 46, 112, 190
Brown, Gov. Joseph E., xiii; and secession movement, 53, 56–57, 68; and Fort Sumter, 107; on conscription, 169; on *habeas corpus,* 214 n., 215; and Magrath, 224, 226–227
Browning, Orville H., 129
Bryan, George S., 76
Buchanan, James, elected President, 9; forts policy, 93–106; and Gist, 94; and South Carolina congressmen, 94–95; and Pickens proposal, 95–96; and commissioners, 97–102; and *Star of the West,* 101–102; and Hayne, 103–106; mentioned, 82 n.
Buell, D. C., orders to Anderson, 97
Buist, Henry, 14, 54–55, 63
Bunch, Robert, British consul, 93

Burt, Armistead, secessionist, 23–24; commissioner to Mississippi, 84 n.; on prospect of war, 133

Butler, Andrew P., 5

Calhoun, A. P., commissioner to Alabama; 84 n.

Calhoun, John C., xviii, 1, 3, 4, 17, 31–32

Camden *Confederate,* 153, 206

Campbell, James B., 184

Campbell, John A., and Fort Sumter negotiations, 120–121, 126–127

Campbell, W. H., secessionist, 62 n.

Cannon, faction of, 64

Cash, E. B., Colonel, 8th South Carolina Volunteers, 115 n., 136

Cass, Lewis, 82, 92–93, 95

Castle Pinckney, 99–111, 116

Catton, Bruce, ix

Cauthen, Andrew Jackson, Jr., xvi

Cauthen, Andrew Jackson, Sr., xvi

Cauthen, Charles Edward, biographical sketch, xv–xx; quoted, xv, xvi, xvii–xviii, xix

Charleston, x, xii; siege of, xiv; election to legislature 1860, 51; secession meeting, 57–58; election to convention, 64–66; fire 1861, 139 and n.; threatened, 178, bombarded, 180; evacuated, 184

Charleston and Savannah Railroad, 43, 151

Charleston *Daily Courier,* in secession movement, 10, 20, 33, 49; quotes Scott, 121; on nitre manufacture, 150; in executive council controversy, 155, 209, 162; on evasion of service, 173–174, 176; on impressment, 182, 185, 212; Ayer letter, 213; on Boyce peace proposal, 219

Charleston *Evening News,* 10

Charleston Free Market, 194 n.

Charleston *Mercury,* ix–x, xiv; on Know-Nothing party, 8; on National Democrats, 14, 16; on Charleston convention, 20; on Lincoln's election, 30; and 1860

Association, 35; on separate secession, 50; for early convention, 52, 57; on coöperation, 53; on Charleston secession meeting, 58 and n.; classifies convention candidates, 69–66; prints secession ordinance, 71 and n.; criticized, 80; on Confederate constitution, 88–89; on Lincoln inaugural, 119; fears reconstruction, 120; on Fort Sumter, 130; predicts no war, 133; on Monarchists, 135 n.; on Pickens, 141; on conscription, 146; on Executive Council, 153–156; on evasion of service, 172–173; on slave labor law; on Davis administration, 201–215, 219–221, 228

Charleston News and Courier, xix

Chase, Salmon P., 120–121

Chesnut, James, Jr., xviii, xix; quoted, x; to Senate, 11; in secession movement, 49–50, 53–54, 64, 66; in secession convention, 70 n., 210; resigns Senate, 61, 70 n.; in Montgomery convention, 85, 86 and n., 87 n., 88; Beauregard aide, 130–131; member Executive Council, 142 n., 143–145 and n., 146–147 and n., 150, 161 and n., 166; mentioned for governor, 162; commands reserves, 194 n., 176

Chesnut, Mary B., 207

Chevis, Langdon, 5

Chew, Robert S., 127

Chicora, gunboat, constructed, 150 and n.; claim for, 198

Chisolm, A. R., Beauregard aide, 131

Churches, support secession, 44, 77

Cincinnati platform, 16–18

Citadel cadets, and *Star of the West,* 102

Civil War, meaning of, ix; in South Carolina, x, xi–xv; South Carolina casualties in, xi

Clay, Henry, 4

Cobb, Howell, and Fort Sumter, 93, 109; requests Orr for commissioner to Georgia, 84 n.

Cohen, Leopold, court case of, 171–172, 222
Colcock, W. F., 14, 58, 82
Cole's Island, abandoned, 151
Columbia, xii, xvi; burning of, xiv, xv, xvi
Columbia College (Columbia, S.C.), xvi
Columbia *Daily South Carolinian,* 20, 28, 32, 80, 219
Columbia *Daily Southern Guardian,* 29, 32
Columbia *Phoenix,* 229
Columbia University (New York, N.Y.), xvii
Committees of Safety, 45–46, 111–112
Compromise of 1850, 4, 8
Confederate conscription, laws, 146, 165, 167, 169, 172, 194 n.; opposed by South Carolina congressmen, 165, 209 n.; believed unconstitutional, 145, 146 n., 209 n., 220; upheld by Magrath, 165; supported by South Carolina, 145, 165–166; and state exemptions, 166–171; evasion of, 171–177
Confederate government, South Carolina and establishment of, 84–91 and n.; commissioners to Washington, 120 ff.; reimburses South Carolina, 188, 197–200; tax controversy with South Carolina, 196 and n.; bond guarantee by states, 199; criticized, 146, 154, 170, 184, 187, 201–216, 220–222
Conner, James, 14, 58
Conner, H. W., 186
Conscription, state, 144, 145 n., 147; Confederate, *see* Confederate conscription, draft, troops
Conventions. *See* South Carolina, secession convention, Democratic party, Southern
Cooper, Thomas, 2
Couch, Jack, deported, 112
Courtenay, W. C., 150 n.
Crawford, Martin J., Confederate commissioner, 120–121, 127

"Crisis," Turnbull's, 2
Cuningham, John, in secession movement, 14, 21, 60; and Fort Sumter, 102

Darlington *Flag,* 9, 29
David, R. L., 77 n.
Davis, Jefferson, xiv; advises secession, 68; elected President, 86–87; and Charleston forts, 96–97, 105, 107, 109; calls for troops, 135, 144, 192 n.; administration endorsed, 91, 145, 164; on South Carolina exemptions, 167; refuses reinforcements, 171; administration criticized, 146, 154, 170, 184, 187, 201–216, 220–222, 228; Boyce letter to, 217–218; and Charleston, 214, 224
Dawkins, T. N., 159 n.
Day, M. C., 77 n.
De Bow, J. D. B., author secession pamphlet, 41–42
De Bow's Review, 35, 37
Declaration of Immediate Causes, 73
Democratic party, national convention at Charleston, 17–19, at Baltimore and Richmond, 25; state conventions, 8, 15–16, 21–24. *See also* National Democrats
Departments, of state government, 81, 143–144
De Saussure, J. M., 186
De Saussure, W. G., on Petigru, 74 n.; South Carolina Secretary of the Treasury, 81, 197
Desertion, 174 ff.
De Stoeckl, Baron Edward, 83, 121
Devine, deported, 112
Dew, Thomas R., 42
Distilling, licensed, 150
Doom of Slavery in the Union, secession pamphlet, 37–38
Dorsey, deported, 112
Douglas, Stephen A., supporters in South Carolina, 14–15; in Charleston convention, 17, 19
Draft, Confederate, xiii–xiv. *See also* Confederate conscription

Drayton, Percival, 76 and n., 137 n.
Drayton, Thomas F., 92, 116 n., 137
Dunkin, B. F., and secession ordi-
  nance, 70 n.
Dunovant, R. G. M., 115, 141
Dupont, S. F., 137

Ebaugh, D. C., 77 n.
Edgefield *Advertiser,* 152
Elections, commissioners to Washington, 97; Confederate Congress,
  206, 208 n., 212, 213 and n.;
  convention 1852, 4–5; secession
  convention, 63–66; proposed
  Southern convention, 5; governor,
  6, 79–80, 162–163 and n., 183 and
  n.; legislature, 6, 28–29, 50–51,
  159, 174; Montgomery convention,
  85; commissioners to cotton states,
  84 n.; U. S. Senate, 10–11
Elliott, S. D., 214
Ellis, Gov. John W:, 53
Elmore, J. A., commissioner to secession convention, 67, 69
Epstein, Phillip, 77 n.
Evans, Josiah, J., 7
Executive Council, created, 142–144;
  measures of, 144 ff., 165–167, 178,
  198; campaign to abolish, 152 ff.;
  defended, 153–154, 157–160; abolished, 161
Exemptions, from Confederate conscription, 166–171

"Fabius," 66
Fairfield *Herald,* 206
*Family Letters of the Three Wade
  Hamptons* (Cauthen), xvii
Farley, Henry S., first shot on Sumter,
  131
Farrow, James, Confederate con-
  gressman, 208 n., 213 n., 222
Fifty-fourth Massachusetts Volunteer
  Infantry (Colored), xiv
Fingal, brings arms, 138
Flag, of South Carolina, adopted,
  81; raised over Fort Sumter,
  133 n.
Flagg, Henry C., censured, 76

Floyd, J. B., and Charleston forts, 93,
  95, 96 n., 97, 100
Foote, H. S., 208–209
Ford, F. W., 77 n.
Ford, W. H., superintendent nitre
  works, 149
Foreigners, and conscription,
  172–173
Forsyth, John, confederate commis-
  sioner, 120, 122
Fort Moultrie, 92, 97, 100–102, 117,
  140, 151. *See also* forts, Fort
  Sumter
Forts, in Charleston harbor, South
  Carolina negotiations for, 92–109;
  congressmen and Buchanan,
  94–95; Hamilton mission, 95–96;
  South Carolina commissioners
  and Buchanan, 97–102; Lincoln's
  policy, 119–129. *See also* Fort
  Moultrie, Fort Sumter
Fort Sumter, bombardment and surrender of, x, xii, xiv, xv, xvi;
  Buchanan policy, 92–106; Pickens
  demands, 95–96; Anderson occu-
  pies, 97–99; reinforcement
  attempt, 102; Hayne negotiations
  for, 103–106; Lincoln policy on,
  119–129; supplies, 123 ff.; surrender, 130–133; Pemberton considers
  evacuation, 151; Federal bombardment, 180. *See also* forts
Forts Walker and Beauregard, 137
Foster, J. G., 96 n.
Fox, Gustavus V., and Fort Sumter,
  urges reinforcement, 125; visits,
  126: relief expedition, 128; con-
  soled by Lincoln, 129
Franco-Carolina Bank, chartered, 22
Fraser, John, and Company, 117, 200
Fraser Trenholm and Company, 83
Frazer, Sidney S., 77 n.
Free Negroes, donate money and
  services, 117 and n.; impressed,
  180
Fremont, John C., 9, 76 n.
Freshley, Joseph, 77 n.
Frost, Edward, South Carolina Sec-
  retary of the Treasury, 81, 141, 197

Furman, C. M., 150 n., 196, 200
Furman, James C., 62 n.; 63
Furman University (Greenville, S.C.), xx

Gadberry, J. M., 22–23
Gardner, J. L., 93
Garlington, A. C., in secession movement, 23 and n., 24 n.; South Carolina Secretary of the Interior, 81; Adjutant and Inspector General, 115; candidate for governor, 183 and n.
Garrison, William L., 33
Gary, Martin W., 56
General Assembly. See legislature
Georgetown, abandoned, 147, 158; customs collector, 82 n.
Georgia, and the Confederate war effort, xiii, xiv; defeats secessionists 1851, 5; influence on South Carolina secession, 53–60; donation, 139 n.
Gibbes, William H., 131 n.
Giddings, Joshua H., quoted, 36–37
Gillmore, Q. A., 228
Gist, States R., xi–xii, 52, 113
Gist, William H., xix; in secession movement, 11, 13, 26, 49 n., 52–53, 56, 59 and n., 67; and Charleston forts, 92–95; and war preparations, 111, 116 n.; predicts short war, 133–134; member Executive Council, 143–144, 150
Gladden, A. H., 114
Goodwin, A. D., 228
Gourdin, Robert N., on Douglas party, 14; on Perry, 28 n.; officer 1860 Association, 34; grand jury foreman, 55; to secession convention, 65–66; and Anderson, 123–124; on tax system, 189
Governors, of South Carolina. See Gist, Pickens, Bonham, Magrath
Gowensville, deserters, 175
Graham, ex parte, 169
Grayson, William J., unionist, 4, 66, 76; opposes reunion, 134
Green, Fletcher M., xvii

Greenville, xii; secession convention election, 63–64
Greenville Southern Enterprise, on secession, 20, 28, 33, 62, 64; on deserters, 176
Greenville Southern Patriot, 5
Gregg, Maxcy, in secession movement, 70 n., 74, 90 n.; Colonel, 1st South Carolina Volunteers, 46 n., 114 and n., 115, 135 and n.; opposes executive council, 143 and n.
Gregg, William, 186
Groceries, offered Anderson, 124
Gunboats, constructed, 150

Habeas corpus, suspension of, 209 n., 211, 212 n., 214 n., 215
Hagood, Johnson, Colonel, 1st South Carolina Volunteers, 114 n., 115 n., 135
Hall, Norman, J., 103
Hamilton, Alexander, 38
Hamilton, D. H., in secession movement, 14, 21, 58; mission to Washington, 96; predicts war, 134; major, 114
Hamlin, Hannibal, 48
Hammond, James H., Senator, xviii, 6, 10; in secession movement, 10–11, 19, 21 and n., 29, 49 and n., 50, 54, 58–59 and n.; resigns United States Senate, 61 and n.; on war, 133; on reunion, 134 n.; on Davis, 136 n., 205, 207; on slave labor for defenses, 148; mentioned for governor, 162; and impressment, 186; on Memminger, 212 n.; mentioned 40–41
Hammond, John F., 76
Hampton, Wade, xi, 60, 135
Hardee, W. J., 177, 221, 224
Harllee, W. W., South Carolina Postmaster General, 81, 83; Lieutenant Governor, 143; member Executive Council, 143, 147, 158
Harper, William, 42, 155
Harrison, J. W., 60
Harvey, James E., 127

Hayne, Isaac W., xix; in secession movement, 14, 22–24, 24 n., 49 and n.; attorney general, 81; mission to Washington, 103–107, 123; on monarchists, 143; member Executive Council, 144, 151 n., 153, 157–158; on liability of aliens, 173

Helper, Hinton R., 13

Heriot, W. B., 150 n.

Hitchings, deported, 112

Hoff, Henry K., censured, 76

Holmes, F. S., 148

Holmes, J. G., 219

Holt, Joseph, and Charleston forts, 100, 105–106, 107 n.

Hood, John B., 226–227

Hooker, Charles E., commissioner of Mississippi, 67, 69

Huff, A.V., Jr., quoted, xx

Huger, Alfred, in secession movement, 14, 20, 75; on Fort Sumter, 107

Huger, Benjamin, 93

Hunter, R. M. T., 15, 18, 68, 97, 101, 120, 203

Hurlbert, William H., threatened, 112

Hurlbut, Stephen A., 76 n.

Hutson, W. F., 70 n., 160

Impressment, of crops, food, and livestock, xii, xiii; of supplies, 184–187, 212, 223, 227; of Negroes, see slave labor

Inglis, J. A., in secession convention, 69, 70 n., 158–159

Institute Hall, 57, 70–71

Interest in Slavery of the Southern Non-Slaveholder, secession pamphlet, 41–42

Jackson, Henry R., pledges Georgia, 57–58

James, George S., first shot on Fort Sumter, 131

James Island, abandoned, 151

Jamison, D. F., in secession convention, 68–69, 71, 73; South Carolina

Secretary of War, 81, 103–116, 141; reconvenes convention, 138–139, 156 and n.; mentioned for governor, 162 n.

Jenkins, Micah, Colonel, 5th South Carolina Volunteers, 115 n., 136

Johnson, B. J., 80 and n.

Johnson, R. B., raises flag over Fort Sumter, 133 n.; slave labor agent, 184

Jones, James, heads Minute Men, 47 n.

Jones, Lewis P., xv

Jones, Sam, 182

Journals of the South Carolina Executive Councils of 1861 and 1862, The (Cauthen), xvii

Kansas, emigrants to, 9 n.

Kansas-Nebraska Act, 7–8, 9 n.

Keitt, Lawrence M., advocates secession, 10, 26–27, 46, 49, 61; resigns United States Congress, 70 n.; in secession convention, 74; in Montgomery convention, 85–86, 88; and Buchanan pledge, 94–95; on Davis, 205

Kendall, Amos, letter from Orr, 26–27

Kenner, Duncan F., 200 n.

Kershaw, J. B., Colonel, 2nd South Carolina Volunteers, 115 n., 135

Kettell, Thomas P., 37

Know-Nothing party, 7

LaBruce, John, 77 n.

Lamon, Ward H., visit to Fort Sumter, 122, 126, 127

Lancaster Ledger, 153

Lane, Joseph, 25, 49

Lapsley, John H., on Lincoln and Fort Sumter, 122, 128

Lead, mined, 149; donated, 149

Lecompton Constitution, 11

LeConte, John, and lead mines, 149

LeConte, Joseph, on secession convention, 68; secessionist, 76; on unionists, 76 n.; and nitre works, 150

Lee, Robert E., 137–138, 171, 221–222

Lee, Stephen D., Beauregard aide, 130–131

Legislature, representation in, 6 n.; considers convention bill, 49–60; removal to Charleston, 71 n.; powers increased, 81; special session 1861, 137; abolishes Executive Council, 160–161; special sessions 1863, 168, 176, 179–181, 185, 192 n.; session 1863, 181, 185; endorses Davis; 206; called at Greenville, 228. *See also* elections

Lesesne, Henry D., in secession movement, 54–56, 66; on *Mercury*, 206

Lieutenant Governors. *See* Harllee, Weston, McCaw

Lincoln, Abraham, election of, xii, xvii; quoted, ix; and Charleston forts, 119–129; mentioned, 26–29, 31, 33, 40, 51, 53, 58, 66

Lopez, David, Superintendent Greenville armory, 150

Lopse, 82 n.

Lost Cause, the, x, xv

Lovell, C. S., censured, 76

Lyles, W. D., 22–23

McAliley, opposes secession, 57, 60

McBeth, Charles, 180

McBride, Rev. T. L., secession sermon, 77

McCaw, Robert G., lieutenant governor, 183 n.

McCrady, Edward, in secession movement, 65–66

McGill, J. D., 77 n.

McGowan, Samuel, in secession movement, 22–23 and n., 24 n., 56; appointed Brigadier General, South Carolina Volunteers, 140 n., 141; candidate for governor, 183 and n.

McGowan, Mrs. W. C., 70 n.

McIver, Henry, in secession convention, 70 n., 90 n.

McKay, Donald, unionist, 76

McQueen, John, in secession movement, 11, 26; and Buchanan pledge, 94–95 and n., 96; resigns United States Congress, 70 n.; South Carolina commissioner to Texas, 84 n.; Confederate Congressman, 208 and n., 209 n., 212 n., 216; defeated 213 n.; suggested for governor, 162

Madison, James, 38

Magrath, Andrew G., xiii; resigns federal judgeship, 55, 61 n.; on Boyce and Orr, 27; advocates secession, 45, 58, 61, 63–65; on cause of secession, 7–72; in secession convention, 66; resigns, 156; candidate commissioner to Washington, 97 n.; South Carolina Secretary of State, 8–83, 103, 105, 107 n., 117, 127, 130 n., 141; Confederate District judge, 165, 171, 172 n.; elected governor, 183 and n., 222; inaugural, 223; and exemptions, 171; requests troops, 177; and slave labor for defenses, 183; and impressment of supplies, 187; on Confederate claims, 199; on arming slaves, 221; requests troops, 223; protests Charleston evacuation, 224; proposals to Southern governors, 224 ff.; withdraws from Columbia, 228; arrest, 228–230

Manassas, battle, 203

Manigault, Gabriel, 43 n., 89–90 and n., 115 n., 210

Manning, John L., elected governor, 6; commissioner to Louisiana, 84 n.; on Pickens, 140; candidate for governor, 162–163; bears Magrath letter to Governor Watts, 227

"March to the Sea," xiv

Martial law, 142, 151

Martin, Luther, 38

Martin, W. E., 218

Mason, George, 38

Mason, J. Y., 68

Means, John H., 1–6, 22